Legal Practice II
Spring 2013
Building on the Fundamentals

Aspen Custom Publishing Series

Legal Practice II
Spring 2013
Building on the Fundamentals

New York Law School Legal Practice Program

Edited by Anne Goldstein

Selected pages from

Legal Writing and Analysis, 3rd Edition
by Linda H. Edwards

*Essential Lawyering Skills: Interviewing, Counseling, Negotiation, and
Persuasive Fact Analysis*, 4th Edition
by Stefan H. Krieger and Richard K. Neumann, Jr.

Basic Legal Research: Tools and Strategies, 5th Edition
by Amy E. Sloan

A Practical Guide to Appellate Advocacy, 3rd Edition
by Mary Beth Beazley

Legal Writing, 2nd Edition
by Richard K. Neumann, Jr. and Sheila Simon

Persuasive Written and Oral Advocacy In Trial and Appellate Courts, 2nd Edition
by Michael R. Fontham, Michael Vitiello and David W. Miller

Clear and Effective Legal Writing, 4th Edition
by Veda R. Charrow, Myra K. Erhardt and Robert P. Charrow

Wolters Kluwer
Law & Business

CONTENTS

PART E

IMPROVING YOUR WRITING   171

21 *13 Steps to Better Writing*   173

═ **PART G** ═

CLIENT COUNSELING   233

═ **24** ═ PREPARING FOR COUNSELING: STRUCTURING THE OPTIONS   235

═ **25** ═ THE COUNSELING MEETING WITH THE CLIENT   251

Acknowledgements

We thank the authors and copyright holders of the following works for permitting their inclusion in this custom book:

Linda H. Edwards, *Legal Writing and Analysis*, 3rd Ed., (2011).

Stefan H. Krieger and Richard K. Neumann, Jr., *Essential Lawyering Skills*, 4th Ed., (2011).

Amy E. Sloan, *Basic Legal Research*, 5th Ed., (2012).

Mary Beth Beazley, *A Practical Guide to Appellate Advocacy*, 3rd Ed., (2010).

Veda R. Charrow, Ph.D., Myra K. Erhardt, Esq. and Robert P. Charrow, Esq., *Clear and Effective Legal Writing*, 4th Ed., (2007).

Richard K. Neumann, Jr. and Sheila Simon, *Legal Writing*, 2nd Ed., (2011).

Michael R. Fontham, Michael Vitiello and David W. Miller *Persuasive Written and Oral Advocacy In Trial and Appellate Courts*, 6th Ed., (2007).

We have organized this custom book into eight parts. Chapters 1, 5, 6, 10–14, 19 and 22 of this custom book are comprised of materials from *A Practical Guide to Appellate Advocacy*, 3rd Ed., (2010), by Mary Beth Beazley. Chapters 4, 15–18, 20, 23, Appendix A and Appendix E of this custom book are comprised of materials from *Legal Writing and Analysis*, 3rd Ed., (2011), by Linda H. Edwards. Chapters 24–33 of this custom book are comprised of materials from *Essential Lawyering Skills*, 4th Ed., (2011), by Stefan H. Krieger and Richard K. Neumann, Jr. Chapter 8 of this custom book is comprised of materials from *Basic Legal Research*, 5th Ed., (2012), by Amy E. Sloan. Chapter 9 and Appendix F are comprised of materials from New York Law School.

Chapter 21 of this custom book is comprised of materials from *Clear and Effective Legal Writing*, 4th Ed., (2007), by Veda R. Charrow, Ph.D., Myra K. Erhardt, Esq. and Robert P. Charrow, Esq. Chapters 2, Appendix B, Appendix C and Appendix D of this custom book are comprised of materials from *Legal Writing*, 2nd Ed., (2011), by Richard K. Neumann, Jr. and Sheila Simon. Chapters 3 and 7 of this custom book are comprised of materials from *Persuasive Written and Oral Advocacy In Trial and Appellate Courts*, 6th Ed., (2007), by Michael R. Fontham, Michael Vitiello and David W. Miller.

INTRODUCTION TO BRIEF WRITING

CHAPTER 1

INTRODUCTION

§1.1 Perspectives

Okay, I'm going to start out by violating a principle of legal writing and ask you a question: Why are you reading this book? Let me guess — because you have to. You've been given a reading assignment in a course, or someone told you that you should read it to improve your writing. As much as the fond author might hope that her readers look forward to reading her book with delight, the hard reality for textbook authors — and brief writers — is that people read their writing for a *purpose*, and not for pleasure. So here's the first lesson. People read differently when they read for a purpose, and because they read differently, you have to write differently.

This book addresses the practical side of advocacy and brief writing, recognizing the limits that every legal writer works with: factual limits, legal limits, and time limits. You will learn to recognize and understand the important decisions that you make every time you write a brief, so that you can do a better job making those decisions.

We all make thousands of decisions every day, both consciously and unconsciously. On some level, you have decided that your eyes are going to move across this page to read these words, and that at the end of each line, you will move your eyes to the left to start reading the next one. Many of your decisions are unconscious, or become unconscious, and they need to be — you would go crazy if you had to decide consciously to read every word or to take every step when you walk. Just being reminded of the decisions we make, however, can help make us conscious of those decisions. I'm guessing, for example, that some of you became conscious of your eyeballs moving from left to right as you read this paragraph.

If we want to be better writers, we need to identify the important decisions that must be made, so that we can make them consciously and thus more effectively. Too many of us go into default mode when we write. We don't think about which issue we want to argue first, second, or third. We don't identify what our best points are, and so we don't consciously decide to state them as effectively as we can or to put them in the places in the document where we know that readers will be paying the most attention.

And that's the other thing most of us don't think about, either: the people who read our briefs. We know that we're writing a brief to a court, but too many of us, I fear, have some vague, dreamy notion that our brief is being read by a panel consisting of Oliver Wendell Holmes, Thurgood Marshall, and Sandra Day O'Connor — at the peak of their judicial and intellectual powers and on a free day with nothing to do but wonder at the fascinating complexities of our arguments.

Well, life's not like that. First of all, many of your briefs will be read by law clerks as well as judges, and sometimes by law clerks alone. Your readers will be real people with real lives. People who have phones that ring and beep, computers that bring them e-mail messages, and colleagues who knock on their doors and interrupt their work. Your readers are people with families and deadlines. They're people a lot like you, except they're a little further down the road than you are now, if you're a law student, or they took a different road from yours, if you're a practitioner.

So instead of reveling in the complexities of your argument or throwing a bunch of authorities at a busy law clerk, you have a different job to do. You have to look at those complexities and make them easy. You need to find and explain the rules and policies that govern your argument and show explicitly how they connect or don't connect to your client's case, and do it so clearly that the judges will wonder why they didn't notice before how obvious the answer is. You'll follow the law, of course — it's no good writing clearly about legal rules that don't exist. You'll follow the court's rules, too, so that unprofessional errors won't distract the reader from your tight, clean argument. And you'll use honest persuasive techniques to make sure that your readers get the best opportunity to read and understand your arguments.

You'll remember that the audience for a brief wears two hats. You have to write for both the *reader* and the *user*. Most of us think of law clerks (and judges) as readers, who read the brief sequentially from beginning to end. At some point, however, they act as users: They are hunting for a particular authority or argument, or they want to know immediately what each sentence, paragraph, or section is about, because if it isn't about what they care about, they want to skip it. So when you write and revise, you have to remember both the reader and the user, and write in a way that helps them both.

§1.2 Know Your Audience

At this point in your law school career, you have probably written at least two kinds of documents: an office memo and a case brief. As you know, a typical office memo is a document that one attorney writes to a supervising attorney in which he or she analyzes one or more legal issues and predicts how a court would rule on those issues. A case brief, in contrast, is an organized set of notes on a court decision, and the writer essentially has himself or herself as an audience. Now you are being asked to write a brief to a court. Briefs of this kind are written to persuade courts to take certain actions or make certain decisions. Although the formal purposes for appellate briefs and motion briefs are different, they are often similar to each other in use of authority and persuasive techniques, and they are both similar to office memoranda in analytical structure.

An *appellate brief* is written to an appellate court. As you know, both state and federal court systems include at least one level of appellate review; most include an intermediate appellate court and a court of last resort. For example, in the federal system, when a federal district court issues a final order, the losing party may appeal to a United States Court of Appeals in the relevant circuit. When the Court of Appeals issues its decision, the losing party may file a writ of certiorari that asks the United States Supreme Court to review the decision of the Court of Appeals.

The party that brings the appeal may be called the *appellant*, because he or she is *appealing* to the higher court to review the decision. The party opposing the appeal is often called the *appellee*. In some courts, the party bringing the appeal is called the *petitioner*, because he or she is *petitioning* to the higher court to ask it to review. In those courts, the other party is often called the *respondent*, because he or she is *responding* to the petition for review.

The audience for a *motion brief*, in contrast, is usually a trial court. Attorneys write motion briefs to argue that a court should *grant* or *deny* a particular *motion*. A motion is a formal request that the court take an action or make a decision relevant to a case before the court. Whenever a party wants the court to take any action in the case (other than the decision on the merits), it must *move* the court or file *a motion*. The parties may file a motion to ask the court to postpone the trial date, to limit the kinds of evidence that may be heard in a case, or to decide in favor of one party or the other without a formal trial. The more significant the motion, the more likely it is that the parties will support the motion with a *motion brief*.[1]

In a motion brief, the attorneys support their arguments by analyzing how the controlling law applies to certain agreed-upon facts (usually the facts that the plaintiff provided in the complaint; sometimes these facts may be supplemented by affidavits or other documents). The party who filed the motion (often the defendant) is sometimes referred to as the *movant* or the *moving party*. The moving party writes the *Brief in Support of the Motion*. The party who did not file the motion, sometimes referred to as the *opponent* or the *non-moving party*, writes the *Brief in Opposition to the Motion*. The parties are also referred to by their categorizations of *plaintiff* or *defendant*, as appropriate. Although many motions are decided on the basis of the briefs alone, the court may ask counsel to participate in an oral argument to help it decide the issues before it.

Whether you are writing to an appellate court or a trial court, you are writing to a busy reader. The United States Supreme Court, for example, hears approximately 80 cases per term. Consider that each case requires reading several

---

[1] Note that these documents are sometimes known under other labels, including *Trial Briefs* and *Memoranda of Points & Authorities*.

documents. The petitioner submits a brief accompanying the petition for writ of certiorari, and the potential respondent often submits a brief in response. If the Court grants the petition, there will usually be three briefs on the merits: petitioner's brief on the merits, respondent's brief on the merits, and petitioner's reply brief on the merits. Furthermore, various parties may submit amicus briefs, and counsel for the parties will submit documents to support or oppose the various motions that may accompany Supreme Court practice.

Thus, even estimating conservatively that each case generates around seven documents, Supreme Court Justices and their clerks are reading over 500 briefs per year. Of course, this statistic does not take into account the reading required when the Justices review the joint appendix (selected elements of the case record) and the statutes, cases, and other sources cited in the briefs. It also does not take into account the time spent reviewing the thousands of certiorari petitions that are ultimately denied or — by the way — the time spent writing opinions.

The numbers are equally impressive in the lower courts. Judge Boyce F. Martin, Jr., of the United States Court of Appeals for the Sixth Circuit, estimated in 1999 that the average judge on the Sixth Circuit sits on 32 panels and hears 192 cases a year.[2] The Federal Court Management Statistics for the United States Court of Appeals reveal that in 2009, the average circuit judge was responsible for deciding 461 cases and writing 156 opinions.[3] At the state-court level, the average intermediate appellate judge writes anywhere from 50 to 100 opinions each year.[4] Presuming that these judges sit on three-judge panels and that the opinion-writing duties are evenly spread, even judges who write fewer opinions hear 168 to 180 cases per year.

An associate justice in Maine's highest court noted that during her first six months on the court, she and her colleagues heard 114 oral arguments and conferenced 181 cases on briefs alone, in addition to reviewing 120 petitions for review of workers' compensation matters.[5] A former Wisconsin Court of Appeals judge estimated that he read 24 *sets* of briefs per month, or almost 300 sets per year.[6] Although cases submitted to lower courts may not generate the same number of documents as cases submitted to the United States Supreme Court, the number is still daunting: The average intermediate court judge will read 600

---

[2] Boyce F. Martin, Jr., *In Defense of Unpublished Opinions*, 60 Ohio St. L.J. 177, 182 (1999).

[3] 2009 Federal Court Management Statistics, http://www.uscourts.gov/cgi-bin/cmsa2009.pl (last visited March 28, 2010). *See also* Honorable Ruggero J. Aldisert, Meehan Rasch & Matthew P. Bartlett, *Opinion Writing and Opinion Readers*, 31 Cardozo L. Rev. 1, 7 (2009) (citing the 2008 report and noting that the average federal circuit judge wrote 152 opinions in 2008).

[4] See 2009 Oregon Court of Appeals Annual Report, http://www.publications.ojd. state.or.us/ 2009CAReport.pdf (last visited Mar. 28, 2010) (noting that in 2009, the ten Oregon Appellate Judges "closed 3,609 cases, issued 2,173 case dispositional decisions, and issued 503 authored opinions"); Honorable Edwin H. Stern, *Frustrations of an Intermediate Appellate Judge (and the Benefits of Being One in New Jersey)*, 60 Rutgers L. Rev. 971, 980 (2008) ("Each judge now writes an average of 108 opinions a year, independent of the cases disposed of by motion, sua sponte, or other order"); Daniel J. Foley, *The Tennessee Court of Criminal Appeals: A Statistical Analysis*, 66 Tenn. L. Rev. 427, 442 (1999) (citing National Ctr. for State Cts., Court Statistics Project, State Court Caseload Statistics, 1994, at 133-36 (1996)).

[5] Leigh Ingalls Saufley, *The Judicial Process: Amphibians and Appellate Courts*, 51 Me. L. Rev. 18, 19 (1999).

[6] William Eich, *Writing the Persuasive Brief*, 76 Wis. Law. 20, 22 (Feb. 2003).

briefs per year, while the average federal circuit judge may read as many as 900 briefs per year.

Writers of motion briefs should not presume that their readers have ample time to read. One trial judge observed that, while hearing and deciding motions is "but a small part" of the work of a trial judge, it has become "overwhelming."[7] A federal district judge noted that "[a]t any given time," on her own docket she carries "approximately 500 civil and another 75 criminal cases."[8] Scholars who analyzed statistics from state and federal courts recently concluded that "[t]rial courts handle approximately 98% of the thirty-five million cases that the federal and state courts resolve each year."[9]

Think about these statistics when you make every decision — from whether to file a motion or an appeal,[10] to the number of issues to argue, to (especially) how to organize and write the brief. Your goal should be to produce a document that can be understood by a busy reader the first time through without reference to outside sources.

§1.3 Follow an Effective Writing Process

Because your reader is so busy, you should keep four policies in mind as you make your brief-writing decisions:

(1) **The *law* upon which you base your argument should be complete and accurate.**   No judge wants to waste time considering arguments that must be rejected. Furthermore, if you have failed to identify a significant legal authority or an important legal, ethical, or policy argument, you should presume that no one else will dig it up either.

(2) **Your arguments must be *organized and written* in a way that makes them easy to read and understand.**   Write with your audience in mind, and presume that your audience is intelligent but ignorant of the specifics of your case. If your point can't be understood without a struggle, it probably won't be understood at all.

(3) **You must avoid *mechanical* problems of all types.**   First, as a matter of professionalism, you should follow the local rules of the court about format requirements and other ancillary matters. In some courts, failure to follow the rules will get a case dismissed; in others, it may result in your brief being returned

---

[7] Honorable Helen E. Hoens, *Writing Persuasively at the Trial Court Level: Practical Tips on Style and Substance*, 210 N.J. Law. 9 (Aug. 2001).

[8] Honorable Sarah Evans Barker, *Beyond Decisional Templates: The Role of Imaginative Justice in the Trial Court* (Hallows Lecture), 92 Marq. L. Rev. 667, 674 (2009).

[9] Chris Guthrie, Jeffrey J. Rachlinski & Andrew J. Wistrich, *Blinking on the Bench: How Judges Decide Cases*, 93 Cornell L. Rev. 1, 4 (2007) (citations omitted).

[10] This book is meant to advise on methods of brief-writing and oral argument. For advice on preserving issues for appeal and deciding whether to appeal, you should consult a reference geared to the jurisdiction in which you are practicing. *See, e.g.,* G. Ronald Darlington, 20 Pennsylvania Appellate Practice 2009-2010 edition, chs. 1-13 (West) ; Paul G. Ulrich, *Federal Appellate Practice: Ninth Circuit* (2d ed., West 1999) (most recent update 2010).

so that you can try again to comply with the rules. Even if you escape these sanctions, you hurt your credibility with the court when you make technical mistakes.[11] Second, proofread carefully to avoid typographical errors, citation form errors, and mistakes in citations (e.g., transposed page or paragraph numbers). Although these errors may not seem legally significant, they waste time and hence annoy the reader.

(4) **You should use *persuasive techniques* that make the most of your facts and your arguments but that do not violate ethical rules or otherwise hamper your credibility with the court.**   If your persuasive methods go too far, all of the work you have devoted to writing a legally valid, well-organized, and error-free document will be wasted. The court may well discount your arguments, or even stop reading your brief, if it believes that you cannot be trusted.

Not coincidentally, these four policies represent four different focuses in the writing process. It is impossible to make each of these focuses totally separate. For example, you cannot help but notice your content while you are reviewing your organization. By forcing yourself to pay special attention to each of these areas, however, you make it easier to create an effective brief.

§1.3.1 Writing Theory

Keeping these concepts in mind may be easier if you connect them to a little bit of writing theory. Although there are many more sophisticated ways of talking about the schools of writing theory, two schools are particularly significant for legal writing. One is the *cognitivist* school, and another is the *social perspective* school.[12]

The cognitivist school teaches that writing is a way to think about things and to learn about them. If you are thinking in cognitivist terms as you write, you are not writing for someone to read your writing; you are merely writing to figure out what you know about something or to generate new knowledge about your topic. Although many people used to think that writing was merely a way for us to record our already completed thoughts,[13] we now realize that writing is more than the hands taking dictation from the brain. When we write, we engage in brainstorming with ourselves. We question and challenge our presumptions, discover new ways of thinking about something, and gain insights that had not occurred to us before we began to write.

The cognitivist theory of writing helps legal writers to understand the benefits of multiple drafts. Writing multiple drafts of the same document allows you to let at least one of the drafts be a "working draft" or a "thinking draft" — that is, a draft you can write without worrying about what the reader thinks or about whether the reader will understand you. In this way you can use the process of writing to

---

[11] *See generally* Judith D. Fischer, *Bareheaded and Barefaced Counsel: Courts React to Unprofessionalism in Lawyers' Papers*, 31 Suffolk U. L. Rev. 1, 20-36 (1997).

[12] *See generally* J. Christopher Rideout & Jill J. Ramsfield, *Legal Writing: A Revised View*, 69 Wash. L. Rev. 35 (1994).

[13] Philip C. Kissam, *Thinking (By Writing) About Legal Writing*, 40 Vand. L. Rev. 135, 138 (1987).

understand your issues better, discover what aspects of your writing need more research and analysis, and clarify your legal thinking.

The second school of writing theory that is particularly relevant to legal writing is the social perspective school. The social perspective school tells us that writers must understand the needs and expectations of their audiences and write in a way that meets those needs and expectations. For example, if you were asked to draft an opinion letter for a client who happens to be a lawyer, you would write it very differently than if you were asked to write a similar letter for a client who is not a lawyer.

The social perspective school of writing theory reminds you to think about "readers" and "users" and about judges' workload and attention span. When legal writers are writing an appellate brief, for example, they may have particular formal requirements that they must meet. They could be required to include a table of contents, a table of authorities, a statement of the case, a statement of the issue, an argument, and a conclusion. Judges and the clerks might be confused, frustrated, or even angry if the brief-writer violated their expectations by not including the required elements.

Writers who keep writing theory in mind will first allow themselves to spend time researching, brainstorming, drafting, and using other techniques to think about the problem in creative ways, so that they fully understand the message that they intend to convey. Only after gaining sufficient understanding of the message will they pay close attention to the reader's needs and requirements. Of course, legal writers should keep the reader's needs in mind from the early stages of the process. Paying attention to many of the reader's needs — for example, the need for clear articulation of the rule, the need for discussion of one issue at a time, the need for an explication of the meaning of the legal rule — will also help the writer in the cognitive stages to gain a fuller understanding of the legal issues that the case presents.

§1.3.2 Conclusion

As you work on all of these tasks, you might keep in mind one of Aesop's lesser-known fables, about an argument between the sun and the wind:

> The Wind and the Sun were disputing which was the stronger. Suddenly they saw a traveler coming down the road, and the Sun said: "I see a way to decide our dispute. Whichever of us can cause that traveler to take off his cloak shall be regarded as the stronger. You begin." So the Sun retired behind a cloud, and the Wind began to blow as hard as it could upon the traveler. But the harder he blew the more closely did the traveler wrap his cloak round him, till at last the Wind had to give up in despair. Then the Sun came out and shone in all his glory upon the traveler, who, finding it too hot to walk with his cloak on, soon took it off.

The moral of this fable is that "kindness effects more than severity,"[14] or, to put it another way, "you catch more flies with honey than with vinegar." Like the

---

[14] http://aesopfables.com/cgi/aesop1.cgi?srch&fabl/TheWindandtheSun (last visited Mar. 28, 2010).

sun and the wind, you are trying to get someone to do something when you act as an advocate. To be most effective as an advocate, however, you must be both the sun *and* the wind. As the wind, you use the law and the facts to show the court that it *must* reach a decision in your client's favor. As the sun, you use persuasive writing techniques to help the court realize that it *wants* to reach that decision.

CHAPTER 2

WHAT PERSUADES A COURT?

What could you write to persuade a judge to give you what you're asking for? What persuades?

§2.1 A Compelling Theory and Theme Persuade

A *theory* is a way of looking at the controversy that makes your client the winner. A *theme* is a sentence or two or even just a phrase that summarizes the theory. You're already familiar with theories and themes in a commercial sense. Think of the businesses or products to which you are loyal. Each of them has been marketed with a theory and theme — sometimes implied rather than stated openly — that has persuaded you to spend money. Here are a few examples:

> iPod and iTouch — so much inside; take it anywhere with all your tunes
> jetBlue — fly on an airline that's fun
> Amazon — stop driving to stores: just click, and it's delivered to you

In law, a persuasive theory is a view of the facts and law — intertwined together — that *justifies* a decision in your favor and that *motivates* a court to render that decision. A persuasive theory

1. relies on the supportive facts;
2. explains why the adverse facts should not prevent a decision in your favor;
3. has a solid basis in law and overcomes your adversary's interpretation of the law;
4. appeals to a judge's sense of fairness and good policy; and
5. can be summarized in one or two easily remembered sentences or a vivid image (the theme).

Unfocused writing can make a judge feel as though she's drowning in detail without a clear idea of how all the detail adds up to a coherent view of the case. Judges complain about lawyers who write that way. *A judge needs a clearly stated theory and a memo or brief sharply focused on proving that theory.*

§2.2 A Compelling Story Persuades

The client's story makes the theory *come alive*. It can do that because — although in a scientific world we expect ourselves to think logically — deep down inside, we think also in terms of stories. You've already experienced something like this. Suppose you're in an audience. Someone is speaking from a podium in the front of the room. For half an hour, that person talks about the logical connection between the Heisenberg uncertainty principle and the invention of chocolate. Your eyelids grow heavy, and you contemplate sleep. Then, the speaker stops talking about logic. To illustrate some point, he tells about a family of ducks who start crossing a busy highway at rush hour — the mother at the head of a long line of ducklings, the father who-knows-where; brakes screeching; Officer O'Leary rushing up waving his arms in air. Suddenly, you are sitting upright on the edge of your seat. Why are you listening differently now? It can't be that chocolate bored you. Instead, the tension in the story has gripped you. Never mind about Heisenberg and his uncertainty. Will the cars hit the ducklings? Will all that slamming of brakes cause a huge chain collision, followed by drivers standing on the pavement and swearing at each other? Will Officer O'Leary be able to prevent all this harm?

Nearly all good stories have tension. The stories lawyers tell courts have tension because they involve conflict. When we start to hear or read a story like that — and if the story is told well — we naturally start asking questions like these: Who's the good person? Who's the bad person? What bad thing did the bad person do? How did it affect the good person? (We're worried.) What happens next? How will the story end?

Every case has a story. You've been reading them in the casebooks in other courses. Actually, every case has at least two stories, one for each side. The one you read in the court's opinion is the winning story. Sometimes, you read the losing story in a dissenting opinion.

How do we know judges are persuaded by stories? The judges say so, in the opinions they write. Judges often tell us, by the way they explain the facts of a case, *how* they have been influenced by a story. For example, here are the first two paragraphs of *BMW v. Gore*,[1] a U.S. Supreme Court case.

> The Due Process Clause of the Fourteenth Amendment prohibits a State from imposing a "grossly excessive" punishment on a tortfeasor. [citation omitted] The wrongdoing involved in this case was the decision by a national distributor of automobiles not to advise its dealers, and hence their customers, of predelivery

---

[1] 517 U.S. 559 (1995).

damage to new cars when the cost of repair amounted to less than 3 percent of the car's suggested retail price. The question presented is whether a $2 million punitive damages award to the purchaser of one of these cars exceeds the constitutional limit.

In January 1990, Dr. Ira Gore, Jr. (respondent), purchased a black BMW sports sedan for $40,750.88 from an authorized BMW dealer in Birmingham, Alabama. After driving the car for approximately nine months, and without noticing any flaws in its appearance, Dr. Gore took the car to "Slick Finish," an independent detailer, to make it look "snazzier than it normally would appear." [citation omitted] Mr. Slick, the proprietor, detected evidence that the car had been repainted. Convinced that he had been cheated, Dr. Gore brought suit against petitioner BMW of North America (BMW), the American distributor of BMW automobiles. Dr. Gore alleged, *inter alia*, that the failure to disclose that the car had been repainted constituted suppression of a material fact. The complaint prayed for $500,000 in compensatory and punitive damages, and costs.

Dr. Gore is going to lose this appeal. We know it already — even though the court hasn't even begun to analyze the law. Here are the clues from the way the court begins:

- Dr. Gore paid about $40,750 to buy the car.
- It took a specialist to notice that the car had been damaged and repaired, and Dr. Gore didn't know about it until the specialist told him.
- He sued for $500,000 in compensatory damages and was awarded $2 million in punitive damages.

The plaintiff's story, which the court rejected, appears in these words in one of the dissents:

> Dr. Gore's experience was not unprecedented among customers who bought BMW vehicles sold as flawless and brand-new. In addition to his own encounter, Gore showed . . . that on 983 other occasions . . . , BMW had shipped new vehicles to dealers without disclosing paint repairs costing at least $300, [and] at least 14 of the repainted vehicles . . . were sold as new and undamaged to consumers in Alabama.[2]

§2.3 Compelling Arguments Persuade

Arguments provide the logical reasons to accept the theory. They're based on the interpretation of statutes and judicial precedent as well as public policy. In all your courses, you've been immersed in arguments since you started law school.

---

[2] *Id.* at 608.

§2.4 How Arguments and Stories Work Together

Suppose you're being asked to believe the last sentence in the paragraph below:

> Almost 80% of the people of India live on less than $2 a day, according to the World Bank, and a typical work day might be 12 or 15 hours long. Millions of Indians are self-employed as farmers or other small producers or as sellers or resellers. *A self-employed Indian in these circumstances can earn dramatically more income and reduce work hours substantially simply by owning a cell phone.*

Assume that you're a government official with a budget. You're besieged by people and organizations asking you to spend money on projects they consider important. For every request you agree to, you will have to turn down a hundred more. You're asked to spend a million dollars in a seed program to get cell phones into the hands of Indian farmers, fishermen, sellers, and resellers. A logical argument in support of this plan appears in the left column below. Read it and ask yourself whether it persuades you and, if so, how *deeply* you are persuaded ("this might work," "it probably will work," or "absolutely will it work!"). Then read the story in the right column.[3]

A Logical Argument

In economics, a market is any system in which buyers and sellers can transact business with each other. In an *efficient* market, all information is available to everybody so that each buyer or seller can make rational decisions. If all information is available to everybody, each person gets the most value out of the market, and waste is minimized. Developing countries are plagued by inefficient markets, where people don't have access to the information they need, and where buyers and sellers have a hard time even finding each other.

The smallest and cheapest medium for transmitting information instantly is a cell phone. It is cheaper than a Blackberry or a laptop and does not require telephone wires or a wifi infrastructure. All it requires is cellular

A Story

Devi Datt Joshi sells fruit and vegetables on the street in New Dehli. He has no store and no refrigerator. He has only a three-wheeled cart and a regular spot on the street where his customers know to find him.

Well before dawn, he goes to a fruit and vegetable wholesale market and buys as much produce as he thinks he can sell that day. That pre-dawn decision of how much to purchase — based on his prediction of how much his customers will want to buy by afternoon — is crucial to whether he will make any money at all that day and how hard he will have to work to make it. Without refrigeration in a hot climate, if he buys more than he can sell, he will have to throw away most of the excess because it will not be fresh the following day. If he buys

---

[3] The details in both columns come from Kevin Sullivan, *Dialing Up a Sea of Change*, Wash. Post, Oct. 15, 2006, at A01, and Kevin Sullivan, *Cell Phone Turns Out To Be Grocer's Best Buy*, Wash. Post, Oct. 14, 2006.

A Logical Argument	*A Story*
transmitting towers, which are being built anyway throughout the world to satisfy the wealthy. A cell phone also does not require any education. A person who does not know how to read or write can operate a cell phone.	too little, he loses sales and risks also losing frustrated customers to some other produce seller.

transmitting towers, which are being
built anyway throughout the world to
satisfy the wealthy. A cell phone also
does not require any education. A
person who does not know how to read
or write can operate a cell phone.

Although the U.S. cost of buying a
cell phone and paying the monthly
service charges would consume most of
an average Indian worker's income,
costs in India are lower than in the
United States. Cell phone air time in
India costs less than one U.S. cent per
minute.

Cell phone subscribers in India have
grown from 1.6 million in 2000 to 125
million in 2006 (when cell phones in
India outnumbered land lines by three
to one).

"One element of poverty is the lack
of information," according to C.K.
Prahalad, a professor in the business
school at the University of Michigan,
who has studied how cell phones can
help people escape poverty. "The cell
phone gives poor people as much
information as the middleman."

Therefore, if small businesses in
India start using cell phones, their
owners, employees, and customers will
all be better off.

too little, he loses sales and risks also
losing frustrated customers to some
other produce seller.

Making this kind of gamble, he used
to earn an average of $3 a day for more
than 12 hours of work. Once his
morning customers had bought what
they wanted, he would have to wander
through the streets looking for buyers
for the produce that was left.

Everything changed when he got a
cell phone.

Customers call him the night before
to place their orders. He knows how
much to buy, and they can depend on
him to supply what they need. He buys
a little extra for customers who do not
call ahead, and he sells that,
too — without having to wander in the
streets.

"The mobile phone has more than
doubled my profits," he told an
American newspaper reporter. He now
earns $8 a day for about eight hours of
work. He still gets up before dawn but
his work day ends before lunch. He has
been able to hire an assistant and put
his children into better schools.

And the food he buys rarely goes to
waste.

Again, you're the government official with a budget. Suppose you hear the story above without the logical argument. The story makes you interested, even excited, about the idea, but you don't yet have confidence that this is a good use of development money. Now you hear the logical argument, which gives you the confidence you didn't have before. The story provided motivation, and the logical argument finished the job by justifying with logic.

The story and the logical argument work together. Neither alone would be sufficient. The story touches us and motivates us to act. The logical argument explains why the story is valid and provides a justification a decision-maker can rely on to explain the decision to someone else. Persuading thus requires telling a good story *and* making an argument that *work together*.

§2.5 Overcoming Your Weaknesses Persuades

Which cases and statutes favor your adversary? Which facts work to your adversary's advantage? What are your adversary's strongest arguments? And what will your adversary say to fight against your arguments? The answers to these questions identify your weaknesses.

Hiding from these problems will not make them slink away in the night. You have to confront and defeat them. "Be truthful in exposing . . . the difficulties in your case," an appellate judge has written. "Tell us what they are and how you expect to deal with them."[4] If you fail to mention your weaknesses, and if you fail to explain why they do not undermine your case, the court probably will hold them against you.

Acknowledging your challenges can preserve your reader's trust in you. Tell the reader the bad news with your spin on it. Think of inviting a friend to your apartment for an impromptu study session. If the apartment is a mess, you might explain — sheepishly and before you bring the guest in — that your place is usually cleaner. Then your guest could still think well of you, despite your mountains of dirty laundry.

§2.6 Solving Judges' Problems Persuades

Make it easy for the judge to rule in your favor.

Imagine an office with a desk, a side table, and book shelves. On the desk and side table, many files are piled up. Each file is very thick and represents a motion or appeal the judge must decide. The judge behind the desk has a huge docket of cases. To decide each of them, the judge must read what the lawyers have submitted — page after page after page of reading — and for most judges there are too few hours in the day to read all that.

Most writing seen by judges has a high word-to-meaning ratio: Many words are used to express a given amount of meaning. If your writing has a low word-to-meaning ratio — no wasted words, every word carrying weight — your work will be more persuasive simply because for the judge it solves a problem instead of creating one. You may have spent days writing a motion memo or brief, but the judge needs to be able to read it — and *completely understand it* — in minutes. To persuade, you will spend more time writing so the judge can spend less time reading.

Think about the other problems a judge might have with your memo or brief, and solve them, too, so that judges find your writing a pleasure. For example, the font should be easy to read, and the headings should look like genuine headings (and not like part of the text). A visually inviting document is more likely to be read with care.

---

[4] Roger J. Miner, *Twenty-five "Dos" for Appellate Brief Writers*, 3 Scribes J. Leg. Writing 19, 24 (1992).

§2.7 Professionalism Persuades

Professionalism generates trust. Judges respect lawyers who hold themselves to high professional standards. One mark of professionalism is to produce memos and briefs that are sharply focused on the issue, carefully reasoned, thoroughly researched, precisely written, and diligently proofread, with careful attention to details.

CHAPTER 3

Meeting the Needs of the Audience

The primary goal of a brief is to persuade, and to be persuasive, a legal argument must be clear, direct, and precise.[1] This observation probably does not surprise you. The more fundamental issue, however, is how to achieve these ends. The starting point is a candid appraisal of your audience to help you determine the type of written product that should most appeal to that audience.

The dockets in both federal and state courts have increased over the past several decades. More litigation means more pretrial litigation, including motions to dismiss, motions for summary judgment, motions for sanctions, and motions to compel discovery. More decisions at the trial level lead to more appeals. Flooded with paperwork, judges do not relish reading a pile of briefs, particularly those that are dull and poorly written. Most judges approach reading briefs with interest and a workmanlike commitment, but they are impatient with poor presentations. By contrast, a good brief wins their respect.

The average judge who reviews your written argument is like the rest of us: other obligations may call her away from the task, she may become distracted, or she may simply daydream. The tedium of reviewing many briefs heightens the tendency to become distracted. Thus, the judge may not read your brief from front to back in a single sitting; instead, she is likely to read it in pieces. Even when the judge reviews your brief in one sitting, she may not always fully understand it. Many briefs contain complex arguments that require a second or third review for full comprehension so the judge may need to reread selected parts. Over time, the judge may again review parts of the brief to refresh her recollection. Thus, she may read and reread your argument piecemeal.

In light of these realities, you should aim to achieve practical goals in reaching your audience. In our discussion of good legal writing, we return to these themes repeatedly. They include the following:

---

[1] *See, e.g.*, Harvey C. Couch, *Writing the Appellate Brief*, Prac. Law., Dec. 1971, at 27, 36.; John C. Godbold, *Twenty Pages and Twenty Minutes — Effective Advocacy on Appeal*, 30 Sw. L.J. 801, 811-12 (1976).

1. **Theme**. The most important aspect of effective legal writing is the identification in advance of your ultimate points — the essential reasons you should win. You should use these reasons, in turn, as your theme, which you should document and develop in the body of your presentation. In a thematic presentation, everything works together to support the overall point, making the material easy to comprehend and remember.

2. **Clarity**. Simple writing is essential to communication. "Getting through" to the court has special importance in modern litigation because of time constraints and the heavy reliance on written submissions. You must ensure that your presentation is well structured. The writing style should be direct. Avoid stuffy language.[2]

3. **Directness**. Your brief should begin by informing the court what the case is about, providing a framework for understanding the rest of the text. Use organizational signposts to ensure that the court can follow the argument and refer easily to specific points. Provide overviews, outlining the points you will explain in the body of each section. Make the theme of each argument evident from the outset.

4. **Interest**. The brief should capture the human side of the case, describe the actors, and evoke sympathy for their concerns. Although you should not overstate your case, you will enliven your writing and engage the court if you demonstrate a sincere enthusiasm for the legal issues. Properly presented, a mixture of the human element and legal theory is intriguing.

5. **Sound Analysis**. You should build your argument with solid, well-supported analysis. Make sure your authorities apply to the facts and your legal arguments are solidly grounded. Document your contentions so they have more than air to support them. Make sure your arguments are consistent and mutually supportive.

6. **Advocacy**. Permeate your brief with personal conviction. You cannot merely set forth the facts and law and hope that the judge will make the necessary connections. Draw conclusions and provide supporting reasons. Your belief in the rightness of your cause should shine through your presentation.

7. **Brevity**. Your brief should include only the material that is truly important to demonstrate your points. Do not worry about "how long" the presentation "has to be"; this mentality will cause you to load the brief with filler. Get to the point, demonstrate the basis for the point, argue the point, and conclude. Argue only the strongest issues; omit questionable arguments. Avoid digressions and shun excess verbiage. Faced with the prospect of reading a stack of legal documents, judges find a long-winded, undirected argument frustrating. They appreciate brevity.

---

[2] Yale law professor Fred Rodell commented that "[t]here are two things wrong with almost all legal writing. One is its style. The other is its contents." Fred Rodell, *Goodbye to Law Reviews*, 23 VA. L. REV. 38, 38 (1936). He is only one of many people to comment unfavorably on the overblown rhetoric of much legal scholarship. *See, e.g.*, Kenneth Lasson, *Scholarship Amok: Excesses in the Pursuit of Truth and Tenure*, 103 HARV. L. REV. 926 (1990).

CHAPTER 4

ETHICS AND THE ADVOCATE'S CRAFT

Language and justice are distinctive attributes of humanity. Human beings reason with language toward resolutions that are just, compassionate, and practical. This connection between language and justice made rhetoric an honored study and practice in classical antiquity, a study and practice whose foundations were formed, in part, by ancients such as Socrates, Aristotle, and Cicero. In writing a brief, today's lawyer takes her place within that honorable tradition. Reasoned argument in the quest for justice is not a mere trade performed for pay, but a craft in the Aristotelian sense, and its right practice helps sustain and advance our common humanity.

Many of the ethical principles that govern the right practice of brief-writing are codified in the professional rules governing lawyers.

1. A brief-writer must not knowingly make a false statement of law.[1] This means, for example, that the writer must not assert that a particular case stands for a proposition of law when no reasonable interpretation of the case would yield that proposition. It also means that the writer cannot fail to disclose that a case has been reversed or overruled. Many law-trained readers maintain that citing an authority is an implicit representation that the writer has read the authority itself (not just the headnotes). Citing an authority you have not read and updated is unprofessional and extraordinarily risky. Never do it.

2. A brief-writer must not knowingly fail to disclose to the court directly adverse legal authority in the controlling jurisdiction.[2] The writer is not required to disclose the adverse authority if it has been disclosed already by other counsel. However, omitting the authority from an opening brief cannot be justified by the argument that the lawyer was simply waiting to see if opposing counsel would raise it in reply[3]

---

[1] Model R. Prof. Conduct 3.3(a)(1) (2007).
[2] Model R. Prof. Conduct 3.3(a)(3) (2007).
[3] *Jorgenson v. County of Volusia*, 846 F.2d 1350 (11th Cir. 1988) (applying Fed. R. Civ. P. 11).

Disclosure is not only ethically required, but it is strategically wise as well. If you wait for the opposing lawyer to raise the adverse authority, you forgo the chance to be the first to interpret the authority and explain its impact. Allowing opposing counsel the first shot at interpreting the authority means that you start out behind and must make up that lost analytical ground.

The scope of the duty to disclose can be articulated in several ways, most often focusing either on the question of whether the case is one that the judge should consider or on the more subjective reactions of a "reasonable judge." In a pre–Model Rules Formal Opinion, the ABA Ethics Committee adopted both articulations:

> The test in every case should be: Is the decision which opposing counsel has overlooked one which the court should clearly consider in deciding the case? Would a reasonable judge properly feel that a lawyer who advanced, as the law, a proposition adverse to the undisclosed decision, was lacking in candor and fairness to him? Might the judge consider himself misled by an implied representation that the lawyer knew of no adverse authority?[4]

The ABA Model Rule expressly requires disclosure only if the authority is in the controlling jurisdiction, but some jurisdictions broaden the requirement. For instance, the New Jersey Supreme Court has required, on federal questions, disclosure of adverse decisions of any federal court[5]

3. A brief-writer must not knowingly make a false statement of fact or fail to disclose a material fact when disclosure is necessary to avoid assisting a criminal or fraudulent act by the client.[6] The duty to refrain from false statements of fact applies throughout the brief, not merely to the section of the brief labeled "Statement of Facts" or "Statement of the Case."[7]

4. A brief-writer must not assert a legal argument unless there is a non-frivolous basis for doing so. A position that argues for an extension, modification, or reversal of existing law is not frivolous. When defending the accused in a criminal matter, it is not frivolous to require that every element of the case be established[8]

A claim is not frivolous merely because the lawyer believes that probably it will fail.[9] But when a lawyer cannot "make a good faith argument on the merits of the action" the claim is frivolous.[10] The attorney's subjective belief is not sufficient to meet the standard. The test is whether a reasonable, competent attorney would believe that the argument could have merit[11]. The meaning of "frivolous" in this context often is subject to debate, even among experienced lawyers. In the early years of law study, while you are still observing the kinds of arguments that

---

[4] ABA Committee on Ethics and Professional Responsibility, Formal Op. 280 (1949).
[5] *In re Greenberg*, 104 A.2d 46 (N.J. 1954).
[6] Model R. Prof. Conduct 3.3(a)(1) and (2) (2007)
[7] *See* Chapter 20.
[8] Model R. Prof. Conduct 3.1 (2007).
[9] Model R. Prof. Conduct 3.1 cmt. 2 (2007)
[10] *Id.*
[11] *See, e.g., Beeman v. Fiester*, 852 F.2d 206, 211 (7th Cir. 1988)

do and do not have persuasive value for judges, you might feel particularly at sea with this standard. When you suspect that you might be approaching the line, consider doing two things: (1) Ask a more experienced lawyer whether the argument might be frivolous.[12] (2) Ask yourself (and the more experienced lawyer) whether making such a marginal argument is good strategy, even if the argument is permissible. If you are wondering whether the argument is so weak that it might be considered frivolous, your position might be stronger without it.

5. *A brief-writer must not communicate ex parte[13] with a judge about the merits of a pending case, unless the particular ex parte communication is specifically permitted by law.*[14] In the context of brief-writing, this means that you must provide each party (through counsel, if any) with a copy of your brief. Court rules require certification that you have done so.[15]

6. *A brief-writer must not intentionally disregard filing requirements or other obligations imposed by court rules.*[16] Virtually all courts operate under rules of procedure that set out the applicable time deadlines and format requirements for your brief. Many courts impose page limits, and some prescribe the margins and number of permissible characters per inch. You can guess the purpose behind these rules. It might be tempting to change the font or ignore the margin requirements so that you can file a longer brief, but it is neither ethical nor wise to do so. Resist the temptation, both in practice *and* in your legal writing course.

---

[12] Take care not to violate any honor code regulations pertaining to your law school assignment or your duty of confidentiality to a client.

[13] Ex parte, in this context, means without notice to other parties in the litigation.

[14] Model R. Prof. Conduct 3.5 (2007).

[15] *See* Fed. R. Civ. P. 5(a).

[16] Model R. Prof. Conduct 3.4 (2007).

RESEARCH BEFORE YOU WRITE

When working on research this semester, you should refer back to the research chapters in your fall semester Legal Practice text. They will provide a solid foundation for getting started on any new research project. The following chapters supplement this foundation with additional techniques and guidance to help you hone your research skills for persuasive advocacy.

CHAPTER 5

PLANNING YOUR RESEARCH

§5.1 Introduction

Naturally, you would not expect to be able to receive a brief-writing assignment and immediately begin to draft the brief. Nor should you expect that you can immediately go online or to the library and begin your legal research. Just as you plan before you write by conducting legal research and by outlining, you must also plan before you begin your formal legal research. The first step is to become familiar with the facts of the case and the issues that the case presents. Next, decide what questions you need to answer and what types of authorities are best suited to provide those answers.

§5.2 Create an Abstract of the Record

The first thing you should do as you prepare to write a brief is to get to know the case to which you have been assigned. If you are preparing a motion brief, it is likely that you were with the case from its inception. If you are preparing an appellate brief, you may also have worked on the case from the initial pleadings onward. Sometimes, however, both in law school and in practice you may arrive on the scene a little later. When that happens, your job is to get to know the facts and the procedure as if they had happened to you. Thus, you should carefully study the "record" of the case. The record can consist of many different elements, depending on the stage of litigation and on the case itself. If you are filing a motion to dismiss, for example, the only "record" you may have is the complaint. If you are filing a motion for summary judgment, the record may include not only pleadings, but also affidavits, depositions, answers to interrogatories, and written admissions or stipulations of fact. If you are writing an appellate brief, the record will also include the decision(s) below, and it may include transcripts of trial testimony, reproductions of exhibits or other evidence offered at trial, and other items.

Whether the record is a joint appendix, a "raw" record and opinions below, or just pleadings and affidavits, your job at this early stage of the writing process is to identify the important facts of the case. One of the best ways to organize this process is to create an abstract of the record. An *abstract* in this sense is a referenced summary of the information contained in the record. The purpose of an abstract is to help the lawyer — or whoever is working on the case — to easily find important information from the record throughout the writing process.

Reading the record materials carefully a few times and creating a good abstract will enable you to learn more about your case now and to find important record information later, while you are conducting legal research or writing the brief.

Like conducting legal research, preparing an abstract is often a recursive process. It is difficult to understand the significance of the case's facts until you know what law applies to the case, but it's difficult to identify the relevant law until you know the facts. Therefore, as preparation for creating an abstract, read over the lower court opinions or the pleadings first to familiarize yourself with the major issues that the case presents. Then, read through any other materials two or three times. You may wish to abstract information as you go through it each time, or you may wish to wait until you have read the documents through once before you begin to abstract the details that you think are important.

To create the actual abstract, make a chart — either on paper or on a word processor — and summarize the important information found in each part of the record or joint appendix as you read through it. Here are some things to look for and to record:

1. Page cites for positive facts, testimony, and other evidence
2. Page cites for negative facts, testimony, and other evidence
3. Page cites for segments of the appendix (e.g., each separate pleading or other type of document) (if a formal joint appendix has been created, this information may appear in its table of contents)
4. Page cites for evidence that establishes needed elements of the crime or cause of action
5. Page cites for findings of fact in the opinions below
6. Page cites for legal findings in the opinions below
7. Page cites for major arguments that each side has made below
8. Page cites for concessions that either side has made below (e.g., in pleadings or in stipulations)
9. Page cites for information that may support any policy arguments you plan to make
10. Page cites for any information you think is important, even if you are not yet sure why it is important[1]

A section of an abstract of the joint appendix in the case of *Adolph Coors Co. v. Bentsen* (later decided as *Rubin v. Coors Brewing Co.*, 514 U.S. 476 (1995)) might

---

[1] *See* Michael R. Fontham, Michael Vitiello, and David W. Miller, *Persuasive Written and Oral Advocacy in Trial and Appellate Courts* §§11.6, 11.7 (2d ed. Aspen 2007).

look like the example that follows. In that case, counsel for Coors was arguing that the First Amendment allowed beer manufacturers to print on beer labels the percentage of alcohol in the beer and that therefore the prohibition-era regulation that forbade this information was unconstitutional. The joint appendix was over 350 pages long, and it contained excerpts of various depositions as well as photographic reproductions of several trial exhibits.

In the excerpts below (from two different parts of the abstract), the attorney has recorded the page number from the joint appendix in the left-hand column. In the right-hand column, the attorney has described the information that can be found on that page. The comments in brackets are what an attorney for Coors might write as a way of using the abstract to think about potential arguments in the case. When the attorney is actually writing the brief, he or she could scan through the abstract to find references to information that might be helpful; the attorney could then quickly find the appropriate page in the joint appendix or opinion below and find specific language, citations, or other information to include in the brief itself.

EXCERPTS FROM ABSTRACT

PAGE #	INFORMATION
135	First page of deposition of Timothy Ambler, alcohol mktg. expert from England
139-40	Testimony re: mandatory disclosure of alcohol on beer labels in Britain and the European Community [Any precedent for following international precedent?]
* * *	* * *
284	Plaintiff's Exh. 3A — Chart showing alcohol % by weight of various beers [Use to show low range of variation among most beers?]
289	U.S. Dept. of HHS, Inspector General's Survey on Youth and Alcohol: "Do they know what they're drinking?"
294	Survey findings: "2/3 students can't distinguish alcoholic beverages from nonalcoholic beverages" [Use to show public benefit of putting alcohol percentage on the label?].

In these days of digital recordkeeping, you may find that some or all of the record materials are available in digital form. In that situation, it may be wise to create links to the full text of the record while creating the abstract. But be sure that you still take the time to include relevant quotations and paraphrases in the abstract itself. Do not let the ease of switching to full text make you skip the important step of reading and re-reading the complete record and creating a careful summary of the information.

Creating an abstract may be time-consuming, but it can actually save time in the long run. The process of creating an abstract helps you get to know the realities of your case and lets you rely on recorded information instead of memory.

During brief-writing, a good abstract makes it easier for you to support your fact statement and your arguments with vital citations to the record. When you prepare for oral argument, you can use your abstract to study the crucial facts, so that you can refer the court to specific record pages as needed.

§5.3 Decide What Questions You Need to Answer

Effective legal research begins before you go to the library or type in your computer-research password. Of course, when you write a brief, you should follow the same research methods that are relevant to any type of legal research. Be thorough. Take good notes. Be sure to check the validity of your authorities. This section will address some basic methods of legal research and some methods that are particularly appropriate to researching briefs.

A good method to use before starting to research any legal issue is to analyze the facts that you have at hand and begin to identify possible search words and possible legally significant categories.[2] Then, create "research questions" based on what you know about the case so far.

Like all statements of legal issues, your research questions should be focused on how the relevant law applies to the legally significant facts. A popular structure for these questions is the so-called Under-Does-When structure.[3] The "under" part of the question identifies the law that governs the legal issue; the "does" part identifies the narrow, yes-or-no legal question that you are trying to answer (whether it is about liability, guilt, or some other legal status or form of legal responsibility); and the "when" part identifies the legally significant facts that relate to the legal issue. Thus, a format for the research question is "Under [relevant law], does [legal status] exist when [legally significant facts] exist?"[4]

Let's presume that you are conducting research on the *Coors* case. From reading the decisions below and the joint appendix, you know that this case is about the constitutionality of a federal statute that prohibits printing alcohol content information on beer labels. If that were all you knew, you'd have a pretty broad "under" clause:

Under the United States Constitution . . .

---

[2] *See, e.g.,* Mary Barnard Ray & Jill J. Ramsfield, *Legal Writing: Getting It Right and Getting It Written* 346-50 (4th ed., Thomson/West 2005) (citing Christopher Wren & Jill R. Wren, *The Legal Research Manual: A Game Plan for Legal Research and Analysis* (2d ed., Legal Education Pub. 1992)).

[3] *See, e.g., id.* at 323-24; Laurel Currie Oates & Anne M. Enquist, *The Legal Writing Handbook* §7.4.2 (4th ed., Aspen 2006). Although your research questions may be similar in format to questions presented, you should not expect that the research questions will be identical to the formal question presented.

[4] Note also that the narrow question may begin with something other than *does*, and that the section about the facts may begin with *include* rather than *when*. For example, you may ask, "Under relevant law, does legal status include legally significant facts?" Or "Under relevant law can a party establish legal status when legally significant facts exist?"

But of course, when you created the abstract, you read the lower court decisions, and so you know that this is a First Amendment case and that the issue is not a matter of political speech but of commercial speech. Thus, the "under" clause can be a little more focused:

> Under the First Amendment's freedom of speech provisions as they pertain to commercial speech . . .

The "does" part of the research question refers to the legal question that your research will answer. In this part of the question, you ask a yes-or-no question — which may or may not begin with the word *does* — that asks whether a certain legal condition has been met or whether a certain legal status exists. This part of the question often focuses on the legal question that the case is about, as in the following example:

> Is 27 U.S.C. §205(e)(2) constitutional when . . .

Of course, your reading of the arguments in the lower courts might lead you to address more narrow questions related to the commercial speech test, and thus you might try to articulate questions that reflect your current understanding of that test and of the relevant arguments, as in the following examples:

> Does prohibiting the printing of alcohol content information on a beer label sufficiently advance the government's interest in preventing strength wars when . . .

> Does prohibiting the printing of alcohol content information on a beer label directly advance the government's interest in preventing consumers from having misleading information when . . .

These core questions help you to focus your research by forcing you to articulate the narrow questions that your research is designed to answer.

In the "when" part of the question, you list the legally significant facts that you (or your opponent) will use to demonstrate that the legal issue should be resolved in a certain way. One caveat about the "facts" part of the research question — what is a "fact" in a legal question may vary from case to case. In many cases, the facts are "real-world" facts that describe behavior or relationships (such as "when the officer did X," or "when the employment contract specified employment at will"). In a statutory analysis case like *Coors*, however, some (or perhaps all) of the facts may consist of the language or requirements of the statute. For example, if the "does" element had asked merely "is 27 U.S.C. §205(e)(2) constitutional?" then the "when" element should at least describe what the statute requires, as in the following example:

> when the statute prohibits beer manufacturers from printing alcohol content information on their beer labels

If the "does" section had been more detailed, the "when" section might be written as follows, based on your predictions as to which arguments the Court would find to be most important:

> when there is no evidence of strength wars in states or countries in which alcohol content information is allowed to be printed on beer labels

> when it is now possible to accurately measure alcohol content in beer and thus the statute is preventing publication of truthful information

These details may or may not be important later; right now they are useful in planning the research for the case.

Of course, in a case in which statutory language is not at issue, the questions would be different. For example, in *State v. Knowles*, 569 N.W.2d 601 (Iowa 1997), the issue was the constitutionality of the behavior of an officer who conducted a complete search of a vehicle stopped for a traffic violation. In that situation, the "when" part of the question could have more real-world details about the parties in the case, as in this example:

> when the officer had no indication that the defendant had broken any law other than a traffic law before he initiated the search of the defendant's car

The "when" part of the question helps to focus your research by helping you to identify relevant authorities. The more familiar you are with the legally significant facts, the more quickly you can identify cases and statutes that are and are not relevant to your client's case.

Putting all of the pieces together, here are three sample research questions for the *Coors* case. The first question could be used alone, while the second and third questions might reveal two different aspects of the case, and thus could be used together:

> Under the First Amendment's freedom of speech provisions as they pertain to commercial speech, is 27 U.S.C. §205(e)(2) constitutional when the statute prohibits beer manufacturers from printing alcohol content information on their beer labels?

> Under the First Amendment's freedom of speech provisions as they pertain to commercial speech, does prohibiting the printing of alcohol content information on a beer label sufficiently advance the government's interest in preventing strength wars when there is no evidence of strength wars in states or countries in which alcohol content information is allowed to be printed on beer labels?

> Under the First Amendment's freedom of speech provisions as they pertain to commercial speech, does prohibiting the printing of alcohol content information on a beer label directly advance the government's interest in preventing consumers from having misleading information when it is now possible to

accurately measure alcohol content in beer and thus the statute is preventing publication of truthful information?

A complete sample question for *Knowles v. Iowa* might look like this:

> Under the Fourth Amendment's search and seizure limitations, does a police officer have the authority to conduct a complete vehicle search of a car that has been stopped for a traffic violation, when the officer had no indication that the defendant had broken any law other than a traffic law before he initiated the search of the defendant's car?

One more caveat. At this early stage of the writing process, don't worry about perfect form or perfection in any way. The important thing is to get some information down in a useful format.

§5.4 Decide What Types of Authorities You Will Look for to Answer Your Questions

§5.4.1 Recognize Relevant Authorities

After you have formulated your research questions, you should take two more steps before you begin researching your specific legal issues. First, evaluate your level of ignorance about the case and do any needed background reading. Second, decide what you're looking for. What are your "ideal" authorities and your "practical" authorities? That is, if you could invent an ideal authority, what would it be? On the other hand, if the ideal authority isn't out there (and it probably isn't), you should decide what types of authorities would be useful in your client's case.

These steps are important because the problem many people have with legal research is not that they can't *find* relevant authorities, it's that they don't *recognize* relevant authorities when they see them. Even people who can eventually recognize relevant authorities often don't recognize them during the initial phase of their research. Perhaps because they don't know enough about the relevant law, they are looking for a case that is the perfect match, and they ignore every authority that is not identical, factually and in every other way. After they realize that they're not going to find the ideal case, they have to retrace their steps to pick up those imperfect authorities that now look a lot better.

§5.4.2 Evaluate Your Level of Ignorance and do Background Reading

Many researchers are able to recognize those valid but imperfect authorities the first time through if they have completed background reading and used their general knowledge about the area of law (whether preexisting or newfound) to help them identify both ideal and practical authorities. To decide what kind of background reading is necessary, consult the "under" clause of any research questions you have drafted to evaluate your level of ignorance. If you have written "under Section 23's limitation provisions," you are pretty well focused on the narrow legal issues. If you are familiar with those provisions and the law governing those provisions, then you do not need to do any background reading before trying to identify what you are looking for. If you are unfamiliar with the statute or the cases governing it, however, you can use narrow search terms to find some worthwhile background reading.

If your "under" clauses are even broader, with such phrases as "under the First Amendment" or "under state and federal employment law," you are obviously pretty unfamiliar with the narrow legal issue that your case presents. In that situation, go to secondary sources first. Do some general background reading by conducting Internet research, by looking for relevant encyclopedia entries, or by reading American Law Reports or law review articles.

Although a search for law review articles in an online database may generate a high number of "hits," remember that unlike case names, law review titles instantly reveal their legal significance. Spending ten minutes scanning through a hundred or more titles may result in finding a title that is exactly on point. Conducting this kind of background reading can help you recognize valid authorities both by teaching you the key terms relevant to your client's legal issues and by giving you a broader understanding of relevant categories of facts and authorities in a particular area of law.

§5.4.3 Tentatively Identify Ideal Authority and Broaden Your Horizon to Identify Practical Authority

Once you have identified or acquired the needed background information, tentatively identify ideal and practical authorities. Identifying ideal authority is simple: It would be great to find a mandatory authority that dictates a decision in your favor, whether that authority is a statute, a constitutional provision, or an on-point case. Finding your ideal authority may be difficult, because the United States Supreme Court and other courts of last resort frequently take up issues that they haven't decided before. Even if you are writing to a trial court, however, you should also consider what nonideal or practical authorities would support your argument and be acceptable to the court.

To identify practical authorities, broaden your horizons. If your client is a nun who was bitten by an aardvark, don't pass by a case about an antelope that bit a priest. That is, instead of looking at the narrow facts of your case, look for legally significant categories that you can use to characterize the parties, events, or issues in your case and that will help you recognize potentially relevant authorities.

§5.4.4 Identify Broad and Narrow Categories of Fact and Law: The Abstraction Ladder

Many legal writers use a theoretical device called the abstraction ladder to help them identify relevant categories. The abstraction ladder is based on the concept that everything in the world can be thought of at various levels of abstraction or concreteness.

First, let's define our terms. The word *abstract* has several meanings and is sometimes hard for people to understand. It is used earlier in this chapter to talk about a written summary of the information in the record or joint appendix. The meaning of *abstract* in the abstraction ladder has perhaps a more familiar definition. In this sense, art is abstract if two people could see different things in the same painting. A word is abstract if two people could perceive two (or more) different meanings from the same word.

For example, if someone asked you what you did before you came in to school or work this morning, you might answer, somewhat abstractly, "I ate." Different people might conjure up different mental images of what kind of food you had from your rather abstract reply. You might be a little less abstract and say, "I had breakfast." Even with this description, some people might picture yogurt, while others would think of bacon and eggs. Or you could be a little more concrete and say, "I had some cereal." Or even more concrete and say, "I had some Cheerios." Or you might be even more concrete and say, "I had one and one quarter cups of multigrain Cheerios and three-quarters of a cup of skim milk." Thus, the words you use to describe something can be placed on a ladder between the extremes of "most abstract" and "most concrete." You might think of the ladder growing wider as it grows taller; the more abstract something is, the more other things share the same rung.

Moving in the other direction, from most concrete to most abstract, you can think of a cow by thinking of Bossy, a particular cow. Or you can be a little more abstract and think of a Holstein. Or you can be a little more abstract and just think of cows in general. Or you could move up the abstraction ladder — or several abstraction ladders — and think of farm animals, or mammals, or farm property, or assets, or wealth. At the top of this (and every) abstraction ladder, you can think of a cow as a "thing."[5]

This concept is important to legal analysis because abstract reasoning helps lawyers to identify analogous authorities. Once you recognize that facts and issues can be put into broader, more abstract categories, you may be better able to see legal similarities between your client's case and relevant authorities. Very frequently, the tension in a legal argument is about whether a rule applies to a broad category that includes a certain person, thing, or event, or whether the rule applies to a narrower group that excludes a certain person, thing, or event. You can use the abstraction ladder to identify both legal and factual categories that may be significant to your argument.

---

[5] S. I. Hayakawa, *Language in Thought and Action* 155 (4th ed., Harcourt, Brace, Jovanovich 1978) (discussing the abstraction ladder in general and the cow example in particular).

§5.4.5 Use the Abstraction Ladder to Expand and Focus Your Research

The good news is that if you move high enough up the abstraction ladder, you can almost always identify some connection between two sets of facts. For example, you could analogize a cow to a horse because they are both farm animals. Or you could analogize a cow to a wheat field because they are both income-producing property for farmers. You could even analogize a cow to a tractor because they are both farm property. Or you could analogize a cow to a pet dog because both are mammals.

The bad news is that after asking whether there is an analogy, you must then ask whether the analogy is legally significant. For example, if a rule governs licensing of pet dogs and cats, that rule probably will not apply to cows on a dairy farm, even though cows, dogs, and cats are all mammals. If, however, a common law rule governed additives to cow feed, you might be able to argue that this rule also should apply to fertilizers on wheat fields because both cow feed and wheat field fertilizer may affect food that consumers purchase. One hint about using the abstraction ladder: Try to go up (i.e., to a more abstract level) only as far as you need to go to find a legally significant analogy and no farther. For example, a goat and a cow are both mammals, but their more legally significant connection in a given case could well be lower on the abstraction ladder: They are both animals that produce milk that may be sold for human consumption.

Thus, before you start researching, look at your case and at your research question(s) and decide what types of authorities you're looking for. If you were researching the *Coors* case, for example, you should plan what to do if you don't find any cases dealing with regulation of beer labels. Going up the abstraction ladder, you might look for regulations about labels of any kind. Or going up farther, you might look for regulations about any kind of advertising.

But "any kind of advertising" might be too broad a concept. What is significant about beer advertising as opposed to the general definition of advertising? One obvious answer is that there are lots of restrictions on beer — as one of my students put it, it's a vice that the government regulates. Thinking in terms of "vices" that the government regulates would broaden your horizons to looking for cases about regulation of advertising about liquor, gambling, smoking, or pornography because they are all legal activities subject to significant governmental regulation ("vices").

Broadening your horizons in this way can make the research process easier because you will be more attuned to the cases that are relevant and helpful even though they are not 100 percent on point. By being more practical about the potential results of your research, you will be more likely to recognize relevant authorities.

§5.4.6 Identify a Theme for Your Argument

As you think broadly about the issues that your case presents, it is a good idea to identify a potential theme or themes for your argument. The theme may develop or change as you continue the research and writing process, but identifying at least a tentative theme early in your research can help to direct your research as well. A theme is particularly important when arguing issues for which no mandatory authority governs the outcome, or when arguing to a court of last resort. If counsel on two sides of a case present legal arguments that are equally plausible from a logical or legal viewpoint, an effective theme may help to carry the day.

A good theme is a statement about the law, the facts, or about how the law and facts intersect, and it is a statement that is true even in the face of your opponent's best argument. Good themes are often policy-based for this reason; although two interpretations of a statute may not be able to coexist, two competing policies often can. When courts must choose between two competing interpretations of the law, they often do so by identifying (explicitly or implicitly) which of two competing policy arguments is more important *in this situation*. The court's decision does not negate the validity of the "losing" theme or policy argument; it merely decides that in this particular circumstance, another policy is more important.

To identify a theme, try to think both broadly and specifically about what your case is about, and try to identify a policy that supports the result you seek. For example, if your client is arguing that a state statute that promises a "safe" workplace entitles him to an injunction banning smoking in and around his office building, possible themes include the importance of protecting non-smokers from secondhand smoke, of protecting the health of workers, or of protecting and promoting public health. In contrast, your opponent might choose as a theme the importance of respecting the autonomy of private employers to make decisions regarding legal activities within the workplace. If both sides present legal arguments of similar validity, the policies behind each theme may help the court to make its decision.

A theme can affect how you write your brief, but it can also help to make your legal research more effective. In the injunction case noted previously, both sides would research the safe workplace statute and its interpreting decisions, as well as authorities relevant to injunctive relief. Going up the abstraction ladder, both sides could research workplace issues in general, and workplace safety issues in particular. Counsel for the employee, however, might spend some time identifying authorities that show the importance of protecting worker health or public health, or the laws and regulations that govern secondhand smoke. Counsel for the employer would try to identify other situations in which legislatures or courts have given employers the autonomy to make workplace decisions that were unpopular with some employees.

Do not close yourself off to other ideas when trying to choose a theme; you may well change your mind as your research and writing progress. By starting to think about possible themes now, however, you make it more likely that you will find authorities that help you to build arguments around your theme.

CHAPTER 6

CONDUCTING YOUR RESEARCH: EVALUATING WHAT YOU FIND AND DECIDING HOW TO USE IT

§6.1 Identifying Valid Authority

When you are writing a brief to a court, you are trying to convince it to do something. On a basic level, your argument consists of assertions that will convince the court to decide in your favor — if it agrees with those assertions. The court will be much more likely to agree with your assertions if it believes in the validity of the authorities you cite as support for your assertions.

The "validity" of each authority depends on several factors. When you are deciding what authorities to cite, realize that most judges are not interested in breaking new ground or making new law: They are interested in not getting reversed. Thus, part of your job is to reassure them that the result you seek is consistent with the mandatory authorities that govern their jurisdiction. Every time you cite to an authority that is not mandatory, the judge may be thinking, "Why do I care about this?" If you are writing to a court of last resort, like the United States Supreme Court, realize that — even though that court has the power to make new law — its first instinct is to look to its own decisions for authority rather than to lower court authorities. If you are writing to a trial court or to an intermediate court of appeals, its first instinct is to look to decisions of the court or courts that have the authority to reverse its decisions.

This principle does not mean that you should ignore nonmandatory authorities; rather, it indicates that you should *first* identify any mandatory authorities because they will have more validity than nonmandatory authorities. The more valid the authorities you cite, the more weight the authority will have with the court. Nonmandatory authorities can persuade, but because they have less weight, you should be sure that your reader knows why he or she should care about the authority. For example, you may be able to use nonmandatory authorities to show how various courts have applied a particular rule from the mandatory authority, particularly if the lower court decisions are more on point than the decisions of the mandatory authority.

Because each case is decided based on the facts and issues unique to it, the validity of an authority can vary depending on both the court you are arguing to and the facts of the case before the court. Therefore, when assessing the validity of authorities during your research, consider the relevance of the facts, the legal issues, and the source of the authority.

§6.1.1 Relevant Facts

First, consider what types of facts might be relevant, and look for authorities that relate to those types of facts. Remember that research is recursive; you may not know what facts are legally significant until after you have completed some of your research. Keep an open mind, and revisit your facts frequently (e.g., by reviewing your abstract of the record). Some cases with similar facts will be easy to recognize, but be sure to consider the different levels of similarity. This is where the lessons of the abstraction ladder become important: Thinking about your facts at various levels of abstraction can help you to recognize facts from other cases whose relevance is not apparent. If your client is seeking to ban smoking in the workplace, for example, you should not limit your research to cases in which plaintiffs tried to ban smoking in the workplace. You might look for cases dealing with other types of toxic fumes in the workplace, other types of dangers in the workplace, or other situations in which an employee tried to enforce public health laws (or other laws) in the workplace.

As noted above, you may have to broaden your concept of what a "fact" is. Many law students think of facts as events that involve human beings — the details of a contract negotiation, a car accident, or a termination of employment. In a statutory construction case, however, the language of a statute can be a "fact" that is significant to your argument. Likewise, the way that particular language within a statute operates can also be a "fact" — or a category of facts — that you need to be aware of so that you can look for similar categories of facts when you conduct your research. For example, if you are arguing that the word "employer" in the Family and Medical Leave Act includes "supervisors" as well as the entity-employer, it may be a legally significant fact that Congress used the terms "employer," "person," and other words in particular ways within certain provisions of the Act. A relevant category of facts in this case could be the way that the legislature used words in the statute. Accordingly, you might find relevant cases that discussed how Congress used a variety of words in a variety of contexts. You may miss the significance of these facts if you limit the concept of "facts" to your client's behavior in the workplace and the conversations the supervisor had with your client before the termination.

§6.1.2 Relevant Legal Issues

Second, consider what types of legal issues might be relevant. Obviously, when choosing authority cases, the more on-point the issue, the better. If your issue involves the meaning of a federal statute, for example, cases interpreting the statute would certainly be relevant. But you might also consider looking for cases that have interpreted other statutes that either use similar (or identical) language or govern similar legal problems. If your client has sued under the Americans with Disabilities Act, for example, you might search for cases interpreting similar aspects of Title VII. Likewise, if your client is being accused of wrongfully discharging an employee in violation of a contract, other categories of wrongful discharge cases can be helpful as well. Further, if your case has several possible sub-issues, authorities that address a sub-issue might be highly relevant for that sub-issue even though they might not be relevant to every issue in your case. For example, if you are analyzing a torts issue, a case addressing foreseeability might be relevant to your case even if the particular tort at issue in that case is irrelevant.

§6.1.3 Relevant Sources

Finally, consider what types of sources might be relevant. The most obvious source for legal authority is a court of law, but some courts will have more validity with the reviewing court. Thus, if you are writing to an Indiana Court of Appeals, opinions of the Indiana Supreme Court would have high relevance. The obvious rule is that mandatory authorities from the relevant jurisdiction will have the most validity with a court.

If there is no mandatory authority exactly on point, however, find out how close the mandatory court has come to addressing the relevant issue and build your argument on those authorities. If the mandatory jurisdiction has not yet considered the precise legal issue in your case, or if nonmandatory decisions are much more on point than any mandatory decisions, you may wish to go beyond cases from the mandatory court. When you decide to include citations to nonmandatory authorities, you can increase the validity of those authorities if you tie them to mandatory authorities or to rules from mandatory authorities.

Thus, if you find that there are few opinions addressing the issue in your case, and none that are on point, first find the opinions in your "mandatory court" that are most on point. If you also wish to cite to a nonmandatory authority, begin your discussion of that issue by citing to the mandatory authority. Only then should you cite the nonmandatory authorities, noting perhaps that the courts in those cases are applying the mandatory rule or (for cases from other jurisdictions) are applying rules that are consistent with or very similar to the mandatory rule. Although, of course, the court is not obligated to follow these cases, you have laid groundwork that will help the court to find the authorities valid.[1]

Some noncourt authorities can also be valid. If you are asking a court to decide on the meaning of federal legislation, the opinion of a federal agency would be relevant if that agency was involved in drafting regulations, enforcing the legislation, or suing to have the legislation enforced. If the area of law is particularly novel, you may have difficulty finding on-point cases or other authorities.

---

[1] *E.g., Vallies v. Sky Bank,* 591 F.3d 152, 154 (3d Cir. 2009) (affirming decision of district court that "follow[ed] persuasive authority from our sister courts of appeals").

In that situation, consider whether any law review articles have been written on the subject. Although most courts would rather rely on cases in which courts have considered the impact that their decisions would have on real-life parties, they may refer to law reviews when case authorities are few or inadequate.[2] If you can cite to a prestigious professor from a prestigious law school, so much the better, but most courts are more interested in the legal analysis that the article presents than in the pedigree of its author.[3]

"As you develop your research skills and take on more advanced legal work, you may also conduct research into "extra-legal" sources, such as statistics concerning the effects of a particular government policy, pertinent news articles, etc."

§6.1.3.1 Internet Sources

The advent of the Internet is changing the way that lawyers and judges find and use legal authorities.[4] Internet research can be an effective way to bring yourself up to speed on an area of law. Be careful, however, when deciding whether to cite Internet materials in a brief. Certainly, valid authorities do not lose validity simply because they can also be found on the Internet; similarly, however, non-valid authorities do not become valid simply because they can be called up on the computer screen of an attorney or a judge. In addition, the ever-changing content on Internet Web pages can affect judges' impressions of the validity of certain source material. If a judge goes to a link within a brief and does not find the cited material, he or she may question the credibility of the source, the attorney, or both. Thus, attorneys conducting legal research on the Internet should keep both validity and accessibility in mind.

There are numerous resources available on the Internet that have a high degree of validity. Many of the extra-legal sources mentioned above may also be found on the Internet. Numerous government agencies have Web pages that contain reports, research studies, or other information that courts would find useful and reliable. On the other hand, an on-point assertion from a random blog may carry little weight.[5] If the Internet simply makes it easier for you to gain access to a report that would have required a trip to the library or to the state capital in days of yore, then the source may well be worth citing. If, in contrast, the source has

---

[2] See generally Deborah J. Merritt & Melanie Putnam, *Symposium on the Trends in Legal Citations and Scholarship: Judges and Scholars: Do Courts and Scholarly Journals Cite the Same Law Review Articles?*, 71 Chi.-Kent. L. Rev. 871 (1996).

[3] *Id.* at 890-92.

[4] *See id.* at 420-22.

[5] Of course, the correct legal standard is often "it depends," and Internet research is no different. Some blogs contain reasoned analysis that is more akin to that found in law reviews. As with law review articles, a blog may be an appropriate citation for a developing legal issue. For example, a dissenting judge in the Eleventh Circuit cited a law professor's blog in the spring of 2005, when interpretation of sentencing guidelines was thrown into disarray by the Supreme Court's decision in *United States v. Booker*, 125 S. Ct. 738 (2005). *See, e.g., United States v. Rodriguez*, 406 F.3d 1261, 1284 (11th Cir. 2005) (Tjoflat, J., dissenting from the denial of reh'g en banc) (citing Douglas A. Berman, *Sorting through the Circuit Circus*, Sentencing Law and Policy, at http://sentencing.type-pad.com/sentencing_law_and_policy/2005/02/sorting_through.html (last visited Feb. 14, 2005)).

come into existence because of the Internet, you may wish to be more circumspect. The most important consideration is the validity of the source.[6]

The fact that Internet Web pages are constantly updated makes them a wonderful research tool, but it can also hurt accessibility for those trying to access "old" citations. One scholar has labeled as "link rot" the persistent problem of links that lead the researcher to defunct Web sites.[7] Thus, whenever you include a Web citation in a brief, be sure to print a copy of the material; you should also attach a copy to your brief to make sure that the court has access to the information.[8] In addition, you may wish to copy the source to your hard drive, to a word processing file, or to both. In these ways, you make sure that the resource is preserved, should you or the court need to find it at a later date.

Assessing the possible relevance of the facts, the legal issues, and the sources of the authorities you plan to cite can help you to predict which authorities the court will find more valid, and to decide where and how to concentrate your research.

§6.2 Researching Statutory Issues

If your case presents an issue of statutory or constitutional construction, you should conduct some research in the text or online versions of the United States Code Annotated or the United States Code Service (or the relevant state court code collections). Note that for some resources, it is easier and faster to use the hard-copy version to survey a wide array of authorities that have cited the relevant statute or constitutional provision. In addition, remember that courts are interested in hearing about interpretations of similar statutes, or even different statutes that use similar phrases or clauses.

For example, if your case involves the federal Age Discrimination in Employment Act, you might look for similar language in Title VII of the Civil Rights Act of 1964, which deals with sex and race discrimination, or in the Americans with Disabilities Act, which deals with discrimination against people with disabilities. If your analysis focuses on the meaning of a particular word or phrase in the statute, try using one or more words from the phrase as a search term, and search in a United States Code database to see if you can find any other statutes with the same or similar language. You may then be able to use authorities that interpret those other statutes when making your arguments.

In essence, when looking for authority on the meaning of statutes, you should consider the three branches of government. First, the executive — has this statute been interpreted by a relevant federal agency? If so, then the court may defer to

---

[6] For excellent advice on using the Internet to conduct effective legal research, consult Laurel Currie Oates & Anne Enquist, *Just Research* (2d ed. Aspen 2009).

[7] Howard A. Denemark, *The Death of Law Reviews Has Been Predicted: What Might Be Lost When the Last Law Review Shuts Down?*, 27 Seton Hall L. Rev. 1, 32 n. 77 (1996) (cited in Barger, *supra* note 13, at 438 n. 67).

[8] Be sure to check the court's local rules to see if they specifically address Internet citations.

the agency's interpretation under the *Chevron* rule.[9] Second, consider the legislative branch: Is there any relevant legislative history? (Keep in mind, however, that many courts look at legislative history with a jaundiced eye.) Finally, and often most importantly, consider the judicial branch: Has a relevant court interpreted this language or analogous language? When you look for interpretations from all three points of view, you may discover analysis that will help you argue that your interpretation is the correct one.

§6.3 Gathering Arguments from Nonmandatory Authorities

If you are writing to a trial court, you need to know first whether a mandatory authority governs the issue directly. If you are writing to a court of last resort, or if there are no mandatory authorities that are directly on point, you may need to look beyond mandatory authorities. First, if you are in a state court or in a federal court other than the Supreme Court, you should determine whether your jurisdiction is within the mainstream. If your jurisdiction is the first to tackle a new interpretation of the law, or a new cause of action entirely, one side or the other may be able to argue that it is now time to return to the old way of doing things. Conversely, if all or most of your sister jurisdictions have made a jurisprudential change, one side can argue that it is time for this jurisdiction to make the change as well.

Whether you are arguing to a trial court, an intermediate court of appeals, or a court of last resort, you need to decide whether to cite nonmandatory, or even nonjursidictional, authorities. If your jurisdiction is within the mainstream and if authorities within your jurisdiction are sufficiently on point to answer your legal question, there may be no need to cite authorities outside of that jurisdiction. If your jurisdiction is out of the mainstream or if there are no authorities that are directly on point, you may want to consult nonmandatory or nonjurisdictional authorities as well.

If you have not already done so, now is a good time to identify "foundational search terms": These are unique statute numbers or legal phrases that always pull up on-point authorities. They may pull up other authorities as well; I call them *foundational* search terms because they include the fundamental, or foundational, legal terms that are relevant to a particular legal issue. Often, you will discover foundational search terms as part of your research, so don't be surprised if you can't identify them until well into your research. For example, if you were arguing that an employer should ban smoking in the workplace, you would discover the term *safe workplace* in a relevant statute. Both the statute number and the term *safe workplace* could be good *foundational search terms*. A Boolean search that looked for the statute number *or* the term *safe workplace* would be a broad search, but if you limit it to the mandatory authority database,[10] you would

---

[9] *See Chevron U.S.A., Inc. v. Natural Resources Defense Council, Inc.*, 467 U.S. 837, 842-44 (1984) (holding that courts must defer to a federal agency interpretation of an ambiguous statute if it is based on a "permissible construction" of the statute). Note that federal agencies sometimes interpret statutes in documents other than formal rulings.

[10] For example, Lexis and Westlaw have search techniques that would allow you to limit your search to just the highest court in the particular jurisdiction.

be sure to find every case in which the court of last resort in your jurisdiction addressed the issue of safe workplaces.

Search the foundational search terms in your mandatory database to make sure you have the last word on how the court of last resort has interpreted the crucial word, phrase, or statute at issue. You should review each case from within the last few years to make sure that you are up to date on the mandatory authority. In addition, you should find the most recent cases in your jurisdiction to have addressed the issue in any way, even if they were not decided by the court of last resort. If your search pulls up too many hits, try using the *when* clause from your research question to help you to identify fact-based search terms to add to your search, which will help you discover the authorities that are most on point. In the smoke-in-the-workplace case, for example, you could add "cigarette or tobacco or smoking or smoke or fumes" to narrow your search.

If there are relevant authorities in your jurisdiction but no authorities that are sufficiently on point, plug your fact-based foundational search into databases outside your jurisdiction. In this way you may be able to discover any cases that are on-point as to issues and facts and that can therefore serve as persuasive authority. Although these cases would be a *source* of an argument rather than an authority for it,[11] courts often find on-point authorities to be helpful guideposts, even when they are not mandatory.

Further, you may be able to "harvest" effective arguments from nonmandatory authorities both within and outside your jurisdiction. When I refer to *harvesting* an argument, I am suggesting that you use the raw materials from an argument or an analysis and then figure out how to *make* that same argument to your court. Harvesting an argument from a nonmandatory or nonjurisdictional authority is a very different thing than *citing* an argument from such an authority. When you harvest an argument, you let nonmandatory or nonjurisdictional sources help to direct your research.

Suppose, for example, that you are arguing that the Americans with Disabilities Act (ADA) forbids your client's employer from requiring her to submit to medical testing. You are arguing the case in a motion brief in a circuit that has no mandatory authority governing the issue. The statutory section at issue, 42 U.S.C. §12112(d)(4)(A), provides:

> Prohibited examinations and inquiries
> A covered entity shall not require a medical examination and shall not make inquiries of an employee as to whether such employee is an individual with a disability or as to the nature or severity of the disability, unless such examination or inquiry is shown to be job-related and consistent with business necessity.

You are arguing that the term *employee* in this section means "any employee," while your opponent is arguing that the term means only "qualified individuals with disabilities." In your research, you discover a case from a nonmandatory authority that looks at the ways that the terms *employee* and *qualified individual*

---

[11] Chapter 19.5.2 explains the difference between "sources" and "authorities."

with a disability are used throughout the statute. That court alludes to statutory and regulatory language that supports your conclusion:

> A plaintiff need not prove that he or she has a disability unknown to his or her employer in order to challenge a medical inquiry or examination under 42 U.S.C. §12112(d)(4)(A). In contrast to other parts of the ADA, the statutory language does not refer to qualified individuals with disabilities, but instead merely to "employees." 42 U.S.C. §12112(d)(4)(A).

McGuffin v. Bernard, 444 F. Supp. 2d 455, 472 (S.D. Ohio 2009).[12]

A writer who merely *cited* that nonjurisdictional case as authority would not use it effectively:

▼ Bad Example

The United States District Court for the Southern District of Ohio has observed that the term "employee" in 42 U.S.C. §12122(d)(4)(A) must refer to all employees and not just to those employees who are qualified individuals with disabilities. <u>McGuffin v. Bernard</u>, 444 F. Supp. 2d 455, 472 (S.D. Ohio 2009). It noted that Congress had used the phrase "qualified individual with disabilities" in other sections of the ADA and could have done so in §12122(d)(4)(A) if it so desired. <u>Id</u>. Therefore, when the ADA forbids medical inquiries directed to "an employee," the term must mean. . . .

To harvest the argument effectively, the writer should let the nonmandatory source direct further research. The writer should observe that the court based its analysis — at least implicitly — on a governing rule that says that when Congress uses the same term in more than one section of a statute, the term should be interpreted consistently, and when Congress chooses a different term, it must have intended the term to mean something different. This observation should lead the writer to conduct research to find an appropriate rule in the mandatory jurisdiction. But that is not enough. It would be ineffective to merely cite the mandatory rule and state the same conclusory analysis. Instead, the writer should also research the language of the statute and figure out how best to apply the rule regarding consistent interpretation of terms to the "fact" of the statutory language:[13]

▲ Good Example

When Congress uses one term in one part of a statute and a different term in another, this court should assume that different meanings were intended. <u>Cucilich Industries v. Perek</u>, 599 F.3d 947, 955 (18th Cir. 2009). In <u>Cucilich</u>

---

[12] The language from this fictional case is adapted from *Lee v. City of Columbus*, 644 F. Supp. 2d 1000, 1011 (S.D. Ohio 2009).

[13] The example mentions fictional case law that is adapted from *Sosa v. Alvarez-Machain*, 542 U.S. 692, 712 (2004) and *APL Co. Pte v. UK Aerosols Ltd.*, 582 F.3d 947, 952 (9th Cir. 2009).

Industries, the Eighteenth Circuit analyzed the Carriage of Goods by Rail Act and noted that "Congress chose to use different terms in [the Act] when referring to the 'shipper' in conjunction with other parties, on the one hand, and the 'shipper' alone, on the other." Id. at 956. Accordingly, the court refused to interpret the term "shipper" in one clause in the same way that it interpreted the phrase "shipper, receiver, or holder of bill of lading." Id. at 958.

When Congress chose to use the term "employee" in 42 U.S.C. §12112(d)(4)(A) of the ADA, it did so in order to refer to all "employees" of the employing entity, and the term should not be interpreted to mean "qualified individual with a disability." The terms "employee" and "qualified individual" are defined separately in the Act, at §§12111(4) and 12111(8), respectively. Section 12114(c) specifies limits that can be imposed on "employees," while other sections speak specifically to qualified individuals with a disability. Section 12122(b)(5)(A), for example, notes that discrimination against a "qualified individual on the basis of disability" includes not making reasonable accommodations for "an otherwise qualified individual with a disability." Similarly, §12112(b)(5)(B) forbids denying employment in certain circumstances to "an otherwise qualified individual with a disability." Accordingly. . . .

Thus, one way to "harvest" an argument is to unpack a relevant legal conclusion from a nonmandatory source. Do some research to find a mandatory rule that would lead to that conclusion, and articulate it and explain it appropriately. Then, apply that rule completely and effectively to the appropriate facts in your client's case.[14]

If you believe that the court you are writing to would find the nonmandatory source to be meaningful, you could include a "see also" citation to that authority, but you should not presume that one is appropriate. In the alternative, if the area of law were novel or the facts or legal issues in the nonmandatory cases were particularly relevant, the writer might follow the citations to the mandatory authorities with a discussion of the nonmandatory authority, perhaps beginning the discussion by noting, "This is just the approach taken by the Fifteenth Circuit in a very similar case. . . ."

To sum up, when designing and executing your research plan, think ahead, but be ready to explore new leads as you learn more about your case and its issues.

---

[14] Of course, it is vitally important to note that plagiarism rules vary greatly in academic settings and in litigation settings in practice. In an academic setting, if you "harvest" an argument from an authority, you should always note the source of the argument. When writing litigation materials in an academic setting, the best course might be to drop a footnote and indicate the nonmandatory source of the argument. Some teachers might give you permission to remove the citation, but presume that you should include the citation unless instructed otherwise.

§6.4 Knowing When to Stop Researching and Start Writing

Most lawyers have a hard time ending their research, perhaps because they don't want to start writing. Researching is fun, and you don't have to make any hard decisions; if you think a case or other authority may be useful, you print it and keep on going. Of course, printing is not research; you must actually read and analyze the sources you have found. For some writers, research is like dating and writing is like marriage: With research, you hope that if you keep looking, you'll find the perfect match right around the next corner. With writing, you just have to take what you have and try to work it out.

Accordingly, when doing your research, you should consciously decide when to stop. No matter how diligent your research, your writing will probably reveal some gaps that need to be filled. Don't try to fill those gaps *before* you start writing. Instead, let the writing reveal the gaps to you and help to direct your follow-up research. Think in terms of a partial stop and a full stop. You should come to a partial stop when you have followed a good research plan, you have updated your authorities,[15] and you are not finding anything new — you keep encountering again and again those almost-relevant cases that you've rejected once or twice before.

You can come to a partial stop when you have achieved four goals: (1) you understand the general area of law and how the relevant courts apply it to cases similar to your client's case; (2) you understand whether your jurisdiction is in the mainstream or is an outlier as to the relevant legal issues; (3) you have found the most recent cases that address the issue in any way from (a) the court of last resort in your jurisdiction, and (b) any court in your jurisdiction; and (4) if appropriate, you have identified relevant cases or other sources from nonmandatory courts or jurisdictions.

As you review these authorities and begin to outline and write your argument, you may decide that some of them are not worth citing. The process of reading and analyzing them, however, can help you to understand your case and to identify valid arguments. Conversely, as you write, you may discover new avenues that you wish to explore, and you can make tactical research strikes to grab cases or other authorities to support the points that come up. Some writers continue these tactical strikes until they are stopped by an outside force: a court-imposed due date.

---

[15] Of course, you should update your authorities frequently during the research process, right up until the day you file your brief, and again as you prepare your oral argument.

CHAPTER 7

PRACTICAL RESEARCH TIPS

To prepare a persuasive legal argument, you must identify those authorities that govern the facts of your dispute. Sometimes this task is easy, as the issue is readily apparent and the controlling law prominent, but at other times categorizing the issue and finding the law requires extensive effort. This section reviews practical methods that may help you locate the law that controls your dispute.

§7.1 The Learning Method

One method of approaching a research problem — the learning method — is to review general information in an area and then move to specific authorities. Start with treatises, encyclopedias, or articles in your general field. This review will give you a perspective for analyzing the issue and provide clues to relevant authority. After your initial review, begin searching for provisions or cases that specifically control your dispute. This search may involve the use of more direct research tools, such as online research and annotations. It may also involve following trials and case notes found in the general authorities.

You will use the learning method most frequently at the beginning of your career and when you encounter a new area of the law. In addition, it is useful when you are uncertain of the best direction to pursue in researching a point. You may know that the issue involves a general area, but not know how to categorize the question for identification in online research or an index. In these instances, a general review of the area may facilitate your categorization of the issue.

The learning method also has the advantage of providing a broad perspective and some analysis of the subject area. Information concerning basic principles, competing theories, and trends in a field should provide you with a foundation for a confident analysis of a problem. This method may also turn up analogous authorities from related areas that you would not find if you used a more direct approach. You should not spend too much time reviewing background, however, because you will need the time to prepare your brief or memorandum.

§7.2 The "Zero-In" Approach

A second research method, which you will use most frequently once you have some experience, is the "zero-in" approach. In this method, you attempt to locate the specific provisions or cases that control a legal point. To make the technique effective, you must categorize the problem accurately and then perform an online search or search the codes, annotations, and digests for cases directly on point. You may have to try a number of categories or key words before you find the right category in the research sources. If you are still unable to locate meaningful authorities, you should use the learning method, using general sources for aid in redefining the problem, clues to direct authority, or analogous citations.

This more direct method of researching a problem, when successful, ensures the most efficient use of time. Since history or background is usually unnecessary in the brief, bypassing the learning step is permissible as long as you understand the issues. Moreover, you usually run across considerable explanation and analysis using the zero-in approach. Court opinions frequently discuss background and attempt to harmonize or distinguish the relevant holdings. The discussion of authorities in an opinion may provide you a lead to more closely applicable decisions. In addition, the headnotes in annotations and digests may provide a perspective as to the holdings in the area. Finally, *Shepardizing* or KeyCiting the cases you read and following leads in those cases can lead you to more recent and more applicable cases.

§7.3 Thoroughly Review the Cases You Rely On

A common and potentially disastrous method of using authorities is to cite a case without reviewing the opinion. We have found too many instances in which a writer relies on a case after reading only a short portion of its text online, a summary of the holding, or the citation of the case in another authority. Unfortunately, cases often contain statements that are unnecessary or counter to the ultimate holdings. The use of this double-edged authority may expose you to a devastating rebuttal.

Another pitfall results from reading only part of a decision. In a multi-issue case, the decisions often contain rulings on more than one of the points in dispute. A given authority may be favorable on one issue but adverse on another. Thus, the use of the decision may be counterproductive, especially if the adverse part of the ruling involves a more important point than the one for which you have cited the case. The court may view the use of the decision as an implicit concession that its holdings are binding. In addition, if the court learns that the brief contains double-edged authorities, it may become skeptical of the strength of your other citations, because this error signals that you have not read the cases.

In some instances, you may have to use a double-edged authority because you lack wholly supportive decisions or because the favorable ruling outweighs the unfavorable aspect of the case. In this situation, explain that the case involves issues other than the one for which you have cited it. You may need to describe both the favorable and adverse holdings to place the decision in its best possible light and to take the sting out of the adverse ruling.

Some opinions are lengthy and involve numerous issues, many of which may have little relevance to the point that you are researching. In this situation, you may be able to scan the parts that are not relevant. But be certain that you have read everything material to the points being analyzed.

§7.4 Look for Leads in the Cases You Find

When you cannot easily categorize an issue, one way to circumvent a "dead end" is to locate cases generally relevant to the issue and follow the leads in those rulings to more specific authority. Opinions frequently discuss special aspects of the holdings they cite, making it easier to determine whether the citations are useful. Thus, you may follow a trail through the cases to find close authorities.

Court opinions frequently refer to holdings that are not listed in reference material. A court's opinion reflects not only the research efforts of the parties, but those of the judge and clerks, which often turn up citations that are omitted from conventional research aids. In addition, these citations may be closely related to the issue decided by the court, providing specific authority for a given point.

Even if you find recent opinions that appear sufficient for the argument, review the cases relied on in these opinions. Frequently the facts of these other cases, or special language in the holdings, make them more helpful than the later decisions.

§7.5 Check Case Histories and Other Developments

One of the most important rules of legal research is that you must check the subsequent histories of the cases, especially those used in your brief. Unfortunately, although we all recognize the importance of *Shepardizing*, we may overlook this step when we are busy.

Shepard's and KeyCite provide the history of a case and all its citations in later published decisions. You can find cases by using the case citations. Listings under the citation include any subsequent history of the case, such as an affirmance or reversal, a Supreme Court denial of certiorari, and the citation of all subsequent decisions that mention the case. Analytical abbreviations indicate whether the subsequent cases followed, overruled, modified, explained, or criticized the main case.

The principal reason for checking subsequent history is to avoid using cases that are no longer good law. Courts do reverse, overrule, modify, or reinterpret a fair number of their earlier decisions. If you rely on a ruling that has been reversed or overruled, your opponent may embarrass you by informing the court that your authority is no longer good law. Even if the court has only modified or reinterpreted the case, your position may be eroded. On the other hand, when you are aware of the legal developments relating to a decision, you can omit the case or explain its meaning in light of subsequent decisions.

You can also use subsequent history as an offensive tool to find recent cases. A review of the history often provides better authority than the decision being *Shepardized*. This use of history is especially helpful since a more recent case is stronger authority than an older case.

§7.6 Record the Turns in the Research Trail

Although you may quickly solve some research problems, you will often have to follow a series of leads. When a problem does not fit the key word or head-note categories, you may have to work through a maze of cases to find relevant authority and make choices as you proceed from one clue to the next. A court's opinion may suggest several avenues of further research, yet you may follow only the one that looks most promising. If the chosen route proves unsuccessful, you must backtrack and pursue the leads that you have not exhausted.

A typical pitfall in this process is that you may lose your position when you turn down a particular research avenue so that you are unable to reconstruct your earlier findings. This difficulty is especially likely in major projects, where the research is comprehensive and requires substantial time. In addition, you may think of new theories as you review authorities, but put the ideas aside to pursue other matters, and forget the new avenues that you hoped to pursue. You may waste time trying to recapture your inspiration.

To avoid these problems, maintain a list of potentially useful authorities and the issues to which they relate. List your potential arguments. This action saves time and avoids needless frustration.

§7.7 Wind Up

Complete research is essential to a good legal argument, but you must know when to stop researching and start writing. In most cases, you have a limited amount of time for completing a project. Regardless of the quality of the research, if you leave too little time for writing, your brief will be inadequate. Thus, you must train yourself to wind up the research in a timely fashion.

Too often students and lawyers get carried away with research projects and pursue lead after lead in the quest for a "magic case" that probably does not exist. The law is only one part of legal analysis; the courts must apply the applicable rules to facts to achieve just results. Since you must explain the application, you have to dedicate sufficient time to planning and preparing your brief. Do not let your research unduly delay that effort.

CHAPTER 8

RESEARCH FLOW CHARTS

Sample Research Plans

The research plans in Figures 8.1 through 8.4 are intended to help you develop a coherent research strategy for four common types of research: state common-law research, state statutory research, federal statutory research, and federal and state procedural research. These plans are representative samples of how you could approach the research process and may provide a useful starting point for your own research planning.

Figure 8.1   Flowchart for State Common-Law Research

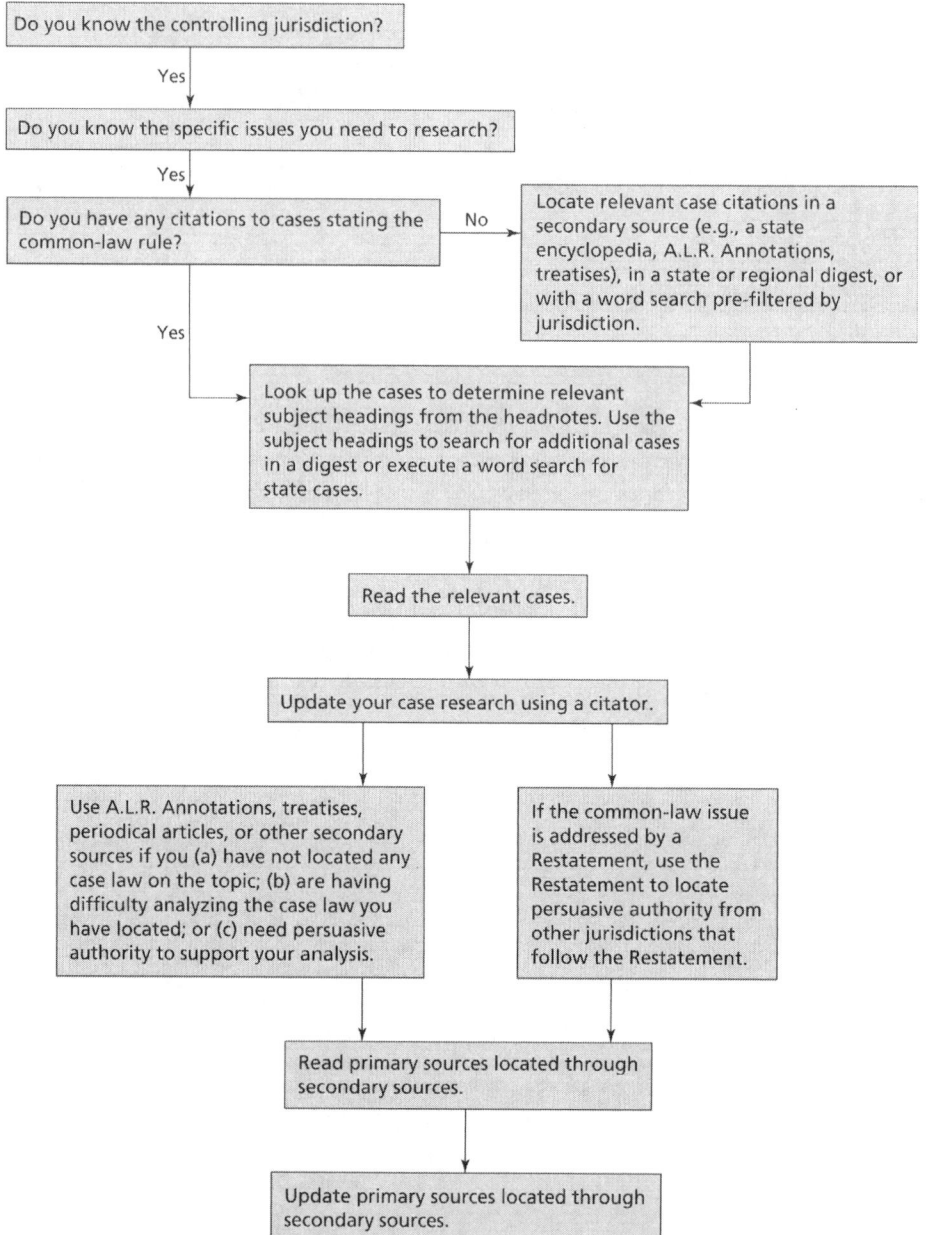

Figure 8.2   Flowchart for State Statutory Research

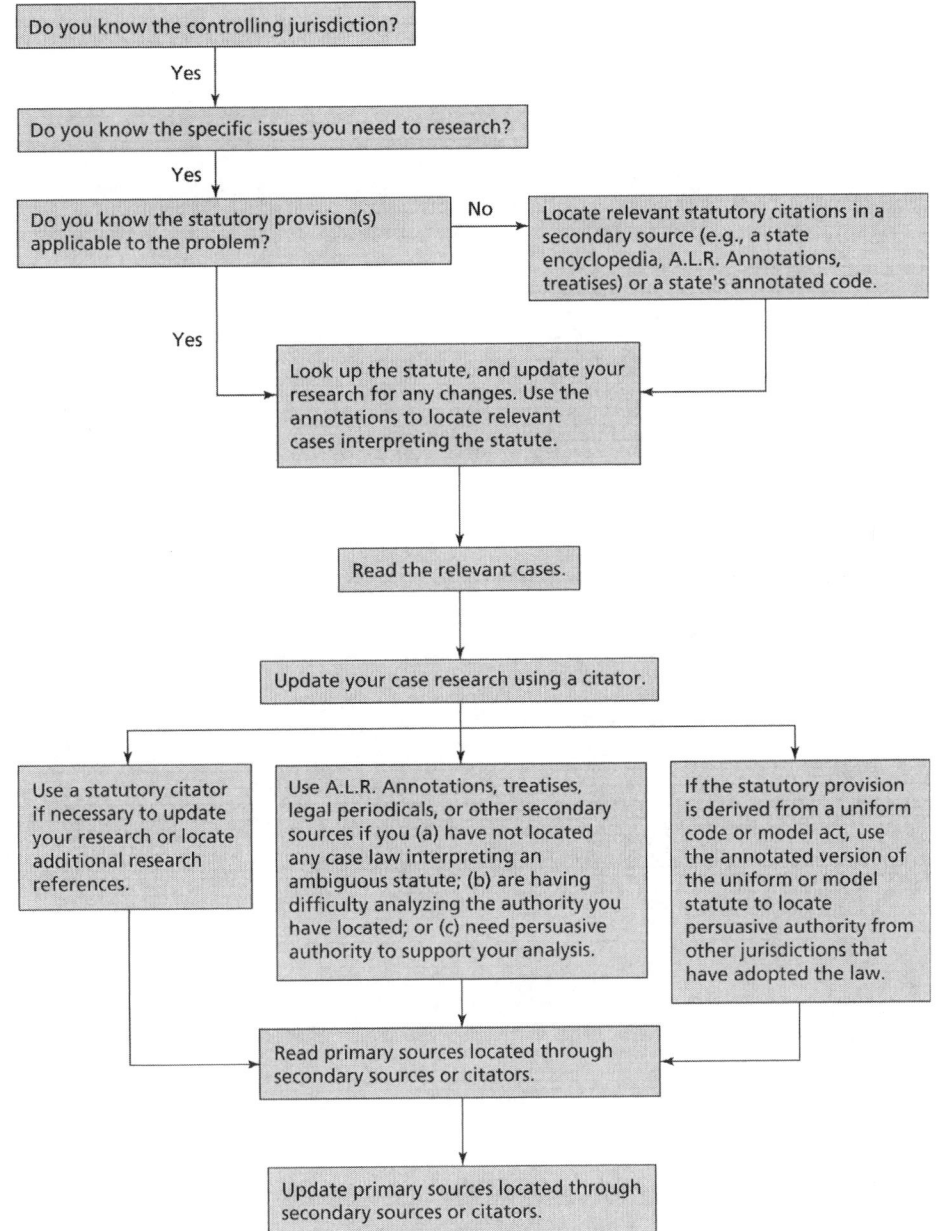

Figure 8.3   Flowchart for Federal Statutory Research

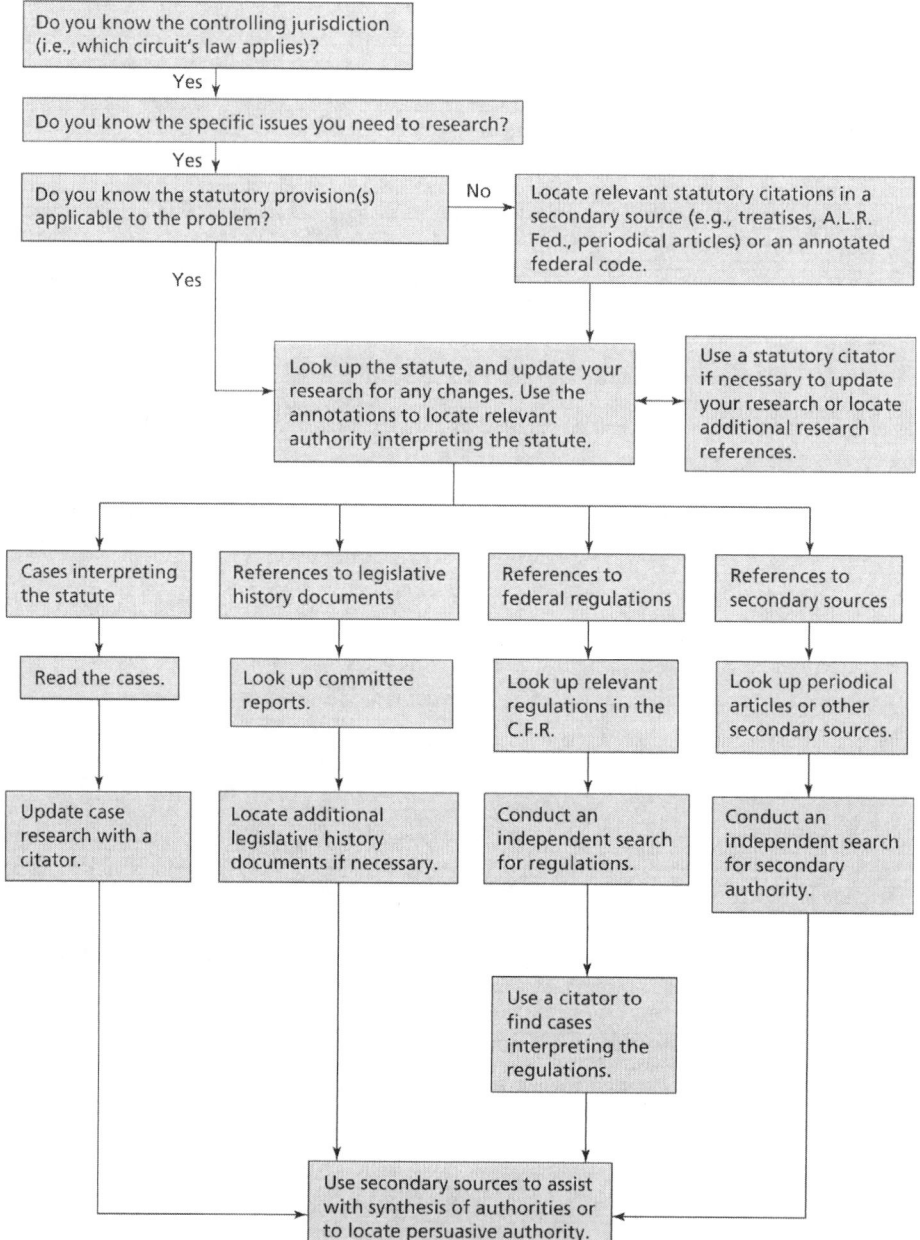

Figure 8.4   Flowchart for Researching Rules of Procedure

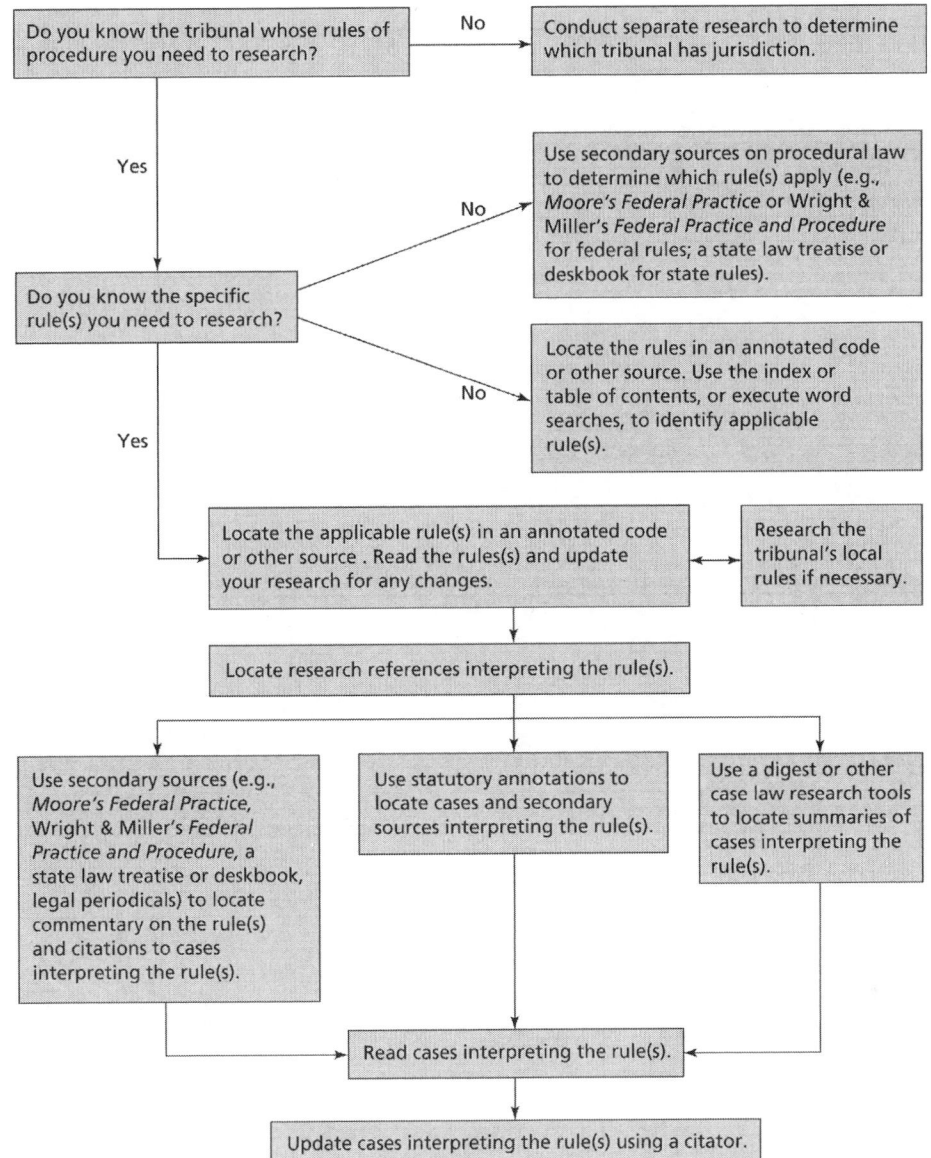

CHAPTER 9

NEW YORK LAW SCHOOL: "DEVELOPING A RESEARCH STRATEGY" FORM

Note: This form is available on the Mendik Library homepage

NEW YORK LAW SCHOOL   **Fall 2012**

> ***DEVELOPING A RESEARCH STRATEGY***
> Use this form as a checklist for your research and to note the sources you review.
> Take notes, keep track of where you have been – where you need to go. Read all of
> the steps first. You may not want or need to do them in order. Expand the sections
> as you work through your problem.

1. **WHAT ARE YOU TRYING TO FIND? WHAT IS THE LEGAL ISSUE? WHAT ARE THE GENERAL RULES OF LAW YOU NEED TO FIND? WHAT ARE THE BASIC CONCEPTS THAT DEFINE THE ISSUE?**

[You should be able to write out your legal issue in one or two sentences. You can come back and edit it as you get more information. Writing it down will help you think through indexing terms, concepts, etc.]

---

2. **WHAT INFORMATION DO YOU HAVE ABOUT THE PROBLEM?**

   - DO YOU HAVE ANY CITATION LEADS?

       - STATUTES?   _____

       - CASE(S)?   _____

       - DIGEST TOPIC & KEY NUMBER INFORMATION?   _____

   - JURISDICTION?

3. **THINK ABOUT THE TYPE OF SOURCES THAT MIGHT BE HELPFUL. WHERE SHOULD YOU START? HOW MUCH DO YOU KNOW ABOUT THE TOPIC?**

   ☐ STARTING WITH AN ENCYCLOPEDIA OR TREATISE CAN HELP TO GROUND YOU AND PROVIDE A GOOD
   INTRODUCTION TO THE ISSUES / STATUTES / CASES AND HOW THEY INTERRELATE.

   < The Library catalog (http://www.lawlib.nyls.edu) will give you a list of treatises, encyclopedias, and other
   sources. The catalog will give you the Call Number so that you can find the source in the stacks. If a source is
   online, the catalog will give you a link to the database. *(Ask a librarian for help.)*

   < If you have the name of the source (e.g., New York Jurisprudence), SEARCH BY TITLE
         For Example: Title: | New York Jurisprudence |

   < If you do not know the name of a book, SEARCH BY KEYWORD
         For Example: Keyword: | New York Negligence |

4. FIND THE SECONDARY SOURCES. Once you find the source, use the Index to find the sections you should read. What are "good" index terms? Review your issue statement (step 1) & see step 5. If you listed a statute or a case name in step 2, check the Tables sections to find specific discussion of that case / statute.

☐ New York Jurisprudence <u>and</u> many treatises have a Table of Statutes & Regulations and a Case Name Table as part of the index. These tables will tell you where the statute, regulation or cases are discussed in the text.

     ENCYCLOPEDIA TOPIC: _____

- An encyclopedia will give you a good overview and help you identify the controlling statute or leading case to work from to find more cases. This is always a great place to start a research project.

- *Take Notes:* Key "terms of art," cases or statutes mentioned, Digest Topic or Key Numbers listed, references to A.L.R. articles.

☐ **LEADING TREATISE ON THE TOPIC:** (Author / Title / Call Number).

    _____

- Check the Treatises link on our web page (under Library Materials) or Ask a Librarian who can guide you to the "leading" (most helpful) treatise on various subjects.

- Treatises are written to explain the law and help you gain a better understanding of the rules and issues. They are more in-depth than encyclopedias. They will help you broaden your understanding of issues.

- *Take Notes:*

5. IDENTIFY THE INDIVIDUAL CONCEPTS WITHIN THE ISSUE THAT <u>MUST</u> BE DISCUSSED IN A DOCUMENT FOR IT TO BE RELEVANT TO YOUR RESEARCH. These will be INDEX terms to use in the statutes, digests or other secondary sources. These terms are also the key to Lexis and Westlaw searching. Consider the ways in which the concepts might be stated: "terms of art" or "general descriptions." Think about synonyms and alternative expressions. Keep a running list of new terms of art / concepts that you did not think of initially. [*Remember*: First look for the "general rules." Searches that are too fact-pattern-specific will almost always exclude relevant material. You may need to argue by analogy or argue from the opposite side of an issue.]

RELEVANT CONCEPTS   **SYNONYMS & ALTERNATIVE EXPRESSIONS**

_____   _____

_____   _____

_____   _____

6. FIND MORE CASES: KEYCITE / SHEPARDIZE: Once you find a "good" case:
- a. make sure it is still good law;
- b. determine how subsequent cases have "treated" the court's reasoning or holding: Followed? Explained? Distinguished? Questioned?
- c. find MORE cases. These are great case-finding tools. Note the CITATIONS that look interesting / worth investigating? *REMEMBER* you can search within the "citing references" for particular words, headnotes, topics, depth of treatment.

7. REVIEW YOUR NOTES ON THE CASES AND STATUTES YOU HAVE READ. EDIT YOUR LEGAL ISSUE. HAVE YOU ANSWERED ALL THE NECESSARY QUESTIONS?

CHAPTER 10

FOR REFERENCE: COURT WEBSITE INFORMATION

Almost every court posts relevant rules on its website. These rules may include the applicable state or federal rules of civil procedure as well as local rules and standing orders.

The rules of the United States Supreme Court, which have been referenced throughout the text, can currently be found at this website: http://www.supreme-court.gov/ctrules/2010RulesoftheCourt.pdf.

Some federal courts combine the generally applicable rules with their own local rules. At the following link, for example, the tenth circuit's local rules are interspersed with the relevant Federal Rules of Appellate Procedure: http://www.ca10.uscourts.gov/downloads/2010-rules.pdf

Other courtsmay post their local rules as a separate document, as this link shows: http://www.state.il.us/court/AppellateCourt/LocalRules/3rd.pdf.

If you are writing a motion brief, remember that many trial courts do not use rules to articulate formal requirements for these briefs. Nevertheless, consult the appropriate civil or criminal rules, the local rules, or the court's standing orders for any existing requirements for motion briefs or oral arguments. This link shows a standing order regarding civil motions for summary judgment: http://www.ohs-d.uscourts.gov/judges/dlott/Standard%20Order.pdf.

If you are looking for the rules of a particular court, search for the court by its full name, and then look on the main page for a link to the court's rules. Be careful when searching. Sites other than the court's official website may give you inaccurate information or no information due to "link rot" or other problems. Be sure to link to the court's official website (perhaps designated with a "dot-gov" url) so that you can be certain to have the most up-to-date rules. Useful search terms include phrases like "standing orders," "standard orders," "general orders," and, of course, "local rules."

UNDERSTANDING STANDARDS OF REVIEW

CHAPTER 11

How and When Appellate Courts Obtain Jurisdiction Over a Case

Understanding some basic principles about the various courts and their powers will help you to make decisions as you prepare your written and oral arguments. Your arguments will be different if you are writing a brief to a trial court as opposed to an appellate court. In the appellate system, you may argue differently to an intermediate court of appeals as opposed to a court of last resort. On the one hand, intermediate courts of appeals must hear every appeal (with few exceptions)[1] and must follow the decisions of the courts above them. Courts of last resort, on the other hand, usually have some authority to decide which cases they will hear[2] and the authority to make new law.

This chapter briefly explains principles of appellate jurisdiction. The chapter that follows discusses how writers can use the appropriate standards of review in both appellate briefs and motion briefs.

§11.1 Jurisdiction in Courts of Last Resort

A "court of last resort" is the highest court in a particular legal system. It is the last court to which litigants can resort when seeking resolution of a legal issue. In the federal system, the United States Supreme Court is the court of last resort, and the majority of its cases come from the United States Courts of Appeals of the various circuits. In state systems, the highest court of appeals — often called the Supreme Court — is the court of last resort, and it generally hears cases from that state's intermediate appellate courts. The United States Supreme Court can hear appeals from state courts of last resort, but only if the issue is a matter of federal law. For example, the Court may hear an appeal in order to determine whether a state court has interpreted a law in a way that may have conflicted with the United States Constitution.

---

[1] *See, e.g.,* Tenn. R. App. P. 3; Fed. R. App. P. 3.
[2] *See, e.g.,* Ohio Sup. Ct. Prac. R. II, §1(A) (listing "appeals of right," "claimed appeals of right," "discretionary appeals," and "certified conflict cases"). *See also* U.S. Sup. Ct. R. 10.

Most courts of last resort are not merely courts of error; that is, they do not take cases simply because one party claims that there was an error of law in a lower court decision. For example, Rule 10 of the Rules of the Supreme Court of the United States explicitly says that "[a] petition for a writ of certiorari [the main method for gaining access to the Court] is rarely granted when the asserted error consists of erroneous factual findings or the misapplication of a properly stated rule of law." Instead, a court of last resort takes cases in order to resolve pressing issues, and it may refuse to take cases unless or until it believes that its intervention is necessary.[3] Two factors make it more likely that the United States Supreme Court, for instance, will grant a petition for a writ of certiorari. First, the Court frequently grants certiorari if it believes that a state court or a lower federal court of appeals is misinterpreting or misapplying the Court's jurisprudence. Second, and more commonly, the Court will grant certiorari when two or more courts are in conflict over an interpretation of the federal Constitution, or when courts are in conflict over a question of federal law.[4]

Interestingly, the Court does not always grant certiorari immediately when either of these factors is present. It is not uncommon for the Court to let a conflict simmer for a few years, with different lower courts writing decisions either way. The Court may use this method purposefully, to benefit from the analysis and reasoning of several different lower courts. By allowing several opinions to be written on a subject, the Court can assess several different resolutions and analyses of the same issue.

Perhaps for these reasons, the Court attaches no precedential value to the denial of a petition for a writ of certiorari. That is, a denial of certiorari does *not* indicate that the Court approves of the decision below. Rather, it means only that the Court did not believe, for whatever reason, that it was an issue that was worthy of its review *at that time.*

§11.2 Jurisdiction in Intermediate Courts of Appeals

The rules are somewhat different in intermediate courts of appeals. Generally, state and federal intermediate courts of appeals will hear any appeal of a final order if the appellant has met specified procedural guidelines.[5] The United States Courts of Appeals have jurisdiction over appeals from all final decisions of the

---

[3] The Ohio Supreme Court, for example, distinguishes between "claimed appeals of right" and "discretionary appeals." Ohio Sup. Ct. Prac. R. II, §1. It then decides whether to grant each type of appeal, depending on whether the appeal meets the court's standards, e.g., whether the appeal involves any "substantial constitutional question" (one standard for claimed appeals of right) or asserts a "question of public or great general interest" (one standard for discretionary appeals). Ohio Sup. Ct. Prac. R. II, §1(A)(2), (A)(3).

[4] *See generally* U.S. Sup. Ct. R. 10.

[5] *See, e.g.,* Ohio R. App. P. tit. II, R. 3; Fed. R. App. P. 3. Appeals of certain criminal appeals may have to meet different standards. In most situations, federal courts of appeals have discretion whether to hear interlocutory appeals according to the guidelines in 28 U.S.C. §1292. *See also Mohawk Indus. v. Carpenter,* 130 S. Ct. 599, 603 (2009) (interlocutory decisions adverse to attorney-client privilege do not qualify for immediate appeal); *Coopers & Lybrand v. Livesay,* 437 U.S. 463, 475 (1978) (describing court discretion).

United States District Courts.[6] The courts of appeals also have jurisdiction to hear appeals from a variety of other judicial and quasi-judicial bodies, including, for example, appeals to enforce or challenge orders of the National Labor Relations Board.[7]

Federal intermediate courts of appeals may decide cases without oral argument. Although, according to the rules, oral argument is presumed, a three-judge panel can vote unanimously that oral argument is unnecessary in a given case for any of the following three reasons:

1. The appeal is frivolous.
2. The dispositive issue or issues have been authoritatively decided.
3. The facts and legal arguments are adequately presented in the briefs and record, and the decisional process would not be significantly aided by oral argument.[8]

What this rule means in practice is that a large percentage of cases are assigned to the so-called summary docket, and many of those are decided based on memoranda submitted by law clerks and staff attorneys who have reviewed the party briefs. The courts' statistics indicate that in 2008, a typical year, more than 65 percent of the appeals terminated on the merits were decided without oral argument.[9] When cases are on the summary docket, some judges make their decisions based on staff memoranda alone; they may not read the briefs in full at all. The practical brief-writer will presume that oral argument will not be granted, and will write a brief that can persuade a law clerk as well as a judge.

---

[6] 28 U.S.C. §1291.

[7] 29 U.S.C. §160(e), (f).

[8] Fed. R. App. P. 34(a)(2).

[9] Federal Judicial Center, *U.S. Courts of Appeals: Appeals Commenced, Terminated, and Pending (Excludes Federal Circuit)*, http://www.uscourts.gov/judicialfactsfigures/2008/Table202.pdf (last visited Mar. 30, 2010). *See also* Patricia M. Wald, *19 Tips from 19 Years on the Appellate Bench*, 1 J. App. Prac. & Proc. 7, 9 (1999) (estimating that 60 percent of cases nationwide are decided without oral argument).

CHAPTER 12

APPELLATE STANDARDS OF REVIEW

§12.1 Introduction

Whether an appellate court is an intermediate court of appeals or a court of last resort, whether it hears an appeal as of right or as a matter of discretion, it agrees only to *review* the decision below. Hearing an appeal does not mean that the court will retry the case. Instead of observing the examination and cross-examination of witnesses, hearing opening and closing arguments, and seeing the attorneys present various evidentiary exhibits all over again, the court *reviews* important evidence (whether findings of fact, testimony, or exhibits) and the attorneys' written arguments — in the form of briefs to the court — about the significance of that evidence. During the oral argument on appeal (if any), the court questions the attorneys about the sufficiency of the evidence, the significance of the arguments, or the impact of a holding one way or the other. The court then decides whether to affirm, to reverse, to reverse and remand, or to vacate the decision below.

When reviewing the decision of any lower court, the court — explicitly or implicitly — applies a certain appellate standard of review to that decision. The *appellate standard of review*[1] is a label that a reviewing court puts on the level of **deference** it gives to the findings of the court below. The appellate standard of review tells the court how "wrong" the lower court has to be before it will be reversed.

The appellate standard of review that the court chooses to apply depends on which aspect of the case is under review: an evidentiary ruling, a finding of fact, a legal ruling, or some other type of decision. Some decisions can be reversed simply if the reviewing court disagrees with the lower court. Others can be reversed only if the reviewing court can identify a serious error on the part of the court below. Generally, courts give high deference to decisions about facts — that is, they are loathe to upset a finding of fact — and low deference to conclusions of law. Because the particular appellate standard of review can significantly affect the arguments that you make to the court, you should consider this issue early in

---

[1] For the sake of clarity, I use the label *appellate standards of review* to refer to these standards. However, as noted below, many courts use the label *standard of review* to refer to appellate standards of review, motion standards of review, and government action standards of review.

your research process and decide what standard the court is likely to apply to the decision that you seek to have reversed or hope to have affirmed.

§12.2 Purpose and Meaning of Appellate Standards of Review

Various public policies support the competing appellate standards of review.[2] Appellate courts use a low deference appellate standard of review for decisions about the law because they believe that those who must use the law benefit from uniformity.[3] Low deference standards give reviewing courts an opportunity to create a consistent body of law, which may be particularly important for issues of constitutional rights.[4] In fact, when a constitutional issue is involved, courts may decide to substitute the low deference de novo standard for a higher deference standard that might normally be appropriate for a given issue.[5]

A high-deference appellate standard of review promotes judicial economy and finality of certain types of decisions. A high-deference standard is also based on the premise that the trial court is in the best position to understand evidence. Particularly in the case of witness testimony, a trial court judge or jury has an opportunity that the court of appeals doesn't have. The judge or jury can observe the witnesses' demeanor, their tone of voice, and their body language, and use its best judgment based on those intangibles when it makes findings of fact.

Although many advocates ignore the standard after articulating it, the appellate standard of review is really the context within which the entire argument rests. Because there is often no controversy about which standard applies, however, some litigators are lulled into complacency on this subject and may miss fertile ground for legal argument.[6]

As a practical lawyer, you should devote serious attention to the standard of review early in the research process in order to determine the role it will play in your case. The discussion that follows describes the most significant appellate standards of review, using the labels most commonly used in federal courts. Although, of course, you must rely on research rather than a textbook to provide

---

[2] For an interesting discussion of the policies behind certain appellate standards of review, see Michael R. Bosse, *Standards of Review: The Meaning of Words*, 49 Me. L. Rev. 367, 374-84 (1997).

[3] *See, e.g., Cooper Indus., Inc. v. Leatherman Tool Group, Inc.*, 532 U.S. 424, 436 (2001); *Ornelas v. United States*, 517 U.S. 690, 698 (1996).

[4] *See generally* Bosse, *supra* note 11, at 383, 397.

[5] *See, e.g., Cooper Indus., Inc. v. Leatherman Tool Group, Inc.*, 532 U.S. 424, 434 (2001) (Court used de novo standard to review a district court determination of the constitutionality of a punitive damages award).

[6] The United States Supreme Court frequently addresses standard of review issues. *See, e.g., Metro. Life Ins. Co. v. Glenn*, 128 S. Ct. 2343, 2348 (2008) (analyzing appropriate standards of review in ERISA appeals); *Gall v. United States*, 552 U.S. 38, 46 (2007) (analyzing use of the abuse of discretion standard of review in sentencing decisions); *Cooper Indus., Inc. v. Leatherman Tool Group, Inc.*, 532 U.S. 424, 434 (2001) (finding that de novo review, rather than abuse of discretion, was appropriate standard of review for district court determination of the constitutionality of a punitive damages award); *Ornelas v. United States*, 517 U.S. 690 (1996) (holding that determinations of "reasonable suspicion" and "probable cause" should be reviewed de novo by appellate courts). *See generally* Bosse, *supra* note 11, at 374-84 (discussing *Ornelas*), and Kelly Kunsch, *Standard of Review (State and Federal): A Primer*, 18 Seattle U. L. Rev. 11, 25 (1994).

support for any standard of review argument, state courts often apply standards that are similar to the federal standards.

§12.2.1 Clearly Erroneous

A clearly erroneous standard applies to findings of facts. Rule 52(a) of the Federal Rules of Civil Procedure provides: "Findings of Fact, whether based on oral or documentary evidence, must not be set aside unless clearly erroneous, and the reviewing court must give due regard to the trial court's opportunity to judge the witnesses' credibility." This standard reflects the attitude that the fact-finder is often in the best position to observe the presentation of the facts. The United States Supreme Court has commented on the importance of the trial judge's opportunities:

> The rationale for deference to the original finder of fact is not limited to the superiority of the trial judge's position to make determinations of credibility. The trial judge's major role is the determination of fact, and with experience in fulfilling that role comes expertise. . . . [T]he trial on the merits should be "the 'main event' . . . rather than a 'tryout on the road.'" . . . When findings are based on determinations regarding the credibility of witnesses, Rule 52(a) demands even greater deference to the trial court's findings; for only the trial judge can be aware of the variations in demeanor and tone of voice that bear so heavily on the listener's understanding of and belief in what is said.[7]

Courts often note that a court should find clear error only when its review of the record leads to "a definite and firm conviction" that the court has committed a mistake.[8] The clearly erroneous standard is a high hurdle for an advocate to overcome. The Seventh Circuit has used a piscatorial metaphor to explain the standard's meaning:

> To be clearly erroneous, a decision must strike us as more than just maybe or probably wrong; it must, as one member of this court recently stated during oral argument, strike us as wrong with the force of a five-week-old, unrefrigerated dead fish.[9]

Although not all courts use such vivid language to describe their reactions, all courts are extremely hesitant to overturn findings of fact.[10]

---

[7] *Anderson v. City of Bessemer City*, 470 U.S. 564, 574, 575 (1985).

[8] *E.g., United States v. U.S. Gypsum Co.*, 333 U.S. 364, 395 (1948); *J. L. v. Mercer Island Sch. Dist.*, 592 F.3d 938, 949 (9th Cir. 2010).

[9] *Parts & Elec. Motors, Inc. v. Sterling Elec. Inc.*, 866 F.2d 228, 233 (7th Cir. 1988).

[10] Note that all federal (and most state) jury findings, which may be hard to separate into distinct questions of law and fact, are usually reviewed under the "substantial evidence" standard per the Seventh Amendment to the United States Constitution, which provides that "no fact tried by a jury shall be otherwise re-examined in any Court of the United States, than according to the rules of the common law." Those "rules of the common law" generally provide that such a finding must have only a "reasonable basis in the law" and have "warrant in the record." *NLRB v. Hearst Publications*, 322 U.S. 111, 131 (1944). Commentators have noted that courts are extremely reluctant to find that there is not "substantial evidence" to support a jury finding. Kunsch, *supra* note 15, at 43. *See also United States v. Ellefson*, 419 F.3d 859, 862-63 (8th Cir. 2005) ("We may reverse a jury's verdict only if 'no reasonable jury could have found the accused guilty beyond a reasonable doubt.'") (citation omitted). *See also United States v. Boria*, 592 F.3d 476, 480 (Fed. Cir. 2010).

§12.2.2 De Novo

Because most decisions that come before appellate courts are based on questions of law, the most commonly applied standard is the **de novo** standard. The de novo standard is a low-deference standard — or, more aptly, a no-deference standard — that applies when courts are reviewing the meaning or application of the controlling law. De novo review is sometimes referred to as "plenary review" because it allows the court to give a full, or plenary, review to the findings below. When courts apply the de novo standard, they look at the legal questions as if no one had yet decided them, giving no deference to legal findings made below. When this standard is applied, the reviewing court is willing to substitute its judgment for that of the trial court or the intermediate court of appeals.

Courts apply the de novo standard not only to questions of law, but also to mixed questions of law and fact. A mixed question of law and fact is often characterized as a question about whether certain agreed-upon facts meet a legal standard. In *Ornelas v. United States*, for example, the United States Supreme Court decided that de novo was an appropriate appellate standard of review when it reviewed a trial court's determination as to whether a police officer indeed had probable cause based on the undisputed facts.[11] The Court justifies the de novo standard in mixed question situations, as it does when it reviews other questions of law, with the goal of unifying precedent and stabilizing legal principles.[12]

If the de novo standard applies, the legal findings of the courts below have *no weight* other than their intrinsic validity. Some novice legal writers make the mistake of citing to the decision under review in order to justify a conclusion that they want the appellate court to accept. It is certainly appropriate to argue that the decision below is correct, but you must support that assertion with citations to authorities other than the decision under review.

§12.2.3 Abuse of Discretion

The **abuse of discretion** standard is typically used to review discretionary decisions such as a judge's procedural rulings during a trial. These decisions might include decisions on nondispositive motions, objections, admissibility of evidence, or general conduct issues.[13] Commentators have noted that language such as "the court may" or "for good cause" are often predictors of an abuse of discretion standard of review.[14] Like the clearly erroneous standard, this standard presumes some expertise on the part of the trial court judge. Some judges see the standard in the same light as the clearly erroneous standard. For example, the United States Court of Appeals for the First Circuit has noted that, as to

---

[11] *Ornelas*, 517 U.S. at 695.

[12] *See generally Ornelas*, 517 U.S. at 697; *United States v. Arvizu*, 534 U.S. 266, 275 (2002).

[13] *See, e.g.*, Kunsch, *supra* note 15, at 34-35.

[14] Kunsch, *supra* note 15, at 35 (citing Maurice Rosenberg, *Judicial Discretion of the Trial Court, Viewed from Above*, 22 Syracuse L. Rev. 635, 655 (1971)). *See also In re Terrorist Bombings of U.S. Embassies in E. Afr. v. Odeh*, 552 F.3d 93, 135 (2d Cir. 2008) (noting use of phrase "the court may" in rule of criminal procedure as signal that abuse of discretion is appropriate standard of review).

evidentiary rulings, "[o]nly rarely — and in extraordinarily compelling circumstances — will we, from the vista of a cold appellate record, reverse a district court's on-the-spot judgment concerning the relative weighing of probative value and unfair effect."[15]

§12.2.4 Other Appellate Standards

Review of administrative agency decisions is governed by the Administrative Procedure Act, which provides at 5 U.S.C. §706 that reviewing courts should "set aside" agency "actions, findings, or conclusions" that are **arbitrary, capricious, an abuse of discretion**, or otherwise not in accordance with law." When an agency holds a formal hearing that creates a record, the reviewing court may set aside agency decisions only when they are **unsupported by substantial evidence**."[16]

§12.3 Identifying the Appropriate Appellate Standard of Review

Of course, knowing the standards is only the first step. You must then decide which standard or standards apply in your case. Some issues are obviously questions of fact (e.g., Did the defendant hit the victim? Did the officer ask a certain question of the defendant?), while others are obviously questions of law (e.g., Did the court apply the correct legal standard? Is a supervisor an "employer" within the meaning of the statute?). Mixed questions are more difficult to identify; courts generally identify a mixed question of law and fact as one that is based on how a legal principle applies to established or agreed-upon facts.

Using one standard over another — for example, a clearly erroneous appellate standard of review rather than a de novo standard — can lead to a vastly different review of the same case. Accordingly, you should study the record below carefully. Identify the decisions, rulings, or findings that are at the crux of your client's case. First, identify who made the ruling. The standard of review depends on whether the decision maker was a judge, a jury, or an administrative body. Second, focus on what kind of decision was made. If it was a ruling on an evidentiary matter, the abuse of discretion standard will probably apply. If it was a finding of fact, the court will apply the clearly erroneous standard. If, as is most likely, it was a decision of law, the court will apply a de novo standard. If you are arguing to a court of last resort, you may look to the court of appeals decision to see what appellate standard of review it applied. If no standard is mentioned in the decision (and the standard is often not mentioned), the court probably applied a de novo standard. Of course, if appropriate, you may decide to argue that the lower court applied the wrong standard of review.[17]

---

[15] *Freeman v. Package Mach. Co.*, 865 F.2d 1331, 1340 (1st Cir. 1988).

[16] *See, e.g.*, Kunsch, *supra* note 15, at 40-41.

[17] *See generally Cooper Indus.*, 532 U.S. at 434 (noting that court below erred when applying an abuse of discretion standard rather than the de novo standard); *Ornelas*, 517 U.S. at 698-99 (noting that court below erred when it applied a deferential appellate standard of review).

If you are in doubt as to the appropriate standard of review for the legal issue your case presents, do a little focused research. You may find precedent as to the standard of review for the narrow legal issue in your case. In addition to conducting primary research, you may find secondary sources helpful. Many practice manuals are geared to attorneys practicing within the courts of a specific jurisdiction; some of these manuals address appellate standards of review as they apply to particular legal issues.[18]

Although the appellate standard of review is usually not controversial, at times it is at the heart of the appellate decision.[19] If the standard of review in your case is de novo, it will have almost no impact on your argument. You will address the standard of review — either in the introductory section or in a separate, labeled section — and then you will spend the rest of the argument discussing the appropriate legal standards and how the appellate court should apply those standards.

If your case could or should be reviewed under a more deferential standard, however, that standard will have a significant impact on your argument. Even if the court you are writing to asks for the standard to be announced in a separate section, you must still incorporate it into your argument. For example, if the clearly erroneous standard applies, your argument must identify the particular finding of fact that you assert to be clearly erroneous, and cite to the record. Then, you must show how the evidence indicates that the finding was clearly erroneous, and show how it changed the outcome of the case. Alternatively, if you must assert that the judge abused his or her discretion, you must identify the particular decision the judge made in error, use appropriate authorities to explain why it was wrong, and specify why and how it changed the outcome of the case.

As you must with any legal argument, make appellate standard of review arguments honestly. Do not create an appellate standard of review issue where none exists. If the standard genuinely makes a difference in the case, however, you can and should use it to demonstrate the justice of the result you seek.

§12.4 Format Considerations

During recent years, many courts have begun using their local rules to ask for a separate statement of the appellate standard of review. The Pennsylvania Rules of Appellate Procedure, for example, require that a statement of "both the scope of review and the standard of review" appear in the appellant's brief, "separately and distinctly entitled," between sections containing the "order or other determination in question" and the "[s]tatement of the questions involved."[20] Similarly, the local rules of the Third Circuit require that "the statement of the standard or

---

[18] *See, e.g., Anderson's Sixth Circuit Federal Practice Manual* ch. 7 (Matthew-Bender & Co., Inc. 2006) (also available at LexisNexis.com).

[19] For an interesting discussion of using policy concerns to drive the discussion of appellate standard of review, *see* Bosse, *supra* note 15, at 374 et seq. If the appropriate appellate standard of review is controversial, you can and should justify your argument with references to policies served by choosing the standard you favor.

[20] 210 Pa. Code Rule 2111.

scope of review for each issue on appeal" should appear "under a separate heading placed before the discussion of the issue."[21] The Rules of Court for the Kansas Supreme Court require that within the Appellant's Brief, "[e]ach issue shall begin with citation to the appropriate standard of appellate review and a reference to the specific location in the record on appeal where the issue was raised and ruled upon."[22] If the local rules do not demand a separate statement, the standard should usually be included in introductory material within the argument. No matter what method is used, you should cite to authority for the standard of review, just as you would for any legal proposition.

In most situations, the statement of the appellate standard of review requires no more than a paragraph. As noted previously, however, if the standard is controversial or if it is otherwise significant to your argument, it should be treated like any other major issue, with appropriate point headings and text used to make the point. This method should be used even if the local rules require a separate, formal statement of the standard.

---

[21] 3d Cir. LAR [Local Appellate Rule] 28.1(b).

[22] Kan. Sup. Ct. R. 6.02(e). Of course, the appellee's brief should reflect any disagreement as to the appropriate standard of review. *See, e.g.,* Kan. Sup. Ct. R. 6.03(d) ("[e]ach issue shall begin with citation to the appropriate standard of appellate review; appellee shall either concur in appellant's citation to the standard of appellate review or offer additional authority.").

CHAPTER 13

"STANDARDS OF REVIEW" IN MOTION BRIEFS

§13.1 Introduction

Many courts use the term *standard of review* to describe the standards used to decide some trial-level motions.[1] Some courts use the term *legal standard* or *pleading standard*, which is perhaps the more accurate term.[2] The term *standard of review* is less accurate in this situation because the trial court cannot be said to be *re*-viewing anything: The motion to the trial court represents the first time that any court has viewed the legal argument. Unlike appellate standards of review, motion standards of review do not ask a court to apply a particular level of deference to the actions of another decision maker. Nevertheless, courts frequently use the phrase *standard of review* in this context.

Many motions address routine matters such as requests for extension of time or for discovery. These motions may require little more than a request for action accompanied by the citation to a statute or rule. Other motions, however, may require formal briefing that is similar to the briefing done for appellate courts. Like appellate briefs, motion briefs may be the sole basis for decision: Trial courts frequently decide motions based on the briefs alone, without oral argument.[3] The standard of review is particularly important for motions like the motion to dismiss

---

[1] E.g., *Stainback v. Mabus*, 671 F. Supp. 2d 12 (D. D.C. 2009) (referring to "standard of review" governing summary judgment motions); *N. Mariana Islands v. United States*, 670 F. Supp. 2d 65, 80 (D. D.C. 2009) (referring to "standard of review" governing motions to dismiss). *See also, e.g.*, David F. Herr, Roger S. Haydock & Jeffrey W. Stempel, *Motion Practice* (4th ed., Aspen 2004), for detailed information on motion practice in litigation.

[2] E.g., *Dukes v. Shinseki*, 671 F. Supp. 2d 106, 110 (D. D.C. 2009) (referring to "legal standards" governing motions to dismiss and for summary judgment); *Ashcroft v. Iqbal*, 129 S. Ct. 1937, 1953 (2009) (court noted, in reference to standards governing motions to dismiss, that "[o]ur decision in *Twombly* expounded the pleading standard for 'all civil actions,' *ibid.*, and it applies to antitrust and discrimination suits alike").

[3] *See* Herr, Haydock & Stempel, *supra* Ch.13 note 1, at §5.02 . *See also* Loc. Civ. & Crim. R. U.S. Dist. Ct. S. Dist. Ohio §III, R. 7.1 (noting presumption that motions will be decided without oral argument and that counsel must apply to the court for permission to present an oral argument on a motion).

(Fed. R. Civ. P. 12(b)(6)) and the motion for summary judgment (Fed. R. Civ. P. 56(c)).[4] These so-called dispositive motions can "dispose" of a case, at least temporarily, and thus present an important opportunity for advocacy.[5]

The standards of review for dispositive motions are based on the trial court's competing needs to allow access to courts on the one hand and to use judicial resources efficiently and prevent frivolous lawsuits on the other. Counsel, in contrast, may use motion practice strategically, to educate the court as to the issues the case presents, or to narrow the factual or legal issues in dispute.[6] Whatever your purpose in filing a dispositive motion — or any motion — it is important to know and use the appropriate motion standard of review. The sections below discuss the standards of review for two of the most common dispositive motions and address general methods for using standards of review in motion briefs.

§13.2 Motions to Dismiss

A motion to dismiss for failure to state a claim upon which relief can be granted is filed in lieu of answering the complaint, pursuant to Rule 12(b)(6). In general terms, this kind of motion can be granted for either of two reasons: the law does not reach the facts, or the facts do not reach the law. That is, a court may grant a motion to dismiss if the law does not support the type of claim made or if the facts pled in the complaint do not indicate that the plaintiff can establish facts that would entitle him or her to relief. The court must take the factual allegations in the complaint as true,[7] but this standard does not apply to legal conclusions.

Two hypothetical Title VII cases can help to illustrate these reasons for dismissing a complaint. Title VII provides that "employers" may not terminate an employee based on race, sex, religion, or other factors. The statute defines an *employer* as someone who employs more than 15 employees. The plaintiff must establish that the employer had knowledge of the protected status at the time of the termination.

First, if a plaintiff filed a Title VII action even though he or she worked for a company with only ten employees, the company would probably file a motion to dismiss. The court would not analyze whether the allegations of discrimination were valid or invalid. Instead, it would consider whether the law reaches the facts by asking, "even if these allegations are true, can this plaintiff recover against this defendant under this statute?" The plaintiff in this example could never recover against this defendant under Title VII, because the law does not support this type

---

[4] Of course, these are not the only kinds of motions that require briefing or that are decided based upon so-called standards of review. *See, e.g., Incantalupo v. Lawrence Union Free Sch. Dist. No. 15,* 652 F. Supp. 2d 314, 322 (E.D.N.Y. 2009) (describing standard of review for motion for preliminary injunction).

[5] Unlike other motions, dispositive motions may dispose of the case by creating a final appealable order. *See, e.g.,* Herr, Haydock & Stempel, *supra* Ch.13 note 1, at §4.03 (detailing the differences between motion practice and appellate advocacy).

[6] Motions for summary judgment or partial summary judgment may often be used strategically in this way. *E.g.,* Herr, Haydock & Stempel, *supra* Ch.13 note 1, at §16.02 (discussing when to use motions for partial summary judgment).

[7] *E.g., Bell Atlantic Corp. v. Twombly,* 550 U.S. 544, 555 (2007).

of claim: Title VII does not apply to employers with fewer than 15 employees. Accordingly, the court would grant the motion to dismiss.

In another case, a plaintiff might file a Title VII claim and allege that he was terminated based on his religion. Suppose that the complaint merely claimed that he had been fired because of his religion (a legal conclusion) but did not allege facts that indicated that the defendant employer had knowledge of the plaintiff's religion. Again, the defendant would probably file a motion to dismiss. The court would consider whether the facts reach the law by evaluating the facts pled in the complaint, asking whether the alleged facts would plausibly allow the plaintiff to establish the fact that defendant knew the plaintiff's religion at the time of the termination.

In general, the standard for a motion to dismiss tries to balance the needs of plaintiffs, of defendants, and of the judicial system. The plaintiff need not specify every detail of his or her claim, but the complaint must give the defendant fair notice and must contain either direct or indirect allegations as to all of the claim's material elements. Two recent cases from the United States Supreme Court may have an effect on how motions to dismiss are analyzed.

In 2007, the United States Supreme Court decided *Bell Atlantic v. Twombly*, 550 U.S. 544 (2007). In that case, a somewhat complex antitrust cause of action, the Court arguably made the plaintiffs' job a little more difficult. The Court seemed to require more than mere notice pleading, holding that while "a complaint attacked by a Rule 12(b)(6) motion to dismiss does not need detailed factual allegations . . . a plaintiff's obligation to provide the 'grounds' of his 'entitle[ment] to relief' requires more than labels and conclusions, and a formulaic recitation of the elements of a cause of action will not do." *Id.* at 555 (citations omitted). The Court noted that "[f]actual allegations must be enough to raise a right to relief above the speculative level" but that "the assumption" is "that all the allegations in the complaint are true." *Id.* (citations omitted). A complaint must include factual allegations that make its legal allegations not merely "conceivable," but "plausible." *Id.* at 570.

Two years later, the Court decided a post-9/11 anti-discrimination case, *Ashcroft v. Iqbal*, 129 S. Ct. 1937 (2009). The Court reaffirmed its decision in *Twombly* and articulated a standard that it called "context-specific" and rooted in "judicial experience and common sense":

> [A] court considering a motion to dismiss can choose to begin by identifying pleadings that, because they are no more than conclusions, are not entitled to the assumption of truth. While legal conclusions can provide the framework of a complaint, they must be supported by factual allegations. When there are well-pleaded factual allegations, a court should assume their veracity and then determine whether they plausibly give rise to an entitlement to relief.[8]

Although the Court took care to say that a "plausibility" requirement is "not akin to a probability requirement," *id.* at 1949, some commentators are concerned that this standard puts too much of a burden on plaintiffs, arguing that many plaintiffs

---

[8] *Ashcroft v. Iqbal*, 129 S. Ct. 1937, 1950 (2009) (citation omitted).

will be unable to craft a "plausible" complaint without discovery.[9] In fact, in 2009, the "Notice Pleading Restoration Act" was introduced in Congress to restore the pre-*Twombly* standard of review.[10]

Accordingly, the careful pleader will be sure to make the complaint's allegations as fact-specific as possible. Even after *Twombly* and *Iqbal*, courts will construe the factual allegations as true. But if the court can be convinced that the plaintiff cannot plausibly establish a set of facts that will entitle him or her to relief — either because the law does not apply to that set of facts or because the set of facts alleged is too speculative, incomplete, or implausible — the court will dismiss the complaint before trial, and often before significant discovery has occurred.

§13.3 Motions for Summary Judgment

The standard of review for a motion for summary judgment is more complicated than the standard for a motion to dismiss. Like a motion to dismiss, a motion for summary judgment may be granted or denied based on issues of fact, issues of law, or both. The plain language of Federal Rule of Civil Procedure 56(c) indicates that the motion should be granted when the evidence shows that there is "no genuine issue as to any material fact" *and* "the moving party is entitled to a judgment as a matter of law." In 1986, however, the United States Supreme Court decided three summary judgment cases that created some initial controversy regarding the standard of review for a motion for summary judgment.[11] The guidelines from these cases, which many state courts have adopted, indicate that a motion for summary judgment requires the nonmoving party to produce substantial evidence on any issue for which that party bears the burden of production at trial.[12] Perhaps obviously, the motion for summary judgment is usually filed after discovery has begun, and sometimes after substantial discovery has been completed. In the alternative, some attorneys use this type of motion to force the other party to bring forth evidence, moving discovery in a particular direction.

Many complaints allege more than one cause of action, and some may be overly optimistic as to the plaintiff's chances of success on some of these causes of action. Defense counsel may file a motion for summary judgment that forces the plaintiff to produce sufficient evidence to support one or more of the allegations. In other cases, a defendant may file a motion for summary judgment supported by its own evidence to counter one or more of the plaintiff's causes of action. A defendant may use this tactic in hopes of forcing a plaintiff to reveal that it has no

---

[9] Edward A. Hartnett, *Taming Twombly, Even After* Iqbal, 158 U. Penn. L. Rev. 473, 474 (2010).

[10] *Id.* at note 7.

[11] *Anderson v. Liberty Lobby, Inc.*, 477 U.S. 242 (1986); *Celotex Corp. v. Catrett*, 477 U.S. 317 (1986); *Matsushita Elec. Indus. Co. v. Zenith Radio Corp.*, 475 U.S. 574 (1986). *See generally* Herr, Haydock & Stempel, *supra* note 32, at §16.01.

[12] *Celotex v. Catrett*, 477 U.S. 317, 322-23 (1986). *See also Wing v. Anchor Media, Ltd. of Tex.*, 570 N.E.2d 1095 (Ohio 1991).

evidence to support certain allegations, leading the court to grant summary judgment to defendant as to those allegations.

If you analogize the adversary nature of the trial to a poker game, defense counsel may use a motion for summary judgment to say, "I call" — in other words, "show me what evidence you have" — or "read 'em and weep" — in other words, "look at the evidence I have; I bet you don't have enough evidence to match it." This technique may force the court to find in defendant's favor or to call an issue into question.

When arguing a motion for summary judgment, be sure to research both how your jurisdiction articulates the standard of review for this type of motion and the relevant burdens of proof for each underlying cause of action.

§13.4 Identifying the Appropriate Motion Standard of Review

With appellate standards of review, a few set standards apply to the many different kinds of decisions that can be reviewed. Motion standards of review, in contrast, are often specific to a particular motion.[13] As with appellate standards of review, the language of the standard may be similar in both state and federal courts, but you should consult the appropriate rules and authorities in the relevant jurisdiction.

Because motion standards of review tend to be motion-specific, identifying the appropriate motion standard of review is usually a more mechanical process than identifying the appellate standard of review. If the motion is mentioned specifically in the civil or criminal rules, that is the place to start, but not end, your research. In addition to consulting the appropriate rules, you should conduct focused research to identify cases in which the relevant courts have applied the standard. Some of these courts may have elaborated on the meaning of the standard, and this "judicial gloss" may have become a part of the standard of review.

As with any legal research, when researching motion standards of review, you should try to identify cases that are recent, on point, in the relevant jurisdiction, and from the highest court possible. On occasion, a particularly germinal case will become "the" case to cite for the boilerplate version of the motion standard of review.[14] When the motion standard and its application are both uncontroversial, it is fine to cite a germinal case for the standard. If either the standard or its

---

[13] There may be some overlap of motion standards of review. For example, under Ohio law, Ohio Rule of Civil Procedure 50 regulates both motions for a directed verdict and motions for judgment notwithstanding the verdict, and the two motions share the same standard of review: "A motion for directed verdict or judgment notwithstanding the verdict is to be granted when, construing the evidence most strongly in favor of the party opposing the motion, the trial court finds that reasonable minds could come to only one conclusion and that conclusion is adverse to the party opposing the motion." *Burns v. Prudential Securities, Inc.*, 857 N.E.2d 621, 631 (Ohio Ct. App. 2006) (citing Rule 50(A)(4)).

[14] For example, in the past, federal courts deciding motions to dismiss under Fed. R. Civ. P. Rule 12(b)(6) frequently cited a 1957 case, *Conley v. Gibson*, 355 U.S. 41 (1957). It remains to be seen whether *Conley* will be replaced by *Bell Atlantic Corp. v. Twombly*, 550 U.S. 544 (2007) or *Ashcroft v. Iqbal*, 129 S. Ct. 1937, 1949-50, 173 L. Ed. 2d 868 (2009).

application is in controversy, however, you should both update and focus your research. Further, be sure to conduct fundamental research to verify that the germinal standard is still valid. Even in 2010, some attorneys have (mistakenly) continued to cite *Conley v. Gibson* as the standard for a motion to dismiss, despite the fact that it was all but overruled for this purpose in 2007.

§13.5 Incorporating Motion Standards into Your Argument

Because motion standards of review are often not controversial, some writers think that they need not articulate the standard or that they may articulate it without citing authority for it. On the contrary, the motion standard of review is the context in which your entire argument takes place, so you must both articulate the standard and cite to meaningful authority for it.[15] If you are arguing in favor of a motion to dismiss, for example, your underlying reason for the request is the language of the standard of review: The court should grant the motion because the plaintiff has not pleaded a set of facts that plausibly give rise to an entitlement to relief. Your argument may focus on case facts and relevant statutes, but it all comes back to the requirements articulated in the motion standard of review.

In many situations, you can merely state and cite the boilerplate language from the standard (whether it comes from a rule, from case law, or from both). With a motion to dismiss, this straightforward use of the standard would be appropriate when, for example, the plaintiff has alleged that the defendant has violated a statute, and the defendant argues that the statute does not apply to the situation. Thus, the focus of the argument would not be the factual question of whether particular facts plausibly exist or have been appropriately included in the complaint, but rather the legal question of whether the statutory language applies to a particular set of facts.

Even in this straightforward situation, however, you should still connect the standard of review to your argument. You may not see much connection between the standard of review for a motion to dismiss and the argument that, for example, supervisors cannot be held individually liable for sexual harassment under Title VII of the Civil Rights Act of 1964. But if you think about it, you will realize that the *reason* the plaintiff's complaint does not plausibly give rise to an entitlement to relief is that Title VII does not allow supervisors to be held individually liable. Thus, even if the facts seem to "plausibly" describe a Title VII violation, Title VII does not allow a plaintiff relief from a supervisor.

You can make the standard of review connection explicit in at least two places: in the roadmap or umbrella paragraphs in which you first articulate the standard, and in your conclusion. Your conclusion will be less effective if you say simply, e.g., "Because supervisors cannot be held individually liable under Title VII, this court should grant Defendant Kobacker's motion to dismiss." Instead,

---

[15] Because most states have enacted state civil rules using language almost identical to federal Rule 12(b)(6) and other federal rules, some students writing briefs to a state court will mistakenly cite to the federal rule or to federal cases articulating the standard. Be sure you are citing authority from the appropriate jurisdiction.

you can explicitly connect the standard of review to your argument by saying, "Title VII does not impose individual liability on supervisors. Therefore, plaintiff has not alleged a set of facts that plausibly give rise to an entitlement to relief against Defendant Kobacker under Title VII, and this court should grant the motion to dismiss."

In the alternative, you may face a situation that allows or requires you to present more in-depth arguments on the application of the motion standard of review. You may wish to argue that the complaint should be dismissed because the facts in the complaint raise a "possibility" of relief rather than a "plausible" "entitlement to relief." In a motion for summary judgment, you may wish to note that the plaintiff has the burden of proof as to the cause of action and argue that it should bring forth evidence in support of one or more of the complaint's allegations. If you are arguing against a motion for summary judgment on an issue for which the moving party had the burden of proof, you may argue that your opponent has not brought forth sufficient evidence. Thus, you may need to expand your standard of review discussion by quoting and citing language from court decisions that explain when the requirements for the motion standard of review have been met.

In the situations noted above — just as with the clearly erroneous and the abuse of discretion appellate standards — the standard will enter into your argument more directly. If you are arguing that the complaint contains only a "formulaic recitation" of the legal conclusions without sufficient facts and that it should therefore be dismissed, the reader will expect you to quote and cite the relevant portions of the complaint, and to cite and discuss appropriate authority to explain why the allegations are insufficient. If the burden of proof issue is significant to your summary judgment motion, you must discuss the specific burden(s) of proof for the relevant cause(s) of action, citing and discussing authority as appropriate. You may wish, for example, to frame your argument by stating that your opponent has "failed to present substantial evidence that would support a favorable verdict by a reasonable jury,"[16] and then explain why the evidence is insufficient, using relevant authority as appropriate.

As these examples show, a motion standard of review can be just as significant as an appellate standard of review. Whenever you file a motion that requires a brief, be sure that you understand the appropriate motion standard of review. Although you may often start your research in the court rules that govern the motion, be sure to go beyond that boilerplate to determine how your jurisdiction uses and applies that standard. Be sure to tie your legal argument to the standard in some way, even if the standard is not controversial. When either the standard or how it applies *is* controversial, however, the motion standard of review becomes an important legal rule that governs your case, and it should be analyzed, explained, and applied as thoroughly as any other important legal rule.

---

[16] Herr, Haydock & Stempel, *supra* Ch.13 note 1, at §16.01[K].

CHAPTER 14

AVOIDING CONFUSION WITH STANDARDS OF REVIEW

§14.1 Introduction

Unfortunately, courts do not always use the term *standard of review* precisely. I have used the phrase *appellate standard of review* to refer to standards that appellate courts apply to their review of lower court decisions, and *motion standard of review* to refer to standards that courts use when deciding particular motions. Courts, however, often use the bare phrase *standard of review*[1] to mean either or both of these things — and to mean other things. Besides its use to refer to appellate and motion standards of review, courts commonly use the phrase *standard of review* in at least one other context: to describe the level of scrutiny that a court may use to review the constitutionality of a state statute or other government action.

Understanding how "government action standards of review" work, and how all three uses of the term may be relevant in a single case, can help you to master the concept of standards of review.

§14.2 Government Action Standards of Review

Courts usually use the phrase *standard of review* to describe the standard that a court will use to review the constitutionality of a state statute or other government action. Some actions will be reviewed under a "strict scrutiny" standard, some under a "heightened scrutiny" standard, and others under a "rational basis" standard. Although these phrases all describe *standards* — standards that are used to *review* — they are not the same thing as appellate standards *of* review. Thinking in terms of "deference," which is so crucial to appellate standards of review, may be helpful. When the court is asked to review the constitutionality of a state

---

[1] As noted above, courts may use the phrase *legal standard* or *pleading standard* to refer to a motion standard of review.

statute or other government action, it is deciding whether to defer to the decision of a state legislature or other government actor. The government action standard of review tells it how closely to scrutinize the government actor's decision when conducting its review.

All types of courts, from the trial court on up through the United States Supreme Court, may use a strict scrutiny, heightened scrutiny, or rational basis standard to review the constitutionality of a government action.

§14.3 Multiple Standards of Review in the Same Case

One way to gain a clearer understanding of different standards of review is to identify which standards are used in which courts, and how multiple standards may occur in one case.

Motion standards of review and government action standards of review can be applied in trial courts, courts of appeals, and courts of last resort. Appellate standards of review can be applied only in courts of appeals and courts of last resort. It is not unusual, in fact, for an appellate court to apply all three types of standards in the same case.[2]

For example, a trial court may grant a motion for summary judgment in a case in which the issue was the constitutionality of a state action. That trial court would have used a motion standard of review and a government action standard of review. The appellate court reviewing that case must use the appropriate (1) appellate standard of review to analyze whether the trial court properly applied the (2) motion standard of review and used the correct (3) government action standard of review. Because the appellate standard in that situation would almost certainly be de novo, the appellate court would, in essence, reapply both the motion standard of review and the government action standard of review as part of its de novo review of the decision below.

Although the use of the same term for three different meanings may be confusing, keep the distinguishing factors in mind: (1) Trial courts may not use appellate standards of review. *Only courts of appeals and courts of last resort* may use appellate standards of review when they review *lower court decisions*. (2) *Any* court (trial or appellate) may use a *motion* standard of review to decide, or to review the validity of a decision on, a *motion*. (3) *Any* court (trial or appellate) may use a *government action* standard of review to review *actions by governmental entities* or to review the validity of a court's decision about the government action. The chart above will help you to understand these three different standards.

---

[2] E.g., *Selevan v. N.Y. Thruway Auth.*, 584 F.3d 82, 88 (2d Cir. 2009) (using a de novo standard to analyze whether a trial court correctly chose to use the rational basis standard as part of its decision to grant a motion to dismiss against plaintiffs who had claimed, among other things, an equal protection violation).

TYPE OF STANDARD OF REVIEW:	MOTION STANDARD OF REVIEW[3]	GOVERNMENT ACTION STANDARD OF REVIEW	APPELLATE STANDARD OF REVIEW
Type of court that may use this standard:	Trial court Intermediate court of appeals Court of last resort	Trial court Intermediate court of appeals Court of last resort	Intermediate court of appeals Court of last resort
Example(s) of this type of standard:	Whether the facts alleged plausibly give rise to an entitlement to relief	Strict scrutiny Heightened scrutiny Rational basis	De novo Clearly erroneous Abuse of discretion
What the court uses this standard to decide:	Whether it's appropriate to grant or deny a **motion**	Whether certain **government action** is constitutional	Whether to affirm, reverse, or vacate a **decision** of a court below
Whose decision the court is being asked to defer to:	N/A	The decision of a **government actor**	The decision of a **lower court**

§14.4 Summary

The type of court that hears your case and the standard of review that the court applies can each make a significant difference in the way that you structure your arguments. Even if the applicable standard is not controversial, you must keep that standard in mind as you conduct your research and write your brief. Be sure to update your research so that you are confident about the standard itself and its judicial gloss. In your brief, be sure to connect the standard explicitly to the legal or factual conclusions that you ask the court to accept. If the standard raises substantive or factual issues, you may well need to address those issues in depth within your argument.

It is likely that most of the appellate cases you argue will be reviewed under a de novo standard. However, do not make this decision on automatic pilot. Carefully consider the record, the issues, and the relevant appellate standards of review so that you can make an informed decision about which standard applies to your case.

---

[3] As noted above, courts also use the terms "legal standard" and "pleading standard."

TRIAL-LEVEL AND APPELLATE BRIEFS

CHAPTER 15

THE COMPONENTS OF A TRIAL-LEVEL BRIEF

Although formats for trial-level briefs vary with the customs of the court and the law firm, the variations are seldom substantively significant. This chapter describes a standard format for a trial-level brief. Refer to the sample trial-level brief in Appendix A for examples of the components described here.

Case Caption and Title of Document. The function of the Caption is simply to identify the court, the case, and the document, for example:

IN THE UNITED STATES DISTRICT COURT FOR THE
SOUTHERN DISTRICT OF TEXAS

CAROLINE MacDONNELL and
BARBARA JAMES,
              Plaintiffs,   Civ. No. 99-8636
    v.
ELLIS PEST CONTROL, INC., and
FORREST MICHIE,
          Defendants.

BRIEF IN SUPPORT OF PLAINTIFFS' MOTION TO COMPEL
THE PRODUCTION OF DOCUMENTS

The Caption must include the docket number (the case number assigned by the court)[1] and the name of the document. In many courts, the captions of cases with multiple parties need list only the first plaintiff and the first defendant

---

[1] *See* Fed. R. Civ. P. 10(a).

followed by "et al."[2] Court rules might require additional information such as the name and address of the attorney or the name of the assigned judge. The Caption can appear on a separate cover sheet or simply at the top of the first page of the brief.

Introduction. The Introduction (sometimes called a "preliminary Statement") introduces the judge to (1) the nature of the case, (2) the parties, (3) the motion or other procedural event that has led to filing of the brief, (4) the party's requested relief, and (5) the primary legal points justifying that relief. All of this information must be conveyed concisely, usually in one or two paragraphs. Here is an example of an Introduction:

Introduction

This is a sexual harassment action brought against Ellis Pest Control, Inc., and its President, Forrest Michie, by Caroline MacDonnell and Barbara James, former employees of the corporate defendant. The action alleges violations of Title VII of the Civil Rights Act of 1964, 42 U.S.C. §2000(e) *et seq.* (1988), and related contract claims.

Plaintiffs file this brief in support of their motion to compel defendants' response to plaintiffs' Requests for Production of Documents, properly filed and served on May 14, 2003. The requests seek production of plaintiffs' employment files and all documents referring to any evaluations of the plaintiffs' job performance. Defendants refuse to provide any of these documents, despite the reasonableness and clearly permissible scope of the requests.

Statement of Facts. This section sets out the facts relevant to the legal issues addressed by the brief, as well as the context necessary for understanding those facts. The Statement of Facts is an important opportunity for advocacy, requiring skillful and careful drafting. Chapter 20 explains how to draft a Statement of Facts.

Question(s) Presented. The Question(s) Presented section states the legal issues addressed by the brief and the factual context in which they have arisen. The questions are phrased favorably to your client's position, suggesting a decision in your favor. Some lawyers include Questions Presented in trial-level briefs and some do not. Chapter 17 of this book explains how to draft Questions Presented.

Argument. The Argument section contains your fully articulated argument on the legal issues. In drafting the argument, you will be drawing on the analytical, organizational and writing skills you learned about and practiced in the fall

---

[2] *Et al.* is an abbreviation for *et alii*, meaning literally "and others." *See* Fed. R. Civ. P. 10(a) and 7(b)(2).

semester of Legal Practice. Chapter 18 provides some suggestions and important reminders for drafting this section.

Remember one special characteristic of trial judges, however. Trial judges are constrained by mandatory precedent. They primarily want to know what those precedents are and how they apply to your case. Authorities from other jurisdictions hold less interest for trial judges, most of whom do not see themselves as free to change the law. Therefore, right up front, the trial judge wants to know whether there are mandatory authorities on your issue, and if so, what they are. Use authorities from other jurisdictions only to fill in any gaps in your jurisdiction's mandatory authority and only after you have explained to the judge why you are presenting these otherwise extraneous authorities.

Conclusion. The Conclusion refers to the arguments set out in the body of the brief and states that the requested relief should be granted. It is followed with a courtesy closing like "Respectfully submitted," a signature line, and the typed name, address, and telephone number of the signing attorney. Two schools of thought exist on the content of conclusions. The more traditional approach is a pro forma statement of the precise relief sought:

> For the foregoing reasons, the Court should grant the Defendant's Motion to Dismiss.

However, if court rules and local customs permit, consider a Conclusion that gives you one last opportunity for advocacy. This sort of Conclusion should still be short — no more than half a double-spaced page — but it could gather together the most compelling arguments in support of the result you seek. Here is an example of a more substantive conclusion:

> Therefore, as this brief has demonstrated, the circumstances of this case render the covenant's terms unreasonable. The covenant would protect Carrolton to a degree far greater than necessary, while devastating both Ms. Watson's fledgling business and her personal finances. Further, it would significantly infringe the public's interest in reasonably priced health care equipment, merchandise vital to the community's well-being. For these reasons, Carrolton's Motion for Summary Judgment should be denied.

Certificate of Service. Ethical rules prohibit ex parte contact with the judge about the merits of a legal matter.[3] Court rules require copies of all filings to be served upon all parties, via their attorneys.[4] The Certificate of Service

---

[3] Model R. Prof. Conduct 3.5(b) (2007).
[4] *See, e.g.,* Fed. R. Civ. P. 5(a).

demonstrates compliance with these rules. The Certificate is placed either after the Conclusion or on a separate page at the end of the brief. It certifies that copies of the brief have been mailed or delivered to the attorneys for all parties. For an example of a Certificate of Service, see the last page of the sample trial brief in Appendix A.

CHAPTER 16

THE COMPONENTS OF AN APPELLATE BRIEF

An appellate brief is a working document for the court, so its sections and format are designed to make it a useful and efficient tool for the judges and law clerks who will work on the case. Requirements for appellate briefs largely are determined by court rules, which vary from court to court. This section describes a standard set of sections and formatting practices. Follow these instructions unless your assignment requires different sections or formats.

Cover Page. The cover page of an appellate brief usually is printed on colored paper of a heavier stock than the rest of the brief. Court rules determine the color of the cover page according to the kind of brief. For instance, the cover sheet on the appellant's brief might be blue and the cover sheet on the appellee's brief might be red. These colors allow the court and the law clerks to distinguish the briefs easily and quickly. On the cover sheet, place the case caption, the docket number, the document's title, and the lawyer's name, address, and telephone number.

Table of Contents. Include all subsequent sections of your brief in the Table of Contents along with the page numbers on which they appear. These section titles (such as "Table of Authorities") should appear in initial caps here, although they will appear in all caps in the body of the brief. The Table of Contents also includes the point headings and subpoint headings, allowing a busy judge to skim the Table for a quick summary of the major points of the argument. Point headings should appear in the Table of Contents in the same typeface as they appear in the text of the Argument; that is, all caps, single-spaced, and not underlined. Similarly, subheadings should appear in the Table of Contents as they appear in the text, that is, in initial caps and underlined. The first page of the Table of Contents should be numbered as page one.

Table of Authorities. Here, provide the titles and citations for all authorities on which you rely in the brief as well as the page number(s) on which they appear in the Argument. If an authority appears on numerous pages, use the term "passim" in place of a page number. Organize the authorities according to categories with labels, such as Cases, Constitutional Provisions, Statutes, Administrative Regulations, Law Review Articles, and Miscellaneous. Beneath each category, the authorities should appear in alphabetical order.

Question(s) Presented. The Question(s) Presented section states the legal issues addressed by the brief and the factual context in which they have arisen. The questions are phrased favorably to your client's position, suggesting a decision in your favor. Chapter 17 will explain in detail how to draft Questions Presented.

Additional Sections. Some courts might require other sections, such as the following: Opinion Below (a complete sentence providing the court with the citation to the opinion from which the appeal is taken); Jurisdictional Statement (a complete sentence providing the citation to the statute on which appellate jurisdiction is based); and Constitutional and Statutory Provisions Involved (a section setting out the text of and the citation to any constitutional provision or statute important to the resolution of the issues).

Statement of the Case. The Statement of the Case is the customary title for the fact statement of an appellate brief. Chapter 20 will explain how to draft a fact statement. You can use subheadings in a complex fact statement, including a section labeled "Statement of Facts" and a section labeled "Procedural History."

Summary of the Argument. Summarize your argument here, allotting approximately one paragraph per issue. Often the judge will read the Summary of the Argument either first or immediately after reading the Question Presented, so this section provides an early opportunity for advocacy. Phrase your summary as persuasively as possible, pulling together your most important points. In an appellate brief, your Conclusion will be a one-sentence, pro forma request for relief, so the Summary of the Argument functions as a substantive conclusion would.

Argument. The Argument section sets out your argument in its complete form. Draw on the analytical, organizational and writing process material from last semester, and on the brief-writing material in this book. Most court rules require an appellate brief to identify the appropriate standard of review for each legal issue the court will decide. Even if you have included a separately labeled section for the standard of review, you might want to state the relevant standard early in the Argument section, especially if it is favorable for your argument. Chapter 18 will provide some important suggestions and reminders about writing this section.

Conclusion. The Conclusion of an appellate brief is a one-line, pro forma request for the relief you seek, for instance: "For the foregoing reasons, the judgment of the District Court should be reversed and the case should be remanded to the District Court for a new trial."

CHAPTER 17

QUESTIONS PRESENTED AND POINT HEADINGS

Two of the potentially most persuasive parts of a brief are the Questions Presented and the Point Headings. This chapter explains their function and tells you how to draft them effectively.

§17.1 Writing the Question Presented

A Question Presented should both apprise the judge of the legal issue to be decided and begin persuading the judge to decide that issue in your client's favor. To draft a Question Presented that accomplishes both purposes, the writer must walk a fine line between neutrality and overzealous advocacy. The goal is to draft a Question that accurately states the issue *and* suggests a favorable answer. For example, here are examples of Questions Presented from opposing briefs:

Question Presented

Is a covenant-not-to-compete enforceable where the covenant was a bargained-for term of the sale of a business, where the term was negotiated as part of the agreement to allow the seller to continue working for the business, and where the sale specifically included the company's customer lists and good will?

Question Presented

May an established business enforce a covenant-not-to-compete where the covenant would eliminate all competition within the market area and where the prohibited activity would affect only four percent of the covenant-holder's profits?

Notice how each accurately recites the legal issue and several key facts while suggesting an answer favorable to the client for whom the brief is written.

Drafting a Question Presented is like creating a haiku. Each of these literary forms requires meticulous attention to word selection and placement, sentence structure, and theme. Unlike poetry, however, no one would argue that obscurity of message is desirable for a Question Presented. Rather, a Question Presented should be a powerful sentence that is easily understandable on first reading.

Keep reworking the Question Presented for readability and subtle persuasiveness. Use the techniques presented in Chapter 21. Try to achieve a concise, clear, and direct style, and a persuasive framing of the Question. The following are some particular suggestions for the Question Presented

Format for a Pure Question of Law. A Question Presented for a pure question of law is a straightforward statement of the legal issue. It should identify the particular legal issue, rather than simply asking whether one side's position is correct. For instance, the first of the following Questions simply asks whether one party's position is correct, without identifying the legal issue. The second actually poses a legal question.

Can Dole bring a claim for malicious prosecution?
Can a criminal defendant bring a civil action for malicious prosecution prior to the resolution of the criminal proceedings that give rise to the claim?

Format for a Question Requiring the Application of Law to Facts. If your legal issue will require the judge to apply the law to your client's facts, your Question Presented should include both law and facts. You can think of the Question in two parts, the first part stating the legal issue and the second part stating the key facts.

Can . . . [state the legal question] . . . where . . . [state the major facts] . . . ?

Both of the examples on the preceding page use this format. Common verbs beginning the Question Presented are: "May . . . ?" "Does . . . ?" "Is . . . ?" and "Did . . . ?" Common words used for the transition to the second part of the Question, referring to facts, are "when" and "where."

A Question Presented also can be phrased as a clause beginning with "whether" and ending with a period:

Question Presented

Whether a large, established business can enforce a covenant-not-to-compete where the covenant would eliminate all competition within the market area and where the prohibited activity would affect only four percent of the covenant holder's profits.

References to Parties. To refer to the parties, a Question Presented can use (1) the parties' names, (2) generic descriptions (property owner, retailer, buyer, lessor), or (3) procedural titles (plaintiff, defendant, appellant, respondent). Procedural titles require the judge to remember who the parties are in this particular case. Thus, they make the Question less readily understandable and, for this reason, some court rules instruct the lawyers to avoid procedural titles.[1] You can use procedural posture, for example:

> Can a criminal defendant bring a civil action for malicious prosecution prior to the resolution of the criminal proceedings that give rise to the claim?

In such a case, the procedural title is actually the generic description of the kind of person to whom the question would pertain.

In other cases, the better choices are generic descriptions or the parties' names. Choose the alternative that will be clearest and that better serves your strategy. Sometimes, using the parties' names can serve the strategic function of humanizing the parties and the legal issues in dispute. Using names can serve a practical function as well, allowing the drafter to use fewer words. For instance, in the third example above, the generic description "an established business" is longer than the name "Carrolton" would have been.

On the other hand, using generic descriptions could allow the writer to give additional helpful information about the party. For instance, in the Carrolton example, the generic description allowed Watson's lawyer the chance to convey some helpful information about Carrolton — that it is an established business. In such a situation, the additional information might be worth the added length. Experiment with both alternatives and select the one that works best for your particular case.

Do Not Avoid the Actual Question the Judge Must Decide. Some writers are tempted to assume the answer to the question the judge must decide, like so:

> May Carrolton enforce the terms of the covenant-not-to-compete where the terms are unreasonable?

Neither party argues that Carrolton can enforce a covenant with unreasonable terms. The governing case law clearly states that Carrolton cannot, and neither party is asking the court to change that rule. Rather, the question the judge must decide is *whether the terms are reasonable.* Perhaps the drafter of this Question Presented was hoping that the assumption would slip past the judge, but it will not. Write a Question Presented that addresses the actual legal issue.

---

[1] *See* Fed. R. App. P. (28)(d).

Phrase the Question in a Way That Suggests a Favorable Answer. Generally, a question that suggests an affirmative answer is more persuasive than a question that suggests a negative answer.[2] Sometimes, however, other rhetorical factors can outweigh the advantage of calling for an affirmative response. For instance, a structure that asks, "Can X force Y to do Z?" implies that X is being oppressive to Y, simply by virtue of the structure of the question. The structure invites the reader to respond with a resounding "No." For example, consider this Question Presented:

> Can an employer, in order to collect urine samples, force employees to urinate in the plain view of a supervisor?

Do Not Overdo the Advocacy. Some court rules require that Questions Presented not be argumentative. Even in the absence of such court rules, overzealous advocacy is counterproductive. It causes the skeptical reader to discount the material because the writer's agenda is too heavy-handed. The goal is to state the question in a way that allows the *facts* to speak for themselves. Facts persuade more effectively than bluster and puffery ever can. Here is a Question Presented that has crossed the line into argumentativeness:

> Can a reckless defendant, whose callous conduct caused the death of a precious new life, escape liability for wrongful death just because the baby's guardians had not yet completed an adoption proceeding?

To avoid argumentative Questions Presented, limit adjectives and adverbs, using facts instead of such descriptors. Edit out language that smacks of name-calling. Stick to facts the opposing party cannot dispute.

> Can legal guardians recover for the wrongful death of a child when the guardians had raised the child as their own for four years, had instituted adoption proceedings two years prior to the child's death, and had believed, reasonably and in good faith, that a final adoption decree had been issued?

Drafting More Than One Question. A brief can raise several questions and thus have several Questions Presented. In such a case, draft a separately

---

[2] John C. Dernbach et al., *A Practical Guide to Legal Writing and Legal Method* 221 (2d ed., Rothman & Co. 1994).

numbered Question Presented for each legal question. Place these Questions Presented in the order in which the issues will appear in the Argument section.

§17.2 Point Headings

§17.2.1 *Identifying Point Headings*

Usually, *a point heading* is the statement of your argument on a *dispositive* legal issue — that is, an independent and freestanding ground that entitles your client to the relief you seek. Here is an example of a point heading:

I. THE WATSON COVENANT SHOULD BE ENFORCED BECAUSE ITS RESTRICTIONS ON DURATION, NATURE, AND SCOPE ARE REASONABLE.

To tell if your argument on an element or set of elements is an independent ground for the relief you seek, ask this: If the judge agrees with me on *only* this component of the rule, is that enough? If yes — if the judge would not need to consider other legal issues before granting the ruling you seek — then your argument on that component of the rule is an independent ground. A heading that states your conclusion on that component is a point heading.

This definition will be clearer if we look at an example. In a burglary case, the state must prove *all* of the elements to win a conviction. Thus, a defense attorney's brief need only show that any one of these elements is missing to show that the state cannot prove the burglary charge. In that brief, each challenged element will constitute an independent ground for the desired result. If the attorney challenges the state's proof on three elements ("nighttime," "intent," and "of another"), the defense attorney will have three independent, freestanding ways to win. The defense attorney can prevail by persuading the judge on any *one* of these elements. Therefore, the argument on each element will constitute a *point*, and the defense attorney's brief will contain three point headings.

However, the prosecution's brief in response must argue that the state can prove all of the elements of burglary. The state cannot obtain the ruling it seeks (submission of the case to the jury) simply by showing that the facts will prove any *one* element; the prosecutor's brief must show that the facts can prove *all* of the challenged elements. In the prosecutor's brief, then, each challenged element will be a subpoint. The prosecutor's brief will have only one *point* heading — a point arguing that all elements are provable. As in an office memo, having only one roman numeral is fine. The roman numerals will identify for the judge the freestanding arguments that entitle your client to the result you seek.

As we said, a point heading is generally a freestanding ground that will entitle your client to the relief she seeks. In brief-writing, this is not a rigid rule, but rather a custom and a general principle of persuasion. In most cases, your reader will expect you to follow this method, and your case usually will be more persuasively presented if you do. Rarely will you have three freestanding grounds for relief that would be more persuasively argued under a single point heading. Instead, you will want to emphasize each by giving each its own point heading. You will want the judge to know at a glance that you are correct for three independent reasons, not just one.

Occasionally, however, you might choose to treat an issue as a point heading even if it is not a freestanding ground for relief. You might want to consider this organizational variation if your case falls into one of the following categories:

- When you have a major threshold issue;
- When you are responding to a brief that has given that issue its own point heading;
- When you must win on two weighty issues that are very different from each other.

Arguing an Important Threshold Issue. Recall that a threshold issue is one that determines the direction of the analysis from that point on. For instance, the question of which standard of review is appropriate would be a threshold issue. The court must decide how much deference to give to the trial court's opinion before the court can consider what decision it will make on the issues you raise.

The question of which law will govern your legal issue would be a threshold issue. Perhaps the court will have to decide whether the law of state *A* or the law of state *B* will govern the situation. Or perhaps your client's legal duty would be different depending on whether a particular statute applies to your client. For instance, under Title VII, an "employer" must not discriminate on the basis of religion.[3] The question of whether your client is an "employer" as defined by the act would constitute a threshold question.

An evidentiary or procedural issue may be a threshold issue. The court might have to decide an evidentiary or other procedural issue before it can consider your argument on the merits. The court might have to consider whether a particular document was properly admitted into evidence before that court can consider whether the trial evidence was sufficient to support the trial court's opinion.

If you have a threshold issue such as one of these, and if you do not have much to say about it, you can simply include it in the umbrella section of another point heading. But if you have a great deal to say about it, you might want to give it a point heading of its own.

Mirroring the Organization of the Opening Brief. If you are filing a brief in response to another brief, you might find that the judge's understanding of your arguments will be improved if you adopt the organizational structure of the opening brief. If the judge will have read your opponent's brief, which uses three point headings, you can consider whether to respond by giving each of those three issues its own point heading in your brief as well. Be careful, though, not to concede structural decisions to your opponent too easily. Sometimes structural decisions carry important implications for persuasion.

---

[3] 42 U.S.C. §2000e-2(b) (2001).

Arguing Two Major Issues. Occasionally you will have to win on two weighty issues, and the analysis of each of those weighty issues will be quite different in nature. For instance, you might have to argue that a particular statute is constitutional and also that your opponent breached its terms. Although you will have to win on both of those issues, you might find that each is a very large issue, that you have a great deal to say about each, and that the nature of your argument for one is quite different from the other (constitutional principles in one case and statutory construction principles in the other). In such a case, you might want to give each of those weighty issues its own point heading. However, do not rush into the decision to separate them. Quite often, your argument on each will be strengthened by a closer association with the other, an association you can emphasize by positioning them as subpoints under a common point heading.

§17.2.2 *Drafting Point Headings*

Headings and subheadings provide the structure of your Argument. They also serve as a tool of persuasion. They can persuade because they assert your position in compelling language; they make visible the persuasive structure you have selected for your rule and your argument; and they allow the judge to find a quick summary of your entire argument by reading only the point headings and subheadings, either in a Table of Contents or by paging through the body of the Argument itself.

Ideally, a point heading should identify, expressly or implicitly, three things: (1) the result you seek, (2) the part of the rule that justifies that result, and (3) the key facts supporting that result.[4] The heading should phrase these items of information as assertions of their correctness. One way to learn to draft point headings is to think of them in halves. The first half asserts the correctness of the result you seek. The second half identifies, at least implicitly, the part of the rule that justifies that result and adds the key facts:

Drafting a Point Heading

[Identify the ruling you seek, asserting its correctness.]

because

[Identify the part of the rule justifying the result and the key facts.]

---

[4] If the issue is a pure question of law, not requiring fact application, then you have no facts to add. However, the heading should still state the supporting rationale.

Here is an example of a burglary point heading. Notice how the second half of the point heading implicitly identifies the part of the rule that determines the desired result and asserts a conclusion about it:

A Burglary Point Heading

<u>The burglary charge should be dismissed</u>
[Identify the ruling you seek, asserting its correctness.]

because

<u>the testimony of the bartender and other bar patrons establishes that Mr. Shaffer arrived at the house earlier than thirty minutes past sunset.</u>
[Identify the key facts and state how they establish the correctness of the ruling.]

When the point heading must cover more than one element, placing the key facts for all those elements in one sentence could result in an unwieldy heading. In that situation, move the facts for each element into the sub-heading dealing with that element. For example, here are the prosecutor's headings for a brief responding to the defendant's challenge of three elements. Because the prosecutor must win on all three challenged elements to prevail, the point heading must cover all three elements, but there are separate *sub* headings for each. Notice that the subheadings expressly identify the components of the rule to be addressed in that subsection and add the key facts.

---

1. THE BURGLARY CHARGE AGAINST THE DEFENDANT SHOULD NOT BE DISMISSED BECAUSE THE EVIDENCE AT TRIAL WILL ESTABLISH ALL OF THE ELEMENTS OF BURGLARY.
   A. The evidence will show that the crime occurred in the nighttime because it occurred at 6:45 P.M., more than thirty minutes past sunset.
   B. The evidence will show that the defendant intended to commit a felony when he entered the house because he alluded to his intent to batter Mrs. Shaffer before he left the bar for her home.
   C. The evidence will show that the dwelling was not the defendant's own because he had waived his claim to the premises and did not retain any right of access.

As you write out the body of the Argument, you will develop even more clarity about which facts are compelling. Revise your point headings to reflect these new insights.

One last point: This section began by stating that point headings "ideally" should include key facts. A situation is less than ideal, however, when the key facts, stated in isolation from other facts and from your explanation of them, are not persuasive. Sometimes the facts of a particular case are persuasive only in a particular context. Or perhaps they require some explanation before their significance will be apparent to the judge. In either case, including the key facts in the point heading probably will hurt rather than help your effort to persuade the judge. In either case, then, leave the facts out of your point heading.

Similarly, a point heading for a pure question of law usually would not include your client's facts. For a question of law, the court will only be deciding what the law is, not how that law applies to your client's facts. In place of facts, however, the point heading should assert the key argument(s) supporting your position on the question of law before the court. Here is an example of a point heading for a pure question of law:

I. THE STATUTORY PROCEDURE FOR DECIDING ZONING AMENDMENT APPLICATIONS COMPLIES WITH DUE PROCESS REQUIREMENTS BECAUSE IT PROVIDES FOR A PETITION FOR RECONSIDERATION AND A SUBSEQUENT APPEAL TO DISTRICT COURT.

§17.2.3 *Editing Point Headings for Readability and Persuasion*

§17.2.3.1 *Editing for Readability*

Often the inclusion of all desirable information in a point heading results in a long, complex, and confusing sentence. Yet a point heading cannot persuade a judge of something she cannot decipher. And readability is especially important for point headings because the format for point headings (all capital letters) already hinders readability.

If you are struggling with readability, use all relevant editing techniques to help simplify and clarify the heading. As a quick checklist, here are some of the techniques most likely to help tame a point heading.

1. *Keep the subject and the verb close together.* In other words, avoid intrusive phrases and clauses.
2. *Avoid nominalizations.* Nominalizations are noun forms of verbs. "Investigate" is a verb; "investigation" is a nominalization. Nominalizations require more words and make sentences harder to understand.
3. *Avoid unnecessary passive-voiced verbs.* Passive verbs make the sentence's subject something other than the actor. These verbs generally require more supporting words and make sentences harder to understand.

4. *Keep the facts and reasoning at the end of the sentence.* Placing the desired result first and the facts and reasoning second often results in a more readable point heading.

5. *Avoid vague words.* Vague words cause the reader to puzzle over the writer's meaning. Purge your point headings of words like these:

this matter	with regard to
it involves	it deals with
it pertains to	it concerns

6. *Avoid negatives.* Negatives, especially multiple negatives, can make a sentence harder to understand.

If you have tried all available editing techniques and still cannot produce a readable point heading, the best solution is to remove one of the items of information. Decide which one, based on persuasiveness and on your assessment of your reader's needs. If the key facts are particularly persuasive, remove the relief requested or the part of the rule at issue. The facts might sufficiently imply the part of the rule at issue, or perhaps the judge is already well aware of the nature of the relief you seek. Regardless, an easily readable point heading that asserts the party's legal argument but lacks supporting facts is more persuasive than a point heading that includes the facts but cannot be understood.

§17.2.3.2 Editing for Persuasion

Editing for persuasion is the final step in the process of drafting point headings. Here are three rhetorical strategies particularly applicable to point headings.

1. Affirmative Language Versus Negative Language. Most briefs focus on certain conduct: Is the conduct lawful? Proper? Desirable? Sometimes the writer can articulate the client's position either by using affirmative language or negative language. In addition to being more readable, affirmative language generally is more forceful and appealing than negative language. Here are examples of two point headings, one using affirmative language and one using negative language.

Negative language	Carrolton's Motion for Summary Judgment should be granted because Watson is unable to show that the terms are unreasonable or that she has not breached those terms.
Affirmative language	Carrolton's Motion for Summary Judgment should be granted because the terms of the covenant-not-to-compete are reasonable and the uncontested facts establish Watson's breach.

2. *Varying the Structure of the Point Heading.* The point heading structure described in this chapter is the easiest structure for learning to draft a readable point heading. It begins with the relief you want and follows with the facts and law supporting that relief. After you have a little practice with drafting point headings, however, you can vary the formula and sometimes achieve a more persuasive version. For instance, consider these versions of a burglary heading. What differences in effectiveness do you notice?

Version 1	The burglary charge against Mr. Shaffer should be dismissed because the alleged breaking and entering occurred at 6:15 P.M., which was earlier than thirty minutes after sunset.
Version 2	Because the alleged breaking and entering occurred at 6:15 P.M., which was earlier than thirty minutes after sunset, the burglary charge against Mr. Shaffer should be dismissed.
Version 3	The alleged breaking and entering occurred at 6:15 P.M., which was less than thirty minutes after sunset, and therefore the burglary charge against Mr. Shaffer should be dismissed.

Tinker with the structure of the point heading until you are satisfied that it is as persuasive as it can be.

3. *Phrasing Alternative Arguments.* When you have more than a single point heading, one or more of the headings may be an alternative argument, presented in case the judge does not agree with the first argument. The challenge here is to avoid seeming to reduce the credibility of the first argument by making an alternative argument. The following example demonstrates this flaw:

I. THE LAW OF THIS JURISDICTION DOES NOT ALLOW RECOVERY FOR THE WRONGFUL DEATH OF A FETUS, EVEN IF THE FETUS IS VIABLE AT THE TIME OF THE INJURY.

II. THE LAW OF THIS JURISDICTION ALLOWS RECOVERY FOR THE WRONGFUL DEATH OF ONLY A *VIABLE* FETUS, AND THE LAWRENCE FETUS WAS NOT VIABLE AT THE TIME OF THE INJURY.

In this pair of headings, a strong first argument is followed by a second argument that seems to undercut the first. Rather than undercutting your own best argument, phrase alternative arguments *in terms that assume the correctness of the first argument.* One way to do this is to restate the first argument expressly, like this:[5]

I. THE NEGLIGENCE CLAIM IS BARRED BY THE STATUTE OF LIMITATIONS BECAUSE THE PLAINTIFF DID NOT FILE THE COMPLAINT UNTIL FOUR YEARS AFTER THE ALLEGED NEGLIGENT ACT.

---

[5] Modified from Girvan Peck, *Writing Persuasive Briefs* 135-136 (Little, Brown Co. 1984).

    II.   NOT ONLY IS THE CLAIM BARRED BY THE STATUTE OF LIMI-
         TATIONS, BUT THE PLAINTIFF'S ASSURANCE THAT HE
         WOULD NOT PURSUE AN ACTION BARS THE CLAIM UNDER
         THE EQUITABLE DOCTRINES OF ESTOPPEL AND WAIVER.

Reiterating the first point in the course of making the second can make the second heading unwieldy, however. Another way to avoid seeming to disavow the first point heading is to use, in the second heading, a verb tense that communicates that any assumption of a flaw in the first point is contrary to fact:

    I.   THE LAW OF THIS JURISDICTION DOES NOT ALLOW RECOV-
        ERY FOR THE WRONGFUL DEATH OF A FETUS, EVEN IF THE
        FETUS IS VIABLE AT THE TIME OF THE INJURY.
    II.   EVEN IF THE LAW *DID* ALLOW RECOVERY FOR THE WRONG-
        FUL DEATH OF A VIABLE FETUS, THE LAWRENCE FETUS
        WAS ONLY IN THE FOURTH MONTH OF GESTATION, AND
        THEREFORE WAS NOT VIABLE.

Notice the use of the subjunctive verb "did." The subjunctive is used when stating something contrary to fact. Therefore, the first clause of the alternative heading affirms your assertion of the first heading rather than disavowing it.

§17.2.4 *Identifying Subheadings*

Use the rule's structure and your annotated outline to create any additional subheadings you desire. Look at the rule's structure first. For example, if the rule is a factors, you can allocate subheadings to each of the factors your brief will discuss.

If the rule does not identify subheadings like factors, you can create your own subheadings based on your major arguments on the point. For instance, if your point heading is a question of statutory interpretation, you can allocate subheadings to the major canons of construction you use or the major policy rationales you assert. Here is an example of such a set of subheadings:

    I.   THE COURT SHOULD DISMISS THE COMPLAINT BECAUSE THE
        PLAINTIFF LIED ON HER EMPLOYMENT APPLICATION AND UNDER
        42 U.S.C. §2000e, A PLAINTIFF CANNOT RECOVER IF SHE OBTAINED
        HER JOB UNDER FALSE PRETENSES.
        A.   The Plain Meaning of the Statute Establishes That Only an Employee
            Who Has Acted in Good Faith Can Recover.
        B.   The Legislature Did Not Intend to Allow a Windfall to an Employee
            Who Lied on the Application.
        C.   Construing the Statute to Allow Recovery Would Encourage Appli-
            cants to Lie and Would Undermine Employers' Efforts to Employ
            Trustworthy Employees.

Use three pages as a rough maximum for a section or subsection. Readers prefer to orient themselves every three pages or so, and new section headings will revive waning attention levels.

§17.3 Conforming Headings to the Standard of Review

The brief's point headings ordinarily should be consistent with the applicable standard of review.[6] Here are examples of headings phrased according to the appropriate standard:

No competent evidence	The burglary conviction should be reversed because the record contains no competent evidence that the breaking and entering occurred later than 30 minutes after sunset.
Clearly erroneous	The judgment should be reversed because the trial court's finding of intent to discriminate was clearly erroneous.
De novo	The judgment entered on the defendant's motion to dismiss should be reversed because this jurisdiction allows recovery for the wrongful death of a fetus.
Abuse of discretion	The trial court abused its discretion when it issued a preliminary injunction prohibiting the defendant from concealing or disposing of his assets.

Notice that the de novo standard does not change the phrasing of the argument because that standard puts no gloss whatsoever on the question. That standard imposes no limitations on the appellate court's decision.

A brief is far more effective when it establishes the most favorable standard of review supportable by the authorities and makes a few points about how that standard should be applied to the pending case. Consider the policy rationales that underlie each standard of review, comparing them to the circumstances of your case. As you write the argument, make whatever points you can in favor of applying the standard most favorable to your position. As Senior United States Circuit Judge Ruggero J. Aldisert explained, "[S]tandards of review are critically important in appellate decision making."[7] Yet many lawyers forget to research the proper standard and to couch their arguments according to its terms. As a matter of fact, Judge Aldisert describes his experience of observing the "psychological block" that seems to prevent some lawyers from recognizing and dealing with the standard of review.[8] If, from the beginning of your practice, you pay careful attention to the standard of review, you will never be one of the lawyers Judge Aldisert describes.

---

[6] If the standard of review is unfavorable, you might not wish to reiterate it in each point heading. A simple acknowledgment of the standard early in the brief might be sufficient.

[7] Ruggero J. Aldisert, *Opinion Writing* 53 (West 1990).

[8] *Id.*

CHAPTER 18

WRITING THE ARGUMENT SECTION

§18.1 Arguments for Different Kinds of Legal Issues

Legal issues, including legal writing assignments, come in several varieties. Drawing on the material in earlier chapters, this section will identify the major kinds of legal issues and provide suggestions for how to handle each. Some of these categories overlap, so be sure to read each section to learn if your assignment falls into more than one category.

§18.1.1 A Pure Question of Law

Some legal issues raise a pure question of law. You have a pure question of law when the only issue meaningfully before the court is *what the law is* — when there is no meaningful issue before the court about *how that law will apply to the facts.* The application of the law to the facts either is not before the court or is essentially uncontested. You can have a pure question of law before either a trial court or an appellate court.

For instance, assume you are representing a plaintiff in a wrongful death action arising from an automobile accident in which your client's wife was killed. At the time of the accident, your client's wife was pregnant with the couple's second child, and the unborn child also died. The defendant might file a motion to dismiss part of your client's claim, arguing that the law in your jurisdiction does not allow recovery for the death of an unborn child. You would file a brief arguing that the law does allow recovery. Both briefs deal with a pure question of *law.* The question of how that law will apply to the *facts* of the case is not yet before the court. That will be a question for the jury to decide.

The same issue also could come before the court on uncontested facts. For instance, the defendant might move for summary judgment in this same wrongful death claim, arguing that the law in your state allows recovery for the death of an unborn child only if the fetus was viable at the time of the injury. If your client's unborn child clearly was not viable at the time of the injury, your only response to the defendant's motion can be to argue that the law does (or should) allow recovery for a fetus not yet viable. You will be arguing a pure question of law — whether the law in your jurisdiction allows recovery for a fetus not viable at the time of the accident. The way the law will apply to your client's facts is not in dispute. The court need only decide the question of law.

For a pure question of law, your introduction or umbrella section will explain to your reader, if necessary, why the facts are not at issue. Then you will proceed with rule explanation. The core of your issue is *what* the law requires — what the governing rule is in this jurisdiction. Once your rule explanation section has proven and explained this governing rule, your work is done. You need not add a rule application section in the usual sense.

You still might be able to use your client's facts to help you persuade the judge on the question of law, however. Consider using your client's facts in your rule explanation section, to demonstrate any policy rationales or important principles on which you rely. You might be able to strengthen these policy or principle-based rationales by showing the results of each possible interpretation of the law in situations like your client's. This strategy would be an exception to the normal practice of avoiding discussion of your client's facts in the rule explanation section.

§18.1.2 *An Issue of Statutory Interpretation*

You have an issue of statutory interpretation when the primary question before the court is what a particular statutory provision means and especially when little case law has arisen defining the provision. In such a situation, the court must interpret the statute itself rather than relying on interpretations other courts have given. The issue might arise because the statute does not directly address your client's legal question or because the statute addresses the question in ambiguous language.

For issues of statutory interpretation, you should use all the relevant tools from you learned last semester. Start with the statutory text — the language and punctuation of the provision itself and other related provisions; any definitions of terms; the titles of the provisions; and the name of the act itself. Consider any arguments you can make from the legislative history or from other indicia of the legislature's intent. Discuss any favorable interpretations by other courts, by an enforcing agency, or by law review authors or other commentators. Argue from any helpful canons of construction. Do not forget to rely on policy and principle-based reasoning. In matters of statutory construction, these arguments can be particularly persuasive.

§18.1.3 *An Issue of Common Law Case Synthesis*

You have an issue of common law case synthesis when you must combine holdings of several cases to formulate the governing rule, to discern the factors courts examine when deciding an issue under the rule, or to discern any exceptions to the rule. For issues of case synthesis, find arguments by using all of the tools in you learned last semester. Consider the following:

- Which cases are most similar to your client's case;
- Whether any of the opinions have subsequently been followed, over-ruled, or questioned;
- Distinctions between a holding and dicta;
- The breadth of the holdings;
- Differences in the precedential values of the cases;
- Differences in the procedural histories of the cases;
- The depth of the courts' analyses and the quality of the courts' reasoning processes;
- The age of the various opinions;
- The weight of authority in your own jurisdiction and in others;
- The evaluations of commentators;
- The comparison between the rule the court announced and the way the court ruled on the facts before it;
- The facts the courts emphasized;
- Any rulings the court declined to make, either expressly or by implication;
- Whether any of the opinions are concurring or dissenting opinions; and
- Whether cases, reviewed chronologically, establish a trend.

For issues of case synthesis, sensitivity to the varying precedential values of cases is critical. The judge will want you to focus on the mandatory authorities and on the cases from the highest courts in your jurisdiction.

Again, do not forget to consider policy and principle-based reasoning. Not only will judges consider the policies and principles implicated by various understandings of the rule of law, but some of the cases whose holdings you must synthesize might raise policy and principle concerns that are different from or closely similar to your client's situation. Those policy and principle-based comparisons can help you justify placing more reliance on some cases than on others.

§18.1.4 A Case of First Impression in Your Jurisdiction

You have a case of first impression if the courts of your jurisdiction have not addressed the legal question you must brief. Usually, the issue has been decided in other jurisdictions, although perhaps inconsistently. For federal issues, this situation is sometimes called a "circuit split," meaning that the circuit courts have issued inconsistent opinions on the questions.

For an issue of first impression, research the holdings of the other jurisdictions to identify the approach most favorable to your client, and argue that this approach is the best. Use all the tools set out above to show why your proposed approach is best and why the other approaches are inferior. If more jurisdictions have adopted the approach you prefer, be sure to point out that the "weight of authority" supports your position. Where possible, use analogies to align your case with similar cases from favorable jurisdictions. Rely on any secondary authorities that have compared the diverse approaches and supported the approach you prefer. You can include interdisciplinary sources that support your position. Also, use policy and principle-based reasoning. When a court must rule on a case of first impression, policy and principle considerations are among the most important parts of your analysis.

§18.1.5 Seeking a Change in the Law

You have an issue asking for a change in the law when the existing law in your jurisdiction is not favorable for your client and you must ask the court to change the rule or to create an exception to it. The strategies for handling such an issue are similar to those used for a pure question of law and a circuit split. You must honestly disclose the existing state of the law but show the court why a change is appropriate. Therefore, your job is to point out the infirmities of the existing rule, propose the change you desire, and explain why your proposal is better. Courts hesitate to change the law without careful thought because the law should be stable and because citizens plan their lives and businesses in reliance on the law. Therefore, address these concerns directly if you can. Also, state clearly the change you propose. A court cannot effectively consider changing the law without understanding the exact nature of the change you request.

Again, policy and principle-based rationales are persuasive. You might draw on persuasive authority from other jurisdictions, the opinions of legal scholars in secondary sources, and available interdisciplinary sources. If you can, use your client's facts as an example of the infirmities of the old rule and the advantages of the rule you propose.

§18.1.6 An Issue Applying Law to Fact

You have an issue applying law to fact when the issue will be resolved primarily by how the court applies the applicable law to your client's facts. Issues of application of law to fact often arise when the governing rule is a factors test or a balancing test or when the language of the governing rule is vague enough to invite speculation about how it might apply to your client's fact. A classic example is the standard for defining negligent conduct: the "reasonable person." If you have taken torts, you probably have had many debates about what conduct would be reasonable in particular circumstances. These debates raise issues of application of law to fact.

Analogical reasoning (analogizing and distinguishing cases) is by far the most important tool for issues such as these. Your analysis should provide the judge with as many examples as possible of cases in which courts have applied the governing rule to situations like your client's and ruled as you hope your judge will rule. Focus primarily on opinions from courts in your jurisdiction. Use opinions from other jurisdictions in a supporting role if necessary to bolster your jurisdiction's case law.

Explicitly state the similarities between your client's facts and the facts of the favorable cases. Distinguish unfavorable cases by showing relevant factual differences. Show similarities or differences of policy and principle as well, thus further aligning your client's case with the favorable cases and distinguishing it from the unfavorable cases. Custom-based reasoning can be effective to show that your client's actions were consistent with customary practices and that the actions of other parties strayed beyond those bounds.

§18.2 Honing your Argument for the Court's Role

The roles of trial court judges and appellate court judges differ significantly. Effective arguments target precisely the role of the judge who will be reading the brief. Let's review the most important differences.

§18.2.1 The Trial Judge

Most trial judges are busy, skeptical, and impatient with squabbling. They are busy, skeptical, and impatient with squabbling. They want to make good decisions that accurately apply the law in their jurisdiction and achieve a fair result. More than any other characteristics in a brief, they want clarity, brevity, and accuracy.

Because trial judges have heavy caseloads, they usually are not familiar with individual cases in the pretrial stages, when most of your briefs will be filed. They might or might not be familiar with the law on your legal issue, depending on how often that issue has arisen in prior cases. Therefore, do not assume that your judge knows the facts and circumstances of your case or even that the judge knows the law on your issue. Your brief must give the judge the factual and legal background necessary to decide your issue.

Finally, trial judges are constrained by mandatory precedent. They primarily want to know what those precedents are and how they apply to your case. Authorities from other jurisdictions hold less interest for trial judges, most of whom do not see themselves as free to change the law. Therefore, right up front, the trial judge wants to know whether there are mandatory authorities on your issue and, if so, what they are. Use authorities from other jurisdictions only to fill in any gaps in your jurisdiction's mandatory authority and only after you have explained to the judge why you are presenting these otherwise extraneous authorities.

§18.2.2 Appellate Judges and the Appellate Process

Both a trial-level brief and an appellate brief are written to persuade a judge to rule favorably on one or more legal issues. But on appeal, the lawyer's job is more complicated and more difficult. First, the appellate court will not review the entire proceeding below. The court will review only the issues the appellant's lawyer has identified for appeal and see only the portions of the trial record the lawyers have designated to be included in the record on appeal.[1] Therefore, the

---

[1] The appellee's lawyer can cross appeal, identifying additional issues for review. For easier reference here, we will refer only to the role of the appellant's lawyer.

appellant's lawyer must first comb the record of the proceedings below to identify issues that might have been decided wrongly.

It might not be enough, however, that the appellate court would have decided the case differently had it been sitting in the trial judge's place. Rather, as section II explains in greater detail, reversal of some kinds of cases would require a finding that (1) the trial judge applied the wrong law, or (2) the record below cannot reasonably be read to support the decision below, even if all inferences are interpreted in the appellee's favor. Further, not every clear error of law or fact will result in appellate relief, but only those that might have made a difference in outcome ("reversible" error). Nor can any additional evidence be submitted,[2] although the appellate court might rely on extrinsic information in making policy judgments.[3] The appellate court will be evaluating whether the record below adequately supported the lower court's decision, so the relevant facts are those that were before the lower court.

Not only does the decision-making process differ on appeal, but the roles and perspectives of the judges differ as well. Appellate judges, especially those sitting on the highest appellate level of their jurisdiction, see themselves as responsible for the law's development. They are more willing to reevaluate the wisdom of a governing rule and therefore more willing to consider policy and principle-based reasoning. Still, they understand the value of stability and the legitimate need of citizens to rely on legal rules. Therefore, they find analogical reasoning (analogizing and distinguishing cases) persuasive because they want their rulings to be consistent with similar prior rulings, if possible. Although they are just as persuaded by stories as are trial judges, they are seeing only the "cold" record, not the actual witnesses, and so will tend to defer to the lower court's subjective interpretations.

Important similarities remain, however. All of the characteristics attributed to trial court judges above apply to appellate judges as well. They are busy with heavy caseloads. They want to issue good, just rulings. More than anything else in a brief, they want clarity, brevity, and accuracy.

§18.3 Suggestions and Reminders

Umbrella Section. If your brief will analyze several rules or several elements of a rule, begin with an umbrella section. An umbrella section should be concise — generally limited to one or two short paragraphs. Its primary function is to introduce the components of the analysis that follows. You can use an umbrella section at the beginning of the Argument section (before the first roman numeral) to introduce the roman numerals or after a point heading to introduce subparts within that point heading.

---

[2] There are some exceptions to this rule, but none that need concern us here.
[3] Ellie Margolis, *Beyond Brandeis*, 34 U.S.F. L. Rev. 197 (2000).

The content of an umbrella section depends on the particular situation and on your own writing decisions. Among the uses for an umbrella section are the following: (1) summarizing the rule and citing the controlling authority defining the rule; (2) providing any favorable principles affecting the application of the rule, such as presumptions, burdens of proof, elevated levels of proof (such as clear and convincing evidence), or policy leanings; (3) explaining the status of any elements not discussed in the brief; (4) providing a one-or two-sentence summary of your argument on each element; and (5) resolving any potential resistance to the order in which you will discuss the issues.

The Standard Paradigm. Because a brief is an advocacy document, it asserts positions (conclusions) at numerous points. The argument begins with a statement of the conclusion the writer hopes the judge will reach. This conclusion, in one form or another, appears in the point heading for that issue, as Chapter 17 explains. It also may appear in the first paragraph of text beneath the heading. A version appears at the beginning of the rule application section, right before the writer shows how the client's facts establish the conclusion. Finally, the conclusion appears at the end of the argument on that issue. This repetition contributes to an orderly route through rule-based reasoning. Also, subtle repetition is an effective technique for emphasis.[4] Here is an overview of the paradigm for the persuasive analysis of a single issue:

Conclusion

- State the conclusion you want the judge to reach on this issue (your thesis).
- Place it in the point heading and in the first paragraph.
- Succinctly state the most important reasons supporting your conclusion.

Rule Statement

- State the applicable legal rule.
- State it in the form and structure most favorable to your client's position.

Rule Explanation

- Explain where the rule comes from so the judge is satisfied that your rule statement is accurate.
- Explain what the rule means and how it applies to your client's facts.
- Explain these characteristics of the rule in the terms most favorable to your client's position.
- Rebut any counter-explanation you can weaken by a preemptive discussion.

---

[4] Mary Barnard Ray & Barbara J. Cox, *Beyond the Basics: A Text for Advanced Legal Writing* 2nd ed. 183 (West 2003).

Factual Conclusion

- State the conclusion you want the judge to reach about how the law applies to your client's facts.

Rule Application

- Discuss how the rule applies to your client's facts.
- Emphasize the favorable facts and de-emphasize or justify the problematic facts.
- Rebut any counter-application you can weaken by a preemptive discussion.

Conclusion

- Restate your conclusion.
- Unless the discussion has been short, summarize the key points supporting the conclusion.

Separating Rule Explanation and Rule Application. Remember that rule explanation generally should remain distinct from rule application, with rule explanation coming first. All of the reasons we saw earlier for keeping rule explanation separate from rule application still apply, but in persuasive writing another important reason applies as well. Presenting the reader with rule explanation first and separate from rule applications capitalizes on a principle of persuasion: Readers are more persuaded by ideas they have first thought of themselves than by an idea first asserted by another. This is especially true when the reader knows that the person doing the asserting is an advocate with an admitted persuasive agenda.

The strategy goes like this. The reader first reads the brief's fact statement and has those facts in mind when reading the rule explanation. During the rule statement and explanation, the reader will be thinking of those facts and anticipating rule application. The reader will be applying each point the writer is explaining about the rule to those facts. Presenting rule explanation first, without explicit application to the facts, allows the rule explanation to lead the reader to the desired conclusions about rule application, *before the writer asserts those conclusions.* Then, when the writer reaches the rule application phase, she is only asserting the conclusions the reader has already reached on his own.

Variations on the Paradigm. Occasionally, later drafts can alter the normal paradigm by combining the rule explanation section for each element into one comprehensive explanation of the rule and then combining the rule application section for each element into a comprehensive application of the rule. However, resist using this variation for the first draft. Let the discipline of separately writing out the rule explanation and rule application for each individual element help you deepen your understanding of that element. After you have mined the depths of possible arguments for each individual element, you can decide whether a combined discussion is appropriate.

Working Labels. As you write your early drafts, feel free to use working labels to help you stay on track and to help you evaluate your early drafts.

Thesis Sentences. Remember to use thesis sentences wherever you can. Because thesis sentences assert positions, they are even more important for a strong *argument* (in a brief) than for an accurate *prediction* (in an office memo).

Citations to the Record. An appellate brief must refer only to facts that are a part of the court record.[5] When the brief recites a fact, it must cite to the location of the fact in the record. The same is true for certain kinds of trial-level briefs. Insert these cites to the record now, as you write your early drafts. Including the citations as you write will save you valuable time later.

Writing the Fact Statement First. You might find it helpful to write out a draft of the Statement of Facts[6] before writing a draft of the Argument section. If you are having trouble getting started, this strategy could help. Also, you might find that immersing yourself in your client's story is excellent preparation for the more linear reasoning required in the Argument section.

§18.4 Rebutting your Opponent's Arguments

Lawyers write both opening briefs and briefs responding to the briefs filed by others. Lawyers often need to rebut their opponent's arguments, both in their own opening brief, where they anticipate opposing arguments, and in responsive and reply briefs filed after those opposing arguments have been made. Often lawyers must rebut both an opposing *explanation* of the law and an opposing *application* of the law to the current situation.

Lawyers struggle with how to treat counter-argument in an opening brief.[7] On the one hand, the writer wants to respond to the arguments she anticipates. On the other hand, she does not want to raise arguments the opposing party might not have thought of or articulate them better than the opposing brief would have. (This concern applies to adverse *arguments*, but not to directly adverse *authorities*. As you know, the lawyer has a duty to disclose directly adverse authorities in the controlling jurisdiction.) Nor does she want to sacrifice her affirmative stance — the primary advantage of the opening brief — by turning her own brief into a defensive document. Resolving these strategic questions is always a case-by-case task, but here are some helpful guidelines:

---

[5] *See* Chapter 20.1.2.

[6] *See* Chapter 20.

[7] An opening brief is the first brief filed on an issue. Usually one side files an opening brief, and the opposing party files a responsive brief. Then, generally, the party who filed the opening brief has an opportunity to file a reply brief.

1. Include counter-argument in an opening brief when you are relatively sure that the opposing brief or the court itself will raise the argument and when you can weaken it by a preemptive discussion. More often than not, a well-crafted preemptive discussion will weaken an opponent's argument.

2. Usually, the most effective forms of counter-argument do not draw attention to opposing argument by labeling it as such ("The defendant may argue that . . . . However, . . ."). Rather, the counter-argument disproves opposing arguments primarily by affirmative proof of the writer's own position ("The Defendant's actions constituted negligence [explain why]. The unreasonableness of the behavior is not justified by . . . or by . . . [explain why].")

3. Articulate your position on that argument in more detail than you use to articulate the opposing party's argument. Detail is a technique for emphasis, and lack of detail is a technique for deemphasis.[8]

4. Do not place an identified counter-argument ahead of your own affirmative argument. Rather, place it after you have made all of your own points. Otherwise, your brief will take on a defensive tone and will lose much of its rhetorical power.

5. After you have a draft of the argument, compare the space devoted to 5. counter-argument with the space devoted to affirmative argument. The great majority of the draft should be devoted to your own affirmative argument.

6. If your opponent has used rhetoric that is either excessive or particularly effective, consider ways to defuse that opposing rhetoric. Confront excessive rhetoric if you think that, left unconfronted, it could influence the judge. Confront particularly effective rhetoric if you can devise a way to remove the rhetoric's power. Usually the best way to remove the power of rhetoric is by using the law or the facts or both. For example:

> Defendant's brief contains broad general conclusions such as "preemptive effect . . . is firmly established in the case law," a "comprehensive network of agency regulations," "pervasive nature of the regulations," and the agency's "specifically stated intent." Def. brief 4. The support and analysis of these grandiose phrases and broad-brush conclusions consists simply of three agency source materials, plus an extensive reliance on one district court opinion, Simon. We now show these authorities do not support these statements . . . .[9]

---

[8] Mary Barnard Ray & Barbara J. Cox, Beyond the Basics: A Text for Advanced Legal Writing 176 (West 1991).

[9] Irwin Alterman, Plain and Accurate Style in Court Papers 125-126 (Student ed. ALIABA 1994).

CHAPTER 19

USING CASE AUTHORITY EFFECTIVELY

One of your brief's most important jobs is showing the court that the law that supports your argument is valid and that the law that supports your opponent's argument is either invalid or not on point. This chapter addresses how to include case authority — the authority used most frequently in briefs — in the most effective way possible.

To use authorities most effectively, you must keep both your reader and your user in mind: The brief should include enough information about the case authorities cited so that any reader can understand their significance. In addition, it must include citations in a way that allows them to be found easily by the user, who may be trying to find the relevant authorities so that he or she can review them and assess their validity.

The practical brief-writer should assume, however, that none of his or her readers will read anything other than the brief itself before deciding the case. Admittedly, at least the judge who writes the opinion, or his or her law clerk, will probably look up each cited case and review it to test whether it adequately supports your argument. Some readers may conduct additional research to further test the validity of the parties' arguments. Because the audience for an appellate brief includes all of the judges who will be voting, however, and because not every judge will have time to consult outside authorities, your brief should include enough information to be useful to those who want to go beyond it, but to be understandable and credible to those who do not.

With these concerns in mind, brief-writers need to pay attention to several different aspects of using case authority: (1) they must provide the reader with an appropriate amount of information about the cases they do cite; (2) they must use quotations effectively; (3) they must use language precisely when they are analogizing and distinguishing cases; (4) they must use unpublished decisions properly; and (5) they must use citations in a way that makes it easy for the judge or the judge's clerk to verify the validity of the rules and authorities in the argument.

§19.1 Providing Appropriate Detail in Case Descriptions

Analyzing authority cases is an essential part of effective written advocacy. Many legal writers neglect this important task, presuming wrongly that citations alone provide adequate support for the assertions in the brief. They seem to have the mistaken impression that judges have all of the needed law at their mental fingertips and that the brief-writer needs only to allude to some of the relevant authorities, drop in some favorite quotations, or provide a string cite of the cases that might have some bearing on the case at bar — certainly the judge and the clerks can fill in the rest. Most readers, however, need more information than the citation can give.

I gladly agree with the premise that judges are extremely intelligent and very knowledgeable about the law. However, there is a difference between a judge's general knowledge and the specific knowledge that is needed to decide a case intelligently. Most judges know and understand the general rules that apply to commonly encountered legal issues. This means that you do not need to discuss the British practice of writs of assistance in the colonies when arguing a Fourth Amendment case or cite to *Marbury v. Madison* if you are asking the court to declare a statute unconstitutional. Having the general knowledge to understand what rules mean and how they apply does *not* suggest, however, that all judges know the particular details of every case that you cite, or why and how each is relevant to your legal argument.

When you cite a case in a brief, it will most likely be for one of two reasons. You may be using the case to provide "rule authority": That is, you are citing the case to provide authority for the existence of a rule. More likely, however, you are citing the case as "illustrative authority": That is, you believe that the case effectively illustrates how the rule has been or should be applied. While the depth of your case description may vary depending on whether it is being used as a rule authority or an illustrative authority, you should provide some description for every case you cite. As a former deputy solicitor general has noted, "[e]very case that is worth citing . . . is worth discussing sufficiently to show why it is particularly on point or sheds analogous light on the question at hand."[1]

The question remains, what is "sufficient" discussion? In most situations, if you are citing a case, the reader should be able to glean four elements from your case description. Notice that I say that the reader should be able to *glean* these four elements. I am not saying that you must devote a sentence to each of these elements or even that you must state each one directly. Your decisions as to which elements to state directly and which to leave unstated will depend, as do most decisions, on the context in which the case descriptions appear.

With that warning, here are the elements:

(1) The issue. Be sure that the reader can identify which of the case's many issues and sub-issues you are using the case to illustrate. You should also provide

---

[1] James vanR. Springer, *Symposium on Supreme Court Advocacy: Some Suggestions on Preparing Briefs on the Merits in the Supreme Court of the United States*, 33 Cath. U. L. Rev. 593, 601 (1984). (The author was a deputy solicitor general of the United States from 1968 to 1971.)

the legal context in which the court analyzed that issue, *if it is different from the context of the case at bar or the cases under discussion in that section of your argument*. If you will be analogizing or distinguishing the case based on some particular facet of the legal issue, be sure to provide sufficient detail so that the reader can understand that facet of the issue.

(2) **The disposition**. Make clear how the court disposed of that narrow issue and, if relevant, how it disposed of the entire case.

(3) **The facts.** Include enough of the legally significant facts for the reader to understand how the court applied the law to reach its holding on the issue and how the case is analogous to the case at bar. If you wish to draw an analogy to these facts or to distinguish your case based on its facts, provide more detail.

(4) **The reasoning.** Include enough information to give the reader a basic understanding of why the court decided the issue before it in the way that it did. If either the case or the reasoning behind the court's decision is significant, provide more detail.

When writing a case description, you should presume that you need to include all four of these elements. Admittedly, on some occasions, it may be appropriate to include only three rather than four of the elements. At times, the facts may be omitted in a section devoted to an issue of law, particularly in a situation in which the writer cites two or more cases with similar fact situations. Likewise, when an argument turns on a question of fact, it may be permissible to omit a court's reasoning. When in doubt, however, include all four elements. Note that including these four elements in a case description is not all that the effective brief writer must do. To ensure that the brief is effective, you must be sure that your case description is as succinct as possible; you must use verb tenses accurately; you must use parenthetical case descriptions effectively and appropriately; and you must be certain that the case description is accurate.

§19.1.1 *Making Case Descriptions as Succinct as Possible*

Including the issue, the holding, the facts, and the reasoning in a case description may seem to require a long description. Actually, all four of these elements can often be conveyed in a parenthetical description, and they can certainly be conveyed in a textual description of two sentences. Of course, if the case is significant or if the argument is controversial, your case description will be lengthier.

There are two keys to succinct case descriptions. The first key is focus. You must understand the focus of the argument you are currently making and make sure that the case description has that same focus. The second key is efficient use of language. Too many case descriptions begin with a wasted sentence that does little more than announce that the case exists. Use your subjects and verbs with care to convey the most information in the fewest words.

§19.1.1.1 Focus

The case descriptions below are from a discussion about the illegality of gender-based classifications in a brief written in support of the petitioner's argument in *Miller v. Albright*, 523 U.S. 420 (1998). Notice how they efficiently include each of the necessary case description elements (signaled by a number after each of the elements appears):

▲ Good Example

❶ Issue
❷ Disposition
❸ Facts
❹ Reasoning

As noted previously, the <u>Virginia</u> Court discredited ❷ governmental justifications for gender-based classifications ❶ as to state-supported military schools ❸ because the justifications were based on overbroad generalizations about the different capabilities of men and women. ❹ 518 U.S. at 533. The <u>J.E.B.</u> Court also categorically rejected ❷ such broad assumptions about men and women's relative capabilities ❹ when it struck down ❷ a state's use of gender-based peremptory challenges to exclude all men from a jury. ❶ & ❸ 511 U.S. at 138-40.

One method you can use to test the focus of your case descriptions is to look for the phrase-that-pays for that section of the document.

If your argument is based in whole or in part on well-established statutory or common law rules, you can structure your argument by looking for each rule's "key terms,"[2] or, as I call them, the "phrases-that-pay." I use this term to label the word or phrase that is the focus of controversy about whether or how a rule applies. You can use phrases-that-pay as an effective organizing principle: By focusing on one "phrase-that-pays" within each subsection of the document, you ensure that you are focusing on one issue or sub-issue at a time, and you make it easier for the court to understand your argument. Thus, if one or more of your legal issues is governed by well-established rules, you can begin to structure your argument by reviewing those rules and identifying the phrases-that-pay that are in controversy in your case.

You can often identify phrases-that-pay by turning your rule into an if-then statement.[3] An "if-then" rule says, in essence, "if a certain condition exists, then a certain legal status results." The phrase-that-pays is almost always the "condition" that you are trying to prove the existence (or nonexistence) of. Thus, look for the phrases-that-pay in the "if" clause; that clause usually contains the narrow point that the writer is trying to explain or prove. For example, the petitioner in *Minnesota v. Carter* might write a rule within its brief as follows:

> While a person's home is, for most purposes, a place where he expects privacy, activities that are exposed "to the 'plain view' of outsiders are not protected" under the Fourth Amendment. Katz v. United States, 389 U.S. 347, 361 (1967) (Harlan, J., concurring).

---

[2] *See, e.g.,* Laurel Currie Oates & Anne M. Enquist, *The Legal Writing Handbook* §§2.2, 3.2(b) (4th ed., Aspen 2006).
[3] Note that you should not necessarily articulate your rule as an if-then statement in the argument itself; this technique is merely a method for identifying the phrases-that-pay.

The same rule stated as an if-then statement would read:

> IF a person exposes activities to the plain view of outsiders, THEN those activities are not protected against observation by the Fourth Amendment's search and seizure limitations.

This writer is arguing that the defendant's activities occurred within the plain view of police officers. Thus, "in plain view" is the phrase-that-pays.

If your case description includes the phrase-that-pays, chances are good that you have at least focused the description on the right legal issue. For example, in the previous example, the phrase-that-pays "gender-based classifications" appears in both case descriptions. In the following example, the brief-writer discusses cases in which the Court allowed or disallowed certain searches based on whether the officers were looking at things that were in "plain view." Note how the brief-writer took care to connect the phrase-that-pays, "plain view," to each of the two case descriptions (the phrase-that-pays is in small capital letters):

▲ Good Example

Illegal activities in PLAIN VIEW from outside the curtilage are not protected even if the police observation is specifically directed at identifying illegal activity. United States v. Dunn, 480 U.S. 294 (1987) (finding that an officer's PLAIN VIEW observation into a barn ❸ was not a Fourth Amendment search ❶ & ❷ , even though the observation was motivated by a law enforcement purpose ❸); Ciraolo, 476 U.S. at 212, 213. In Ciraolo, the defendant was growing marijuana in a 15-by-25 foot plot in his backyard. He surrounded the yard with a 6-foot outer fence and a 10-foot inner fence. ❸ Id. at 209. Officers flew over the defendant's house in a private airplane and readily identified the illegal plants using only the naked eye. ❸ Id.

❶ Issue
❷ Disposition
❸ Facts
❹ Reasoning

The government in Ciraolo argued that the observation was analogous to looking through a knothole or an opening in a fence: "If there is an opening, the police may look." Id. at 220. This Court agreed with the government, holding that the officers violated no expectation of privacy and that the observation was not a Fourth Amendment search. ❶ & ❷ Id. at 215. The airspace was outside the curtilage of the apartment, and the Court reasoned that the scene would have been in PLAIN VIEW to any member of the public flying in the same airspace. ❹ Id. at 213-14.

If the court has not been thoughtful enough to use the phrase-that-pays that you have identified for that section of the argument, you can make the connection yourself, as long as you do it honestly. If you do make the connection yourself, be sure to justify the connection in the way you describe the case, or with language that you quote. The word *apparently* is often helpful when describing a connection that is implicit rather than explicit, as in this description of a court's reasoning in a fictional case:

▲ Good Example

The court apparently believed that the search was justified by the fact that the defendant was smoking marijuana in PLAIN VIEW of the arresting officer, because it noted that "police officers need not turn away when they encounter illegal behavior right under their noses." Ohio v. McGuffin, 101 U.S. 101, 103 (2013).

When trying to decide how much detail to give the reader, first assess how you are using the case. If you are using the case as rule authority and plan to discuss it in depth in your explanation section, you may give only a "naked cite." On the other hand, you may be using a case as rule authority only because it is from a court of mandatory jurisdiction or it is well known as the source of a particular rule, rather than because of its relevance to your client's case. (Presumably, you plan to use other cases to illustrate the rule.) If that is the situation, you should provide a parenthetical description, as shown above with the writer's use of the *Dunn* case.

§19.1.1.2 Using Language Effectively

Even when using a textual case description or when you must give the reader more detail, do not make your case description needlessly long. Provide only the information that the reader needs about each of the four elements. The description of the *Ciraolo* case above is somewhat lengthy, but its length is concentrated in the facts and the reasoning. The plain view issue is fact specific, and thus the details about cases in which plain view was or was not established were particularly important in that case.

In many case descriptions, writers run into trouble in the first sentence. One way to avoid this trouble is to concentrate on the subject-verb combination. The first sentence you write about a case should tell the reader something that the court did or something about why the court did what it did. It should *not* tell the reader what the case *involved, regarded,* or *concerned,* or what the court *addressed, considered, examined,* or *dealt with.* Notice how the first sentence in the following case description wastes the reader's (scarce) time and energy:

▼ Bad Example

In J.E.B. v. T.B., 511 U.S. 127 (1994), this Court examined the issue of sex discrimination in the selection of jurors.

This description tells the reader that the court examined an issue, but leaves the reader in suspense as to what happened as a result of the examination. Suspense is the enemy of good legal writing. Instead of saying only that the court "examined" the issue, the writer should say something about a court's ultimate ruling or, if relevant, a particular finding in the case. Verbs such as *held* and *found* are more likely to get your reader to the point of the case:

▲ Good Example

In 1994, this Court held that sex-based ❶ peremptory challenges ❸ violate ❷ jurors' rights to equal protection. ❶ <u>J.E.B. v. T.B.</u>, 511 U.S. 127, 138-40 (1994).

❶ Issue
❷ Disposition
❸ Facts

The bad example told the reader only the issue that the court addressed in *J.E.B.* The good example, on the other hand, tells the reader the issue, the legally significant facts, and the disposition of the issue. The writer can add any needed reasoning in a second sentence.[4]

§19.1.1.3 *Verb Tense in Case Descriptions*

Many writers get confused as to the appropriate verb tense when describing cases. This confusion results when courts mix legal rules that are currently in force — properly stated in the present tense — with case facts, findings, and holdings — properly stated in some form of the past tense.[5]

Within a case description, use an appropriate form of past tense to describe events that happened before the case began as well as events that happened in the case. The court's holdings as to specific parties should also be described using the past tense:

▲ Good Examples

The plaintiff claimed that the defendant had assaulted him.

The advertisement had not specified the need for a college education.

Defendant had sought outside counsel before deciding to terminate the plaintiff.

The plaintiff alleged . . .

The defendant argued . . .

The court found . . .

The court reasoned . . .

The court held that Officer Thielen had violated the Fourth Amendment when he observed the defendants through a gap in a window blind.

When you are stating a general rule that the court articulated, however, use the past tense only to describe the court's action, and use the present tense for the rule itself:

▲ Good Example

The Court held that police officers do not violate the Fourth Amendment when they are able to observe criminal activity from a lawful vantage point without the aid of special equipment.

---

[4] For information on avoiding wordiness generally, see Anne Enquist & Laurel Currie Oates, *Just Writing: Grammar, Punctuation, and Style for the Legal Writer* §6.2 (3d ed., Aspen 2009).

[5] A detailed discussion of the sequence of tenses is beyond the scope of this book; for an excellent explanation of how verb tenses are used in legal writing, *see* Enquist & Oates, *supra* note 2, at §§8.3, 10.1.1.

The correct verb tense may not make or break your argument, but using the wrong verb tense distracts the reader at best. At worst, it confuses the reader and slows down his or her comprehension.

§19.1.2 *Writing and Using Effective Parenthetical Descriptions*

Many writers use parenthetical case descriptions to give the reader information about authority cases more efficiently. Parenthetical descriptions can save both space and the reader's time, and they are often a good choice. However, it is just as important to keep the principles of focus and completeness in mind when writing parenthetical descriptions as it is when writing textual descriptions. Ineffective parentheticals tend to give only a snippet of information. Often, unfortunately, the snippet does not contain enough information to make the case useful to the reader, who must decide whether the cited case provides authority for a ruling in the case at bar:

▼ Bad Example

See generally Virginia, 518 U.S. at 533 (plaintiff challenged gender-based classifications in state-run military schools); J.E.B. v. T.B., 511 U.S. at 138-40 (male juror questioned sex-based peremptory challenge).

These parentheticals tell the reader something about the issue (gender-based classifications) and the facts (the classifications occurred in a military school and in peremptory challenges to jury selection), but they do not tell the reader how the court resolved the issue or why the court resolved it the way it did. This type of snippet parenthetical may be effective, but only if the surrounding text — usually the text before the citation — supplies sufficient context. For a parenthetical to be effective, either the parenthetical alone *or* the parenthetical and the preceding text will give the reader information about at least three, and preferably four, of the required elements: the issue, the disposition, the facts, and the reasoning. In the first example below, the text before the citations provides the disposition, the issue, and the reasoning; the parentheticals, therefore, need include only the legally significant facts. In the second example, in contrast, which has no introductory text, the parenthetical includes all four elements:

▲ Good Examples

❶ Issue
❷ Disposition
❸ Facts
❹ Reasoning

Courts have justified striking down ❷ a variety of gender-based classifications ❶ when those classifications were based on "overbroad generalizations about the different capabilities of men and women." ❹ See, e.g., Virginia, 518 U.S. at 533(single-sex state-run military schools) ❸; J.E.B. v. T.B., 511 U.S. at 138-40 (gender-based peremptory challenges in jury selection). ❸

J.E.B. v. T.B., 511 U.S. 127, 138-40 (1994) ("categorically" rejecting broad assumptions about capabilities of men and women ❹ to strike down ❷ sex-based ❶ peremptory challenges ❸).

As with textual descriptions, using language effectively and focusing on the phrase-that-pays can help to make parenthetical descriptions more useful.

Knowing how to write effective parenthetical case descriptions is important, but the writer must also know *when* to use a parenthetical description. Deciding when to use a textual or a parenthetical description for a cited case is really a question about how much detail to provide. If little detail is needed, as when you are citing to a case only for rule authority, you can easily use a parenthetical description. Ultimately, your decision will be based on the answers to two questions: (1) How is the case significant to your argument? (2) What information does the reader need to have to understand the case's significance? The more significant an authority case is, and the more important it is for the reader to understand its facts and reasoning, the more detail you need to provide *in your argument*. If the issue or the authority case is more straightforward, on the other hand, you can provide a shorter textual description *or* a parenthetical description. Note that you should generally *not* provide both a parenthetical and a textual description for the same case. You may appropriately have a sentence with introductory text that precedes a citation with a parenthetical description. Generally, however, you should not follow a parenthetical case description with further textual description of a case.

The ideal explanation section within each unit of discourse in your argument includes at least one case in which a court found that the rule applied to a certain set of facts, and at least one case in which a court found that the rule did *not* apply to a certain different set of facts. In most situations, you will want to provide a textual description of both of those cases. A sensible compromise is to provide one or two more detailed case descriptions, followed up — when needed — by citation to one or more illustrative cases with parenthetical descriptions.

Do not use this method as an excuse to bombard the reader with eight authorities when one would suffice. Cite an additional authority only when it illustrates some aspect of the case that your previous authorities did not illustrate, or when it proves that the interpretation you are illustrating is well established.

The following example is an excerpt from a respondent's brief in *Minnesota v. Carter*, 525 U.S. 83 (1998). The brief-writer is using four cases to explain the rule that a person has a legitimate expectation of privacy in a location if that person can demonstrate an expectation that his or her activities would be private, and if society will accept that expectation as reasonable. This example shows the "conclusion, rule, explanation" part of the formula. The writer begins by articulating the rule and citing to authority, and follows by stating in a summary fashion how the rule should apply to the client's facts. The writer then proceeds to explain the rule, using the rule authority and other cases. In one of the cases, the Supreme Court found that no legitimate expectation of privacy existed. Some writers seem to think it is dangerous to let the court see any case in which a court ruled "against" their client's interest. Effective writers, however, realize that if a so-called negative case is distinguishable, it can be used very effectively to argue against a particular result. Notice how the writer of this example gives details from the *Rakas* Court's reasoning that he can use to distinguish the defendant in *Rakas* from his clients, who are claiming an expectation of privacy in an apartment that they visited for the purpose of packaging illegal drugs: ·

▲ Good Example

This Court has held that people will be recognized as having a legitimate expectation of privacy if they demonstrate an expectation that their activities are treated as private, and if it can be shown that society will find that expectation to be reasonable in a given situation. <u>Katz v. United States</u>, 389 U.S. 347, 361 (1967) (Harlan, J., concurring). ❶ In this case, Respondents demonstrated their expectation of privacy when they lowered the blinds to the apartment's window. Society should be prepared to recognize this expectation of privacy in a friend's apartment as reasonable.

This Court has allowed Fourth Amendment protections to extend beyond the home when the defendants have legitimate expectations of privacy and society can accept those expectations as legitimate. <u>See, e.g., Minnesota v. Olson</u>, 495 U.S. 91, 98 (1990). ❷ In <u>Olson</u>, this Court held that the unwarranted arrest of defendant, an overnight guest, was an illegal seizure. <u>Id</u>. The Court recognized that overnight guests have a sufficient interest in the privacy of the host's home to be free from unwarranted search and seizure. <u>Id</u>. at 96-97. Furthermore, the defendant's subjective expectation of privacy was found to be reasonable because society is known to recognize the social custom of staying overnight in another's home: "We will all be hosts and we will all be guests many times in our lives. From either perspective, we think that society recognizes that a houseguest has a legitimate expectation of privacy in his host's home." <u>Id</u>. at 98. The Court specifically noted that it is a "mistaken premise" that a place "must be one's 'home' in order for one to have a legitimate expectation of privacy there." <u>Id</u>. at 96.

Indeed, this Court has consistently found that legitimate expectations of privacy exist outside the home, as long as the circumstances are those in which most people would normally expect to enjoy a feeling of privacy. <u>Olson</u>, 495 U.S. at 96-97. Accordingly, this Court has found that defendants did not have a legitimate expectation of privacy in the contents of a car in which they were merely passengers, and where they had expressed no expectation of privacy in the areas of the car searched. <u>Rakas v. Illinois</u>, 439 U.S. 128, 148-49 (1978). The <u>Rakas</u> Court specifically refused to make a finding as to whether guests in houses or apartments would be treated similarly, noting that "cars are not to be treated identically with houses or apartments for Fourth Amendment purposes."<u>Id</u>. at 148 (citations omitted). <u>See also Katz v. United States</u>, 389 U.S. 347, 348 (1967) (defendant found to have legitimate expectation of privacy in conversations in a closed phone booth); <u>McGuffin v. United States</u>, 362 U.S. 257, 265 (1960) (defendant has standing to challenge a search warrant used to arrest him while in a friend's apartment).

❶ Rule authority that will be used later in this section as illustrative authority and then described in full.

❷ Illustrative authority

The writer highlights the fact that the *Rakas* Court said that houses and apartments should receive special treatment under the Fourth Amendment. The writer can use this point to argue that guests in an apartment, unlike passengers in a car, are entitled to assert an expectation of privacy.

§19.1.3 *Accuracy in Case Descriptions*

As noted above, an effective case description includes the relevant issue, disposition, facts, and reasoning. It should go without saying that legal writers should not misrepresent any of these elements. Say it I must, however. When I chat with judges and law clerks and quiz them about their legal writing pet peeves, many mention wordiness and poor organization. Almost all of them, however, complain about attorneys who misrepresent the facts or the law. Law clerks describe the many times that they have read in a brief that a case stands for one proposition, only to consult the case and find that it stood for some wholly unrelated point, or worse, that it contradicted the very point the attorney was using the case to make.

So the first thing you need to remember about accuracy is that someone will be checking your work. And don't count on escaping scrutiny if you are submitting a brief to an overworked and understaffed trial court; at the very least, your opponent should be checking the validity of your cited cases.[6] Don't be tempted to misrepresent case law, either through negligence or willfulness. The momentary satisfaction of presenting an argument with a veneer of validity is not worth the cost in reputation and future credibility. Further, you may face sanctions; model rule 3.3(a) provides that a lawyer shall not "knowingly make a false statement of fact or law to a tribunal." Accordingly, let us presume that you are not going to knowingly misrepresent cases; how can you avoid doing so negligently? First, avoid two common shortcuts that often lead to mistakes; second, be careful to avoid characterizing dicta as holdings, particularly when describing certain categories of cases.

One shortcut to avoid is relying on how others have characterized cases. If you read a memo, brief, or court opinion that characterizes a case in a certain way, it is tempting to repeat that characterization yourself.[7] Certainly, you may reason, that attorney or that judge would not have misrepresented the law. Resist the temptation. Take the time to click through to the cited case and to read it for yourself to verify that it says what you think it says. Further, be sure to use Shepard's and Keycite and conduct further research to verify that the case is still valid law. Even if the judge or attorney did not misrepresent the law, more recent authorities may have changed the validity of that case. Thus, read it and update it yourself; don't rely on the work of others.

---

[6] Admittedly, some lawyers do not take this seemingly obvious step. Take note, and be sure to do so with your own opponents. It is both satisfying and effective to be able to say to a court — in an oral argument, a responding brief, or a reply brief — that the very case that your opponent cites actually hurts rather than helps his or her argument.

[7] Of course, in law school, an academic honor code may forbid you to consult attorney briefs, or to use them without citing them as the source of your analysis. Even if it were permissible to use them without citation, however, you should not rely on their validity.

Another shortcut to avoid is using a case as authority when you have read only an isolated paragraph or two. Modern computer research can often send legal researchers on a cavalcade of clicking, jumping from one source to another to another. If you are not careful, you can end up citing a dissenting opinion as authority. One reason that this happens is that every paragraph of a case looks the same on a computer screen; if a hotlink takes you to the middle of an opinion, you have no way of immediately telling from that paragraph if you are reading a majority opinion, a concurrence, or a dissent.[8] If you don't take the time to discern the relevant issue, disposition, facts, and reasoning, you may not discover that you are reading something other than the majority opinion.

The second way that writers may negligently misrepresent the law is by failing to distinguish dicta from holdings, especially in what I refer to as *kickback cases*. A kickback case is a case that comes to a court of appeals after the trial court has granted a motion to dismiss or a motion for summary judgment. If the court of appeals reverses and remands the decision, it in essence "kicks it back" to the court below. But a decision to reverse and remand does not necessarily mean that the court made any *findings* as to the merits regarding how the law applies to the facts. In reversing a grant of a motion for summary judgment, the court may be doing no more than finding that a dispute exists as to the material facts. When reversing a grant of a motion to dismiss, the court is merely finding that the pleadings were sufficient to state a claim, not that the pleadings were true or that the plaintiff will necessarily succeed in his or her cause of action. It is particularly important to remember that the standard of review for a motion to dismiss requires a court to presume that a complaint's factual allegations are true. This presumption does *not* mean, however, that the allegations are in fact true or that the plaintiff will be able to establish at trial that they are true.

For example, in a 1991 case,[9] the plaintiffs had alleged that police officers had owed a duty to protect a man made helpless by drunkenness when they interfered with acquaintances who were helping the intoxicated man. These acquaintances left the scene when the officers took control of the situation, the complaint alleged, and the man later fell to his death after the officers ordered him to walk home alone. In granting (and affirming the granting of) defendants' motion to dismiss, the trial court and the court of appeals found that the defendants owed no duty to the plaintiff's decedent under the facts alleged. The state supreme court reversed the decision, noting that the Restatement of Torts provides that a person owes a helpless person a duty of care when he or she "takes charge" of that person and then leaves the person in a worse situation. Accordingly, the court reversed the decision below.

A careless writer, trying to explain the rule about taking charge of a helpless individual, might misrepresent the court's holding by quoting a partial sentence with a misleading introduction:

---

[8] As of this writing, no computer databases use color, shading, or another graphic means to signal researchers when they are not reading part of a majority opinion. Even if they do, however, you should never rely on a case without verifying that the language you are relying on is part of the majority opinion.

[9] *Russell v. City of Columbia*, 406 S.E.2d 338 (S.C. 1991).

▼ Bad Example

The court held that "once the police officers took control of the situation and preempted individuals already attempting to aid the petitioner's obviously injured and intoxicated decedent, respondents incurred a duty to follow through and finish what was begun." <u>Russell v. City of Columbia</u>, 406 S.E.2d 338, 339 (S.C. 1991).

The *language* is quoted accurately; the context, however, is not accurate. A law clerk who went to read the decision would find that three words missing from the sentence create a vastly different impression of the case (the emphasis is added):

> *Petitioner argues that* once the police officers took control of the situation and preempted individuals already attempting to aid the petitioner's obviously injured and intoxicated decedent, respondents incurred a duty to follow through and finish what was begun.

The state supreme court did not find that the officers had incurred a duty of care or that the facts were accurate as pleaded. It merely restated the petitioner's argument and found that the complaint was adequate to state a cause of action. In contrast, notice how the writer in this example accurately portrays the disposition of the issue and uses the word "may" to indicate the lack of a legal holding:

▲ Good Example

Persons may incur a duty to a helpless person when they send away others who are rendering aid. <u>Russell v. City of Columbia</u>, 406 S.E.2d 338, 339 (S.C. 1991) (complaint sufficient to state cause of action as to duty when it alleged that officers questioning intoxicated man sent away persons who were trying to help him).

Thus, you can still cite to a kickback case; you must, however, accurately portray the issue and its disposition in any case description.

Accurately describing authority cases is one of the best ways to educate a court about the meaning of the law. You will increase your chances of doing so both effectively and accurately if you make sure to (1) provide sufficient information about the issue, disposition, facts, and reasoning; (2) focus the information on the issue currently under discussion; (3) use language efficiently to avoid unnecessary wordiness; (4) use parentheticals as needed for rule authorities or less significant cases; and (5) take care to avoid misrepresenting the cases you cite.

§19.2 Using Quotations Effectively in Case Descriptions

Quotations can be used very effectively to provide proof and support for the brief-writer's assertions. When using quotations from cases, however, it's good to keep a couple of points in mind. First of all, you should usually paraphrase rather than quote language from cases. Quotation marks draw the reader's attention, and you want to save that special attention for important statements. Generally, use direct quotations only when you are stating rules or other language at issue, or when you are justifying a conclusion you have drawn about the meaning of an authority. Of course, whether you are quoting or paraphrasing, be sure to provide appropriate citations.

Writers' problems with quotations from cases tend to fall into the two categories of "not enough" and "too much." Some writers drop quotations into their arguments without giving the reader enough information about the case. Without sufficient context, the quotation is meaningless. Other writers give the reader too much quoted language, leaving the reader to complete the writer's job of sifting through the language and sorting out its meaning. Police your writing to avoid these problems.

§19.2.1 *Not Enough Context*

Legend has it that Marie Antoinette once said, "Let them eat cake!" If you don't know the context of that remark, she sounds like a pretty nice person. She sounds a lot less friendly, however, once you learn that she supposedly said it while looking down at the peasants in the street who were crying for bread.

Keep Marie in mind when you are tempted to drop a pithy quote from an obscure case into the middle of your rule explanation section. If the judge doesn't know what that court was looking at — i.e., the issue, the rule, and the facts — when it made that statement, he or she can't begin to understand the significance of the quote without looking the case up. And since most judges don't have time to read the cases cited in the briefs, the quote may have a negative impact: The judge will be annoyed at being given insufficient or misleading information.

Thus, when using a quotation from a case, be sure you have provided the reader with the context. Do not drop a quotation into your argument like a chocolate chip into batter:

▼ Bad Example

This Court has noted that generalizations "concerning parent-child relations . . . become less acceptable as the age of the child increase[s]." Caban v. Mohammed, 441 U.S. 380, 382 (1979). Thus, the gender-based generalizations in this case are invalid.

An altered quotation with an unaccompanied citation does not fill the court with confidence about the validity of your argument. Instead, include the details that will give context for the quotation:

▲ Good Example

As far back as 1979, this Court struck down a statute that characterized parent-child relationships between unwed fathers and their children differently from those of unwed mothers. <u>Caban v. Mohammed</u>, 441 U.S. 380, 382 (1979). While conceding that unwed mothers might be closer to their children at birth, the Court stated that the generalization would become "less acceptable as a basis for legislative distinctions" as the age of the child increased. <u>Id</u>.

Quotations can also be used effectively in a parenthetical:

> As far back as 1979, this Court struck down a statute that characterized parent-child relationships between unwed fathers and their children differently from those of unwed mothers. <u>Caban v. Mohammed</u>, 441 U.S. 380, 382 (1979) (noting that any generalizations would become "less acceptable as a basis for legislative distinctions" as the child grew older).

By making a quotation part of a coherent case description, you make it more likely that the quotation will do the job of convincing the court that the case stands for the proposition you say it does.

§19.2.2 Too Much Quoted Language

Some writers are so enamored with the court's language that they are loathe to paraphrase. Instead, they simply provide page after page of excerpted quotes and let the reader determine the significance of the quoted language. "Overquoting" creates two problems. First, the writer is not doing his or her job. The writer is not supposed to provide the raw material to the readers and let them sort out what it all means. The writer's job is to research the law, synthesize the available information, and write up the analysis in a way that allows the reader to understand the situation with a minimum of effort.

The second problem is related to the first. A reader — a judge in this context — who is constantly asked to consume and digest lengthy quotations may lose the thread of the argument. As a practical matter, many readers (including some of the people reading this book) skip long quotations. Judges who are reading briefs may do so because they know that the quotation says nothing about the case currently before the court; instead, it talks about another case, which must some how be connected to the current case. Writers who overuse long quotes frequently do so because they have not figured out that connection and thus cannot make the connection within the argument. They compensate by giving the reader background reading that may, with luck and some work, allow the reader to reach the conclusion that the writer espouses. Since the writer, rather than the reader, is supposed to do the work, it is usually ineffective to use lengthy quotations.

The following example is from a student-written brief written in the case of *Chicago v. Morales*, 527 U.S. 41 (1999). In that case, the city of Chicago argued in favor of the constitutionality of a statute that allowed the arrest of people who "loitered" with gang members and who refused to disperse on police order. The writer of the following example apparently wanted the reader to use the quoted language to draw the conclusion that laws that promote "peace and quiet" are constitutional:

▼ Bad Example

This Court has provided almost absolute protection to speech of a political nature. In 1969, the Court found the arrest of demonstrators for disorderly conduct to be unconstitutional under the First Amendment. Gregory v. Chicago, 394 U.S. 111, 116 (1969). The Court made this finding in favor of political speech even though the picketers' actions led to a disruption of the peace and quiet of a neighborhood by picketing in front of the mayor's home.Id. at 111. A concurring opinion stressed the lawfulness and peacefulness of the demonstration as well as the petitioners' First Amendment right to engage in that activity.Id. at 121 (Black, J., concurring). However, Justice Black also declared:

> Plainly, however, no mandate in our Constitution leaves States and governmental units powerless to pass laws to protect the public from the kind of boisterous and threatening conduct that disturbs the tranquility of spots selected by the people either for homes, wherein they can escape the hurly-burly of the outside business and political world, or for public and other buildings that require peace and quiet to carry out their functions, such as courts, libraries, schools, and hospitals.

> Id. at 118 (Black, J., concurring). Therefore, even if loitering were treated as a fundamental right, Petitioner possesses a significant, legitimate interest in limiting criminal street gang members' right to loiter for no purpose.

Readers who skipped the quote would have no way of knowing where the writer's "therefore" came from. Even readers who read the quote would have to figure out for themselves the significance of the quoted language. If you are tempted to use a lengthy quotation, try one of two tactics to help ensure that your readers will understand your message.

The first and perhaps most obvious solution is to try to shorten the quote. Start by underlining the language that is most significant to your argument:

> Plainly, however, <u>no mandate in our Constitution</u> leaves States and governmental units powerless to pass laws to protect the public from the kind of boisterous and <u>threatening conduct</u> that <u>disturbs the tranquility</u> of spots selected by the people either for homes, where in they can escape the hurly-burly of the outside business and political world, or for public and other buildings that require peace and quiet to carry out their functions, such as courts, libraries, schools, and hospitals.

Then, quote only the underlined material (after removing the underlining), and incorporate a paraphrase of the rest of the quotation into your argument:

▲ Good Example

This Court has provided almost absolute protection to speech of a political nature. Gregory v. Chicago, 394 U.S. 111, 116 (1969). In Gregory, the

Court found the arrest of demonstrators for disorderly conduct to be unconstitutional under the First Amendment.Id. The Court made this finding in favor of political speech even though the picketers' actions led to a disruption of the peace and quiet of a neighborhood by picketing in front of the mayor's home.Id. at 111. A concurring opinion stressed the lawfulness and peacefulness of the demonstration as well as the petitioners' First Amendment right to engage in that activity.Id. at 121 (Black, J., concurring). However, Justice Black also declared that "no mandate in our Constitution" prevents states from passing laws that protect the public from "threatening conduct" that "disturbs the tranquility" of homes or certain public buildings.Id. at 118 (Black, J., concurring). Therefore, even if loitering were treated as a fundamental right, Petitioner possesses a significant, legitimate interest in limiting criminal street gang members' right to loiter for no purpose.

In the alternative, you may determine that the lengthy quote is absolutely necessary for your argument. If this is the case, promote the effectiveness of the quotation by articulating the conclusions you want the reader to draw from it and putting those conclusions into the body of your argument. I recommend using what I refer to as a *Katie Couric Introduction* before the quotation.

A Katie Couric Introduction is an introduction that focuses the reader's attention on the point the writer is using the quotation to prove or establish. I call it that because Katie Couric and other newscasters constantly introduce little snippets of interviews or public events. In much the same way, a long quote is a little snippet of an opinion or other legal document. Legal writers, unfortunately, often give readers unfocused introductions like, "The Court noted," or, as in the previous illustration, "Justice Black also declared." In contrast, newscasters almost never give introductions like, "The President said," or "The Senator noted." Instead, they give the audience some context and essentially tell them what to listen for when they hear the quoted language.

The illustration below is from a broadcast in which Katie Couric excerpted pieces of interviews with Captain Chesley Sullenberger and other crew members of U.S. Airways flight 1584. Captain Sullenberger and the crew achieved fame in 2009, when they safely landed a disabled jet on the Hudson River and safely evacuated all of the passengers. The excerpt below is from the beginning of the story, and it focuses on Captain Sullenberger's feelings when he realized the danger of the situation. Notice how the (italicized) language leading up to the quotation gives the audience context and prepares it for what is to come:

▲ Good Example

KATIE COURIC: When U.S. Airways flight 1549 landed in New York's Hudson River on January 15th, what seemed destined to be a tragedy became an extraordinary tale of success and survival. By the time all 155 people were pulled from the icy waters by a flotilla of rescue boats, a story began to emerge of a highly trained pro with a cool demeanor who had deftly guided his doomed aircraft to safety. In an instant, Captain

Chesley "Sully" Sullenberger found himself at the heart of an uplifting news story people all over the world wanted to celebrate. In February, *just two weeks later, Captain Sullenberger gave his first account of the harrowing five minutes in the sky over New York City*:

CAPTAIN CHESLEY SULLENBERGER: It was the worst, sickening, pit-of-your-stomach, falling-through-the-floor feeling I've ever felt in my life. I knew immediately it was very bad.[10]

In the same way, you should prepare your audience for a long quotation by stating the conclusion you want the reader to draw from it:

▲ Good Example

However, Justice Black also pointed out that governments can prohibit certain behaviors in public places to protect the public:

> Plainly, however, no mandate in our Constitution leaves States and governmental units powerless to pass laws to protect the public from the kind of boisterous and threatening conduct that disturbs the tranquility of spots selected by the people either for homes, wherein they can escape the hurly-burly of the outside business and political world, or for public and other buildings that require peace and quiet to carry out their functions, such as courts, libraries, schools, and hospitals.

Id. at 118 (Black, J., concurring). Therefore, it is possible for municipalities to protect both the Constitution and the peace and quiet of their communities with appropriate legislation.

Use a Katie Couric Introduction to help the reader to get the most out of lengthy quotations. The focused introduction will encourage the reader to read the quote by directing his or her attention and making it easier to understand the point of the quotation. Even if the reader does skip the quote, the writer has still articulated the point of the quotation in a place that the reader will see it and in a way that the reader can understand.

§19.3 Using Language Precisely When Analogizing and Distinguishing Cases

Analogizing and distinguishing relevant authority cases can be a vital part of the application sections of your argument. By showing the reader how a case is like or unlike a relevant case, a writer can convince the reader to apply the rule in a way that will achieve the desired result. Note that your application section should not *begin* with the analogy or distinction. Instead, begin with an explicit

---

[10] Video available at http://www.cbsnews.com/video/watch/?id=4784012n&tag=mncol;lst;1 (last accessed May 5, 2010).

assertion about how the law applies to the facts (generally, "phrase-that-pays equals or does not equal case facts"). Use the relevant cases to support that assertion. Do not begin your application this way:

▼ **Bad Example**

This case is like <u>McGuffin</u>.

Instead, begin by telling the reader how the law applies to the facts:

▲ **Good Example**

Mr. Pillion had a reasonable expectation of privacy. Like the defendant in <u>McGuffin</u>, . . .

Your case analogies and distinctions will be most effective if they are *precise*. Do not analogize a specific fact to a whole case:

▼ **Bad Example**

Like <u>Robinson</u>, the Defendant here had committed an arrestable offense.

This comparison is inapt because one defendant, by definition, cannot be "like" a whole case. Make your analogy or distinction specific. Compare defendants to defendants, and other actors and things to their specific counterparts in the authority case. These illustrations make the comparisons explicit:

▲ **Good Examples**

In the present case, Respondents, like the defendants in <u>Lewis</u> and <u>Hicks</u>, were present on property for the sole purpose of conducting criminal business.

Like the officer in <u>Lewis</u>, Officer Thielen observed only activities that were a necessary part of Respondents' illegal business. During the entire time Officer Thielen watched the apartment occupants, the occupants did nothing but divide and package cocaine. <u>See</u> Record at E-2, G-14.

Unlike the car at issue in <u>Rakas</u>, an apartment is a private dwelling not normally open to the public view.

These examples also provide details from the client's case that make the analogies vivid. The writer must do more than make the bare statement that "this case is like (or unlike) *McGuffin*" if the reader is to see the connection or the disconnection between the two cases. In the next example, the writer takes care to provide the details that will clarify the distinctions between the two cases:

▲ **Good Example**

Unlike the defendant in <u>Katz</u>, who argued that he sought privacy by closing the door to his phone booth, Respondents introduced no evidence of conduct that demonstrated an intent to keep their activities private. Though the blinds were drawn, there is no indication that Respondents drew them. <u>See</u> Record at E-2, E-10. On the night in question, Respondents were present in a first-floor apartment that had several windows <u>at</u> ground level. Record G-26. The windows faced a public area that apartment residents and nonresidents frequented. Record G-69, G-70. As darkness fell in early evening, Respondents sat illuminated under a chandelier light at a table directly in front of one of these windows. Record G-13. Only a pane of glass and a set of blinds that featured a series of laths, Record G-50, separated Respondents from the adjacent common area. On the night in question, the blinds, though drawn, had a gap in them; the gap was large enough for a citizen who passed by and an officer who stood a foot or more from the window to view easily the entire illuminated interior scene. Record G-13.

Individuals in Respondents' position would have known and expected that a passerby could look through the gaps in the blinds and see into the illuminated kitchen. Thus, Respondents could not have actually expected that their illegal activities would go unnoticed.

This application is somewhat long, but the details are necessary for the reader to understand how the law applies to the facts. Although analogies and distinctions are not always needed, make sure that when you do include them, you focus them on the specific people or things that you want to compare. Second, make sure that you provide the details that allow the reader to understand both the comparison and the application of law to facts.

§19.4 Dealing with Nonprecedential, Or "Unpublished" Opinions

In recent years, the "publication" and use of unpublished opinions — now more commonly referred to as "nonprecedential opinions" — has become controversial, with some courts forbidding their citation, others allowing them with some restrictions, and one court holding that rules limiting use of unpublished decisions are unconstitutional.[11] A recent change to the Federal Rules of Appellate Procedure has mandated that no court may limit the citation of any federal case decided after January 1, 2007. Because the rules about citation of nonprecedential opinions vary from jurisdiction to jurisdiction,[12] the most important thing to do is to consult both the rules of the jurisdiction and the local rules of the court when deciding whether to cite to them.

All United States Supreme Court opinions are published, as are virtually all opinions of state supreme courts. State and federal trial courts and intermediate

---

[11] *Anastasoff v. United States*, 223 F.3d 898, 899 (8th Cir. 2000), *vacated as moot on reh'g en banc*, 235 F.3d 1054 (8th Cir. 2000).

[12] For example, the Minnesota Rules of Civil Appellate Procedure provide that "[u]npublished opinions and order opinions are not precedential except as law of the case, res judicata or collateral estoppel, and may be cited only as provided in Minnesota Statutes, section 480A.08, subd. 3 (1996)." Minn. R. Civ. App. Proc. 136.01(b) (2010).

appellate courts, however, currently designate a significant percentage of their opinions as nonprecedential or unpublished. Professor Amy Sloan reports that, overall, "84% of opinions issued by the federal courts of appeals are nonprecedential."[13] Actually, because of the availability of opinions on the Internet and on research services such as Lexis and Westlaw, many so-called unpublished decisions are not unpublished in the real sense. Instead, they are decisions that the court has decided to designate as nonprecedential, perhaps because the judges believe that they address routine issues that will not add significantly to the body of law.[14]

The local rules of the various federal appellate courts and of the various state courts treat nonprecedential decisions in a variety of ways. Some courts have promulgated rules that seem to favor the issuance of precedential decisions, while others disfavor their issuance, and still others are silent.[15] Illinois Supreme Court Rule 23, for example, designates categories of appellate court decisions as precedential or nonprecedential, and section (a) of that rule explains which decisions are appropriate for "full opinions":

> The decision of the Appellate Court may be expressed in one of the following forms: a full opinion, a concise written order, or a summary order conforming to the provisions of this rule. All dispositive opinions and orders shall contain the names of the judges who rendered the opinion or order. Only opinions of the court will be published.
>
> (a) Opinions. A case may be disposed of by an opinion only when a majority of the panel deciding the case determines that at least one of the following criteria is satisfied, subject to the limitations contained in the accompanying administrative order:
>
> (1) the decision establishes a new rule of law or modifies, explains or criticizes an existing rule of law; or
> (2) the decision resolves, creates, or avoids an apparent conflict of authority within the Appellate Court.

Further, in contrast to the federal rule, this state court rule (at 23(e)) forbids citation of nonprecedential decisions except in limited circumstances:

> (e) Effect of Orders. An unpublished order of the court is not precedential and may not be cited by any party except to support contentions of double jeopardy, *res judicata*, collateral estoppel or law of the case. When cited for these purposes, a copy of the order shall be furnished to all other counsel and the court.

---

[13] Amy E. Sloan, *If You Can't Beat 'em, Join 'em: A Pragmatic Approach to Nonprecedential Opinions in the Federal Appellate Courts*, 86 Neb. L. Rev. 895, 898 (2008) (citing Statistics Div., Admin. Office of the U.S. Courts, 2006 Annual Report of the Director: Judicial Business of the United States Courts 52 (2007)).

[14] E.g., K. K. DuVivier, *Are Some Words Better Left Unpublished? Precedent and the Role of Unpublished Decisions*, 3 J. App. Prac. & Process 397, 399 (2001).

[15] Sloan, *supra* n.13, at 909-10.

Because a search on the Internet or on Westlaw or Lexis may turn up non-precedential opinions, you must know what the rules are in the court to which you are writing. If you don't know the rules, find out. Check the library or the court's Web site, or call the clerk of the court. If the court does allow citation to nonprecedential opinions, and you cite any in your brief, be sure to attach copies of them as needed to the briefs that you serve on the court and on opposing counsel. Federal Rule of Appellate Procedure 32.1, for example, mandates that a party who cites any federal "written disposition that is not available in a publicly accessible electronic database" must file and serve a copy of the document with the brief or other document submitted to the court. The comments to the rule indicate that "commercial databases" are considered to be "publicly accessible," so any decision available on Lexis or Westlaw presumably would not need to be filed.

Nonprecedential opinions require different citation forms. The *ALWD Citation Manual*, Rule 12.18, for example, requires that when citing opinions that are available only in slip form, the author provide the case name, the docket number, the court abbreviation, and the exact date of disposition:

> Operator Serv. Co. v. Croteau, No. CL961672A1 (Fla. 15th Cir. Aug. 5, 1996).[16]

Particularly if the case is a recent decision, you may decide to provide additional parenthetical material to distinguish a decision that is unpublished because it is so recent from a decision that is unpublished because the court designated it as nonprecedential:

> McGuffin v. Coleman, No. LCW25890856 (Fla. 15th Cir. Jun. 13, 2010) (court-designated nonprecedential decision) (copy attached).

In addition or in the alternative, you may want to state explicitly that you are citing to an nonprecedential decision in the text of your argument:

> The Ninth District Court of Appeals, in a nonprecedential decision, endorsed just this interpretation in 1992. Pillion v. McGuffin, No. AB9123561A4 (Ohio App. 9th Dist. Jan. 24, 1992) (copy attached).

Regardless of formal citation rules, many courts designate a nonprecedential opinion by putting the word "unpublished" in a parenthetical at the end of the citation. Try to find out about local rules and local customs when deciding whether and how to cite nonprecedential opinions. When citing them, err on the side of giving too much information to avoid violating court rules.

---

[16] Association of Legal Writing Directors & Darby Dickerson, *ALWD Citation Manual: A Professional System of Citation* (4th ed., Aspen 2010). Rule 12.12 addresses methods for citing cases published only on Lexis or Westlaw.

§19.5 Using Citations Effectively

§19.5.1 When to Cite

The first challenge for many legal writers is figuring out when citations are necessary. Generally, you *must* include a citation at the end of every sentence in which you state a legal proposition, refer to a new authority, or quote or paraphrase information from a court opinion (or other source). One of the few occasions on which you may *omit* a citation is when you have already analyzed an authority and are applying that authority's rule to your case. For example, the statement that "the *McGuffin* rule applies here" does not need a citation in a discussion in which the writer has already introduced and cited *McGuffin*.

Some legal propositions are so basic that they may seem self-evident. If you are asking a court to apply such a legal principle to your client's case, however, you should cite an authority that controls in that court's jurisdiction.

▼ Bad Example

It is well known that the Fifth Amendment's protection against compelled self-incrimination applies to the states.

▲ Good Example

The Fifth Amendment's protection against compelled self-incrimination applies to the states through the Fourteenth Amendment's Due Process Clause. See Malloy v. Hogan, 378 U.S. 1, 6 (1964).

Legal writing is referenced writing, and readers expect frequent citation. You can use short citation forms and effective sentence structures to keep your writing readable, but you must include citations whenever you state a legal proposition, refer to an authority for the first time, or quote or paraphrase material from a source. This means that within the rule explanation section, for example, every sentence may have a citation after it. Many of the citations may be in the "Id." form, but the reader will still expect and need citations.

§19.5.2 Distinguishing Between Authorities and Sources

Although this text, and many legal writers, often refer to all cases, statutes, and the like as "authorities," the reality is that some are only "sources": They contain information that the court may find interesting and relevant, but the source has no *authority* over the court reading the brief. Too many legal writers do not make this distinction, and they annoy and frustrate courts by their imprecise use of citations.

I do not mean to imply that you can cite only to cases, for example, that are written by authoritative courts. Rather, you need to recognize that there are at least three different possible meanings for a citation, some of which may overlap. The citation may mean simply, "I am not the person who first said or thought of this statement." This kind of citation is used to give appropriate credit to the originator of an idea and to avoid charges of plagiarism. A citation may also mean, "Here is the source of the law, facts, or policy I just mentioned, so you can find it if you want." This kind of citation — and its accuracy — is very important for judges and their clerks. Finally, a citation can mean, "This statement is *the law*." This use of citation is very important for the brief-writer because it is used to justify and support legal arguments.

Unfortunately, the same citation forms are used for all three of these categories of citations, and so brief-writers must be sure that their text makes the distinction. If the writer says nothing, the reader's instinct is to presume that a cited statement is authoritative, and the reader may be startled or frustrated when he or she looks at the citation and realizes that the cited case (or other source) is not authoritative.

Writers who quote or paraphrase relevant legal assertions from law review articles and nonmandatory courts must make the necessary distinction by introducing the material with a phrase indicating that an authoritative court did not make the statement. Here are some bad examples from a brief written to a federal district court within the First Circuit:

▼ Bad Examples

Refusing to allow individual liability for supervisors under Title VII is "manifestly inconsistent" with Title VII's "underlying rationale and primary goals." Tracy L. Gonos, <u>A Policy Analysis of Individual Liability — The Case for Amending Title VII to Hold Individuals Personally Liable for Their Illegal Discriminatory Actions</u>, 2 N.Y.U. J. Legis. & Pub. Poly. 265, 270 (1998-1999).

With Title VII, Congress intended not only to make discriminatory acts by both employers and their agents actionable, but also to make "those who discriminate" — both employers and their agents — jointly and severally liable for their discriminatory acts. <u>Wyss v. General Dynamics Corp.</u>, 24 F. Supp. 2d 202, 206 (D.R.I. 1998) (citation omitted).

With both of these examples, the statements are relevant legal assertions that are followed by a citation and are not preceded by a qualifier. In both situations, the reader would instinctively presume that the citation provides authority for the validity of the statement, and would be frustrated to see the nonauthoritative citation following the statement. To avoid this problem, simply use qualifying language that reveals that the source is not authoritative. Generally, the best way to do this is to mention or refer to the source; you need not announce to the court that a particular source is not authoritative:

▼ Bad Examples

Although not authoritative, a commentator has noted that refusing to allow individual liability for supervisors under Title VII is "manifestly inconsistent" with Title VII's "underlying rationale and primary goals." Tracy L. Gonos, <u>A</u>

Policy Analysis of Individual Liability — The Case for Amending Title VII to Hold Individuals Personally Liable for Their Illegal Discriminatory Actions, 2 N.Y.U. J. Legis. & Pub. Poly. 265, 270 (1998-1999).

A persuasive court has found that Congress intended for Title VII not only to make discriminatory acts by both employers and their agents actionable, but also to make "those who discriminate" — both employers and their agents — jointly and severally liable for their discriminatory acts. Wyss v. General Dynamics Corp., 24 F. Supp. 2d 202, 206 (D.R.I. 1998) (citation omitted).

The judge or his or her clerk knows that commentators and nonauthoritative courts are only persuasive authority. The best way to make them aware of the nonauthoritative nature of the statement is to succinctly reveal the source in text. If possible, you should also give the court a reason to find value in the statement:

▲ Good Examples

One commentator has argued that refusing to allow individual liability for supervisors under Title VII is "manifestly inconsistent" with Title VII's "underlying rationale and primary goals." Tracy L. Gonos, A Policy Analysis of Individual Liability — The Case for Amending Title VII to Hold Individuals Personally Liable for Their Illegal Discriminatory Actions, 2 N.Y.U. J. Legis. & Pub. Poly. 265, 270 (1998-1999). Title VII's underlying rationale is revealed in Section. . . .

Another district court in the First Circuit has faced this same issue and agreed that Congress intended to make discriminatory acts by both employers and their agents actionable under Title VII. Wyss v. General Dynamics Corp., 24 F. Supp. 2d 202, 206 (D.R.I. 1998) (citation omitted). That court further noted that Congress also intended to make "those who discriminate" — both employers and their agents — jointly and severally liable for their discriminatory acts. Id.

In the first example, the writer tries to increase the value of the source by tying its assertion to specific statutory language. In the second example, the writer tells the court why it should care about this nonauthoritative source by stating that the court was addressing the same issue as the issue the court is currently addressing. Citing to a mandatory authority is almost always preferable. When other citations are necessary, however, the practical brief-writer does not try to hide the use of nonmandatory authority, but instead uses effective writing techniques to try to increase the value of nonmandatory sources.

§19.5.3 *Where to Cite*

As noted previously, citations in a brief will sometimes be citations to sources rather than citations to authorities. For this reason, writers should place their citations in text in almost all situations. Use footnotes for citations only on rare occasions (e.g., for occasions when a string citation is necessary). Placing citations in text allows readers to identify immediately which citations are and are not authoritative citations. The reader's immediate need to understand a source's validity makes it more important for brief-writers to place citations in text than it is for any other kind of legal writer. Only the brief-writer has the job of marshaling mandatory and nonmandatory authorities, synthesizing rules from those authorities, applying them to facts, and presenting them to a decision maker. The brief-writer, much more than the legal commentator or the judge, asks the reader to accept or reject legal arguments based on the authoritativeness of his or her citations. The journal-writer, in contrast, may assemble citations from a variety of jurisdictions to posit a theory; the judge derives authority from his or her judicial appointment.[17] The reader of a brief, unlike the reader of a law review article or of an opinion, must reserve judgment about the validity of any legal proposition until the authoritativeness of the citation is known. Putting citations in footnotes needlessly frustrates the reader of a brief.

A reader who encounters a brief with citations in footnotes has three choices for deciding what to do, and all of them are bad. First, the reader can presume that the writer is citing an authoritative source. This choice is bad because the reader may be wrong and may overvalue the validity of the writer's argument. Second, the reader can presume that the writer is *not* citing an authoritative source. This choice is bad for the same reason — the reader may be wrong — only this time, the reader will undervalue the validity of the writer's argument. Third, the reader can check each footnote to see if the citation provides an authoritative source or not. Of course, not every footnoted statement will be a legal assertion; the reader will therefore be checking footnotes that do nothing more than provide needed page numbers for quoted or paraphrased statements of fact. These citations could be passed over easily if they were in text, but in a footnote they require the same two "finding actions" that every footnote requires: First, the reader must check the number of the footnote and find the corresponding number at the bottom of the page. Second, the reader must return to the text and find the place where he or she stopped reading.

Although at least one judge prefers that citations appear in footnotes,[18] others say quite pointedly that footnotes interfere with effective reading. Speaking of footnotes in general, former Justice Arthur J. Goldberg praises elimination of all footnotes from judicial opinions in the name of increased readability.[19] Judge Abner Mikva notes that "[i]f footnotes were a rational form of communication, Darwinian selection would have resulted in the eyes being set vertically rather than on an inefficient horizontal plane."[20] More recently, both Judge Posner and

---

[17] This statement is most true about judges who sit on courts of last resort. The opinions of a trial judge or of an intermediate appellate judge, in contrast, may be more likely to be affirmed or reversed depending upon the authoritativeness of cases and other sources that they rely on.

[18] Mark Painter, *The Legal Writer: 40 Rules for the Art of Legal Writing* 47 (2d ed., Jardyce & Jardyce 2003).

[19] Arthur J. Goldberg, *The Rise and Fall (We Hope) of Footnotes*, 69 A.B.A. J. 255, 255 (1983).

[20] Abner Mikva, *Goodbye to Footnotes*, 56 U. Colo. L. Rev. 647, 647 (1985) (quoting Professor Rodell, quoted in Kenneth Lasson, *Scholarship Amok: Excesses in the Pursuit of Truth and Tenure*, 103 Harv. L. Rev. 926, 942 (1990)).

Justice Scalia have protested the placement of citations in footnotes.[21] A reader who wants to read a brief responsibly — i.e., understanding the validity of legal assertions — will find footnoted citations just as distracting as any other footnotes.

The practical brief-writer will remember the old saw that the only person who likes to be interrupted in the middle of a sentence is a prisoner. Presume that all citations should be incorporated in the text, and make exceptions only rarely.

§19.5.4 *Using Effective Sentence Structures to Accommodate Citation Form*

Incorporating citations into text is the best way to promote easy identification of the value of your authority. You will help both your reader and your user, however, if you use effective sentence structures to accommodate citations. Many writers instinctively introduce a new case by beginning a sentence with a long-form citation:

▼ **Bad Example**

In J.E.B. v. T.B., 511 U.S. 127, 138-40 (1994), this Court held that sex-based peremptory challenges violate jurors' rights to equal protection.

This sentence is difficult to read because the citation takes up a lot of space within the sentence. Furthermore, this structure puts too much emphasis on the citation and not enough emphasis on the substance of the sentence. To solve this problem, some writers mistakenly separate the case name from the rest of the citation:

▼ **Bad Example**

In J.E.B. v. T.B., this Court held that sex-based peremptory challenges violate jurors' rights to equal protection. 511 U.S. 127, 138-40 (1994).

This "separated long-form" structure is also not optimal. Although some citation rules may condone this separation, it can confuse the reader, who could be expecting a long-form citation because he or she does not recall reading about the case earlier. The best way to write a readable sentence and still use correct citation form is to put the citation in a separate citation sentence:

▲ **Good Example**

This Court has held that sex-based peremptory challenges violate jurors' rights to equal protection. J.E.B. v. T.B., 511 U.S. 127, 138-40 (1994).

Thus, instead of focusing the attention in your sentence on the citation, you focus it on the court that took the action or, as in this next example, on the rule itself:

---

[21] J.H. Huebert, *How to Persuade Judges in the Real World*, 35 Ohio N.U. L. Rev. 829, 831 (2009) (book review of Antonin Scalia & Bryan Garner, *Making Your Case: The Art of Persuading Judges* (2008), which cites Scalia & Garner, at 35, and Richard A. Posner, *Against Footnotes*, 38 Court Rev. 24, 24 (2001)).

▲ Good Example

Sex-based peremptory challenges violate jurors' rights to equal protection. J.E.B. v. T.B., 511 U.S. 127, 138-40 (1994).

This structure lets the citation do its work of telling the reader the name of the case, the court, and the year of decision, but keeps it from intruding on the sentence itself. Including a case name alone in your sentence is appropriate only if you have already cited the case in full in that same discussion:

▲ Good Example

This Court has held that sex-based peremptory challenges violate jurors' rights to equal protection. J.E.B. v. T.B., 511 U.S. 127, 138-40 (1994). In J.E.B., the Court found peremptory challenges invalid because they were based on broad assumptions about men's and women's relative capabilities. Id.

Thus, structure your sentences so that all citations, and particularly long-form citations, can be placed in their own citation sentences. You can accomplish this goal by keeping the focus on the substance of the cited material rather than on the citation.

§19.5.5 Avoiding String Citations

Judges are almost uniformly against the use of string citations. As Judge Boyce Martin notes, "When I read a lengthy string cite in a brief or slip opinion, I often find that I have lost the gist of the argument after fighting through line after line of gobbledygook."[22] Admittedly, string citations are useful on rare occasions. For example, if you need to illustrate a trend in the law, give a brief overview of a still-developing area of law, or establish that multiple authorities in a variety of jurisdictions have followed or not followed a particular rule, a string citation may be appropriate. Two warnings: First, most cases you write briefs for will not present any of these situations, so presume that you will not need a string cite. Second, the longer the string cite, the less likely it is that anyone will look at it except the unfortunate judge's clerk who has been assigned to review all of the cited cases. You will make more friends if you have fewer string cites.

When a string cite is unavoidable, put as much information as possible into the sentence preceding the string cite. Most readers would have to struggle to pick up any information in phrases and clauses interspersed among the citations. One problem with a string citation is that it inevitably creates a very long sentence, and, psychologically, the reader tries to keep that sentence "going" in his or her brain. A sentence with text and citations interspersed is probably the hardest thing for a reader to read:

---

[22] Boyce F. Martin, Jr., *Judges on Judging: In Defense of Unpublished Opinions*, 60 Ohio St. L.J. 177, 193 (1999).

▼ **Bad Example**

Several courts of appeals have considered the issue of whether a transient visitor has a legitimate expectation of privacy while within the residence of another, see, e.g., United States v. Gale, 136 F.3d 192 (D.C. Cir. 1998), and they have considered this issue in a variety of contexts and using a variety of factors in reaching their decisions, including the frequency of rent payments, id. at 193; the lack of an overnight stay, United States v. Maddox, 944 F.2d 1223, 1234 (6th Cir. 1991); the use of another's hotel room, United States v. Carr, 939 F.2d 1442, 1446 (10th Cir. 1991); the lack of evidence of connection to the residence, United States v. Antone, 753 F.2d 1301, 1313 (5th Cir. 1985); and mere presence in a hotel room, United States v. Irizarry, 673 F.2d 554, 558 (1st Cir. 1982).

To make this information easier to digest, write a sentence informing the reader of the significance of the cases, and then end it with a period. Depending on the circumstances, the string citation could be placed in a footnote; even if it is in the text, using this technique will make the citation string easier for the reader to read:

▲ **Good Example**

Several courts of appeals have decided that a transient visitor has no legitimate expectation of privacy while within the residence of another, whether the residence was a home or a hotel room, when the visitor did not have sufficient connection to the residence. See, e.g., United States v. Gale, 136 F.3d 192, 193 (D.C. Cir. 1998) (current day visitor's one rent payment seven months ago not enough to establish sufficient connection); United States v. Maddox, 944 F.2d 1223, 1234 (6th Cir. 1991) (attendance at drug party without overnight stay does not establish sufficient connection); United States v. Carr, 939 F.2d 1442, 1446 (10th Cir. 1991) (guest in another's hotel room does not have sufficient connection); United States v. Antone, 753 F.2d 1301, 1313 (5th Cir. 1985) (fingerprints on book not enough to establish daytime visitor's connection to residence); United States v. Irizarry, 673 F.2d 554, 558 (1st Cir. 1982) ("mere presence" in hotel room not sufficient to establish connection).

The best solution is one that avoids the string cite entirely. If you are using the string cite to point out the well-established fact that many courts have already agreed with a legal rule, you may be able to use a parenthetical to accomplish the goal of the string cite. Often, one of the most recent cases in a "string" will have addressed the fact that the rule is well established, and may have cited most or all of the other cases. In that situation, you may tell the reader that the cases exist and give him or her access to those cases by citing only the most recent one:

▲ **Good Example**

Since 1978, every Ohio court that has addressed this issue has decided in favor of the employee. See, e.g., Sanders v. McGuffin Corp., 901 N.E.2d 911, 933 (Ohio 2009) (citing cases).

This citation supports an accurate statement — that every Ohio court has decided a certain type of case in a certain way — and it allows the judge or the judge's clerk to find all those decisions if needed by citing to a decision that cites them. Use this method with care. It cannot be used unless the text of your argument accurately reflects what the cited case has said about the list of cases cited. Furthermore, you should not use this method if information from each authority is important to your argument. When this method is appropriate, however, the legal writer is able to simultaneously avoid a string cite and give the reader access to multiple authorities that support his or her argument.

§19.5.6 *Cases That Cite Other Cases*

A citation dilemma for many legal writers is what to do when citing an excerpt of a case that has quoted another case. Both *ALWD* Rule 47.7(c)(2)[23] and *Bluebook* Rule 5.2[24] indicate that the writer should cite the original source, as the writer does in the following example:

▼ Bad Example

A person possesses a reasonable expectation of privacy, and thus a search occurs when an officer makes an observation from a location within the curtilage of a private home. See Oliver v. United States, 466 U.S. 170, 180 (1984). Curtilage, "the land immediately surrounding and associated with the home," is "the area to which extends the intimate activity associated with the 'sanctity of a man's home and the privacies of life.'"Id. (quoting Boyd v. United States, 116 U.S. 616, 630 (1886)).

Although this guideline may be appropriate for law review articles and other publications, it is not always the best rule for brief-writing. In this situation, it is doubtful that the court needs to know about an 1886 case that is the origin of the "sanctity" language.

Of course, a legal writer may need or want to cite the original source to give added credence to a discussion of a case decided by a nonmandatory court. In the example below, from a petitioner's brief in *Minnesota v. Carter*, the writer is discussing a California case that applied *Minnesota v. Olson*, a significant United States Supreme Court case that had been previously cited in that same section of the brief:

▲ Good Example

In 1992, a California court found that a defendant who moved to suppress items seized at his brother's apartment while the defendant was babysitting there had a legitimate expectation of privacy. People v. Moreno, 3 Cal. Rptr.

---

[23] ALWD & Dickerson, *supra* note 16, at 393.
[24] *The Bluebook: A Uniform System of Citation* 45 (18th ed., Harv. L. Rev. Assn. 2008).

2d 66, 70 (Cal. Ct. App. 1992). The court cited <u>Olson</u> and indicated that, "[l]ike 'staying overnight in another's home,' babysitting 'is a longstanding social custom that serves functions recognized as valuable by society.'"<u>Id</u>. at 70 (quoting Olson, 495 U.S. at 98).

Noting that the California court was basing its decision on United States Supreme Court authority may give that California decision more weight in a brief written to the United States Supreme Court. Thus, if knowing the origin of the cited language could affect the Court's understanding of your argument, identify that source. This situation does not occur regularly in legal writing; generally, if the origin of the language is significant, the writer should go to the original source and cite that authority in addition or instead. It is only when the relationship between the two sources is significant — as it is when an on-point nonmandatory court applies a rule from a mandatory court — that the reader is likely to be interested in the origin of the quoted language.

In most other situations, however, judges looking at the citations supporting an argument want to know only that a valid court made that statement in an analogous case. They usually have little or no interest in the original source of particular words or phrases. If the cited opinion is a valid authority for that quote, it matters only that an authoritative court made the statement in its majority opinion and that the statement is not dicta. Even if that court misinterpreted the original language, what matters is that the court believed that the language was appropriate to apply to the particular set of facts that was before it. Thus, determine whether the court you are writing to would better understand your argument if it knew the original source of the quoted language. If knowing the source would not improve the court's understanding, you can omit the citation, as long as you inform the court that you are doing so:

▲ Good Example

Curtilage, "the land immediately surrounding and associated with the home," is "the area to which extends the intimate activity associated with the 'sanctity of a man's home and the privacies of life.'" <u>Id</u>. (citation omitted).

Substituting the "citation omitted" parenthetical phrase for the full citation will allow those who wish to track the original language the opportunity to do so. Most judges and clerks, however, will be grateful that you have not cluttered the brief with irrelevant citations.

§19.5.7 *Importance of Pinpoint Citations*

A pinpoint citation is a citation to the specific page on which quoted or cited language appeared. Some legal writers use the phrases *pin cite*, *pinpoint*, or *jump cite* to mean the same thing. You must include pinpoint citations *every time* you cite to a case.

Do not convince yourself that you are citing the case only "generally" and thus do not need to include a citation to the specific page. If you want your readers to be able to verify that the authorities you cite stand for the propositions you say they do, you must make it incredibly easy for them to find the law that is the source of your argument. Remember that the clerk of the judge who is writing the opinion will often be given the task of verifying the truth of the assertions in the briefs. If you do not give pinpoint citations, you may force the clerk to wade through 30- or 40-page opinions, trying to find the legal principle that you said was in there. If you cite a case for its main holding, find the page on which the court articulated that holding: That is the pinpoint page. Even if you are citing to the first page of the opinion (a rare event, since many reporters fill the first page with headnotes and other editorial information), you must still provide a pinpoint citation:

▲ Good Example

McGuffin v. Wood, 101 F.3d 115, 115 (6th Cir. 2015).

Think of the judges and their clerks whenever you are making a citation decision. Whenever you can make it easier for them to understand your argument by putting a little more information into the brief, you should do so.

§19.6 Summary

The practical brief-writer has a lot to remember when trying to use case authorities effectively. Remembering the needs of the judges and clerks who must use your brief will help you (1) to include all of the authorities that are necessary; (2) to give enough information about those authorities, but not too much; (3) to present that information accurately and in a helpful way; and (4) to cite that information in a way that provides sufficient information without needlessly intruding on the text.

CHAPTER 20

WRITING A FACT STATEMENT

There is an adage among trial lawyers: If you have to choose between the law and the facts, take the facts. The adage reflects the experience of many lawyers that a judge or jury convinced of the justice of your cause will find a way around unfavorable law. Conversely, if the judge or jury perceives that justice is on the other side, favorable law might not be enough.

The Statement of Facts (sometimes called the "Statement of the Case") is the primary place where your reader's sense of justice about the case will be formed. As a general rule, narrative is more effective at creating attitudes than is intellectual analysis. *The Jungle* persuaded countless readers of the inhumanity of the meat-packing industry. *Cry, the Beloved Country* convinced people around the world of the injustice of apartheid.

Consider your own reactions. Imagine reading a well-reasoned analysis arguing that Hitler should not have imprisoned and killed European Jews. The analysis explains and applies certain abstract moral principles. Imagine your response. Now compare it to your response to *The Diary of Anne Frank* or *Schindler's List* or *Sophie's Choice*. Which would you find more powerful: the rational analysis or the stories of the people who lived the facts? Which would you remember longer? Which would persuade you more?

Stories grab us, persuade us, motivate us. Your client's story can persuade a judge, just as a movie or book can persuade you. But to be persuasive, your client's story must be told skillfully. Many lawyers believe that the brief that tells the most effective story is the most likely to prevail. But writing this key part of the brief is more challenging than writing a short story or novel. It is harder because you cannot make up desirable facts or imagine away undesirable facts, and because you must use the facts to persuade without *appearing* to do so. You must recite the facts objectively enough to be fair and yet persuasively enough to be compelling. As Professors Ray and Cox put it:

> If briefs to the court were gymnastics events, their statements of facts would be performed on the balance beam. Writing a persuasive statement is accomplished not

by following one set of rules, but by balancing your use of various techniques to maintain credibility while achieving the stance needed to highlight favorable facts. It does not require the brute force of emphatic language so much as a subtle blend of strength and control of structure and detail. It involves much thought, consideration of alternatives, and monitoring the interactions of various techniques. Yet an excellent statement of facts looks natural and effortless, just like a complex routine looks easy when performed by a skilled gymnast.[1]

§20.1 Fact Ethics, Readers, and the Conventions of Fact Statements

§20.1.1 Fact Ethics

Remember from Chapter 4 that a lawyer must not misrepresent facts.[2] Misrepresentation includes both stating facts untruthfully and omitting material facts when the result of the omission is to create a false inference. The rule further requires lawyers to disclose material facts when disclosure is necessary to avoid assisting the client in a criminal or fraudulent act.

In virtually every case, you will find some facts you wish were not there. The more material the facts are, the more you wish they would go away. But they exist nonetheless, and leaving them out of your Fact Statement will not make them disappear, for they will certainly appear in the opposing brief. Omitting them from your brief will only damage your credibility before the judge, causing the judge to wonder how much she can rely on the other facts you assert and on the legal analysis you propose. Few things make a judge angrier than feeling misled by a lawyer.

The omission of important facts also forces the judge to use the opposing party's Fact Statement, rather than yours, as the court's primary factual reference. These consequences are serious for both lawyer and client. Therefore, both good ethics and good strategy require inclusion of all material facts, favorable or not.[3]

§20.1.2 The Conventions of a Statement of Facts

Certain formal requirements and generally accepted conventions apply to the Statement of Facts. Refer to the Statement of Facts of the briefs in Appendices C and D for examples of how a Statement of Facts employs the following conventions:

1. An appellate brief must refer only to facts that are a part of the court record. Facts cannot be added to the record.[4] Because the point of an appeal is to decide

---

[1] Mary Barnard Ray & Barbara J. Cox, *Beyond the Basics: A Text for Advanced Legal Writing* 167 (2d ed. West 2003).

[2] A lawyer shall not knowingly make a false statement of fact or fail to disclose a material fact when disclosure is necessary to avoid assisting a criminal or fraudulent act by the client. Model R. Prof. Conduct 3.3(a)(1) and (2) (2007).

[3] Later sections in this chapter identify ways to neutralize or deemphasize unfavorable facts.

[4] There are rare exceptions to this rule, but none that we need to worry about here.

whether the lower court's decision on a certain point was supported by the facts and the law *before that court,* the appellate court may consider only the factual record that was before the lower court at the time of the decision from which the appeal has been taken.

The Statement of Facts must cite the location of the fact in the record.[5] The citation allows the judge to verify that the fact actually appears in the record and to check that the writer's descriptions of the fact and its context are not misleading. Judges *do* check the facts. For an appellate brief, the most common form for these citations to the record is "R. at [page number]."

2. A Statement of Facts is a part of a legal document and retains the formal style of the rest of the brief. Although a Statement of Facts tells the story of the legal dispute, its style is not like a short story. You do not want the style of the fact statement to cause the judge to wonder if she is reading fiction. Therefore, present the facts in an objective style, avoiding obvious appeals to emotion, grand description, dramatic literary devices, and other obvious attempts to manipulate the reader. The style should be dignified and courteous, never sarcastic or angry.

3. A Statement of Facts does not discuss law. It sets out all of the facts the rule makes important, but it does not explain the rule or the rule's relationship to the facts. Rule explanation and application come in the Argument section. The only exception to this convention is that the last paragraph of the fact statement may segue into the legal argument by stating the legal issue the Argument will address.[6]

4. A Statement of Facts does not contain overt argument, whether legal or factual. The facts are presented in an objective style, and the writer does not expressly assert factual conclusions. For instance, for a case involving medical malpractice, the Fact Statement might relate the patient's vital signs, the medical test results, the patient's medical history, and the nurse's observations, but the writer would not argue that the doctor breached the applicable standard of care.

Note that this restriction applies to conclusions drawn by the *writer,* but the writer *is* permitted to relate the conclusion of another. For instance, whereas the writer cannot assert that the doctor breached the applicable standard of care, the writer can report the testimony of an expert witness who asserted this conclusion. The testimony of the witness is a *fact* that occurred at a deposition or at trial. Reporting the conclusions of others is sometimes called "masked editorializing."[7] Quotations, used in moderation, are appropriate in a Statement of Facts, and often are effective.

A Statement of Facts also can point out the *absence* of certain facts from the record. The absence of a fact from the record is itself a fact. Thus it is fair game to include in the Statement of Facts the following:

---

[5] Fed. R. App. P. 28(a)(7).
[6] *See* section IIIB.
[7] *See* Louis J. Sirico & Nancy Schultz, *Persuasive Writing for Lawyers and the Legal Profession, Second Edition,* 81 (Lexis Nexis 2001).

At trial, three officers testified that they were stationed at the building's entrance between 5:00 and 6:00. However, no witness testified to seeing the janitor enter or leave the building.

Pointing out a fact's absence can allow the writer to make a point about the evidence while remaining within the legitimate bounds of fact-reporting. One of the most common and most unfortunate errors lawyers make is neglecting to notice important *absent* facts.

§20.2 Developing a Theory of the Case and Selecting Facts

Although some facts must be included no matter what theory of the case or theme the lawyer selects, other fact-selection decisions are tied directly to the theme the lawyer will develop. This section explores these two interrelated lawyering tasks.

§20.2.1 Developing a Theory of the Case

Lawyers use the term "theory of the case" to refer to the theme they will weave throughout the facts, the theme that will explain the facts from their client's perspective. The theme should be sympathetic to the client. It should help the judge understand who the client is, why the client acted in the way he did, feels the way he does, and needs the things he needs. At the least, a good theory of the case assures the judge that a ruling in favor of your client will not be unjust. At best, the theory convinces the judge that justice requires a ruling for your client.

Of course, a theory of the case must be consistent with the key facts. Creating a theory is easy when the facts are generally favorable and much more difficult when they are not. For troublesome facts, you must work even harder to see and *feel* the story from your client's perspective.

To find an effective theory of the case, try to look at the facts from your client's perspective and look for narrative themes. Professors Brian Foley and Ruth Anne Robbins have pointed out seven common kinds of narrative themes: (1) a person against another person, (2) a person against herself, (3) a person against nature, (4) a person against society, (5) a person against a machine, (6) a person against God, and (7) a person against everybody else.[8] Might one of these stock themes describe your client's struggle? If so, explore possible theories of the case that would communicate that narrative theme.

You might find that several of these themes could describe your client's story. People are complex, after all, and seldom are we motivated by only one need, feeling, or goal. For presentation of the facts in a legal proceeding, however,

---

[8] Brian Foley & Ruth Anne Robbins, *Fiction 101: A Primer for Lawyers on How to Use Fiction Writing Techniques to Write Persuasive Fact Sections*, 32 Rutgers L.J. 459 (2001) (citing Josip Novakovich, *Fiction Writer's Workshop* 74-75 (1995)).

beware of trying to present several themes at once. The medium of a brief generally is better suited to handle one consistent theme rather than several themes intermixed. The effort to combine several themes might leave the reader with no coherent theory at all; so pick the theme that is most compelling and best supported by the facts.

The best way to find an effective theory of the case is by talking with your client. However, your client might not be good at communicating the heart of his position and might not even be consciously aware of it himself, so you will need also to use your imagination. Try to put yourself in his position. Imagine what it must have been like, what it must be like now. Try to understand who this person is and who the other key characters are. Mull it over in the shower, on your morning run, on your way to the grocery store. Try to fill in the blanks of the following statement: "This is a story about a (man) (woman) who (is)(was) . . . [describe client] . . . and who is struggling to . . . ." If you can do so without breaching client confidentiality, try telling the story orally. Go to lunch with another lawyer from your firm and tell her your client's story. Telling the story and then talking about it with another person often gives you a fresh perspective. After you have developed a clearer sense of your client and the situation, what helps you understand your client's behavior? What moves you about the story? What might move the judge?

Once you have an idea, try articulating it in a few sentences, like so:

> Carrolton bought Watson's company, the only provider of health care products in the area, and immediately began to take advantage of the company's customers by raising prices, limiting product lines, and allowing long delays for special-order items. Because the customers had nowhere else to go for their health care products, they had no choice but to pay the prices and put up with the limited service. Watson, who had continued to work at the business, had to sit by and watch as Carrolton took advantage of her neighbors and longtime customers. Many of them even thought that Watson was intentionally profiting at their expense, as she was still the customer contact person in the office — the only face her old customers saw. This situation was personally distressing to Watson. She also became increasingly convinced that it just wasn't right.

A good theory of the case should be consistent with the facts and with a common sense notion of fairness. It should explain as many of the unfavorable facts as possible, and it should cast your client in a sympathetic light.

§20.2.2 Selecting and Citing to Facts

Once you have developed your theory of the case, select the facts you will include in the Statement of Facts. Include facts that fall into the following categories:

1. Facts that fit the theory of the case
2. All facts mentioned in the
3. Argument section of the brief
4. All legally significant facts, whether favorable or unfavorable

5.   Significant background facts
6.   Emotionally significant facts

Note the location of each fact in the record. In the final draft of a trial-level brief, the citations should appear like so:

> On January 20, 1995, Carrolton filed a complaint in state court alleging that Watson was violating the terms of the covenant-not-to-compete. (Compl. ¶27.) Carrolton's Vice President, Justin Bakker, stated that the Complaint was fi led within one month of Carrolton's discovery of Watson's business activity. (Bakker Aff. ¶14.)

§20.3 Organization

§20.3.1 Formats

The most common organizational formats for fact statements are organizing chronologically, by topics, or by theories of the case.

Chronological. For simple facts, a chronological presentation is often best. For instance, in a simple collection matter, the facts will usually set out the events giving rise to the debt, the default, the plaintiff's demand that the defendant cure the default, and the amount owed. These simple facts are best presented chronologically.

Topical. For more complex facts, the topical format might work best. Set out the facts according to relevant topics. For example, in an employment discrimination case, the plaintiff's facts might be organized according to these topics: the nature of the defendant's business, the defendant's usual hiring process, the defendant's usual employee evaluation procedure, the procedures used in selecting employees for layoffs, the hiring process for the plaintiff's position, the terms of the plaintiff's employment, the plaintiff's employee evaluations, the business conditions that necessitated layoffs, the selection of plaintiff for layoff, and the defendant's efforts to assist laid-off employees to find other jobs. The topics should be ordered logically, perhaps chronologically. For lengthy Fact Statements, consider using subheadings to help your reader follow the topics.

Theory of the Case. This format might be effective when the opposing party has some powerful facts that seem to support her position, but you have some key facts or a compelling theory of the case that will explain away those opposing facts. The format first sets out the powerful facts that seem to support your opponent's theory of the case, and then neutralizes them by setting out the facts that explain or justify the opposition's facts.

Organizing by theory of the case is a more daring choice for several reasons. First, as a general rule, the beginning of a section soaks up more reader attention than does later material.[9] Second, there is the risk that a busy judge might not

---

[9] Other lawyers believe that the position of greater emphasis is the end. But nearly everyone agrees that the position of least emphasis is the middle.

finish reading the Fact Statement. Third, the writer who selects this organization is betting a large stake that the supporting facts will defeat the opposing facts. Because the format sets up such a direct and express juxtaposition of these facts, the writer had better be right.

When this organizational format works, however, it is extraordinarily effective. Having heard the worst facts and having decided that they do not necessarily mean what they seem to mean, the reader is far less likely to be impressed on reading them in the opposing brief or on hearing them at oral argument or at trial. So, be aware that this organizational format is an option, but choose it only after careful evaluation.

§20.3.2 Procedural History

No matter which format you choose, you will need to decide where to place the procedural history. Court rules or the instructions for your assignment might make this decision for you.[10] Or the rules or instructions might require a Preliminary Statement or Introduction, in which case the procedural history goes there, in its own section.

If court rules or your instructions have not identified the location for the procedural history, the two most common places for it are at the beginning or the end of the Fact Statement. At the beginning, it can help to establish the context for the facts that follow. At the end, it can serve as a natural segue into the Argument section. Either way, consider using subheadings to divide the Statement of the Case into at least two subsections: the "Factual History" and the "Procedural History." Because the procedural history will seldom comprise a compelling part of the theory of the case, using subheadings can put the dull procedural facts out of the way of the theme you hope to deliver with the facts.

§20.4 Techniques for Persuasion

§20.4.1 General Principles

1. Clarity is more important than using sophisticated techniques for persuasion. Judges will not be persuaded by a fact statement they cannot understand. If a technique impedes clarity, do not use it.

2. Do not use a technique that the reader will notice. An effective technique must be invisible, or nearly so. Once a reader recognizes a technique, it has lost its power because the reader's attention is on the technique and not the fact. For instance, assume that you have used the technique of repetition to emphasize a favorable fact. You hoped that it would encourage the reader to realize the significance of the fact, to let it sink in. If, instead, your reader's Commentator observes, "Ah, look, the writer is repeating this fact to try to get me to notice it," the reader will be thinking about the technique and the writer's goals rather than the fact.

---

[10] *See, e.g.,* Fed. R. App. P. 28(a)(6).

Your Fact Statement would have been more persuasive if you had not used the technique at all.

3. Do not overuse any technique. Overuse creates monotony, decreases the technique's power, and increases the chances that the reader will notice the technique rather than the facts.

4. Any technique for emphasizing one fact or group of facts deemphasizes the remaining facts. To the extent you try to use techniques of emphasis for nearly all of the facts, your strategy will fail. You have to pick the few facts you want most to emphasize and allow the others to serve as the background.

5. Some of the techniques described below are inconsistent with each other. The inconsistency does not mean that one is right and the other wrong, but only that each has its advantages and disadvantages. The writer's job is to select the technique that will work best for the needs of a particular fact statement.

§20.4.2 Large-Scale Organization

The Beginning

6. Unless you know differently, assume that the judge is not already familiar with the case. The beginning of the Statement of Facts should establish the context for the facts that follow. Otherwise, the judge might find herself reading a chronological account of a series of events without knowing why these events are important. Context can be provided by a procedural history or by a short summary of what the case is about, written to be consistent with your theory of the case. Here is an example written on behalf of Carrolton:

> This is an action to enforce the terms of a covenant-not-to-compete. As part of the sale of her business to Carrolton Company, the defendant promised that for the three years immediately following the sale she would not compete with Carrolton in the three counties closest to Carrolton's headquarters. Eighteen months after the sale was completed, the defendant opened a competing business just one mile from Carrolton's office. She has been competing directly with Carrolton in the three prohibited counties ever since. This action seeks to enjoin her continued breach of the covenant-not-to-compete.

7. The reader's attention level is greatest in the first few paragraphs. When you can find a way to do so logically, capitalize on this increased attention level by selecting an organization that allows you to place there material you want to emphasize. This strategy can be consistent with a summary of the case drafted from your client's perspective, like the one above.

8. Aim for a beginning that will spark the reader's interest. Journalists call this "the lead." The conventions of a legal document do not allow for some of the more dramatic forms of grabbing attention, but you do want the reader to be drawn into the story and want to read on. For example, a prosecutor's brief might begin with the facts of the crime rather than with the procedural history of the appeal.

The Middle

9. Here is the place for the facts you want to deemphasize. Normally, a reader's attention level is at its lowest about three-fourths of the way through the section.[11]

The End

10. Readers might pay more attention to the material at the beginning, but they remember longest the material at the end. Readers tend to take a mental break to let the story sink in, and when they do, the last sentence lingers in their minds. Try to select an organization that allows you to place at the end material you most want the reader to remember.

11. The last paragraph should have the "feel" of a concluding paragraph. One way to accomplish this is to close with a transition into the legal argument to follow by identifying the legal positions staked out by the parties. Be careful not to include overt legal argument. Limit yourself to identifying the positions each side will take on the legal dispute. Avoid stating the opposing position any more favorably than you have to. Keeping in mind that the last sentence lingers in the reader's mind, end with your legal position rather than your opponent's. Here is an example of such a transition:

> The bank has admitted that it did not disclose the effective interest rate to the Turners. However, it claims that disclosure was not required, arguing that the transaction was not a "consumer loan" under the Consumer Protection Act. This brief will show that the transaction was, indeed, a "consumer loan" and that the bank's failure to disclose to the Turners the effective interest rate was a violation of the Act.

§20.4.3 Paragraph Organization

12. A reader devotes more attention to the beginning and the end of a paragraph than to the middle. Put facts you want to emphasize in the first sentence or in the last clause or phrase of the last sentence. Deemphasize unfavorable facts by placing them in the middle.

13. Be conscious of paragraph length. In sections where you want to emphasize the facts, keep paragraphs relatively short. Where you want to deemphasize facts, let the paragraphs get longer, and put the facts you particularly want to deemphasize deep in the paragraph.

§20.4.4 Techniques with Sentences

14. As a general rule, reduce clutter by eliminating surplus verbiage. Clutter reduces clarity, irritates the reader, and deemphasizes the important facts. Occasionally, you can allow just a bit of clutter to surround an unfavorable fact. The

---

[11] Mary Barnard Ray & Barbara J. Cox, *Beyond the Basics: A Text for Advanced Legal Writing, Second Edition* 171 (West 2003).

clutter will reduce emphasis by lengthening the sentence and by making it less striking. Use this technique sparingly.

15. Use active verbs for emphasis and passive verbs for deemphasis or to avoid focus on the identity of the person who took the action.

a.   *To encourage focus on the person taking the action:*

> Shaffer kicked in the front door of the house and attacked his estranged wife, breaking her forearm.
> *[Here the prosecutor wants all attention on Shaffer as he takes these violent actions.]*

b.   *To avoid focus on the person taking the action:*

> Acme Health Equipment was formed and began operation on April 22, 1995.
> *[Here the writer seeks to defl ect attention away from the person who formed and ran Acme — Watson.]*

c.   *To focus on a person other than the one taking the action:*

> In the early morning of January 1, 1995, after attending several New Year's Eve parties, the defendant was stopped for a routine sobriety test.
> *[Here the writer is not so much trying to keep attention away from the police officer who stopped the defendant as to keep the focus on the defendant who was stopped.]*

16. Place favorable facts in main clauses and unfavorable facts in dependent clauses. Consider this sentence in a brief for Watson:

> Although Acme's business does compete with Carrolton [dependent clause], the competition only extends to three small product lines and could only impact, at the most, four percent of Carrolton's profits [main clause].

17. If an unfavorable fact *must* go in the first or last sentence of a paragraph, place the dependent clause carrying the unfavorable fact toward the interior of the paragraph. Thus, for the first sentence of the paragraph, a dependent clause carrying an unfavorable fact should go at the end of the sentence. Which party's brief would contain this sentence?

> Acme competes directly with Carrolton in the three prohibited counties [main clause], although the competition presently extends only to three product lines [dependent clause] . . . [paragraph continues by setting out the facts of the competition].

For the last sentence of the paragraph, try putting the dependent clause at the beginning:

[The paragraph has set out the facts establishing the competition.] Thus, while the competition extends only to three product lines [dependent clause], Acme directly and openly competes presently with Carrolton in the three prohibited counties [main clause].

18. Occasionally, when you want the reader to slow down and take in the significance of the material in all parts of the sentence, place a phrase or dependent clause in the middle of the sentence, interrupting the reader's usual path from the subject directly to the verb.

Watson, who admits that she is intentionally violating the terms of her covenant, asks this Court to use its equitable powers to relieve her of the consequences of her own actions.

Use this technique sparingly because it makes sentences less readable.

19. Use shorter sentences for material you want to emphasize and longer sentences for material you want to deemphasize.

Longer Sentences for Less Emphasis
   On July 1, while Mr. and Mrs. Emilio and their daughter Ashley were driving south on Interstate 75 toward Valdosta, a car swerved across the median and hit the Emilio car. Mr. and Mrs. Emilio survived, although they were seriously injured. Their daughter, who had been riding in the back seat, died as a result of the injuries she sustained in the accident.

Shorter Sentences for Greater Emphasis
   On July 1, Mr. and Mrs. Emilio were driving south on Interstate 75 toward Valdosta. Their daughter Ashley was riding in the back seat. A car swerved across the median and hit the Emilio car. Mr. and Mrs. Emilio survived, though seriously injured. Ashley, however, died.

§20.4.5 Other Small-Scale Techniques

20. Compress the space you devote to unfavorable facts, and expand the space you devote to favorable facts. The more material you provide about the favorable facts, the more emphasis they soak up.

21. Use detail to describe the material you want to emphasize. Conversely, limit the detail of your discussion of the unfavorable facts, although of course you cannot omit any significant facts.

22. Use *visual* facts and images to describe favorable facts; avoid them for unfavorable facts. Visual images carry particular power for placing the reader, mentally, at the scene.

On July 1, Mr. and Mrs. Emilio were driving south on Interstate 75 toward Valdosta. Their daughter Ashley was riding in the back seat. A car swerved across the median and crashed into the Emilios. The front of the other car hit the Emilio car at the left rear door, precisely where Ashley was sitting, strapped in by her seat belt.

The force of the impact carried the other car's engine well into the passenger cabin of the Emilio car. It ripped Ashley from her seat belt, pinned her against the opposite door, and crushed her thoracic cavity.

Mr. and Mrs. Emilio survived, though seriously injured. Ashley, however, died at the scene.

23. Short quotations (a sentence or two) or snippet quotations (just a word or a phrase) can be powerful facts. If the words of the witness or document are particularly helpful, quote them.

> Shaffer left the bar, declaring "I'm going to go talk to my wife, and she'll need a doctor before I'm through."

Avoid overquoting, however. Overquoting will result in a disjointed story and will cause the most effective quotes to fade into the pack with the rest of the quotes.

24. When you can repeat key facts *unobtrusively*, the repetition serves to emphasize those facts or concepts. For instance, the first sentence of the paragraph might summarize the facts, and the remaining sentences could set out the facts in more detail. Or the beginning of a sentence might refer to the facts of the prior sentence as a transition.

> Marie Claxton, the expert witness who testified on behalf of Pyle, concluded that a reasonable and prudent lawyer would have checked the deed for easements. Claxton explained that deeds often contain restrictions that signifi cantly affect the use of the property. She testifi ed that any prudent lawyer would know that such restrictions are common. According to Claxton, Gavin's failure to check the deed fell below the standard of professional skill and diligence of a reasonable and prudent lawyer.

Do not just repeat particular facts, seemingly for no reason, however. It will bore and irritate your reader. Remember that the Argument section gives you a natural opportunity to repeat the key facts.

25. Place unfavorable facts in a favorable or mitigating context. You can juxtapose the unfavorable fact with favorable facts or you can place the unfavorable fact in a context that negates some of the unfavorable inferences the fact might otherwise invite.

Juxtaposing an Unfavorable Fact with Favorable Facts

> Although Acme's business does compete with Carrolton, the competition only extends to three small product lines and could only impact, at the most, four percent of Carrolton's profi ts.

Placing the Unfavorable Fact in a More Favorable Context

> While the demonstrations against the abortion clinic are disruptive to the other tenants, the landlords cannot prevent the demonstrations; nor can they force the clinic to move until the clinic's lease term expires.

26. Humanize your client. The most important way to do this is by telling the story from the client's perspective, as your theory of the case will already accomplish. Include, where possible, a description of the client's feelings, responses, and motivations. It is also helpful to refer to your client by name and use titles that communicate respect, like "Mr.," "Ms.," "Dr.," or "Officer."

It is especially important to humanize corporate clients. Remember that every story involving a corporation is really a story about people. Identify the people who took the actions, and humanize those people. Portray them in a sympathetic light by setting out the context for their actions.

27. Generally, do not humanize opposing parties. Where there is no need to use the names of opposing individuals, consider using generic descriptions instead ("the officer," "the insurance agent," "the electrician"). Generic descriptions can be especially helpful where the description has unsympathetic connotations, such as "the finance company," "the insurance company," or "the corporation." However, humanize when your theory of the case depends on showing the judge not only the sympathetic facts about your client but also the outrageously bad behavior of one or more of the opposing parties. In such a case, you might need to humanize the opposing party so you can show the outrageousness of his or her behavior.

28. Use graphic words, especially verbs, for facts you want to emphasize.

> The van *crashed into* [instead of "hit"] the taxi, and the force of the impact *shattered* [instead of "broke"] the driver's spine.

29. Refrain from name-calling. Name-calling tells your reader that you do not have good facts, so you are compelled to resort to derogatory characterizations.

30. Where possible, delete adverbs in favor of additional facts and more vivid verbs. Vivid verbs, alone, are much more powerful than a ho-hum verb with an adverb. Avoid such artificial intensifiers as "very" or "extremely."

31. Pay careful attention to common connotations of words. Choose words with helpful connotations and avoid those with unhelpful connotations.

A Word with Potentially Troubling Connotations

> Mr. and Mrs. McMann were *anxiously* awaiting the birth of their first child. ["Anxiously" carries the connotation of worry. Use it if the connotation helps your theory, but avoid it if the connotation either impedes the theory or might distract the reader into wondering what they were worried about.]

An Option with a Better Connotation

Mr. and Mrs. McMann were *anticipating* the birth of their first child.

Finally, put the draft down for a few hours and then read it afresh. Try not to look for the techniques you used, but rather read openly, as you hope your reader will. Notice your reactions and fix anything that troubles you.

CHECKLIST FOR FACT STATEMENTS

Large-Scale Organization

- Does the organization present the facts clearly? Is it easy to follow?
- Does the organizational format allow you to put most of the unfavorable facts in the middle and put some of the favorable facts at the beginning and some at the end? (The "theory of the case" format is an intentional exception to this principle.)
- Does the material at the beginning catch the reader's interest?
- If your reader needs context, does the material at the beginning provide it?
- Does the draft communicate your theory of the case?
- Does the draft include all significant facts and all facts mentioned in your Argument?
- Does the draft include enough context to allow the reader to understand the dispute and your theory of the case, but no more?
- Does the draft place the procedural history at an appropriate location?
- Does the last paragraph have the "feel" of an ending?
- Does the draft end with a sentence that you want the reader to remember?

Paragraph Organization

- Are your best facts on the outside ends of the paragraph, while your least favorable facts are in the middle?
- Does the last phrase or clause of the paragraph contain favorable information?
- Are the paragraphs with facts you want to emphasize relatively short? Are those with facts you want to neutralize longer?

Techniques with Sentences

- Are the sentences (except one or two carrying unfavorable facts) free of clutter?
- Do the passive-voiced verbs serve a purpose? Are there any actions you would like to deemphasize by changing to passive?

- Where appropriate, are unfavorable facts in dependent clauses juxta-posed with more favorable facts or explanatory context?
- Do the shorter sentences carry favorable facts? Where appropriate, are the unfavorable facts in longer sentences?
- Using brackets in the margins of the draft, identify the text that deals with favorable topics and the text that deals with unfavorable topics. How does the total allocation of space to each compare?
- Notice where you have used detail and visual images. Notice where you have not.
- Do the quotations really help?
- If you have used the technique of repetition, is it too obvious?
- How have you referred to your client? To the opposing parties?
- At spots where you are presenting favorable material, are there any verbs you can switch for more powerful or graphic synonyms?

IMPROVING YOUR WRITING

CHAPTER 21

13 Steps to Better Writing

This chapter contains 13 guidelines for clear legal writing. They have been selected because they are particularly useful for writing and reviewing all types of legal documents, including exams, memoranda, briefs, pleadings, client letters, legislation, contracts, and leases. These guidelines are tools for you to use when you want to write for a specific audience or audiences, accomplish a well-defined purpose or purposes, and create well-organized, logical legal documents.

Note that the sentences and paragraphs used as bad examples and exercises for revision were, for the most part, taken from real legal documents, modified to eliminate the identities of the attorneys who wrote them. You will thus be learning from the mistakes of others, and will — if you learn these guidelines well — be spared the shame of writing such embarrassing material yourself.

Thirteen Guidelines for Clear Legal Writing

1. Write short sentences.
2. Put the parts of each sentence in a logical order.
3. Avoid intrusive phrases and clauses.
4. Untangle complex conditionals.
5. Use the active voice whenever possible.
6. Use verb clauses and adjectives instead of nominalizations.
7. Use the positive unless you want to emphasize the negative.
8. Use parallel structure.
9. Avoid ambiguity in words and sentences.
10. Choose vocabulary with care.
11. Avoid noun strings.
12. Eliminate redundancy and extraneous words; avoid overspecificity.
13. Use an appropriate style.

§21.1 Guideline 1: Write Short Sentences

You will often see two-and three-hundred-word sentences in all forms of legal writing, from hornbooks to judicial opinions, briefs, and memos. Probably no other single characteristic does more to needlessly complicate legal writing than these long sentences.

Research in linguistics and psychology has shown that the average reader can hold only a few ideas at a time in short-term memory.[1] After two or three ideas, the reader needs to pause and put together what he or she has read. The period at the end of a sentence is one signal for such a pause. When there are no periods in long strings of thoughts, the reader will try to break up the sentence into smaller pieces in order to understand it. However, the reader may not know where to pause or which ideas to group together. Readers often get lost in very long sentences.

In addition to the burden imposed by sheer length, most long sentences violate other guidelines for writing clearly. Structural complexities such as complex conditionals, passive verbs, unclear references, and nonparallel constructions add to the reader's difficulties.

Although you see long sentences in all kinds of traditional legal writing, there is nothing in the nature of the law itself that requires you to express all of your thoughts in one sentence. Your writing can be legally accurate whether you use one sentence or several sentences. Legal convention, however, will sometimes require you to put a lot of information in one sentence. For example, you may have to put each issue statement in a brief in its own sentence. This convention has resulted in some of the longest, most cumbersome sentences you will see in legal writing.

Here are two examples of overly long sentences that we have revised. The first example is a subsection from a will that we have broken into several sentences.

POOR: The trustee may pay all or part of the income to or for the benefit of the beneficiary or may accumulate all or part of the income, distribute trust principal (even all of it if necessary) to or for the benefit of the beneficiary for the beneficiary's maintenance, support, education, comfortable living, business or professional needs, or general welfare, and if there is more than one beneficiary, pay income or distribute principal to or for the benefit of the beneficiaries as it determines (even excluding one or more of the beneficiaries) without regard to any principle of law requiring impartiality among beneficiaries of the trust.

BETTER: The trustee may pay all or part of the income to or for the benefit of the beneficiary or may accumulate all or part of the income. The trustee may distribute trust principal (even all of it, if necessary) to or for the benefit of the beneficiary for the beneficiary's maintenance, support, education, comfortable living, business or professional needs, or general welfare. If there is more than one

---

[1] Miller, The Magical Number Seven, Plus or Minus Two: Some Limits on Our Capacity for Processing Information, 63 Psychological Review 81 (1956).

beneficiary, the trustee may pay income or distribute principal to or for the benefit of the beneficiaries as it determines (even excluding one or more of the beneficiaries), without regard to any principle of law requiring impartiality among beneficiaries of the trust.

Notice that just dividing the passage into shorter sentences makes it easier to read. Breaking up the last sentence and making it into a new paragraph can further clarify the drafter's meaning.

> If there is more than one beneficiary, the trustee, in addition to the powers noted above, may pay income or distribute principal to or for the benefit of one or more of the beneficiaries, as the trustee determines. The trustee may exclude one or more of the beneficiaries from these payments or distributions, even if the law requires that the trustee treat all beneficiaries equally.

Sometimes breaking up a long sentence into shorter sentences makes the entire passage longer. There is nothing wrong with this: The goal is *clarity*, not brevity for its own sake.

The second example is an issue statement, which we have rewritten so that it is shorter and easier to understand. It can be very difficult to put an issue statement into one sentence. If you create a sentence that is very long and very complex, keep rewriting it until you have put the parts of the sentence in a logical order and have removed all extraneous words.

POOR: The district court was correct in holding that the statute of limitations for medical malpractice begins to run at the time of the tort or when treatment ceases which was prior to the plaintiff's conception thereby foreclosing the right for her to bring a cause of action.

BETTER: Since the district court was correct in holding that the statute of limitations for medical malpractice begins to run at the time of the tort or when treatment ends, and since the plaintiff was conceived after both of these events, the plaintiff has no right on which to base a cause of action.

EXERCISES

Break up the following long sentences into shorter sentences. Rearrange the parts of the sentences and add words if necessary.

1. To remit a controversy like this to the circuit court of appeals where it properly belongs is not to be indifferent to claims of importance but to be uncompromising in safeguarding the conditions which alone will enable this court to discharge well the duties entrusted exclusively to us.

2. Following the *Hirota* decision at the 1948 term, a series of motions for leave to file petitions in war crime cases were again denied by an evenly divided court,

with four justices returning to their pre-*Hirota* ground of lack of original jurisdiction and the other four amending their notation to state the opinion that argument should be heard on the motions for leave to file the petitions in order to settle the issue of what remedy, if any, the petitioners have.

3. A court order forcing the student editor of the Lincoln Weekly Star to publish candidate Jones' advertisements would clearly violate and destroy the discretionary editorial privilege guaranteed to newspapers by the First Amendment and consistently upheld by the Supreme Court of the United States.

4. Where, upon the trial of such a case as is indicated above, there was evidence from which the jury was authorized to find that the defendant's agent went to the plaintiff's home and knowing that she, a child of 11 years of age, was at home alone, attempted to gain entrance to the home for the announced purpose of repossessing a television set, and when the child refused to admit him by the front door that he went to the rear door and wrote a note which he exhibited to the child through a window of the door and in which he threatened to go for the police and have her put in jail if she did not admit him so that he could take possession of the television set, and that the child became so frightened by this threat that she became extremely nervous, fearful of leaving the house, and unable to sleep at night, the jury would be authorized to find that the conduct of the defendant's agent, who was acting within the scope of his authority, was willful misconduct under the circumstances, and that the child's resulting nervousness and distress was a natural and probable consequence of such willful misconduct. (203 words)

5. In the case of a State Medicaid plan that the Secretary of Health and Human Services determines requires State legislation (other than legislation appropriating funds), in order for the plan to meet the additional requirements imposed by such amendment, the State plan shall not be regarded as failing to comply with the requirements imposed by such amendment solely on the basis of its failure to meet these additional requirements before the first day of the first calendar quarter beginning after the close of the first regular session of the State legislature that begins after the date of the enactment of this Act. For purposes of the preceding sentence, in the case of a State that has a two-year legislative session, each year of such session shall be deemed to be a separate regular session of the State legislature. (138 words)

§21.2 Guideline 2: Put the Parts of Each Sentence in a Logical Order

Some sentences are ineffective or difficult to read because they lack internal logic. It is very important to put the parts of a sentence in a logical order. Start each sentence with information that is familiar to your audience or that will tell the reader where you are going with the sentence. If the sentence is the first in your document, begin it with information that will provide a context. If the sentence is in the middle of a document, begin the sentence by tying it to the information in the previous sentences or paragraphs. The following opening sentence from a letter provides the reader with a context that ties the content of the letter to the reader's own past action.

> *In response to your request of April 10, 2001,* I am sending you copies of the pleadings and some additional documents.

Don't make your reader read through an entire sentence in order to discover its purpose.

Here is an example from a student memo. It is the opening paragraph of the student's Discussion section.

> Since the instant action arose in Connecticut (the employer and employee are located in Virginia, but the alleged discrimination occurred in Connecticut), the initial issue to be resolved in determining what limitations period applies in a section 1981 action in federal court in Virginia is which state's law applies.

The main idea in this sentence — the initial issue that will be considered in the memo — is buried in the middle of the sentence. The student should have begun the sentence with a statement of the issue and then recounted the specific facts of the case.

> The issue in this case is what limitations statute applies in a section 1981 action brought in federal court in one state if the cause of action arose in another state. In this case, the suit was brought in federal court in Virginia. The employer and the employees are located in Virginia, but the alleged discrimination occurred in Connecticut.

This guideline applies to groups of several sentences, or even paragraphs, as well. Look for a *logical sequence* — a time sequence, a cause-and-effect relationship, an order of priority — and arrange the sentences or paragraphs in that order. As with a single, longer sentence, begin with information that the reader already knows or that will explain where you are headed and use that as a context for information that follows. Tie the sentences to each other with the proper transitions (and, but, because, however, moreover, nonetheless, furthermore, therefore, thus, and so on).

EXERCISES

Put the parts of each sentence into a more logical order.

1. The fact that the *Rutgers* publication was a newspaper and the present publication is a law review and requires special selection of the type and quality of

its articles is what distinguishes the two cases and will probably be the crucial factor in the court's decision.

2. The ultimate verification of the inquiries at the hospital was the damaging factor.

3. Whether or not the method of gathering data would be objectionable to the reasonable person is the question that must be asked by the court.

4. The court of appeals in holding that the doubt rule contravenes the Administrative Procedure Act, ruled correctly.

5. Whether the "true doubt" rule is identical to this view overruled by *Del-Vecchio v. Bowers, supra* and rejected by Congress in enacting F.R.Evid. 301 which, moreover, is fundamentally antagonistic not only to federal law but all American law, is not considered by the agency.

§21.3 Guideline 3: Avoid Intrusive Phrases and Clauses

One reason that a sentence can be too long is that it may contain a phrase or clause that has been inserted into the middle of the main clause. These additions, exceptions, or pieces of incidental material disrupt the logical flow of the sentence and make it difficult for readers to understand what is meant.

Sometimes even relatively short sentences contain intrusive phrases or clauses. The italicized words in the example below are not part of the main sentence. The date comes in the middle of the verb. The address comes between the verb and its object.

POOR: Interested attorneys may, *on or before (date)*, submit *to the Clerk, (address)*, written comments *regarding the proposed change in court procedures*.

Notice how much clearer even a short sentence can become when the intrusive phrases have been moved so that they no longer separate the parts of the main clause (subject, verb, and object).

GOOD: Interested attorneys who want to comment on the proposed change in court procedures may send comments in writing to the Clerk, (address), by (date).

Intrusive phrases occur in abundance in all kinds of legal documents. In the following example from a law student's memo, the student tried to cram too much information into one sentence.

POOR: One of the main questions presented in this memo is whether 28 U.S.C. §636(b)(1)(B), *which allows a district court to decide a suppression motion based on the record developed before a magistrate, the magistrate's proposed findings of fact and recommendations, and the defendant's written and oral objections before the district court,* violates the Due Process Clause.

The italicized information is inserted in such a way that it interferes with the continuity of the main part of the sentence. Because the subject of the sentence is separated from the verb by 37 words, the reader does not know where the sentence is going until the very end. The student should have broken up the sentence and reordered the information logically.

BETTER: One of the main questions presented in this memo is whether 28 U.S.C. §636(b)(1)(B) violates the Due Process Clause. This section allows the district court to decide a suppression motion based on the record developed before a magistrate, the magistrate's proposed findings of fact and recommendations, and the defendant's written and oral objections before the district court.

The reader of the rewritten version knows immediately what the point of the passage is. A related problem is illustrated by the following sentence.

POOR: Petitioner's argument *that exclusion of the press from the trial and subsequent denial of access to the trial transcripts is, in effect, a prior restraint* is contrary to the facts.

In this sentence, the subordinate clause, which is in italics, intrudes into the middle of the main clause. The verb phrase of the subordinate clause ("is . . . a prior restraint") is perilously close to the verb phrase of the main clause ("is contrary to the facts") and makes the sentence very confusing to read. This type of subordinate clause construction is called *self-embedding,* and psycholinguistic research[2] has shown that self-embedding is very difficult for readers' minds to process. The writer could easily have avoided self-embedding in that sentence.

BETTER: Petitioner argued that excluding the press from the trial and subsequently denying access to the trial transcripts is, in effect, a prior restraint. This argument is contrary to the facts.

In general, the best way to deal with any type of sentence with intrusive phrases is to remove the inserted material and put it into a new sentence.

---

[2] Psycholinguistic research is the study of how language is perceived and understood, using the methods of experimental psychology. *See* Miller & Isard, Free Recall of Self-Embedded English Sentences, 7 Information and Control 292 (1964); and Schwartz, Sparkman, and Deese, The Process of Understanding and Judgment of Comprehensibility, 9 Journal of Verbal Learning and Verbal Behavior 87 (1970).

EXERCISES

Underline the intrusive phrase(s) and rewrite the sentence.

1. No outpatient health care, which is ordinarily available to people in this category and must be obtained through the HMO, will be available after this date.
2. Some people, especially those receiving services that are covered by insurance and who have to pay only a nominal co-payment, over utilize certain services.
3. Moreover, the rule which without question was applied is invalid as petitioner, because it offers a substitute, must be assumed to agree.
4. On May 23, 2006, petitioners (hereafter plaintiffs), consisting of 16 minors, suing as public school students, and seven parents of students attending public schools, brought the underlying action against real parties in interest (hereafter defendants) in respondent superior court claiming a deprivation of rights in violation of the Elementary and Secondary Education Act of 1965.
5. In light of the prevailing jurisprudence, including that of the District of Columbia, contrary to our position that the district court should look to District of Columbia law (jurisdiction where the action arose), I conclude that a summary judgment motion relying on the applicability of the limitations provisions of the forum state (Maryland) is more likely to succeed than one relying on the law of the state in which the action arose.
6. The court held that the agreement whereby she would support him financially and provide household services while he wrote a German textbook, in return for which he would support her when he reestablished his professional career, was enforceable.
7. Although the Court stated that it need not reach the question of whether strict scrutiny was required because even under the most exacting standard of review the Minority Business Enterprises (MBE) provision passes constitutional muster, nowhere in the court's opinion is there any indication that it applied the strict scrutiny necessary to determine whether the MBE provision was in fact constitutional.
8. Moreover, although claimant's edema theory about which the fact finder expressed grave doubt and therefore indicated no difficulty in evaluating can be said to have been probative, independent of its believability, since any tendency to make the existence of a fact more probable, he made no finding that it was credible.

§21.4 Guideline 4: Untangle Complex Conditionals

A conditional is a statement that establishes an *if... then* relationship between pieces of information; a complex conditional is a conditional with many conditions (*if* statements) or many rules or consequences (*then* statements). A conditional or complex conditional may not always contain the word *if*. Some conditionals introduce a condition with *when, where, whether,* or other words or phrases. Many conditionals also lack the word *then* in the rule or consequence statement. For example,

When both parties are residents of the same state, there is no diversity of citizenship.

This sentence could be rewritten:

If both parties are residents of the same state, *then* there is no diversity of citizenship.

As long as the sentence states a condition and a rule or consequence, it is a conditional.

Readers often have problems understanding complex conditionals. The more conditions or rules and the more combinations of *ands* and *ors* that a sentence contains, the more difficult it is to understand.

Here is an example of a complex conditional from the Federal Rules of Civil Procedure, Rule 6(b).

POOR:	*Enlargement.* When by these rules or by a notice given there under or by order of court an act is required or allowed to be done within a specified time, the court for cause shown may at any time in its discretion (1) with or without motion or notice order the period enlarged if request therefor is made before the expiration of the period originally prescribed or as extended by a previous order, or (2) upon motion made after the expiration of the specified period permit the act to be done where the failure to act was the result of excusable neglect.	**Condition** **Rule or Consequence**

To untangle a complex conditional like this one, it is often useful to list each provision. It can also help to physically separate each condition and rule on the page itself. This rule would be much easier to understand if it were rewritten with these suggestions in mind.

GOOD:	*Extending a time period.* This rule applies to acts that may or must be done within a certain time when that time is specified by:	**Condition**

- the Federal Rules *or*
- a notice issued under the Federal Rules *or*
- a court order.

If a party wishes to extend the time period, the party must show cause to the court to do so. The court may then, at its discretion, extend the time under two different sets of circumstances:

Rule or Consequence

1. *If the request is made before the time period expires*, then the court may extend the original time period (or a previously extended time period) with or without motion or notice.
2. *If the request is made after the time period expires*, then the court may extend the original time period, but only if failure to act was the result of excusable neglect and if a motion is made.

EXERCISES

Rewrite the following complex conditionals so that they are easier to understand.

1. In a patent infringement action commenced in a district where the defendant is not a resident but has a regular and established business, service of process, summons, or subpoena upon such defendant may be made upon the defendant himself, his agent, or agent's representative conducting such business.
2. If a plaintiff who has once dismissed an action in any court commences an action based upon or including the same claim against the same defendant, the court may make such order for the payment of costs of the action previously dismissed as it may deem proper and may stay the proceedings in the action until the plaintiff has complied with the order.
3. When actions involving a common question of law or fact are pending before the court, it may order a joint hearing or trial of any or all the matters in issue in the actions; it may order all the actions consolidated; and it may make such orders concerning proceedings therein as may tend to avoid unnecessary costs or delay.
4. The court, in furtherance of convenience or to avoid prejudice, or when separate trials will be conducive to expedition and economy, may order a separate trial of any claim, cross-claim, counterclaim, or third-party claim, or of any separate issue or of any number of claims, cross-claims, counterclaims, third-party claims, or issues, always preserving inviolate the right of trial by jury as declared by the Seventh Amendment to the Constitution or as given by a statute of the United States.
5. When a presumption such as Longshore Act Section 20(a), which provides that it "shall be presumed in absence of substantial evidence to the contrary — [t]hat the claim comes within the provisions of the chapter" exists — if presumptions are "evidence," i.e., if they do not disappear upon presentation of proof sufficient to justify a contrary result but add weight after rebuttal supporting a finding of any fact presumed — the burden of persuasion, because in every case opposing evidence must be stronger, is transferred from the party in whose favor the presumption was created (the claimant who therefore must be assumed to originally have had it) to the disfavored party (the employer).

§21.5 Guideline 5: Use the Active Voice Whenever Possible

The *passive voice* is an interesting grammatical construction. It is a way of changing the *focus* of a sentence without changing its meaning, by rearranging and adding words. Here are examples of active sentences and their passive counterparts.

Active: John *hit* Morris.
Passive: Morris *was hit* by John.

Active: Alice *will eat* the entire pizza.
Passive: The entire pizza *will be eaten* by Alice.

The passive voice allows the writer to focus on the object of the (original active) sentence rather than on the "doer" or the "agent" of the action. A passive construction can be in any tense; it can refer to a single action or to continuous action. For example:

Those buildings *will have been destroyed* by flooding by the time the governor decides to act (future perfect tense).

Even as we speak, the supplies *are being eaten* by rats (present continuous tense).

Because the passive voice does something unusual to the focus of a sentence, a passive sentence can be difficult for the reader to understand. Use the passive voice only when you want to focus on the object of the original active sentence.

When you use the passive voice, it is possible to *truncate* the sentence by leaving out the doer of the action. For example, the full passive sentence

Morris was hit by John

can be made into the truncated passive

Morris was hit [   ].

The full passive

Those buildings will have been destroyed by flooding by the time the governor decides to act.

becomes the truncated passive

Those buildings will have been destroyed [   ] by the time the governor decides to act.

Using a truncated passive allows a writer to speak in general terms in cases in which it does not matter who performed the action. For example:

> In most law schools, law is *taught* by means of the Socratic method.

The writer can also avoid stating who is responsible for the action when the identity of the actor does matter. The writer may intentionally "pass the buck" linguistically or may simply forget to identify the actor.

The effects of using the passive voice inappropriately can be particularly significant in legal writing. Much of legal writing deals with the rights and responsibilities that govern the past, present, or future actions of specific individuals or entities. A contract, for example, spells out the rights and responsibilities of individuals under certain carefully defined circumstances. However, this vital information can be obscured by the use of verbs in the passive voice, especially if the constructions are truncated.

The following passage is an example of a very familiar kind of contract: It is part of an insurance policy. One of its major purposes is to describe the rights and responsibilities of the insurer and of the insured. However, the passage fails to focus on this important information. It is unclear who "incurred," who "lost," who "earned," and who "made payments."

> The company will pay, in accordance with Chapter 670 of the Acts of 1970 of the Commonwealth of Massachusetts and all Acts amendatory thereof or supplementary thereto, subject to any applicable deductible, all reasonable expenses *incurred* within two years from the date of accident for necessary medical, surgical, X-ray, and dental services, including prosthetic devices, and necessary ambulance, hospital, professional nursing, and funeral services, and, in the case of persons employed or self-employed at the time of an accident, any amounts actually *lost* by reason of inability to work and earn wages or salary or their equivalent, but not other income, that would otherwise have been *earned* in the normal course of an injured person's employment, and for payments in fact *made* to others, not members of the injured person's household and reasonably *incurred* in obtaining from those others ordinary and necessary services in lieu of those that, had he not been injured, the injured person would have performed not for income but for the benefit of himself or members of his household (emphasis added).

Similarly, when an attorney describes the past actions of an individual in the fact statement or analysis section of a memo or brief, it is important that the reader know exactly who did what. The passive voice may do more than just confuse the reader about each individual's actions; the passive voice can dilute the impact the attorney is trying to achieve. A plaintiff's attorney should describe the actions of the defendant so that they seem real and direct. The attorney wants the court to know that a particular individual committed the act that caused injury to the plaintiff. If the attorney writes in the passive voice, the focus will be on the act instead of on the person who committed the act.

Here is an example: The plaintiff, Jean, is suing her mother's doctor because the doctor prescribed the drug DES for her mother, Mrs. *M*, six months before

Mrs. *M* became pregnant with Jean. The fact statement in the plaintiff's brief contained the following passage:

> On January 15, 1958, the plaintiff's mother, Mrs. *M*, consulted the defendant about the medical complications that she had experienced as the result of a miscarriage in March of 1957. Since Mrs.*M* was again pregnant, the drug DES *was prescribed* for her to take orally to prevent another miscarriage. Assurances *were made* to Mrs. *M* that the drug was completely safe. The prescribed drug *was taken* from January 16, 1958, until approximately February 28, 1958, when another miscarriage occurred. In August of 1958, Mrs. *M* became pregnant with the plaintiff.

This passage becomes far more effective when the passive voice is replaced by the active voice. It becomes clear who did the prescribing and assuring and who took the prescription and acted on the assurance. As a result, the defendant is directly indicted.

> Since Mrs. *M* was again pregnant, *the defendant prescribed the drug* DES for her to take orally to prevent another miscarriage. The *defendant assured* Mrs. *M* that the drug was completely safe. Mrs. *M* took the prescribed drug from January 16, 1958, until approximately February 28, 1958, when Mrs. *M* had another miscarriage. In August of 1958, Mrs. *M* became pregnant with the plaintiff.

You can use the active voice as part of your strategy to persuade your audience when you write documents like briefs and memoranda. As you begin to consciously identify the passive voice in legal documents, you will see the subtle effects you can achieve with this grammatical construction. Be attuned to writers who use the passive indiscriminately, because these writers may be diluting the forcefulness of their arguments and analyses. Being aware of the passive is especially important when you analyze an opponent's brief.

Learn to make your own arguments more convincing by following these rules:

1. Use the active voice whenever possible.
2. Avoid truncated passives. Reveal who is responsible for a particular action and put this "doer" into the sentence.
3. Use the passive voice only when you are speaking in general terms, when you want to stress the receiver of the action and not the actor, or when you want to downplay the actor.

EXERCISES

Identify the passive verbs in the following sentences. Rewrite the sentences in the active voice. If the original sentence is ambiguous or just unclear, make a reasonable assumption and rewrite the sentence accordingly.

1. No request was made by the defendants for a separate trial of the federal claims nor was the judge asked to stay trial or to dismiss the state claims.
2. An opinion was rendered by the court after completion of the trial in which no evidence was found to support either the 10b-5 claim or the plaintiff's claim of violation of the margin requirements by the defendant.
3. It was held by the court that the requisite amount in controversy-was lacking.
4. Dismissal for want of jurisdiction has been imposed where transparently inflated damages resulting from a minor injury, such as a minor whiplash, have been claimed by the plaintiff.
5. A renewal clause was incorporated into the contract by the parties as well as the changes that were made in the delivery dates.
6. It can be argued that since the building wasn't owned but was leased by our client, permanent occupancy was not intended.
7. An official file shall be established for each client. To the extent that retained copies of documents do not represent all significant actions taken, suitable memoranda or summary statements of such undocumented actions must be prepared promptly and retained in the file.

§21.6 Guideline 6: Use Verb Clauses and Adjectives Instead of Nominalizations

Another interesting construction that is overused in legal documents is known as nominalization — the creation of nouns from verbs and adjectives.

The verb	*can be made into the noun*
determine	determination
resolve	resolution
apply	application
enforce	enforcement
inquire	inquiry
reverse	reversal

The adjective	*can be made into the noun*
enforceable	enforceability
distinguishable	distinguishability
applicable	applicability
specific	specificity
important	importance

As with the passive voice, these constructions are grammatical and so are the sentences that contain them. But, as with the passive voice, writers who overuse nominalizations weaken their writing.

Nominalizations make sentences difficult to understand, because they do not communicate a scenario that the reader can picture. Like truncated passives, nominalizations eliminate information about who did what.

Nominalizations make sentences less persuasive. Because nominalizations are nouns, they are *static*, giving the reader little or no feeling that an *action* is involved. For the reader to fully grasp that someone *did* something, it is necessary to use verbs. Here are a few examples of sentences containing nominalizations. Notice how direct the sentences become once the nominalizations are replaced with verb clauses.

POOR:	*Recovery* by our client is predicated upon *circumvention* of the current *interpretation* of the adultery statute.
GOOD:	Our client can *recover* if he *circumvents* the current interpretation of the adultery statute. (Note that some nominalizations are appropriate, such as *interpretation* in this sentence, because it cannot easily be replaced with a verb clause.)
POOR:	Appellant did not authorize the *compilation* or *dissemination* of her credit report expressly or by *implication* when she submitted her *application* for insurance.
GOOD:	The appellant did not expressly or implicitly authorize [whom?] to *compile* or *disseminate* her credit report when she *applied* for insurance.
POOR:	The case's *significance* is in the fact that it demonstrates the court's *recognition* of the great *importance* of the right to privacy.
GOOD:	The case is *significant* because it demonstrates that the court *recognizes* the importance of the right to privacy. (Here, too, one nominalization, *importance*, is appropriate.)

As you can see in the second of these examples, nominalizations often lead to other awkward or wordy constructions. Here, the simple verb *applied* has become *submitted her application*. Similarly, *decide* may become *make a decision; interpret* may become *construct an interpretation; sign* may become *affix one's signature*, and so on. After making a noun out of the meaningful verb, the writer has to hunt around for another verb to make the sentence or clause grammatical. Often, the writer ends up using an "empty" verb, one that has no specific meaning: for example, *do, make, give, necessitate*. This type of writing makes the action seem remote from the actors in the sentence; this, in turn, makes it harder for the reader to picture the scene. If you find nominalizations in your own writing, try converting them into their original form as verbs or adjectives. In most cases this will make your sentence more direct, easier to understand, and more forceful.

EXERCISES

Identify the nominalizations in the following sentences. Rewrite the sentences to eliminate them.

1. We believe that the Act contains an underlying recognition that disclosure of the workings of a government bureaucracy can be of benefit to the public.
2. There are rules covering the preclusion of certain kinds of employment by the attorney after acceptance of these cases for purposes of the avoidance of any suggestion of a conflict of interest.
3. During the representation of a criminal defendant, an attorney must demonstrate an adherence at all times to the rules of professional conduct.
4. Disability arising at work or after years of employment due to employee susceptibility should not be the employer's liability.
5. The appellee and W. C. Frederick entered into a contract for the delivery of ice by the appellee to Frederick and, before the expiration of the contract, Frederick executed an assignment of the contract to the appellant; and on the refusal of the appellee to deliver ice to the assignee it brought an action on the contract against the appellee.

§21.7 Guideline 7: Use the Positive Unless You Want to Emphasize the Negative

Most people can easily understand a strong negative imperative ("Do not do that"). Negative statements, however, are generally more difficult for readers to process than positive statements. Furthermore, two negatives within a single clause are more than twice as difficult to understand as the corresponding positive statement.

Occasionally it is legitimate to use double negatives to capture subtleties of meaning. When you say that you are "not unhappy," for example, you do not necessarily mean that you are happy. The double negative expresses a state that is between happy and unhappy.

The words *unless, except,* and *until* are negatives, as are words such as *failure, absent,* and *deny*. Here is a very simple example.

POOR: Plaintiff contends that it could *not* properly demand an equitable adjustment *until* after the completion of the project.

GOOD: Plaintiff contends that it could properly demand an equitable adjustment only after the project is completed.

You may occasionally want to use double negatives to make a command or proscription more forceful. For example, in some circumstances you might use the double negative:

No client letter is to be sent out *unless* a senior partner has approved it.

Rather than the more positive form:

A client letter is to be sent out *only after* a senior partner has approved it.

In general, however, you should avoid using two negatives when you can make a positive statement.

More than two negatives make a clause exceedingly difficult or even impossible to understand. Yet legal writing is full of multiple negatives. Take a look at this example from a jury instruction:

POOR: *Failure* of recollection is common. Innocent *mis*recollection is *not uncommon.*[3]

BETTER: Failure of recollection is common. Innocent misrecollection is also common.

Following is an example of a triple negative from a law student's memo:

POOR: It is *un*likely that a Maryland district court would *ignore* the clear language of these opinions in the *absence* of convincing authority to the effect that a different rule applies where the action arose outside of the forum state.

GOOD: A Maryland district court would probably follow the clear language in these opinions unless there is convincing authority that a different rule applies where the action arose outside of the forum state.

Multiple negatives can be found in even longer passages than the above. Following is a penalty provision from a federal regulation.

POOR: The penalty provided in subsection (c) shall not apply to the disclosure of any information received under this subsection, except that such penalty shall apply to the disclosure (by the agency receiving such information) of any such information described in paragraph (1) unless such disclosure is made in a judicial, administrative, or other formal legal proceeding resulting from an investigation conducted by the agency receiving the information.

---

[3] California Jury Instructions — Civil — Book of Approved Jury Instructions §2.21 (1993).

Untangling this type of sentence imposes a particularly heavy burden on the reader and can lead to misinterpretation and legal errors. The following revision deals with the multiple negatives (*not . . . except . . . unless*) by breaking up the passage into three separate sentences:

BETTER: The penalty provided in section (c) generally does not apply to the disclosure of information received under this subsection. However, the penalty does apply if an agency that received information described in paragraph (1) discloses any of it. But that agency may disclose the information without penalty in a judicial or administrative proceeding or other formal legal proceeding that resulted from the agency's own investigation.

Notice that untangling the multiple negatives and other difficult constructions brings to light a number of problems in the original clause. For example, the nominalization in "unless such *disclosure . . .*" leaves unclear whether, to avoid the penalty, the information must be disclosed only by the agency receiving the information or whether it could be disclosed by any one else in the course of the legal proceeding. These problems are far less likely to arise if you avoid convoluted constructions containing multiple negatives in the first place.

EXERCISES

Rewrite the following sentences in the positive, if possible.

1. We cannot but think that the Court in *Robson v. Drummond* went to the utmost length to which the principle can be carried.
2. A will shall not be valid unless it is signed by two witnesses.
3. There are few lawyers who would not agree that there are situations where "it is more important that the applicable rule of law be settled than that it be settled right."
4. With the vendor number being retroactively set to the original date of revocation, the agency cannot ascertain that the Company would not take responsibility for breach of the Vendor Standards.

§21.8 Guideline 8: Use Parallel Structure

Sentences or clauses that bear the same conceptual relationship to some major idea should have parallel grammatical structure, for example, all infinitives, all active voice, all gerunds (the *-ing* form of the verb, used as a noun), and so on. Sentences with parallel structure are much easier to read and remember. Here is a simple example:

POOR: To write a legal memo

- Identify the legal issues (imperative)
- Doing the correct research is your first priority (gerund and copula)
- You should make sure to read all cases and statutes with care (active sentence)
- Shepardize any cases that you use in your memo (imperative)
- It is important to use the correct citation form (stative sentence)

GOOD: (all   To write a legal memo
imperatives)

- Identify the legal issues
- Do the correct research
- Read all cases and statutes with care
- Shepardize any cases that you use in your memo
- Use the correct citation form

Parallel structure is important in lists. It is also important within a sentence and among sentences in a paragraph. Following is an example from a student memo. The student is discussing whether or not certain items in a rental property would be considered to be fixtures:

POOR: Mr. Smith *used* the carpeting in his store, the air conditioner *was used* to cool the store, and the toilet in the back room *was intended for use* in the store.

The student used both the active and passive voice. The sentence is more effective and easier to understand if all the verbs are simple active verbs.

BETTER: Mr. Smith *used* the carpeting in his store, *used* the air conditioner to cool the store, and *intended* to have the toilet in the back room available for use in the store.

Parallelism is one of the best devices for effective, persuasive writing. First, a writer can use parallelism to test the cogency of his or her reasoning. Putting ideas into a parallel structure can help reveal to the writer whether those ideas are actually parallel. Once several ideas are lined up in a series, with the same grammatical structure, the writer can often tell whether he or she has forced dissimilar ideas into the same framework.

Second, a repeated grammatical structure emphasizes important information. When the arrangement of words in one sentence is repeated in another sentence, the repeated structure tends to stand out. In fact, a writer can achieve an emotional impact by arranging words, phrases, or sentences in structurally similar groupings. By repeating these groupings, the writer can build a powerful statement.[4]

Here is an example of an artful use of parallelism. It is from a speech by Winston Churchill to the House of Commons at the start of World War II. Notice how Churchill used parallelism in the overall structure of the passage by asking a question and then answering it. This provides a powerful framework for his ideas. He also used parallelism within sentences to emphasize concepts and to build them to a climax. The parallel structures are italicized.

> *You ask, what is our policy? I will say:* It is *to wage* war, by sea, land, and air, *with all* our might and *with all* the strength that God can give us; *to wage* against a monstrous tyranny, never surpassed in the dark, lamentable catalogue of human crime. That is our policy. *You ask, what is our aim? I can answer* in one word: Victory — *victory* at all costs, *victory* in spite of all terror; *victory*, however long and hard the road may be; for without *victory*, there is no survival. Let that be realised; *no survival* for the British Empire; *no survival* for all that the British Empire has stood for, *no survival* for the urge and impulse of the ages, that mankind will move forward towards its goal. But I take up my task with buoyancy and hope. I feel sure that our cause will not be suffered to fail among men. At this time I feel entitled to claim the aid of all, and I say, "Come, then, let us go forward together with our united strength."[5]

EXERCISES

Correct the lack of parallelism in the following passages.

1. Upon vacating, the Tenant agrees to pay for all utilities services due and have same discontinued; to see that the property is swept out and all trash or other refuse is removed from the premises; that the doors and windows are properly locked or fastened; and that the key is returned to the Landlord or Agent.

2. The test used in determining whether the bookcases could be removed from the rental property was whether or not they became a fixture under the tests used in determining fixtures:
   1. alterations made to the property to facilitate installations of equipment;
   2. who bore the cost of expense;
   3. removal without damage to the premises;

---

[4] For more details on parallelism, *see* L. Oates, A. Enquist, & K. Kunsch, The Legal Writing Handbook 764-771 (1993), and the sample memorandum of points and authorities.

[5] Churchill, Speech to the House of Commons, May 13, 1940, reprinted in Their Finest Hour 22 (1977).

4. whether the item is particularly adapted to the particular present use — in that it would not be equally useful elsewhere.

3. The trend is toward recognizing the rights of citizens to privacy and for punishing unwarranted intrusions thereon.

§21.9 Guideline 9: Avoid Ambiguity in Words and Sentences

An ambiguous word or sentence is one that can be interpreted in more than one way. If you want to be certain the reader understands your meaning, you should know the causes of ambiguity and how to deal with them.

§21.9.1 Ambiguity at the Word Level

There are many kinds of ambiguity. Ambiguity at the word level is prevalent in legal language because the law gives common, everyday words special legal meanings. For example, a motion in legal language is a particular type of pleading, not a movement or gesture, nor a proposal for action in a parliamentary setting.

When words have different meanings in different contexts, readers will understand exactly what is meant only when they are familiar with the context. This applies not only to legal language itself, but to technical words and phrases that you may use in drafting a legal document for a particular trade.[6] Shipping or construction contracts, for example, may use terms that mean something different in that trade than in everyday usage. It is important that the trade meaning be clear — not only for the benefit of the parties to the contract, but in case it is ever necessary to interpret rights and obligations under the contract.

Avoid using *shall*.   One source of ambiguity is the use of the word *shall*. In writing legal documents, it is traditional to use *shall* to establish a legal obligation. However, many lawyers use *shall* incorrectly. They use it inconsistently — to mean both *must* (obligatory or mandatory action) and *will* (future action). This ambiguous use can cause legal problems.

To complicate matters further, lawyers sometimes use *shall* along with *must* and *will* in the same document. Because most people do not use *shall* in ordinary speech or writing and therefore do not use it properly in legal documents, we suggest that you do not use it at all. Use *must* when you mean the action is obligatory; use *will* when you intend future (nonobligatory) action; use *may* for permissible action. In the negative, use *must not*; *will not*; and *need not* or *does not have to*.

---

[6] *See* Frigaliment Importing Co. v. B.N.S. International Sales Corp., 190 F. Supp. 116 (S.D.N.Y. 1960), where one party to a contract thought that the word "chicken" in the contract referred only to broiling and frying chickens, while the other party insisted that in the trade the term also included stewing chickens. *See also* Nashville v. K. R. Co. v. Davis, 78 S.W. 1050 (Tenn. 1902) (holding that a goose was not "an animal," within the meaning of a state statute that required railroad engineers to take evasive action when "an animal or obstruction" appeared on the track).

May not is often ambiguous. It can mean either "must not" or "does not have to." For example, the following sentence can be interpreted in two ways.

> If you give incorrect information on your application to take the bar exam, we may not accept your application.

The sentence can mean "we are barred from accepting it" or "we have the option of refusing it."

Don't use elegant variation.   In legal documents it is important to use only one term for any concept. Call the car that struck your client "the car" every time you mention it; don't refer to it as "the car" in one place and as "the vehicle" in another place. As Mark Twain said, "Eschew elegant variation." Referring to the same thing by different names may confuse the reader; it may also create legal problems. For example:

> I conclude that we should argue that the limitations period of the forum state applies, rather than that of the *state where the action arose*. However, if we argue for the limitations period of the *accrual state*, we will have to rethink our strategy.

The writer assumed that the reader would understand that the state where the action arose and the accrual state are the same thing, but the reader may assume that they are two distinct states or become confused enough to give up trying to understand the passage.

§21.9.2 *Ambiguity at the Sentence Level*

Misplaced words or unclear structure.   Ambiguity can also occur at the sentence level. If you misplace words or fail to indicate what a word or phrase refers to, you will confuse the reader.

Misplacing words such as *only* and *exclusively* can make a sentence ambiguous. For example:

> Describe the client's property only in section II of the will.

Does this mean describe the property and no other asset in section II, or describe the property in section II and nowhere else? *Only* is a useful word, but depending on where it is placed, it can create ambiguity.

You can also create ambiguity by using *more than* or *less than* carelessly. Be sure that the reader knows what is being compared. Consider, for example, this line from an old commercial:

> I love Devil Dogs more than Marcia.

It can mean either "more than I love Marcia" or "more than Marcia loves Devil Dogs." If the meaning of a sentence with *more than* or *less than* is not clear, fill in the missing words that will make it clear.

Pronouns.   You must also be careful when you use pronouns. Make sure the reader will know which noun the pronoun refers to. If you have not made it clear which noun is the pronoun's antecedent, you can confuse the reader. For example:

> If the argument is made that the Secretary's regulation applies in our case, I believe that *it* will be attacked by our opponent.

The reader may be unsure whether the pronoun *it* refers to the Secretary's regulation (will the opponent attack the validity of the regulation) or to the argument that the regulation applies in the case at issue (will the opponent attack the validity of the argument?).

Here is a particularly egregious example, based on an actual federal statute:

> Physicians can invest in securities of corporations provided they meet the following standards.

It is not clear whether *they* refers to the physicians, the corporations, or the securities. Sentences like this not only manifest poor writing; they may also indicate fuzzy thinking.

You must also make sure each pronoun is in the same person (he, she, it) and number (he, they) as the noun it refers to. Not doing so will give readers a poor impression of you. For example, in the following sentence the pronouns *they* and *their* do not agree with the antecedent *one*.

> If one of the expert witnesses were to be used in this trial, they would be asked to show their qualifications.

Misplaced clauses.   Yet another type of ambiguity arises from misplacing subordinate clauses. Position a subordinate clause so that it is clear which words you want the clause to modify. For example:

> The second type of fringe benefit is the receipt of goods, services, or money, not as a salary, *which is indirectly related to the performance by the employee of his duties on his job.*

> Our client is questioning the $2,000 requested for heat treatments for the plaintiff's arm *based upon Dr. Smith's itemized medical report.*

In each of these sentences, it is unclear exactly what the subordinate clause refers to. Does "which is indirectly related" in the first sentence refer to "salary" or "receipt" or "benefit"? Does "based upon Dr. Smith's itemized medical report" in the second sentence modify "the $2,000" or "requested" or "heat treatments"? Each sentence should be rewritten so that only one interpretation is possible.

Conditionals.   Conditionals can be especially ambiguous if they contain both *ands* and *ors*. For example:

> If a client is receiving alimony or is receiving child support and has been divorced for more than one year, then this section of the rule does not apply.

This sentence can be interpreted two ways. It can mean:

> This section of the rule does not apply if the client
> 1. Is receiving either alimony or child support *and*
> 2. Has been divorced for more than one year.

Or the sentence can mean:

> This section of the rule does not apply if the client
> 1. Is receiving alimony *or*
> 2. Is receiving child support and has been divorced for more than one year.

Nothing in the original sentence tells the reader which conditions belong together.

To avoid ambiguity in conditionals, make it clear where conditions begin and end. You can use punctuation, but that is not the best solution. A better solution is to use *syntax* to clarify the message. For example, you can repeat the subject of the sentence before each full condition.

> *If the client* is receiving either alimony or child support and *if the client* has been divorced for more than one year, then this section of the rule does not apply.

Or you can use *layout* to make the conditions clear. We used layout above to demonstrate the two possible interpretations of the alimony example. The best solution is to use a combination of syntax and layout to get your message across unambiguously.

Exceptions require even more care. Exceptions are negative conditions (if not ... then; if ... then don't). Exceptions cause confusion because the reader must shift gears from "apply this rule" to "don't apply this rule." A shift like this can be particularly confusing if the exception appears in the same sentence as the rule.

POOR: The same cost accounting period shall be used for accumulating costs in an indirect cost pool as for establishing its allocation base, *except* that the contracting parties may agree to use a different period for establishing an allocation base, provided:

1. The practice is necessary ...
2. The practice ... *etc.*

Rather than joining exceptions into the same sentence as the rule, you should state the rule and then start a new sentence with "However, if ..." or "Nonetheless, if ..." The above example would be much clearer if it were rewritten as follows:

BETTER: Use the same cost accounting period for accumulating costs in an indirect cost pool as for establishing the allocation base for that period. However, the contracting parties may agree to use a different period for establishing an allocation base, if all of (or any one of) the following conditions hold:

1. The practice is necessary
2. The practice . . . etc.

§21.9.3 *Intentional Ambiguity*

Ambiguity can have a valid place in legal writing. Legislation is often designed to be ambiguous so that it will be flexible enough to cover unforeseen circumstances. Ambiguity can also be useful to the writer who *wants* to obscure his or her meaning, as in the case of an attorney who is answering interrogatories. However, using intentional ambiguity takes a great deal of skill and care: Inappropriate or unsophisticated use can backfire. A piece of ambiguous legislation, for example, could exclude or include the wrong conditions, situations, or people. Unskillfully drafted answers to interrogatories may obscure neutral pieces of information while revealing too much about sensitive issues.

EXERCISES

Find and eliminate the ambiguities in the following sentences. Also use the other guidelines to make the sentences clearer.

1. This statute applies to any individual who is at least 65 years of age or who is disabled and has a spouse living at home.
2. If you have taken into account all of your clients and their unique concerns when completing the interrogatories or conducting depositions, then it is likely that you have been successful with them.
3. No person shall be a representative who shall not have attained to the age of 25 years, and been 7 years a citizen of the United States, and who shall not, when elected, be an inhabitant of that state in which he shall be chosen.[7]

---

[7] *See* Art. I, §2, cl.2 and Art. I, §3, cl.3, Constitution of the United States. These clauses set the qualifications for Representatives and Senators, respectively. The meaning of these clauses was at the heart of the constitutional dispute over whether a state could impose term limits on members of its congressional delegation. *See* U.S. Term Limits, Inc. v. Thornton, 514 U.S. 779 (1995). One of the issues in Thornton was whether these clauses set out the exclusive qualifications or merely the minimum qualifications. The double negative ("No Person . . . who shall not have attained. . . .") in each clause added to its ambiguity. Compare the language in Art. I, §2, cl.2 with the clearer language in Art. VI, cl.3, which states that "no religious Test shall ever be required as a Qualification to any Office or public Trust under the United States." Disagreements over the meaning of Art. I, §2, cl.2 persist. *See* Campbell v. Davidson, 233 F.3d 1229 (10th Cir. 2000) (holding that a state statute requiring congressional candidates to be registered voters in the congressional district in which the person seeks election violates Art. I, §2, cl.2).

§21.10 Guideline 10: Choose Vocabulary with Care

From law school onward, members of the legal profession often unthinkingly emulate the writing they encounter in legal treatises, opinions, and casebooks. And often the language used in these documents is ungrammatical, unnecessarily complex, or archaic. Choose your vocabulary carefully. Try not to indiscriminately follow the models you see just because they look and sound "legal."

§21.10.1 Eliminate or Change Archaic or Unnecessary Words

There are a number of archaic words that commonly occur in legal documents. These words can often be left out entirely. If, for the sake of precision, you can't just leave them out, replace them with commonplace words or phrases (e.g., henceforth = from this day forward; hereinbefore = previously in this document). The following is by no means an exhaustive list of words of this kind. You will no doubt come across others. Try to keep them out of your own writing.

aforesaid	hereinbefore
henceforth	hereinafter
herein	heretofore
hereafter	thereto
thereby	thereunto

verbs ending in -*eth*
said, same, such (when you mean *the*)
one (before a person's name)

§21.10.2 Replace Difficult Words or Legal Jargon with Words Your Readers Will Know

This principle is often stated as "use short words," but it is not really length that causes problems. It is unfamiliarity that causes problems. As it happens, of course, less familiar words tend to be longer than common words.

This principle should be tempered by your knowledge of your audience. The purpose of a document is to communicate to the people who must read it. When people write only for other people in their field, it is appropriate to use technical words and specialized ways of communicating. Brevity and precision are both served by the use of specialized language if the reader and the writer give the same interpretation to that language. However, even lawyers can have trouble understanding specialized legal terms. For example, a criminal lawyer might have trouble understanding a document meant for tax lawyers.

Furthermore, many of the documents that lawyers produce are meant to be read by nonlawyers, who are unlikely to understand legal vocabulary and terms of art. The lay audience may also be confused by words or phrases that look familiar but that have a special meaning to lawyers. The list shown in Table 21.1 will give you an idea of how you can substitute simpler terms for complex or specialized

Table 21.1   Some Words and Phrases You Can Change

Don't use this word	if this word will work as well	Don't use this word	if this word will work as well
accord	give	in the event that	if
adequate amount	enough	maintain	keep, continue,
afford	give		support
aggregate	total	necessitate	require
allocate	give, divide	on or about	on
applicable	that applies	on or before	by
as to	about, relating to	on the part of	by
attain	reach	originate	start
attributable to	from, by	per annum	a year
by reason of	because of	prior to	before
cease	stop	procure	get
commence	begin	promulgate	issue
constitute	make up	provided that	however if
deem	consider	pursuant to	under
effectuate	carry out	retain	keep
exclusively	only	render	make, give
expiration	end	shall	must, may, will
for the duration of	during	solely	only, alone
for the purpose of	to, for	sufficient	enough
for the reason that	because	submit	send, give, contend
furnish	give, provide	subsequent to	after
has the option of	may	said, same, such	the, this, that
indicate	show	terminate	end, finish
in excess of	more than	unto	to
initiate	begin	utilize	use
in lieu of	instead of	without the United States	outside the United States
institute	begin		

terms. The words in this list will not always be perfectly interchangeable. Nevertheless, it is a good rule of thumb to try the simpler term first to see if it works as well as the more difficult one. You will find that your audience will not be insulted if you use *after* instead of *subsequent to*, no matter how sophisticated that audience is.

§21.10.3 *Define or Explain Technical Terms*

There are times when you cannot eliminate or change technical terms or legal terms of art, even though you know that some part of your audience will not be familiar with those terms. A definition, explanation, or example can help. If the definition for a technical term is fairly short, you can insert it right after the technical term the first time that term appears. You can do this with or without parentheses.

The following excerpt from a bank's loan note includes two examples of technical terms that are defined or explained in the sentence ("refinanced" and "rule of 78").

> *Prepayment of Whole Note:* Even though I needn't pay more than the fixed installments, I have the right to prepay the whole outstanding amount of this note at any time. If I do, or if this loan is *refinanced — that is, if I take out a new loan to pay off my old loan —* you will refund the unearned finance charge, figured by *the rule of 78 — a commonly used formula for figuring rebates on installment loans.* However, you can charge a minimum finance charge of $10.

You can provide a fuller explanation or example by making it a main part of the text itself, as in the following rewritten jury instruction.

> There is a type of negligence that involves the conduct of the plaintiff, rather than the defendant. It is called *contributory negligence.*
>
> If a plaintiff is negligent, and his negligence helps cause his own injury, we say that the plaintiff is contributorily negligent.
>
> A plaintiff who is contributorily negligent cannot recover money for his injury.

The following explanation of *default* from the rewritten bank note also illustrates how a term can be defined or explained within the main part of the text.

Default:　　I'll be in default

　　　　　1.　If I don't pay an installment on time; *or*
　　　　　2.　If any other creditor tries by legal process to take any money of mine in your possession.

EXERCISES

1.　Underline the inappropriate or unnecessarily difficult vocabulary in this passage. Rewrite the passage.

Consent of Minor Child to Adoption

I, Jane Smith, age 11, born on March 1, 1989, do hereby consent to my adoption by John Jones. I understand that if this adoption is granted, the relationship of parent and child will be established between myself and John Jones the same as if I had been born to him and further that all rights of my mother, Mary Jones, will be reserved unto her. I further consent to the change of my name to Jane Jones.

2. Underline and mark with the appropriate letter any words or phrases that you think are: a) totally unnecessary; b) necessary but need to be defined or translated.

Know all Men by these Presents

That the undersigned, individually and as parents or guardians of John Smith, a minor of the age of 12 years, residing at 1800 Oak Street, for and in consideration of the sum of Eight Thousand Dollars lawful money of the United States of America, to them in hand paid for and on behalf of said minor, the receipt whereof is hereby acknowledged, do hereby remise, release, and forever discharge Asa Luntz from any and all claims which are a result of a certain accident or event which occurred on or about June 5th, 1994, at 4700 Chestnut Street.

---

§21.11 Guideline 11: Avoid Noun Strings

In addition to allowing its users to create verbs from nouns and adjectives (nominalizations), the English language also allows the use of nouns as adjectives. For example, in the phrase *client interview form*, the first two nouns modify the final noun, *form*. Two or more nouns in a row are often called a noun string.

When a writer strings together more than two nouns, especially with an occasional adjective added to the string, it becomes difficult for the reader to understand the relationships among the nouns. Noun strings are (usually) grammatical, but the longer the string, the harder it is for the reader to understand what is going on. Some of the worst noun strings appear as the names of institutions or programs: consider *Family Planning Services Delivery Improvement Research Grants Program*. Here are other examples of noun strings from student memos and briefs:

- Qualified scholarship funding bonds
- The District of Columbia Human Rights Law limitations period
- Intrusive pretrial discovery methods

This is what one of these noun strings looks like in the context of a sentence:

> There is no precedent to support our position that the District of Columbia Human Rights Law limitations period applies to section 1981 actions.

Noun strings lack the "little words" — usually prepositions, sometimes the possessive *'s* — that clarify *how* the nouns are related. Noun strings may shorten a sentence, which may appear to simplify it, but removing the little words actually makes the sentence more complex. The reader has to laboriously untangle the noun string and reconstruct the original relationships. The reader puts back the prepositions or possessives mentally, and that takes time and energy. Noun strings can also make a sentence ambiguous, so that readers sometimes untangle them incorrectly. A good example is the name *International Ladies Garment Workers Union*. Is this a union of ladies who work on garments or a union of workers who work on ladies' garments? Are the ladies, the union, the workers, or the garments international?[8]

The solution is to unstring noun strings whenever possible. For example,

POOR: There is no precedent to support our position that the *District of Columbia Human Rights Law limitations period* applies to section 1981 actions.

GOOD: There is no precedent to support our position that the limitations period of the District of Columbia Human Rights Law applies to section 1981 actions.

POOR: Not all information is available to the consumer for *consumption or purchasing choice decisions*.

GOOD: Consumers do not have all the information they need to decide what to use or what to buy.

Notice that noun strings often include nominalizations. When you unstring the noun string, you should also look for the verb underlying the noun and make sure that it is necessary. In the last example, for instance, "consumption" comes from the verb *consume*, which really means to use up or to eat; "purchasing" comes from the verb *purchase*, which really means to buy; and "choice" comes from the verb *choose*, which is redundant here because it means the same as *decide*, which appears as the noun "decisions."

EXERCISES

Identify the noun strings in the following sentences and unstring them. Correct any other errors you may find.

1. The State bar client grievance committee is an attempt at a voluntary professional self-regulation program.
2. The Supreme Court held in *Ohralik v. Ohio State Bar Association*, 436 U.S. 447 (1978), that the state could prohibit attorney in-person client solicitations.
3. This is a request for public comment on a proposal for an industry self-regulated voluntary informational labeling program.
4. The company shall facilitate communication, collaboration, and coordination for Data Report Production activities within the group, as specified in its contract.

---

[8] Another example is *Federal Employers Liability Act*. Is this an act that regulates federal employers or a federal act that regulates certain employers?

5. For section 508 compliance, it may be necessary for an agency to outsource accessibility efforts, such as PDF document and forms accessibility, and to install a Web-service enabled accessibility checker.

§21.12 Guideline 12: Eliminate Redundancy and Extraneous Words; Avoid Overspecificity

Legal drafters often use two words that have almost identical meanings where one is really enough (aid and abet, false and untrue). There is a historical reason for these pairs. One term is usually Anglo-Saxon, while the other is Latin-based, derived through Norman French. In the Middle Ages when British common law had to deal with English-speaking yeomen and French-speaking aristocrats, doublets like these may have been necessary. In twenty-first-century America, they usually only add redundancy. Here are some of the more common pairs to be aware of:

each and every	false and untrue
any and all	excess and unnecessary
aid and abet	final and conclusive
authorized and empowered	type and kind
full and complete	absolutely and completely
order and direct	null and void

Bureaucrats and academicians are also guilty of using two words where one will do. The temptation to say things twice is often very hard to fight, but extra words that do not add any information should be left out. For example:

personal opinion	honest opinion
next subsequent	positive benefits

Some of these examples are truly redundant. You could not use the opposite of the adjective and have a meaningful phrase. For instance, what are negative benefits? In other cases, the adjective is informative only if you are stressing that attribute, for example, "This is my personal opinion, not that of the group."

The use of extraneous words can also overload a sentence and obscure its meaning. Extraneous words often appear as meaningless sentence introductions.

It is possible that you may not be able to file your brief on time.
This is to inform you that your case has been put on the docket.
There are four people *who* would like to testify.
It was in the fall of 1990 *that* she revised her will.

You can tell that an introduction is extraneous if you can remove it and still communicate the same information.

Extraneous words can appear anywhere in a sentence. For example, one law student wrote:

> The *matter presented* for this Court's *determination in the case at bar* is the *question* of *allowing* a cause of action for a preconception tort in Minnesota.

The student could have eliminated many of the italicized words and rewritten the sentence as follows:

> The court must decide whether the plaintiff can recover under Minnesota law for negligence that occurred before the plaintiff was conceived.

A good way to edit out extraneous words is to think of how you would express the concept orally. Often this will enable you to eliminate words that only serve to pad your sentences.

Another, related problem is overspecificity — that is, listing every possible instance of a general concept. Some attorneys fear that they won't be "covered" unless they list every possibility.

Know All Men by these Presents

That John Smith, hereinafter designated as the Releasor, for and in consideration of the sum of $8,000, the receipt whereof is hereby acknowledged, has *remised, released, and forever discharged,* and by these presents *does remise, release, and forever discharge* the said Releasee *of* and *from* all *debts, obligations, reckonings, promises, covenants, agreements, contracts, endorsements, bonds, specialties, controversies, suits, actions, causes of actions, trespasses, variances, judgments, extents, executions, damages, claims, or demands,* in law or in equity, which against the said Releasee, the Releasor *ever had, now has,* or hereafter *can, shall, or may have, for, upon, or by reason of* any *matter, cause, or thing* whatsoever, from the beginning of the world to the day of the date of these Presents.

Not only is this overspecificity unnecessary, it can be dangerous: The drafter can easily leave out an important item or action, and because he or she has been so specific, the omission would probably be interpreted as intentional. If a litigated document contains such omissions, the omissions can be used by your opponents to their advantage.

Rather than specifying every instance, we suggest that you use a general term and perhaps one or two examples, or several general terms, for example, "... released from all obligations, suits and other claims...." Remember that under the rule of ejusdem generis, courts will often construe general terms that follow terms of a particular or specific meaning as being defined or limited by these specific terms. That is, the general terms will be interpreted as applying only to things that fall into the same class as those specifically mentioned first. For example, if a list includes "dogs, cats, and other animals," "other animals" would probably exclude amoebas. The more general item is limited by the prior terms.

EXERCISES

Eliminate redundancy, superfluous words, or overspecificity in the following exercises. Also replace or eliminate any unnecessary legal jargon.

1. Any and all persons operating motor vehicles of any type and kind whatsoever in the District of Columbia shall obtain liability insurance.
2. The findings and determinations hereinafter set forth are supplementary and in addition to the findings and determinations previously made in connection with the issuance of the aforesaid order and of the previously issued amendments thereto; and all of the said previous findings and determinations are hereby ratified and affirmed, except insofar as such findings and determinations may be in conflict with the findings and determinations set forth herein.
3. §550.10 Trees, shrubs, plants, grass, and other vegetation. (a) General injury. No person shall prune, cut, carry away, pull up, dig, fell, bore, chop, saw, chip, pick, move, sever, climb, molest, take, break, deface, destroy, set fire to, burn, scorch, carve, paint, mark, or in any manner interfere with, tamper, mutilate, misuse, disturb, or damage any tree, shrub, plant, grass, flower, or part thereof, nor shall any person permit any chemical, whether solid, fluid, or gaseous, to seep, drip, drain or be emptied, sprayed, dusted or injected upon, about, or into any tree, shrub, plant, grass, flower, or part thereof, except when specifically authorized by competent authority; nor shall any person build fires, or station, or use any tar kettle, heater, road roller or other engine within an area covered by this part in such a manner that the vapor, fumes, or heat therefrom may injure any tree or other vegetation.

§21.13 Guideline 13: Use an Appropriate Style

It is important to choose the right style when you write legal documents. The style you use will depend on your audience and your purpose. Once you choose an appropriate style, stick with it throughout the document. Following are several guidelines to the style you should use when you write memos, briefs, letters, and other documents.

§21.13.1 Use the Correct Point of View, Labels, and Pronouns

The point of view, labels, and pronouns you use in legal writing will depend on the type of document you are writing. For example, the rules are slightly different for briefs and memos. You should generally write briefs in the third person (he, she, or it) from the point of view of an observer of the facts and the law. This will give the document a professional tone that will help convince your reader that you have drawn your conclusions from research and reasoning rather than by relying on your own biases and emotions.

This means that you should avoid referring to yourself with the personal pronoun *I* or *me* or to yourself and your client as *we* or *us*. Instead, formally refer to the client as petitioner, respondent, appellant or appellee, or, better still, use the client's last name. Also avoid using phrases that suggest that your statements are your personal observations: *I feel, It is my opinion, It is our belief.* Present your contentions more objectively by referring to yourself and your client in the third person: *Petitioner contends, Appellee suggests.* Be careful about being overly cautious in the way you present your contentions. Do not use phrases such as *It appears that, It seems likely that, It is suggested* to keep from committing yourself. Although cautious statements are occasionally necessary, they are usually used as a safety device, that is, the user of such a statement cannot later be proved wrong. The consequence of hedging your bet this way is that the reader perceives the statement as just what it is — an equivocation. Your assertion is robbed of force. This is especially undesirable in a brief, where you are trying to persuade your audience.

POOR: Now that I have reviewed the facts, it appears that the petitioners have failed to establish undue influence, overreaching, and misrepresentation.

GOOD: The evidence shows that the petitioners have failed to establish undue influence, overreaching, and misrepresentation.

You should use the same style when you write memos. Even though you are not writing for an adversary or for the court, you still want to convince your audience that your analysis is impersonal and well reasoned. However, because memos are often internal documents, you may have more leeway for informality. For example, a law firm may allow you, or even expect you, to express your conclusions or recommendations as your own opinions. For instance, you might offer the following conclusion:

> It is my opinion that the petitioners have failed to establish undue influence, over-reaching, and misrepresentation.

When you are writing letters to a client or a loan agreement for consumers, you can relax the rules presented above. In fact, it may be quite appropriate to present your document in the first person (I) or in the second person (you).

You can also use personal pronouns to give a document a tone of directness and personal interest. People may be more motivated to read a document that they feel is addressed to them. Using personal pronouns will also force you to write active rather than passive sentences (see Guideline 5). In a regulation or set of instructions, you can define *you* to mean all of the various participants. This can save space by making it unnecessary to repeat a cumbersome list many times.

In the revised regulations for Citizens Band (CB) radio operators (47 C.F.R. Part 95, Subpart D (1993)), the heading of each section is a question that the CB owner might ask. The body of each section is the answer. The first person pronouns (I, my) and the second person pronouns (you, your) refer to the CB owner in the questions and the answers, respectively.

> **§95.404 (CB Rule 4) Do I need a license?**   You do not need an individual license to operate a CB station. You are authorized by this rule to operate your CB station in accordance with the rules in this subpart.

In some revised bank forms and insurance policies, the company is writing to the consumer. *We* refers to the company and *you* means the consumer. Compare these two versions from a homeowners' insurance policy:

BEFORE: *Company's options.* It shall be optional with this Company to take all, or any part, of the property at the agreed or appraised value and to repair, rebuild, or replace the property destroyed or damaged with other of like kind and quality within a reasonable time, on giving notice of its intention to do so within 30 days after the receipt of the proof of loss herein required.

AFTER: *Our option.* If we give you written notice within 30 days after your signed, sworn statement of loss, we may repair or replace any part of the property damaged with equivalent property.

Unfortunately, there is no standard way to use pronouns. Sometimes the consumer is *I* and the company is *you*. This lack of consistency in the use of pronouns from one document to the next may be confusing to readers. There is also some evidence that readers find it difficult to remember who is who as they get further and further into a document that has both *we* and *you* in it. For most documents a good solution is to call the reader *you* and refer to your firm, company, or agency by name or initials.

§21.13.2 Use the Correct Tense

Legal writing has specific rules for when you should use the present and past tenses in memos and briefs.

1. If you are writing your own argument or analysis or if you are writing about your opponent's argument, use the present tense.

> Petitioners *argue* that common sense *dictates* that respondent's activities be classified as commercial.

2. If you are writing about a rule or statute that is still in force, use the present tense.

> According to §2-513 of the Uniform Commercial Code, a person who *buys* goods *has* a right to inspect the goods before *accepting* or *paying* for them.

3. If you are writing about a case that the court has already decided, use the past tense.

    In *Weisberg v. Williams, Connolly & Califano*, 399 A.2d 992, 995 (D.C. 1978), the court *held* that the statute of limitations for legal malpractice will not run if the defendant fraudulently concealed improprieties.

4. If you are writing about the actions of the people involved in a case, use the past tense, unless the actions are still going on. Discuss ongoing actions in the present tense.

    While it *is true* that the respondent *might have profited* from her activities, this *was not* the respondent's primary motive.

§21.13.3 Use a Formal but Not Pompous Style

Aim for a style that is neither too chatty and colloquial nor too formal or inflated. It is difficult to describe the happy medium between these two extremes. To get an idea of the proper style, look at the sample memos and brief presented later in this book. Here, however, we point out a few characteristics to avoid.

1. Avoid inappropriately "chatty" language.

    The most recent appellate court decision wasn't very good for our side. It will be a lot of trouble for us to argue around it.

2. Try to avoid inflated language. Using an inflated term like "telephonic communications" for telephone calls can give your writing a pompous tone.

    The attorney's subsequent *telephonic communications* were nothing more than the further dissemination of information to a special group.

3. Avoid cliches and mixed metaphors. You can damage your credibility if you use them. Cliches tell the reader that your thinking is not original. Metaphors are difficult to create, and if your metaphor doesn't work, or if you mix metaphors, you risk looking foolish. Here are examples from student memos that contain cliches and mixed metaphors. Note that in the second one the student also misquotes the metaphor, using *unchartered* instead of *uncharted*.

    A recurring theme in petitioner's appeal is that the courts have been flexible in their response to changing times. That flexibility is evidenced by *the slow and grudging wheels of Justice* is but a romantic notion of Justice responding to *every hue and cry*.

    Whether this small number of jurisdictions represents a trend or a *minority rushing blindly into unchartered waters* remains to be seen.

§21.13.4 Use an Appropriate Approach

Begin your analysis or argument by dealing directly with the facts and law. Do not begin an analysis or argument with philosophical discussions, as in the following example from a memo.

> Since a lawyer's primary function is protecting and advising a client in the client's best interest, it is always of the utmost importance to first determine what it is, exactly, that the client needs or wants. Before assuming lawsuits and potential liability it is necessary to examine alternative procedures that may, in fact, serve the client as well or better than winning a particular day in court.

Legal briefs and memos are not term papers; don't write them like term papers. For term papers, students are usually expected to do library research on a topic and then write up all that they have discovered about that topic. The student may be encouraged to philosophize, cite people's opinions, or give a history of the topic. Here is an example in which a student used a term paper approach. The student was arguing that recognizing the specific tort of invasion of privacy is not necessary, because a plaintiff can currently use other tort actions and existing statutes to enforce the right of privacy.

> The right of privacy is an important value which has been gleaned from the Bill of Rights and developed throughout our nation's history. Arguing against it is like arguing against American notions of freedom, liberty, and justice.
>   Historically, a tort action of privacy never existed in common law. Kalven, Privacy in Tort Law — Were Warren and Brandeis Wrong?, 31 L. & Contemp. Prob. 326, 327 (1978). The first major work done on the subject was motivated by the author's displeasure with stories of his daughter's marriage. Warren & Brandeis, The Right to Privacy, 4 Harv. L. Rev. 192 (1890). Out of this article arose the tort called invasion of privacy, which some courts began recognizing some thirty years later.

In the law, the reader's expectations are different, and hence the writer's approach must be different. The writer should include only information that is necessary for analyzing the facts and the law. The writer should leave out irrelevant material, no matter how interesting it may seem.

REVIEW EXERCISES

Identify all of the problems in each sentence and then rewrite the sentence.

1. Recent developments in Wisconsin law have made some progress in clearing up the problems encountered in the construction of the drunk driving statute and will aid the resolution of our client's problem.
2. In *Marsh v. Alabama*, 326 U.S. 501 (1946), it was found that the town was not unlike others in its accessibility and functions to the public.

3. In this determination, state membership or representation on policymaking bodies and state powers over institutional decision making would be important factors for examination.
4. To examine more closely the objectionable methods of data gathering, reflect upon the attainment of private mental records from a state entity.
5. The agency's argument for deference is as a result based upon claim that the "X" rule, which requires that the evidence be first determined to be "otherwise in equipoise" ("Question Presented") — or a prior version or versions thereof not significantly different — was created by the courts of appeals and has long been sound law; which, if true, would mean that deference to its determination concerning the statute which it administers is not relevant.

CHAPTER 22

HOW TO PROOFREAD

Unfortunately, many writers lose interest when they read advice about polishing the mechanics of a document because they think that people do not notice mechanics or that their administrative assistants will take care of mechanical problems. First of all, people do notice "the small stuff." Judge Wald, of the D.C. Circuit, has recommended that counsel "proofread with a passion":

> You cannot imagine how disquieting it is to find several spelling or grammatical errors in an otherwise competent brief. It makes the judge go back to square one in evaluating the counsel. It says — worst of all — the author never bothered to read the whole thing through, but she expects us to.[1]

Fairly or unfairly, many readers see mechanical mistakes as a sign of overall incompetence; too many typographical errors may lead the judge to mistrust the validity of the legal analysis. Justice Ginsburg has observed that if a brief is "sloppy" in regard to mechanics, "the judge may suspect its reliability in other respects as well."[2] In a 1994 case, a federal district judge dismissing a complaint ordered a sanctions hearing for the plaintiff's attorney, noting that the attorney's mechanical errors were evidence of a lack of due care:

> [Counsel] continues to submit documents to this Court with grammatical errors and misstatements. . . . Moreover, throughout the Amended Complaint [the attorney] repeatedly refers to his client as "he" instead of "she." These types of errors strongly suggest that Mr. Williams has not taken the appropriate care to avoid errors before submitting documents to this Court.[3]

---

[1] Patricia M. Wald, *19 Tips from 19 Years on the Appellate Bench*, 1 J. App. Prac. & Process 7, 22 (1999).

[2] Ruth Bader Ginsburg, *Remarks on Appellate Advocacy*, 50 S.C. L. Rev. 567, 568 (1999).

[3] *Styles v. Philadelphia Elec. Co.*, No. CIV. A. 93-4593, 1994 WL 245469, at *3 (E.D. Pa. June 6, 1994) (cited in Judith D. Fischer, *Bareheaded and Barefaced Counsel: Courts React to Unprofessionalism in Lawyers' Papers*, 31 Suffolk U. L. Rev. 1, 27 (1997)).

To take a more practical view, failure to take care with polishing may cost you money. In a case that received wide publicity (including a story in the *New York Times*), an attorney whose courtroom work was praised had his fees for his written work cut in half — from $300 to $150 per hour — due in large part to sloppy proofreading.[4] When he was interviewed about the case, the federal judge who decided on the award of attorneys' fees commented that "no matter how good you are in front of the jury, most of your reputation's going to be built on what you write."[5]

The second reason you must learn polishing skills is that you probably cannot afford an assistant who can do this level of polishing. You must take responsibility for polishing the mechanics of your legal documents because your document reflects on your client and on your competence.

Polishing is hard for the same reason that revision is hard. Most people don't really see their writing when they review it. Instead, they see the document that they meant to write; their short-term memory interferes with their ability to see typographical errors or other problems. For that reason, this chapter identifies some objective methods for polishing that will help you to break up that relationship between your short-term memory and your document, and help you to catch mistakes in both your writing and your analysis.

The best way to proofread effectively is to put your writing away for a while. If you've ever gone back and read a document that you wrote last year, or even last month, you've probably noticed several mistakes or style problems that you missed when you wrote it. If you are trying to polish a document that you wrote this morning, your short-term memory makes it hard for you to see your mistakes. It knows what you wanted to say, and it tends to gloss over the mistakes.[6] Therefore, if you can get a draft done a week before your deadline, *don't* reread it and edit it every day. Instead, wait three days and do a thorough edit, and then wait three more days and do a final edit.[7] Even a little time can make some difference. In a crunch, that might mean taking a 15-minute walk and then coming back to edit, but taking some time can make a difference.

A second effective polishing technique is to "start in the middle" when reviewing your work. Most writing teachers find that mechanical mistakes and other weaknesses show up more often in the second half of the document than in the first half. That's because many writers get bored with editing or polishing as they get closer to the end of the document; many give up before finishing the job.

---

[4] *DeVore v. City of Philadelphia*, 2004 U.S. Dist. LEXIS 3635, at *6 (E.D. Pa. Feb. 20, 2004). The court noted that counsel's lack of care "caused the court, and I am sure, defense counsel, to expend an inordinate amount of time deciphering the arguments." *Id.* at *6-7.

[5] *All Things Considered*, "Magistrate Judge Jacob P. Hart Discusses His Fight to Get Lawyers to Clean Up Their Written Work" (NPR Mar. 4, 2004) (radio broadcast).

[6] Of course, getting a friend or colleague to review the document can also be helpful, since that person will not have the information in his or her short-term memory. In an academic setting, you should not use this method unless you have *specific* permission from your teacher. In a professional setting, asking a friend to review your work is fine; finding someone who has the time to help you is the hard part.

[7] *See also* Judge Stephen J. Dwyer, Leonard J. Feldman & Ryan P. McBride, *How to Write, Edit, and Review Persuasive Briefs: Seven Guidelines from One Judge and Two Lawyers*, 31 Seattle L. Rev. 417, 425 (2008).

Even conscientious editors should give fresh eyes to different parts of the document at different times.

Generally, it is ineffective to proofread by reading the entire document very slowly once or twice, trying to catch every type of error. Instead, you should read the document through several times on the computer and several times in hard-copy form. Make surgical strikes, focusing on only one or two aspects of the document at a time. For example, you can review the document once just looking at citation form, another time just looking at topic sentences, and so on. This chapter discusses proofreading techniques for both the electronic and hard copy versions of the document.

§22.1 Methods to Use on the Computer

You can do some proofreading while your document is still in electronic form. First, you may want to enlarge the font size while you proofread. Enlarging the font (say, to 20- or 22-point size) can have two benefits. First, you can focus more easily because you will have a smaller number of words on the screen at a time. Second, it will be easier to distance yourself from the text because the font change will significantly change the way the document looks. Proofreading electronically also allows you to use your computer software's Find and Replace feature to your advantage. Although your eyes get tired, the computer never misses on a search, presuming you are searching precisely.

1. Pronoun search.   Use the Find and Replace feature to search for *he, she, it, they*, and so on. Stop when you hit a pronoun and scrutinize it to make sure that the reader will have *no doubt* about the noun you are referring to (the antecedent). Also, make sure that you have not mistakenly used *they* in place of *it*. For example, both courts and corporations should be referred to in the singular as *it*.

2. Apostrophe search.   If you tend to use too many apostrophes, use the Find and Replace feature to search for *s[apostrophe]* or *[apostrophe]s* so that you can scrutinize whether you've used each apostrophe correctly. If you use too few apostrophes, your task is a little harder. You could use the Find and Replace feature to find words that end in *s* by searching for *s[space]* or *s.[space]*. Once you are zeroed in on the potential problem words, consult grammar guidelines to see if you are using apostrophes correctly. Appendix A [Mary Beth Beazley, A Practical Guide to Appellate Advocacy, 3rd ed., (2010)] includes advice about the most common apostrophe problems.

3. Quotation mark search.   The rule in American English is that periods and commas *always* go inside quotation marks, even if you are quoting only one word or one letter:

▼ **Bad Example**

Judge Wald has noted that finding errors in a brief makes her "go back to square one in evaluating the counsel".

▲ Good Example

Judge Wald has noted that finding errors in a brief makes her "go back to square one in evaluating the counsel."

▼ Bad Example

The word "Aspen", which refers to both trees and a publisher, begins with the letter "A".

▲ Good Example

The word "Aspen," which refers to both trees and a publisher, begins with the letter "A."

To find errors of this type, use the Find and Replace feature to search for quotation marks, and check your punctuation. Also, check to make sure that all quotation marks come in pairs. Too often, when writers block and copy quotations, they place an opening quotation mark, then copy the language into the text, and neglect to insert the closing quotation mark. This is the punctuation equivalent of leaving the refrigerator door open, and it is very annoying to readers. Be sure to proofread specifically for this problem.

4. Citation search.   To review your citations, search *[begin underline]* or *[begin italics]* or even *v.* to help you find citations and scrutinize them in isolation. Three types of errors are particularly common: (1) incorrect volume or page numbers, (2) misspelled party names, and (3) missing pinpoint page numbers. As noted earlier, presume that every citation should have a pinpoint. Even if you are just citing to a general principle from the case, find a page on which that general principle appears, and use it as the pinpoint.

5. Spell-check.   Run the spell-check early and often, but keep a few things in mind. First, keep your hand away from the mouse, or your finger off the button, so that you don't hit Replace or Skip by mistake. Second, don't hit Skip as soon as you see a party name or a case name; make sure that you've spelled each one properly and consistently.

Third, after completing spell-check, use the Find and Replace feature to search for typos that the spell-check function won't catch. In every document, look for *statue* for *statute*, *untied* for *united*, *form* for *from* (and vice versa), *reasonable* for *reasonably* (and vice versa), and *probable* for *probably* (and vice versa). You might consider setting your Quick Correct feature to change *pubic* to *public* to avoid that potentially embarrassing error. If your document is about *probable cause* or *reasonable doubt*, it is even more important to do this kind of search. I have read several briefs in which students claim that there was no "probably cause" for the defendant's arrest, or that the defense could not establish "reasonably doubt." Because both forms of certain problem words could appear in the text, search for each form separately and make sure each use is proper.

As you can see, the Find and Replace feature can help you to proofread on the computer in many different ways. You may be able to figure out other ways to make the computer's tireless brain work for you.

§22.2 Methods to Use on the Hard Copy

Plan to print out a hard copy several times before you must file the document. Because your brain works differently when you are looking at a computer screen than when you are looking at a hard copy, you will undoubtedly find errors on the hard copy that you missed when reading the document on the computer.

1. Check paragraph length. You may have created some overlong paragraphs as you revised; they will be evident on the hard copy. Remember that there are two reasons to create a paragraph break: substance and graphics. Even if you have not moved on to a new subject, the reader may need the brief visual rest that a paragraph break provides. A good default is to look for at least two paragraph breaks per page (more is fine). If you have only one paragraph break, you must find a place to insert a hard return. Note that if you create an artificial paragraph break in this way, you may need to add a topic sentence to ensure that the reader can instantly understand how the paragraph is relevant to the point under discussion.

2. Check sentence length. If you have a problem with overlong sentences, edit for them by looking for periods. Take a pencil and make a slash mark at every period; you can do this without even reading the text. When you're done, review the slash marks. If you see several sentences in a row that are over four lines long, review them and try to shorten at least one. One good way to shorten long sentences is to look for verbs. If you have three verbs in one sentence, try giving each verb a subject and its own sentence. If you see several sentences that are only one line long — and you're not using short sentences for occasional, dramatic effect — try to combine a couple of the short sentences.[8]

3. Review the verbs. Readers subconsciously pay more attention to information in the verb position. Thus, go through your document and circle all of your verbs, trying not to read the sentences. You should scrutinize all vague verbs, including *is, are, was, were, made, involved, concerned, had,* and the like. Unless you are using them purposefully — e.g., in a persuasive document to deemphasize information, or because you are using passive voice to avoid an unusually long subject — you should look for the better verb hidden in the sentence and revise accordingly.

4. Review the signals to the reader. Look at the first paragraph (or two) of each heading section for needed legal backstory and roadmap. Look at the last paragraph of each heading section for a concluding statement connecting the analysis to the point being covered within that unit of discourse. Scan the first sentence of each paragraph to see how often your paragraphs begin with main points and include the phrase-that-pays. Scan through the document to make sure there

---

[8] *See* Mary Barnard Ray & Jill J. Ramsfield, *Legal Writing: Getting It Right and Getting It Written* 371-72 (4th ed., Thomson/West 2005).

are enough headings. If you go more than three or four pages without a new heading, scrutinize that section. Can you break that section down into two subsections? Have you gone onto a new point without labeling it with a heading? Similarly, review each roadmap and mini-roadmap, and then compare it to your headings. The roadmap should predict precisely the headings that follow.

5. Do a ruler-read.   After you have taken these steps, read a hard copy aloud (as slowly as you can) backwards and forwards *with a ruler under each line as you read it.* Using the ruler helps to separate you from your text, breaking up that cozy relationship between your short-term memory and your document. When doing this ruler-read, include all extraneous materials like cover pages and tables; these sections often get short shrift when it comes to proofreading.

6. Repeat any or all of the above as needed.   If you keep finding new mistakes when using these techniques, you need to keep proofreading. Do not print the final version of the document until you can read it through and find *no* mistakes.

§22.3 Proofreading Your Revisions

Word processors have greatly improved the quality of written documents, but they are also responsible for a new type of editing error. In the past, when a writer revised a document, someone had to type the whole thing over again, and so it was fairly easy to substitute the new words and to leave the old words out. Now, with the constant editing that word processors allow, it is not uncommon to see both old and new versions of a phrase within a document: The writer typed the new phrase and forgot to delete the old one. Further, writers who carelessly use the Find and Replace feature frequently find sentences like this in their writing:

▼ Bad Example

On Saturday, the Mr. Johnson returned home.

The best way to avoid these types of errors is, once again, to focus on proofreading. After each round of edits, print out the hard copy and highlight the words, lines, or paragraphs in which edits occurred. Read those sections in isolation, so that you don't get caught up in the meaning of the words. In addition, *never* use the Replace All feature; doing so causes mistakes like the one shown above because it's difficult to envision all of the contexts in which a word or phrase might appear. Instead, look at each use of the word you are replacing to avoid mistakes.

§22.4 The Last Thing to Do with the Document

This section is really about the second-to-the-last thing to do with the document. The last thing you should do is file it with the court. But the last proofreading method you should use with your document is to read it aloud, out of order.

Either start in the middle, start on the last page and then read the second-to-the-last page, and so on, or mix up the pages and read them in a random order. Whichever method you use, your goal is to pay attention to individual words and sentences rather than to get swept away by your no doubt fascinating discussion of the law.

§22.5 Summary

In practice, you will often need to write and file documents in a hurry, without time to polish and proofread in a leisurely way. Take the time now to develop an effective polishing process. When you submit documents that demonstrate professionalism in both content and presentation, you enhance your credibility and increase your opportunities for success in law practice.

ORAL ADVOCACY

CHAPTER 23

ORAL ARGUMENT

This chapter and your first law school oral argument provide only a glimpse of appellate practice. Appellate lawyers must know much more than this introduction can provide. Consider taking a course in appellate practice and procedure. The first time you handle a case on appeal, you will be glad to have had that important training.

These next sections present material designed for a law school oral argument. In actual law practice, some of the details of presentation and formality expected in a particular court might differ from those expected in a law school setting. However, the fundamental concepts presented here will be equally applicable. In actual law practice, you can adjust your presentation to that expected in a particular court by observing a few oral arguments before you present your own. You will not find these small differences to be a problem.

This chapter describes an appellate argument rather than a trial-level argument. Again, the fundamental principles of delivering a trial-level argument and an appellate argument are the same, and you will be able to adapt your presentation by observing arguments by other lawyers in a trial-court setting.

§23.1 The Purpose of Oral Argument

Before you plunge into preparing your oral argument, consider its purpose. An oral argument is not simply an opportunity to say orally what you have already said in writing. If that were the purpose of oral argument, the judges would not waste your time or theirs. They would simply read your brief and issue a ruling.

Rather, an oral argument is *an opportunity for the judges to ask you questions*. They want to clarify their understanding of your arguments. They want to give you a chance to alleviate their concerns about adopting the position you advocate. They want to have a conversation. As your only chance to speak directly with those who will decide your case, oral argument is an important opportunity.

Oral argument also provides you a chance to return the judges' deliberation to the big picture and to emphasize the narrative themes and policy rationales that underlie your legal argument — the themes that show not just how the law *does* support your position, but also why it *should*. Direct, eyeto-eye contact often is the best way to bring home the importance of those fundamental aspects of your argument.

§23.2 Formalities and Organization of Oral Argument

The first step in preparing for oral argument is to understand the formalities you will encounter and the overall organization your argument should follow. Here is an overview of the oral argument:

§23.2.1 *Preliminary Formalities*

Usually you will be seated at counsel table, waiting for the judges to enter and call your case. A bailiff will announce the entry of the judges by saying something like this:

> Oyez, oyez, oyez. All rise. The First Circuit Court of . . . is now in session. All those with business before this Honorable Court may now draw near.

As soon as the bailiff begins this speech, stand up and remain standing until the judges are seated and the Chief Judge tells you to be seated. The Chief Judge will then call your case and ask if the lawyers are ready, saying something like this:

> The Court calls the case of *Jones v. Brown.* Is counsel for the appellant ready? . . . Is counsel for the appellee ready?

When the judge asks you if you are ready, stand up and say "Ready, Your Honor." The Chief Judge will then instruct counsel for the appellant to proceed.

§23.2.2 *The Appellant's Argument*

As the lawyer for the moving party, counsel for the appellant goes first. You might be the only lawyer for the appellant, or you could have co-counsel arguing one of the issues. Use the following structure, leaving out the mention of co-counsel if you are arguing alone:

> May it please the Court. My name is Russell Stege, and along with my co-counsel, Susan Marks, I represent the Appellant, Paul Giray. I would ask the Court for permission to reserve two minutes for rebuttal. [Pause to allow the Chief Justice to respond.]
>
> Thank you, your Honor. Mr. Giray respectfully asks this Court to . . . [state in one or two phrases the ruling you seek, for example, "reverse the trial court's entry of summary judgment and remand the case for trial"].

The issue(s) before the Court is/are whether . . . [state each issue in one sentence, phrased favorably to your side[1]]. Ms. Marks will argue the damages issue, and I will argue the adverse possession issue.

Then give the Court a short overview of the arguments you will make.

Your Honors, Mr. Giray will show that the undisputed facts in this case simply are not adequate to establish the elements of adverse possession. [In two or three sentences, state a summary of your argument so the judges will have a sense of the arguments you will make and the order in which you will present them. This is also a good spot to introduce your narrative theme, as described in section III below.]

Your Honors, the facts are these: . . . [Inform the Court of the relevant facts, and then begin the main section of your argument, as described in section III.]

§23.2.3 Argument of Co-Counsel for the Appellant

If you are co-counsel arguing a second issue for the Appellant, you will argue next. Go to the podium as soon as your co-counsel leaves it without waiting for an invitation from the judges. If the judges are still writing or conversing when you arrive at the podium, wait a moment until they are ready or until one of them tells you that you may begin. Then introduce yourself and identify your client, as the first lawyer did. You do not need to introduce your co-counsel from whom the Court has already heard. Nor do you need to repeat the request to reserve time for rebuttal. Proceed to a short overview of the arguments you will make:

May it please the Court, my name is Susan Marks, and I also represent Paul Giray. I will argue the issue of the adequacy of money damages in this case. Your Honors, even if the undisputed facts were sufficient to establish a claim for adverse possession, an award of money damages would be more than sufficient in this case. [In two or three sentences, state a summary of your argument.]

Your co-counsel has already stated the facts, so you do not need to repeat them. Simply begin your legal argument, perhaps starting with your narrative theme. The rest of your argument should proceed just as described above for the first advocate.

§23.2.4 The Appellee's Argument

Go to the podium as soon as counsel for the Appellant leaves it. If the judges are still writing or conversing, wait a moment until they are ready or until one of them tells you that you may begin. Then introduce yourself, your co-counsel, if any, and your client, just as the first lawyer did. As counsel for the appellee, you do not have a rebuttal, so you do not need to reserve any time. Then give the Court a short overview of the arguments you will make:

---

[1] Use the same techniques you used to phrase favorably the Questions Presented in your brief. See Chapter 17.

> May it please the Court, my name is Elizabeth Tunnesen, and along with Jason Kennedy, I represent Carol Cole. Ms. Cole requests the Court to affirm the trial court's order granting summary judgment. Mr. Kennedy will argue the damages issue, and I will argue the adverse possession issue. I will show that the undisputed facts are more than sufficient to establish each element of adverse possession.

Give the Court a short overview of the arguments you will make, perhaps introducing your narrative theme. Counsel for the appellant has already provided the facts of the case, so you need only add or clarify any *important* fact omitted from the appellant's fact statement.

> Ms. Cole agrees with the facts as stated by the Appellant. However, the Court should also be aware that . . .

If you do not need to clarify or add an important fact, simply proceed to the rest of your argument, following the format described above.

§23.2.5 *Argument of Co-Counsel for the Appellee*

Your argument should follow the format described for the second lawyer for the appellant.

§23.2.6 *Concluding the Argument*

No matter whether you argue for the appellant or the appellee, you will have to reach a graceful and persuasive ending while negotiating the constraints of the time cards. Prepare a conclusion consisting of a short summary (three to five sentences) of your best points, phrased compellingly, and a request for the relief you seek:

> [A summary of your strongest arguments] . . . . Therefore, the appellant requests that the Court reverse the trial court's entry of summary judgment and remand the case for trial on the adverse possession claim. Thank you, Your Honors.

Try to be ready to begin your conclusion when the one-minute card goes up. When the "zero" card is raised, you may finish your sentence, but then you must stop. Simply say, "Thank you, Your Honors," and sit down. If you are in the middle of answering a judge's question when the zero card goes up, stop and say to the Chief Judge:

> Your Honor, I see that my time is up. May I finish answering Judge Nottingham's question and have a moment to conclude?

The Chief Judge will probably say "Yes." If so, finish your answer and take *no more than forty-five seconds* to deliver your conclusion. If the Chief Judge declines your request, simply say "Thank you, Your Honors," and sit down.

§23.2.7 *Rebuttal*

After counsel for the appellee has finished arguing, one of the lawyers for the appellant will deliver the rebuttal. If you will be delivering the rebuttal, listen carefully during the appellee's argument to identify a weak point or a point on which opposing counsel has damaged your case but that you can remedy with a strong, extremely brief rebuttal. When counsel for the appellee concludes, go to the podium and deliver your rebuttal in one to two minutes, say, "Thank you, Your Honors," and sit down. The goal is to make your point in a compelling way and to sit down without prompting further questioning from the bench. Have one rebuttal prepared in advance, and use this prepared rebuttal in case you panic and cannot put together a compelling rebuttal based on what you have heard in the appellant's argument.

§23.3 The Content of Argument

The following procedural facets of your case will be crucial to the success of your oral argument. You must know how these procedural concepts apply to your case, and you must be able to phrase your arguments accurately in light of those effects.

§23.3.1 *The Standard of Review*

The standard of review governs how much deference the appellate court must give to the decision of the judge or jury at the trial level. Review the material on the standard of review in Part C of this book. If the standard of review is favorable to your side, be especially sure to phrase your argument in its terms. No matter how much you choose to emphasize the standard, be ready to respond clearly and succinctly to a judge's question regarding the appropriate standard.

§23.3.2 *The Burden of Proof*

Be sure you know the relevant burden of proof on the issue you are arguing. The burden of proof identifies the party who has the responsibility of proving the necessary facts and persuading the trial court. Usually, the plaintiff bears the burden of proving the elements of the cause of action, and the defendant bears the burden of proving an affirmative defense. On a procedural issue, the moving party often bears the burden. For instance, on a motion to compel discovery, the moving party would bear the burden of proof. Check the authorities on your legal issue to be sure you know which party bears the burden of proving each aspect of the case.

§23.3.3 *The Trial-Level Procedural Posture*

Finally, your argument could be affected by the trial-level procedural posture of the ruling from which the appeal arose. The trial-level procedural posture defined the appropriate legal question in the trial court, and it is the decision on that legal question that is now on appeal. For instance, if the appeal is from a ruling granting summary judgment, the question before the trial court judge was whether the undisputed facts entitled the moving party to judgment without the necessity of a trial. Therefore, the role of the appellate court is to decide whether the trial judge ruled correctly *on that legal question*. If the appeal is from a judge's decision after a bench trial, the question is whether the facts in the trial record are sufficient to sustain the ruling (in other words, whether a reasonable judge, reviewing that trial record, could have decided the case in the way this judge did). Therefore, the role of the appellate court is to decide whether the trial judge ruled correctly *on that legal question*. Check the authorities to be sure of the implications of your case's trial-level procedural posture, and frame your arguments and your answers with that posture in mind.

§23.3.4 Themes

Your case needs a theme, an overriding point to which you repeatedly return. Your theme should be the most persuasive big-picture point you have. Commonly, themes are based in the case's narrative (narrative reasoning), in the policies implicated by the case (policy-based reasoning), in the strength of the doctrinal law (rule-based and analogical reasoning), or in the case's procedural posture. Select a narrative theme if the most powerful part of your argument is based on your client's compelling facts:

> Your Honors, this is a case about a record title-holder who sat by and watched his neighbor build a garage, knowing that the neighbor believed the garage to be properly located on his own land. Then, just as the garage was completed, the record title-holder told his neighbor that the garage was six inches over the property line and demanded that the neighbor tear it down.

If the most compelling point of your argument is a policy implication, select a theme based on that policy:

> Even if a minor is less than completely candid about his age, the law should still require a merchant to take the remarkably simple precaution of asking to see the minor's driver's license. Such a requirement does not burden the merchant at all, and it protects against the very real danger that a merchant might find it profitable to be too easily convinced of an eager young customer's age.

If the most compelling part of your argument is the strength of the law on your side, select a theme that capitalizes on this strength:

> Despite the plaintiff's admittedly sympathetic facts, the law in this jurisdiction could not be more clear. A wrongful death action simply cannot be sustained for the death of a nonviable fetus. The legislature of this state has expressly declared this to be the law, and no fewer than five rulings of the Supreme Court have agreed.

If the most compelling part of your argument is the procedural posture of the trial court decision on which the appeal is based, select a theme that keeps bringing the discussion back to that procedural posture:

> The defendant strenuously disagrees with the inferences the plaintiff asks the Court to draw from the affidavits. However, even if the affidavits did support the plaintiff's inferences, the fact remains that this case comes before the Court on appeal from a summary judgment ruling. The question is not whether the plaintiff's inferences are possible, or even whether they are the most likely, but rather whether they are the *only* possible inferences. Clearly they are not.

§23.4 Preparation

§23.4.1 *The Record*

Thoroughly know the facts in the Record. For the important facts, be able to cite the page on which they appear. Do not overstate the facts, and do not state as facts the inferences you ask the court to draw from the facts. If you misstate facts, you will have lost credibility with the court, and if you mis-state facts intentionally, you will have acted unethically.

§23.4.2 *Outline Your Argument*

Usually the outline of your argument should mirror the large-scale organization of your brief. The first level of headings should articulate your position on each relevant element of the governing rule. Under each heading, place as subheadings each argument you will make on that element, and under that subheading, place each point you will make in that part of the argument.

§23.4.3 *Prepare Your Folder*

Prepare a folder with your notes for oral argument. You can use a file folder and small index cards. Open the folder and use both sides for your opening and closing language (in case you panic), for important factual information to which you might need to refer (for example, dates and relevant numbers you might not remember), and for the outline of your argument.

Consider including two outlines, one for a cold bench (a bench that asks few questions) and one for a hot bench (a bench that leaves you little time for your scripted material). The outline for the cold bench is your expanded outline — the one you will use if the judges are quiet and you have time to present most of your prepared material. The outline for the hot bench is compressed into just the main points you want to make in case you have only a few minutes. You can start with the expanded outline but shift to the compressed outline as necessary during the argument.

Reserve one area of the folder for the index cards. For each important case, statute, or regulation, summarize on a card the important information from that source and quote any key language. Tape the cards on top of each other with the bottom of each card protruding a quarter of an inch from beneath the card on top of it. Tape the cards to the folder along the card's top edge, so the cards can be flipped up like an address file. In the visible space on the bottom of each card, write the name or the case, statute, or regulation. Practice finding the information on the cards and in the other parts of the folder quickly and easily.

§23.4.4   Script the Entire Opening, the Conclusion, and Your Prepared Rebuttal

Although you cannot and should not try to script the body of the argument, the opening and closing should be scripted, essentially memorized, delivered with full eye contact, and spoken as if they were not memorized. This preparation will guarantee that you say what you want to say and that you say it smoothly and effectively. Your extemporaneous responses might not always be smooth, but your beginnings and endings can and should achieve a high level of poise and persuasion.

§23.4.5   Practice

Practice delivering your argument to friends. Have the friends question you just as they would if they were the judges before whom you will argue. Practice at least five or six times, and more if possible. Go through the whole argument each time, and then ask for feedback. Use these practice benches to improve both your knowledge of the case and the smoothness of your delivery.

§23.4.6   Visit the Courtroom

Familiarize yourself with the room where you will argue. Imagine yourself delivering your argument there, and remind yourself that you belong there, advocating for your client. Psychologically claim the space.

§23.5   Handling Questions from the Bench

Because a primary purpose of oral argument is to answer the judges' questions, a big part of your preparation should consist of getting ready to provide those answers. Here are some important points to guide your preparation.

§23.5.1   Anticipating Questions

Ask yourself what you would want to know if you were a judge hearing the case. What parts of the argument would be hard to accept and why? What will your opponent argue? What key cases or statutes will the court be most concerned about? Also, pay close attention to the questions you receive in your practice rounds. Prepare answers for all of these questions.

§23.5.2 *Attitude*

The judges will ask you questions, and they will often interrupt you to do it. This is part of the role of a judge. It is efficient and it saves you precious time. When a judge interrupts you, stop talking *immediately* and listen to what the judge is saying. Then answer the judge's question as best you can. Treat the question for what it is — a valuable opportunity to clarify a point about which the judge is concerned. Do not appear to be rushing through the answer so you can get back into your prepared argument. The judge's question is more important than your prepared argument.

The right to interrupt belongs only to the judge, however. Never interrupt a judge. No matter how badly you want to speak, wait patiently until the judge has finished speaking before you utter a sound.

§23.5.3 *Recognizing Types of Questions*

You will encounter three basic kinds of questions: friendly questions, questions genuinely seeking clarification of information, and adversarial questions.

A friendly question is designed to help you present your argument or make an additional point. A judge might want you to make a certain point primarily for the benefit of another judge, or a judge might simply be pleased to have thought of another point and might want to share it. Be sure to recognize a friendly question and to make use of the opportunity it gives you to agree with a judge and to articulate and validate the judge's point.

A question genuinely seeking information is an opportunity to be helpful to a judge who needs a point clarified. Do so willingly. Then, if you have a point to make about the subject of the inquiry, you can use this chance to make it, but only after you have answered the judge's question.

You might find that most of the questions you receive are adversarial, designed to test your arguments. Despite their threatening nature, these are the questions you should welcome most because these are the questions that allow you to resolve the concerns that could stand in the way of achieving the result you seek. Often these questions will be politely phrased, but sometimes a judge will deliver the question in an intimidating, angry, or even rude manner. Your job is to answer politely but firmly, ignoring the packaging of the question and responding only to its content. Do not respond in anger, even if you are feeling angry. Remain calm, at least outwardly, and answer the question as best you can.

Your Honor, I must respectfully disagree. In the *Jones* case, the Supreme Court did not hold that . . . . Rather , ... And this is precisely why . . . .

§23.5.4 Listening Carefully to the Question

You might find that your nervousness impedes your ability to listen carefully to the question. After you hear the first part of the question, you might assume that you know what the judge will be asking, and your nervousness could cause you to begin scrambling to formulate an answer. Yet you cannot answer a question that you have misunderstood. When a judge begins to speak, remember to listen carefully to the whole question before you answer.

§23.5.5 Clarifying the Question

Sometimes you will not understand a question even when you have listened carefully. This could happen because you are nervous or because the judge has not articulated the question clearly. Simply admit that you did not understand the question, apologize, and ask the judge to repeat it. If you think that you might have understood it but you are not sure, you can clarify your understanding: "Is Your Honor asking whether . . . ?"

§23.5.6 Beginning with a Clear, Direct Answer

Usually you will want to say a number of things in response to a question. However, you should always begin with a very short, direct answer to the question in the form in which the judge posed it: "Yes, Your Honor," or "No, Your Honor, I must respectfully disagree," or "Your Honor, that has sometimes been the case, but not always." After you have responded directly, you can go on to explain your answer, but the judge should know within roughly your first ten words what your answer to the question will be.

§23.5.7 Returning to Your Prepared Presentation

When you have finished answering a question, return immediately to your prepared presentation. Do not wait for the judge to respond or to give you permission to return to your prepared material. Try to find a way to connect the ending of your answer to an entry point into your argument so that the answer seamlessly weaves you right back into your prepared material. However, if you cannot think of a connection on the spot, simply return to your argument.

§23.5.8 Handling Questions on Your Co-Counsel's Issue

Sometimes a judge will ask you a question about the issue your co-counsel has already argued or will shortly argue. Try to answer it if you can, but qualify your answer by admitting that your co-counsel might be able to provide a better answer. This should minimize the chance that the judge will pursue the matter further.

Your Honor, because *Home Finders* dealt with the issue of sufficiency of money damages, my co-counsel might be the best person to assist the Court on this question. However, I believe that the court there held that . . . .

§23.5.9 *Handling a Question for Which You Do Not Have an Answer*

Your hard work should prepare you for most questions, but you might be asked a question for which you do not have an answer. A judge might ask you about a case or a statute with which you are not familiar, about how your issue compares to the comparable issue in some other area of law, or about how some particular procedural practice would affect your position. Even experienced appellate attorneys do not know all aspects of the law. If you do not know the answer to a judge's question, admit it. You can offer to find the answer and provide it to the court promptly after the argument concludes:

> Your Honor, I regret that I am not familiar with *Hatcher v. Norman*. However, if the Court allows, I will provide the Court with an answer to this question within twenty-four hours after today's argument concludes.

§23.5.10 *Agreeing When You Can*

Remember that you will probably receive a friendly question here and there, so do not automatically disagree each time the judge engages you. You can even agree partially with the concerns underlying some adversary questions as well, but go on to show why that valid concern does not defeat your position:

> Yes, Your Honor, I agree that this is a legitimate concern. However, . . .

§23.5.11 *Referring to Earlier Questions or Comments from the Bench*

Remember the questions directed to you or to your opponent; you can refer to them when appropriate in your argument. If a judge has asked you a friendly question or made a friendly comment, you can refer to it later in the argument. You can refer also to the adversarial questions or comments directed to opposing counsel.

> As Justice Bailey pointed out, . . .

Use this technique sparingly, however. Some judges might be irritated to hear their own words used in this manner more than once or, at most, twice during an argument.

§23.6 Presentation

§23.6.1 Dress

Wear a conservative suit.

§23.6.2 Body, Hands, and Eyes

Stand straight, with your weight equally placed on both feet, and remain behind the podium. Maintain eye contact with the judges, and include the whole bench in that eye contact. Do not read your argument. Rather, speak to the judges conversationally, looking down at your notes now and then. Lay your hands on the podium, and use them only moderately for occasional small gestures. Do not grip the podium. Do not put your hands in your pockets or clasp them behind your back.

§23.6.3 Voice

Speak at a moderate pace. Do not allow your nervousness to cause you to speak too quickly, but do speak with a degree of energy appropriate for discussion of an important matter about which you and your client care deeply. Speak firmly and loudly enough to be heard.

§23.6.4 References

Refer to the bench as "Your Honors" or "the Court." Refer to individual judges as "Your Honor" or "Justice [last name]." Refer to clients by their last name preceded by "Mr." or "Ms." or by other appropriate titles, such as "Dr." Refer to other lawyers as "counsel for Appellant/Appellee" or as "opposing counsel."

§23.6.5 Nervousness

Oral argument will probably make you a little nervous, but remember that judges are human beings. Like you, they are trying to do a hard job well, and they will sometimes fall short. Although they have more experience than you do at this point in your legal career, they probably remember when they did not. All they ask of you, and all you need ask of yourself, is to do your best.

CLIENT COUNSELING

Before reading this chapter and the chapters on client counseling that follow, please review the chapters in the section of your Fall Legal Practice text entitled: *Introduction to Client-Centered Lawyering.* The chapters in that section are a necessary foundation for this section about client counseling. In particular, before continuing, read the chapter entitled *What Happens When a Lawyer Counsels a Client.*

CHAPTER 24

PREPARING FOR COUNSELING: STRUCTURING THE OPTIONS

The process of preparation is outlined in the Fall textbook. You identify: the client's goals and preferences; gather and evaluate relevant information about both the law and the facts; generate alternative potential solutions that, to varying degrees, might accomplish those goals; and analyze the advantages, costs, risks, and chances of success of each potential solution.

§24.1 Focusing On Client Goals and Preferences

Transactional goals. Make sure that you have clear answers to the following questions: "What do you [the client] want to gain out of this transaction? What should we try to make sure that you get? How does this transaction fit into your overall plans for the future?"

Do not assume you know the client's goals. Even two clients who want the same kind of transaction might want it for very different reasons and therefore have very different goals. A client whom you are helping to buy land last week might have wanted it to preserve wilderness (you might have represented the Nature Conservancy). Another client whom you are helping to buy a different plot of land this week want it for reasons that would have the opposite effect (you might be representing a developer of shopping centers).

Clients who do not use lawyers very often are sometimes unsure of their goals and instead seem to have a vague feeling that the transaction at hand is just called for by the circumstances. This is especially frequent in estate planning. It sometimes helps to ask the client to imagine the scene after the transaction and its effects and consequences have run their course: "This may seem indelicate, but could I ask you to imagine how the people in your life would be managing if you were to pass away? What would be their needs? Is there anything you would like to do about what you imagine?" It can also help to mention the sorts of things that clients generally seem to want in such situations: "People with young children usually want to designate a guardian in case both parents pass away. Is that something you would want to do?"

Virtually all transaction clients will want to minimize any taxes or legal liability that might grow out of the transaction.

Dispute resolution goals. If the client has suffered a loss, what might she want? The possibilities include money or other measures to make up for that loss (damages, etc.); something that would prevent the defendant and others from causing similar losses in the future (punitive damages, an injunction, legislation); an official and public finding that the defendant acted wrongfully (a favorable judgment); and punishment for the defendant (punitive damages, publicity from the judgment). One client might want one or two of these things, while another client might want them all.

If the client is being sued or prosecuted, the primary goal usually is a successful defense. But the client might want more than a technical victory. The client might want victory in a form that clears the client's name. Often, a name-clearing victory can be gotten only with more risk — such as at trial — than a technical victory, which might come out of negotiations or pretrial motions that are hard for the public to understand.

Ranking client goals. You need to know how important each goal is to the client. Sometimes it is necessary to sacrifice what the client wants to get what the client needs. You are not in a position to counsel until you know where the client would draw the line between those two things.

Client preferences. A goal is what the client hired you to get. A preference is something the client would like you to do or not do while pursuing goals. "If you can avoid it, don't call my Aunt Sally as a witness" is a preference. The client did not hire you to prevent Aunt Sally from testifying. The client hired you to obtain something else and would prefer that the cost not include Aunt Sally's testimony. Some common client preferences include avoiding trials and other confrontations, avoiding taking time off from a job or other occupation, and avoiding publicity (although some clients want publicity). You can assume that all clients would prefer to get money owed to them sooner rather than later and to pay as little as possible in attorney's fees and other expenses.

Client preferences are important because they will affect each potential solution's value to the client. You need to know not only the preferences, but also how intense they are. There's a big difference between "If you can avoid it . . ." and "Under no circumstances . . ." And you need to know why the preference exists. One client might prefer to get money soon because, once invested, early money earns more in interest, dividends, and capital gains than late money does. Another client might prefer to get money soon to pay mounting medical bills — a much more compelling reason.

For many clients, the most important preference is represented by their tolerance or intolerance for risk (see §24.4).

§24.2 Developing Potential Solutions

Solutions do not leap out of a law book. The lawyer creates them by combining a number of raw ingredients. Some of the raw ingredients come from law books, and some come from common sense and an understanding of the business practicalities of the situation.

The lesson is this: Do not simply itemize the solutions that are obvious ("the law will let you do X, but it will not let you do Y"). Find ways to *create* solutions that — without your imagination and strategic skills — would not otherwise exist. More than anything else, that is what clients believe they are paying you to do.) may have special attractiveness for the client and are often the most long-lasting and satisfying solutions.

What clients want from you are practical solutions that produce good results. Do not limit yourself to how the law will treat the client. Think in bigger terms. Consider the people involved and their human needs. If money is involved, think about the wisest way to deal with it, taking into account all the costs and the way the relevant markets and financial institutions operate. Think in practical terms. Use good judgment and good common sense.

§24.3 Predicting What Each Potential Solution Would Cause

Ben Franklin said that complicated decisions are hard to make because:

> all the reasons pro and con are not present in the mind at the same time; but sometimes one set present themselves, and at other times another, the first being out of sight . . . [and] uncertainty . . . perplexes us.
>
> To get over this, my way is to divide half a sheet of paper by a line into two columns; writing over the one Pro, and over the other Con. Then, . . . I [write] down under the different head[ing]s short hints of the different motives, that at different times occur to me, for or against the measure. When I have thus got them all together in one view, I endeavor to estimate their respective weights . . . and thus proceeding I find at length where the balance lies. . . .
>
> And, though the weight of reasons cannot be taken with the precision of algebraic quantities, . . . when each is thus considered, separately and comparatively, and the whole lies before me, I think I can judge better, and am less liable to make a rash step. . . . [1]

This is solution-evaluation as explained in the Fall text. You estimate — in detail — the advantages, costs, risks, and chances of success of each option. That requires you to make predictions. You can express a prediction either in descriptive phrases (such as "a good chance of success" or "highly likely") or in numbers ("odds of about two out of three" or "a 50/50 chance of success"). Both methods have problems.

---

[1] Letter from Franklin to Joseph Priestley, from *The Benjamin Franklin Sampler* (1956).

Descriptive phrases might be too vague to be meaningful to the client, or even to you. An optimistic client might hear "the chances are good" to mean "we are definitely going to win." And how much probability do we have when there is "an excellent chance of success"? A client making one of the most important decisions of her life should want a more meaningful measurement of probability.

On the other hand, numbers can imply a precision that is not really there. Predictive estimates are by nature inexact, and a prediction that something is 65% likely to happen is not significantly different from a prediction that it is 60% or 70% likely to happen — although a client could easily think otherwise because you are using exact numbers. Unless you have done a detailed predictive analysis, it would be better to avoid predicting in percentage terms and instead limit yourself to more general statements expressed in fractions, such as "odds of three in four." Without a detailed predictive analysis using a decision tree or similar device, you cannot really be more accurate than odds expressed in fifths ("two chances in five"), and you should resist the temptation to use smaller fractions. The only exception is where you believe the odds are even: it's hard to say that without using a phrase like "a 50/50 chance."

Predicting is frightening business. How can you possibly assure a client that you know what the future will bring? You cannot, but you have to predict anyway. It might help to remember that every day trillions of dollars are invested, lent, or otherwise committed based on predictions of whether customers will like a product or hate it, whether stock prices or interest rates will rise or fall, whether Congress will do this or that, or even whether there will be lots of rain or only a little over the next few months in the wheat belt or the corn belt or the cotton belt or some other place where crops are grown. Many of those predictions turn out to be wrong. The earth will not swallow you up if a prediction you make turns out to be inaccurate. But people whose predictions tend mostly to be right gain the loyalty and respect of their clients, both in investing and in law.

Out of fear of being wrong, you may want to hedge, which might be either bad or good. One form of hedging — waffling — makes your advice less useful to a client, who must make a decision and needs the best prediction you are capable of. From the client's point of view if you waffle, you are not really predicting. Another form of hedging — adding qualifications or conditions — makes your prediction *more* precise because qualifications and conditions identify variables that might change and alter your prediction ("we stand less than a 50/50 chance at trial unless we can get the Britz letter into evidence").

Often, you will have to predict without complete knowledge of the facts or the law. Some facts might not become available to you until later, or only at some expense, or only after fighting with an adversary, or never. And as you know, some parts of the law are unsettled. When you predict, you need to identify not only what you know, but also what you do not know. And where you see a gap in knowledge, you need to define exactly how the gap would influence the prediction and estimate how and when that gap can be filled and how much it would cost to do so. (Sometimes the cost of filling the gap will exceed the value to be gained in making the prediction more accurate.)

Predictions cannot be set in stone. They evolve as you learn more about the facts and as other things change. Your prediction about the results at trial might change when you find out who the judge will be, and it might change again after you have chosen a jury. Even the law itself can change in the midst of your representation of a client. But when a client has to make a decision, the client has to work with the predictions you are able to make at the time the decision must be made.

To make a good decision, the client will need to know what variables might change enough to alter your prediction as well as any gaps in the facts or the law that qualify your prediction. If you fail to make these qualifications clear to a client, you risk the kind of misunderstanding that leads to ethics complaints and malpractice actions.

And your predictions should be frank and disinterested. If there is bad news, the client needs to know it. Hiding it from the client does neither her nor you a favor (and again, risks the kind of misunderstanding that can turn into an ethics complaint or a malpractice action).

You should be able to articulate a reason for each prediction. When you meet with the client, you will have to explain that reason. And if you force yourself to articulate it now, while preparing, your predictions will be more accurate because the act of articulating will force you to bring your unconscious thinking out in the open where you will notice its gaps and inconsistencies.

For two reasons, it may be a good idea to reduce to writing your predictions and the reasoning behind them. The first is preservation for the future, in case there is any later misunderstanding about the advice you gave the client. The second reason is that the act of writing improves the quality of the prediction. The writing process and the thinking process are inseparable. When an idea is spoken about, it might be half-formed, but if it is written about with care, it will have to become fully developed. The number of variables to be considered can make predictive judgments so complex that a lawyer can easily become lost unless thoughts can be worked out on paper. It is not unusual for a lawyer to start writing on the basis of a tentative prediction already made, only to find, after much writing — and rewriting — that the prediction "won't write" and must be changed. Depending on the complexity and importance of the issues, the writing could range from handwritten (but careful and complete) notes for the file to a formal office memorandum of law.

§24.3.1 *The Potential Solution's Chances of Achieving the Client's Goals*

Construct three scenarios for each option: the best case, the worst case, and the most likely case. Imagine the best result that could *reasonably* happen and the worst result that could reasonably happen. Neither of these should be far-fetched. They should define the range of what is genuinely possible — the range of things that really could happen to the client. Now imagine the result you think most likely to happen.

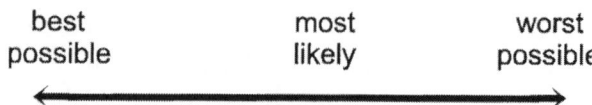

In especially important situations, you might want to construct five scenarios: the three above, plus two more that define a range of *probability*. What is the best result that would not surprise you? What is the worst result that would not surprise you?

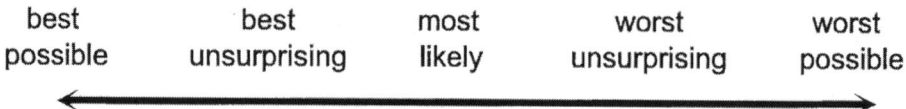

The range of outcomes that would not surprise you helps the client put your "most likely" scenario into a sharper context. What happens if your estimate of what is most likely turns out to be wrong? Into what range of probability will you and the client be falling back? In less important situations, you can dispense with the "best unsurprising" and "worst unsurprising" scenarios if you explain to the client that any prediction contains a plus-or-minus factor: your "most likely" prediction implies at least some margin of error on both sides.

Because legal reasoning is so difficult to learn, law school inadvertently encourages students to think formalistically — to think that courts will rule in a certain way once the legal tests have been satisfied. But in prediction, there is a step that comes after formal legal reasoning. After analogizing, distinguishing, focusing on policy, synthesizing fragmented authority, and reconciling conflicting or adverse authority, step back from what you are doing and test the result of your reasoning for realism. That requires taking into account how judges, juries, and administrative agencies think.

For issues to be decided by a judge, ask yourself whether the result you predict will seem right to the judge who will rule (if you know who that judge will be) or to the typical judge. The experience of adjudicating creates what Roscoe Pound called "the trained intuition of the judge,"[2] an instinct for how the law ought to treat each set of facts. If the result of your reasoning would strike the judicial mind as unrealistic and unreasonable, that mind will reject what you have done no matter how nice your reasoning is. Karl Llewellyn wrote that "rules *guide*, but they do not *control* decision. There is no precedent that the judge may not at his need either file down to razor thinness or expand into a bludgeon."[3] Or, put less delicately: judges first decide what they think is right and then dress it up with legal argument so that it looks presentable (although what they think is right can also be influenced by legal argument).

---

[2] Roscoe Pound, *The Theory of Judicial Decision*, 36 Harv. L. Rev. 940, 951 (1923).
[3] Karl N. Llewellyn, *The Bramble Bush* 180 (1930).

Llewellyn also wrote two other things that are particularly important here. The first is that law *as practicing lawyers know it* is "[w]hat officials [including judges] do about disputes"[4] — and not what statutes and cases say they should do about disputes. The second is that " 'rights' which cannot be realized are worse than useless; they are traps of delay, expense, and heartache."[5] Your client might seem to have rights under a literal reading of a statute, but if judges will find ways to rule otherwise, you will not help your client by counseling with false optimism.

Thus, you need to evaluate not only the strength and weakness of the case in terms of legal abstractions, but also predict what the actual court involved would decide. For example, in a high-volume eviction or consumer credit court, although case law may support the dismissal of a complaint for failure to plead a specific element, a particular trial judge may ignore this precedent to expedite the trial of cases. Or, in a criminal case, while appellate cases may strongly require the suppression of certain evidence, many trial court judges will find ways of ignoring this authority if a ruling to suppress would lead to dismissal of the case. These kinds of predictions are fairly easy if you have had experience with a particular judge or with typical local juries.

If you know who the judge will be but have never litigated before that judge, ask the advice of lawyers who have. Use Lexis or Westlaw to find and read the judge's opinions on similar issues. And visit the judge's courtroom to get a sense of her personality.

If you do not know who the judge will be, try to think realistically about judges and how they view the world. You might respond that all law school has taught you is legal argument and that you do not know any judges, or at least enough judges for you to be able to generalize about what they would do in the infinite variety of cases that clients will bring you. Certainly, it will take a long time for you to understand fully how "the trained intuition of the judge" operates. But you can, in a rudimentary way, test your predictions for realism by thinking of one or more persons you do know very well who seem typical of respected and responsible people in their 40's, 50's, and 60's (which is the age of most judges). It would help if these people were lawyers, but that is not essential. It is much more important that these people are instinctively responsible and that their good common sense naturally gains the respect of others. After you have worked out the legal reasoning, ask yourself how these people would react to the result you predict. Would they scoff at it? Or would they say that it is nice to see the law coming to the result it ought to? This is not going to give you the same feel for judicial realism that a good lawyer has after ten years of experience. But it can help you break out of the abstract view of law that legal education sometimes inadvertently encourages.

For issues to be decided by a jury, you have a different problem. Juries are randomly selected groups of people and often behave in unpredictable ways. But over time, juries from the same community tend to render verdicts in a range that roughly reflects some of the values of the community. And you can make

---

[4] *Id.* at 3.
[5] *Id.* at 9.

approximate predictions by (1) "determining the distribution of verdicts in similar claims" tried in the same community, (2) "adjusting the distributions of verdicts in similar claims to reflect the unique facts of" the client's claim, and (3) "adjusting the revised distribution to reflect transaction costs."[6] In addition, if the client is deciding whether to settle or go to trial, the two options have to be compared in terms of expected value, the time value of money, and the effect of taxes. All of this is explained below.

How do you find out what *verdicts juries have returned in similar cases?* Lawyers who practice in large urban areas can subscribe to verdict reporting services. There are also some national services,[7] but the verdicts they report might be more or less generous to plaintiffs than juries typical of your community might return. If you are on the defense side of a tort action and are being paid by an insurance company, the company itself might have a database on past jury verdicts. If none of these sources produces the information you need, you might ask the advice of a lawyer who has long experience litigating your kind of case in your community.[8] In predicting personal injury verdicts, some attorneys use "rule of thumb" formulas such as "three times specials" or other multiples of the plaintiff's out-of-pocket expenses. In many instances, these rough estimates ignore the unique facts in the case and over-simplify.[9]

Once you have gotten data on other jury verdicts, how do you *adjust to get something comparable to your case?* Ask yourself the following questions: Are the facts of your case more or less favorable than the facts of prior verdicts? Are the injuries being remedied more or less egregious than the injuries in your case? How do the jurisdictions and communities involved compare with yours? (Other jurisdictions might have different law, and other communities might produce different kinds of jurors.) How recent are the verdicts you are comparing to your case? In some communities, juries have over time grown more generous to plaintiffs, while in others the opposite has happened. And how many verdicts are you comparing? The smaller the number, the less reliable the sample is as a basis for prediction. The most reliable sample would be a large one in which most of the juries appear to be behaving consistently with one another.

§24.3.2 *Transaction Costs, Expected Value, the Time Value of Money, and Tax*

Suppose you predict that the jury will return a verdict for your client, the plaintiff, of $100,000; that the judge will enter a judgment in your client's favor in

---

[6] Peter Toll Hoffman, *Valuation of Cases for Settlement: Theory and Practice*, 1991 J. Disp. Resol. 1, 7. The next few paragraphs in the text rely heavily on pages 10–31 of Professor Hoffman's thorough article.

[7] See, for example, Association of Trial Lawyers of America, Jury Verdicts & Settlements (available in the Lexis Verdict library) and National Jury Review & Analysis (available in the Lexis Verdict library).

[8] If you have to go outside your law firm to get this kind of advice, you might have to pay for it. You are taking up another lawyer's time, although some lawyers will talk to you informally for free as a professional courtesy.

[9] Donald G. Gifford, *Legal Negotiation: Theory and Applications* 53 (1989).

that amount; and that the defendant will lose any appeal. Should your client start looking for ways to spend $100,000? Suppose the defendant makes an offer to settle now for $65,000. Which is more valuable — a $100,000 judgment in the future or $65,000 now?

To understand the value today of a predicted gain of money in the future, or to compare a predicted future gain of money with a competing possible gain of money now, or to know how much of a gain can be kept, your calculations need to take into account four facts of financial life:

1. it costs money to get money (*transaction costs*), and those expenses reduce the value of a financial gain;
2. unless you are 100% confident that a future gain will occur, its real value today (its *expected value*) is reduced because of doubt;
3. the value of money differs over time (the *time value of money*) because future money will suffer from inflation and because money you have now could be invested and grow in the future; and
4. whenever money changes hands, a government might — or might not — take some of it to pay for things like streets, schools, and national defense (*tax*).

Let's consider each of these concepts as well as how to use them.

Transaction costs.   How do you adjust to reflect transaction costs? The most obvious transaction cost is what the client would have to pay to go to trial and get the verdict you predict. How much would the client have to pay you, and how much would your client have to pay for things like expert witnesses and deposition transcripts? (These estimates merit precision, at least within a range. When a lawyer gives an off-the-cuff guess and costs steadily mount until they greatly exceed that guess, the client can justifiably become distrustful and angry.) If there is an appeal, how much would the client have to pay to defend the verdict? If the client is a plaintiff and if the judgment would not be chargeable to an insurance company or some other party that promptly satisfies judgments, how much would the client have to pay to enforce the judgment you predict? (Some defendants go to elaborate lengths to hide their assets.) For that matter — and this is critically important — do you have good reason to believe that the defendant actually has the assets or insurance to satisfy the judgment you predict? And how much of the client's own time and effort would all this litigation consume? Some transaction costs are not financial. An example is the emotional drain of being a litigant.

Expected value.   If you have a lottery ticket that will pay $5 million, its value as you walk away from the lottery counter is much less than $5 million because your odds of winning are low. If a total of ten million tickets have been sold, your ticket is worth fifty cents, computed by the future payout multiplied by your chances of getting it ($5 million multiplied by 1/10,000,000 or 0.0000001). If you paid a dollar for the ticket, a financial analyst would tell you that you paid more than it was worth. But if only two tickets have been sold, which means that your odds of winning are 50%, your one dollar ticket is worth $2.5 million ($5 million multiplied by 0.50).

But if you win, you get $5 million, and if you lose, you get nothing. Why is the expected value more than nothing and less than $5 million — the only two things that could happen in the future? (Either you will get $5 million or you will get nothing.) The reason is that we need some way of assigning value to a speculative gain, and the math outlined above is used in a wide variety of situations — from valuing frequent flyer miles to valuing a company's legal claim against another company when the first company is being sold and its assets (including legal claims against others) need to be assessed.

A predicted verdict can be compared to a proposed settlement by computing the expected value of the verdict. If you predict that there are two chances in three that a jury would return a verdict in a plaintiff's favor, and that such a verdict would be for $100,000, the verdict's expected value is $67,000. This is more meaningful to frequent litigants such as insurance companies, because over time their bets even out. But it can still be meaningful to an individual client who otherwise would have no real way of comparing the worth and risk of a predicted verdict with the certainty of a settlement offer.

The time value of money.   Money's value differs over time. Money delivered now is worth more than the same amount delivered later because the money you get now can be invested and will grow in the meantime. If the client is choosing between going to trial and accepting a settlement offer, you have to estimate how long it would take to get payment on a judgment and what investment income the amount offered in settlement would earn in the meantime. A safe assumable investment income is the current annualized rate paid by Treasury bills or money market funds, which can be found in the business sections of daily newspapers.

Suppose you believe the most likely result at trial would be a $100,000 judgment in favor of the client, the plaintiff, who would not receive that money until three years from now. What is the present value of that $100,000? We will ignore temporarily the other three variables: transaction costs, expected value, and tax. In other words, we are assuming that attorney's fees and other expenses are not being paid by the client, that the odds of winning the $100,000 are 100%, and that no part of it will be taxed. Realistically, there will be transaction costs, the odds will be less than 100%, and there might be tax. But the only way to illustrate present value is to ignore the other variables — temporarily. Let's also assume that a relatively risk-free investment would earn 6% interest annually over the next three years.

The present value of $100,000 under these circumstances is $83,962. Put another way, if today you invested $83,962 at 6% interest, compounded annually, you would have $100,000 in three years. (More frequent compounding would change that, but we are trying to keep the illustration simple.) Here's the formula for computing the present value of a future amount:

$$FV \ divided \ by \ (1+i)^n = PV$$

If you are mathphobic, don't panic. We'll walk you through this. Here's what the abbreviations mean: FV = future value; i = the interest rate; n = the number of years between now and the future payment; and PV = present value. Now here's the formula applied to the $100,000 judgment that we are convinced our client will get in three years

$$\$100,000 \ divided \ by \ (1 + 0.06 = 1.06)^3 = \$83,962$$

Here's the same calculation in words: Add 0.06 (6%) to 1 to get 1.06. Multiply 1.06 by 1.06 by 1.06 (because of the three years) to get 1.191016. Do *not* multiply 1.06 by 3. That's because the interest will *compound* annually. Divide $100,000 by 1.191016 to get $83,962.

Business calculators (which cost a little more than ordinary pocket calculators) and spreadsheets will do this calculation for you, but if you are mathphobic you might have a hard time understanding their instructions. If you don't have a business calculator and don't know how to use a spreadsheet, just follow the formula above.

Tax.   Because some kinds of awards are taxed and others are not, the effect of taxes might be different depending on how a case is settled. In a verdict, the client is taxed according to the kind of award the jury provides. For example, compensatory damages for personal physical injury or property loss are not taxable. But the client will pay taxes on damages for breach of contract, compensation for lost income, or punitive damages. In a negotiated settlement, on the other hand, the parties can sometimes limit the taxes one or both of them will pay.

For example, suppose a plaintiff has sued for $120,000 in compensatory damages for personal physical injury and $80,000 in punitive damages. The defendant is willing to settle for half of the total $200,000 sought by the plaintiff. If the parties agree to allocate that settlement proportionately between the two categories of damages — producing $60,000 in compensatory damages for personal physical injury and $40,000 in punitive damages — the plaintiff will pay federal income taxes (and possibly state income taxes as well) on $40,000 because punitive damages are taxable. But if all of the settlement is allocated to compensatory damages, and if the evidence supports compensatory damages in the range of $100,000, the plaintiff will pay no federal income tax on any of the settlement because compensatory damages for personal physical injury are not taxable.

Although you may be able to reduce taxes by the way you develop options, the converse can be frightening. If you *ignore* the tax consequences of the options you offer a client in counseling, you commit malpractice. And a client who later must pay a surprising tax bill will be highly motivated to sue you.

If the options are valued in monetary terms, even only partially, you *must* do the math to determine what each option is really worth. For example, if in a damages lawsuit the client will decide whether to accept a settlement offer or go to trial, the client has no way of choosing between the two unless you place a value — in *numbers of dollars* — on each option.

To do the math, you need to answer two questions. *Is it taxed?* And if so, *at what rate?* Some income is taxed by the federal government at 15%; other income is taxed at well over 30%. For federal tax, the ultimate answers to these questions are in the tax code, IRS regulations, and cases interpreting them, although reading a tax service, like CCH's, will usually give you the answers faster. For state tax, the answers are in state tax statutes, regulations, and cases.

Let's go back to the question posed at the beginning of this question: which is financially more valuable — the $100,000 judgment we predict or the $65,000 offer to settle? The client has suffered a physical injury, which means that compensation for it will not be taxed. The contingency fee agreement provides that attorney's fees will be 25% of a negotiated settlement and 33% of a judgment achieved through trial. (There are a few other transaction costs, but they are small enough that we can ignore them in this illustration.) The predicted judgment minus transaction costs is $67,000 ($100,000 times 0.67, which is what's left after deducting your 0.33). Using the formula illustrated above, the present value of $67,000 is $56,254. Suppose that you believe the likelihood of that verdict is three chances in four, or 75%. The expected value of the judgment is $42,191 (0.75 times $56,254).

The $65,000 settlement offer is immediate (it already is a present value), certain (it has 100% expected value), and as tax-free as the judgment. The only thing to deduct is transaction costs of 25%, which reduce its real value to the client to $48,750 ($65,000 times 0.75). That is more — but not dramatically more — that the $42,191 value we assigned to the predicted judgment.

All of this ignores other, nonfinancial considerations, such as the client's feelings about risk, the emotional toll and client effort required by further litigation, the client's need for or fear of public adjudication, and other factors listed below in §24.3.3. They may be more important to the client than the exact amounts of money involved. But doing these calculations is the only way we can assign numerical values to separate financial options that differ in likelihood, time of delivery, and transaction costs. Sometimes, they will also differ in tax consequences.

§24.3.3 Side-Effects — Desirable and Undesirable

In dispute resolution counseling, consider the following:

- Would a lawsuit or other confrontational option disrupt relationships the client considers important? Would it give the adversary an opportunity to impugn the client's character? If the client's honesty or another character trait could be made an issue, you can be sure that the adversary will do so.
- Would continued conflict build up stress to a level that the client would want to be relieved of? Most individual clients experience litigation as "emotional turmoil,"[10] but some do not care.
- Could litigation compound harm the client has already suffered? For example, if the client has been defamed, but the damage to reputation has been limited to a small circle of people, litigation — and especially a trial — could give the defamatory claims much wider circulation.
- Could a verdict provide a public vindication important to the client?

---

[10] *Id.* at 33.

- Is vengeance ("making them pay") important to the client? One of law's functions is give people an avenue of vengeance more socially acceptable than murder or mayhem. But there are limits. You learned in first-year Civil Procedure that in federal court you may not use a paper filed in court "for any improper purpose, such as to harass or to cause unnecessary delay or needless increase in the cost of litigation."[11] Nearly all state courts have similar provisions. And ethical rules everywhere impose other constraints and provide mechanisms for you to decline to pursue client goals under some circumstances.

- If the client is a frequent litigant (such as an insurance company) or an attractive target for litigation (such as a newspaper that aspires to print the truth no matter whom it offends), is it important to force plaintiffs to trial in order to discourage the impression that the client is a "soft touch"?

- In a criminal case in which the client is being offered a plea bargain, what problems, aside from the sentence itself, would the resulting conviction or other disposition cause the client? Does the client risk deportation or loss of a license or a job?

Finally, consider the moral dimension. We are too used to assuming that when people act in their own self-interest, they will act selfishly. In a world where material success and conspicuous consumption are so important, people are led to believe that in many situations, especially where lawyers are involved, maximizing their own gain is what they are *supposed* to do. But for more clients than you might suppose, doing the morally right thing can be in their own self-interest. Being fair or even generous can be a pleasure for its own sake, and for some clients it can introduce a degree of inner peace into an experience that might otherwise be more distressful. Years after the decision the client is about to make, will the client feel guilt, shame, or a loss of self-respect remembering how others suffered because the client chose to maximize her own gain? Or, if the client tries to do the morally right thing now, will the client look back on it later with satisfaction?

Some clients are open to this kind of counseling, while others are not. The best way to find out how a client will react is to raise the subject gradually. For example, you might point out the ways in which another person in the dispute or transaction will suffer if the client chooses a certain option and then ask whether that is something the client wants to consider. The answer, and the tone and body language that accompany it, will tell you whether it is worth continuing down that path.

§24.4 Adapting To the Client's Tolerance For Risk

Some people will bet small amounts of money — $5 on a lottery ticket or $25 on the office World Series or Superbowl pool. Some people will not bet at all; they have no taste for it, or it violates their convictions. Some people feel comfortable staking relatively large bets, such as $1,000 in a poker game. Some people bet with money they cannot afford to lose.

---

[11] Fed. R. Civ. P. 11(b)(1).

If you think of gambling as limited to lotteries, office pools, poker, and the like, you will probably say that you do not gamble often or that you never gamble. But the fact is that every time you make a decision based on a prediction of the future, you are gambling.

You gamble every day in small ways. If it takes you 20 minutes to drive to school and if your first class of the day is with a teacher who will not tolerate tardiness, you're gambling that you will have no trouble finding a parking space when you leave home 25 minutes before class. And you have gambled in big ways. When you decided to go to law school, you were gambling that you would enjoy the work and that it would pay what you need or want to earn.

We win a lot of the small gambles of everyday life, but we also lose a lot of them. In the end, it doesn't matter much because both the benefits of winning and the costs of losing are not terribly great. You're embarrassed if you walk into class five minutes late, and the embarrassment might cause you to stop making that particular gamble. But you still have your family and friends, your net worth is unchanged, and you have not significantly added to the amount of injustice in the world. Even if you win, what have you won? Maybe an extra five minutes at home.

The big gambles are much more frightening. What happens if after graduation you find that there are things about the practice of law that you cannot stand? If you lose this gamble, the cost in time and money could be staggering. On the other hand, if you win this gamble, you might acquire the largest thing most people could own: an emotionally satisfying career that also produces a lifetime of reasonable income.

A person who is comfortable making substantial bets is said to have a high tolerance for risk. This might be either realistic or foolish. Some investment managers and some bettors at horse races know how to find the long shot that pays off. There are also others who think they know how to do that but really do not have the skill.

Most people do not have high tolerances for risk. They might instead have a medium amount of tolerance, only a little, or none at all. Sometimes this reflects a prudent reluctance to bet things that one cannot afford to lose. Sometimes it just reflects fear.

Tolerance for risk decreases as the stakes get bigger. A person who will casually bet $20 on a horse race might be a lot more hesitant if three zeros were added to that amount. And the size of the stake is always relative. To some people with very large financial resources, even a $20,000 bet is not significant enough to cause anxiety. And to others in precarious circumstances, $20 can be a lot of money.

Whatever the client's tolerance for risk, it is entitled to your respect. The client, after all, must live with the consequences of the decision long after you have disappeared from the client's life. (You do, however, have an obligation to point out the disadvantages of betting to clients with high tolerances for risk and the disadvantages of not betting to clients with low tolerances.)

How can you structure the options to take the client's level of tolerance into account? First, you can make sure that the menu of choices you offer addresses the client's level of tolerance. If you offer four risky options and one safe one to a client who has a low tolerance, your creativity may have been focused on the wrong end of the scale. Might there have been more than one safe option?

Second, if money or something else quantifiable is at the heart of the matter, you can calculate the expected value of each option. (See §24.3.1.)

Third, you can help a client understand whether her or his tolerance for risk is realistic *in this situation*. A client with a high tolerance who wants to make an unrealistic gamble might gain insight if you explain that you think most clients would not bet that steeply against the odds, and *why* most clients would not do that. (But do not claim more than you know. If you do not have much experience with client decision-making, ask a senior attorney whether most clients would make that bet.) On the other hand, it might be overbearing, if not oppressive, to tell a person with a low tolerance for risk that most clients would make a bet the client does not want to make.

§24.5 Why Do Some Clients Exclude Their Lawyers From Important Decisions?

Lani Guinier tells the following story about a construction company, Bovis General Contractors, and an office building:

> Before beginning construction, but after the contracts were formally negotiated by the lawyers, a team from Bovis arranged a meeting attended by the [future] owners of the building, the architects, the engineers, and those who would be using the building. The Bovis team encouraged those present to identify important issues at the outset. Everyone agreed they wanted the project to come in on time and under budget; to meet the needs of the building's users; and to lead to long-term relationships with each of the other parties.
>
> Most poignant is that these business people *did not invite lawyers* to their meeting. The lawyers negotiated the contract under which everyone was operating, but the [meeting] participants negotiated duties without ever referring to or consulting [that] contract. . . . The lawyers' approach, which is understandably based on avoiding client [liability] in the event things go awry, often forecloses the *human interaction* — the pleasant exchanges and gestures — *which assure that things go right*. Indeed, *Bovis boasts that it has never had a lawsuit filed when it leaves lawyers out of the room and negotiates interpersonal agreements among the participants themselves.*[12]

Some clients believe that lawyers listen too little, dominate conversations, poison relationships by generating conflict, and raise objections when they should be developing solutions. Business people call this kind of lawyer a "deal killer" — a lawyer who can sabotage a deal the client really wants. Why do some lawyers behave this way? Here are some possibilities:

First, some lawyers think bureaucratically, dividing everything into what is legal and what is illegal, even though a large gray area, where the law is unclear, exists between the plainly legal and the plainly illegal. An early twentieth-century lawyer named Elihu Root is often cited for the statement that most of the practice of law is telling clients that they are acting like fools and should stop. There is some truth in

---

[12] Lani Guinier, *Lessons and Challenges of Becoming Gentlemen*, 24 Rev. of L. & Soc. Change 1, 13–14 (1998) (emphasis added).

that, and a wise lawyer knows how to deliver that kind of advice in a way the client can accept. But perhaps a more important quote is this: "I don't want a lawyer to tell me what I cannot do; I hire him to tell me *how* to do what I want to do." That quote has an unattractive reputation because of the person who said it — J. P. Morgan, a robber-baron financier who was a contemporary of Root. But stripped of that association, it actually states what all clients want from their lawyers — not just the rich and powerful but also clients who are oppressed by society.

Second, some lawyers — especially inexperienced ones — do not know when or how to take risks, even necessary ones. Business people cannot make money without taking risks, and the most effective business people are good at separating profitable risks from pointless ones. People at the top of large organizations (such as generals) can sometimes feel the same way, even where profit is not an issue (as in the Army), because they can see the bigger picture and more easily balance need against risk.

Third, law school teaches students how to read cases and statutes, but not necessarily how to solve problems. Our job is to "find" or *create solutions*. We should say no only when there truly are no viable solutions. Lawyers who say no too easily need to develop solution-generation skill. Clients view them as obstructionists. A few students go to the opposite extreme: they confidently propose off-the-wall solutions that have almost no chance of success. These students might be good at solution-generation but not at solution-evaluation.

Fourth, law school so emphasizes shooting down ideas that some students may think that that is the heart of what lawyers are paid to do. But shooting down potentially valuable ideas makes a lawyer a destructive presence rather than a constructive one. Some business people say that when confronted with an idea that has some faults, the bureaucratic mind will reject it to avoid risk while the entrepreneurial mind will find a way to improve it to create an opportunity. By that measure, the lawyer who reflexively shoots down every idea with a fault in it subtracts value from a situation rather than adding it.

CHAPTER 25

THE COUNSELING MEETING WITH THE CLIENT

§25.1 Mood, Setting, and the Lawyer's Affect

A client who is making a momentous decision will be presented with a large amount of information while under stress. Remembering that *how* you say something has an enormous effect on how people respond, what should you be careful about in this situation?

Involve the client so that you have a genuine conversation. This is collaborative decision-making. Do not be a talking head. Suppose you are at home, looking at the television, surfing channels with the remote control in your hand. On the screen you see two or three people sitting in easy chairs in a television studio, talking about the great issues of the day. How long will you watch this before moving on to the next channel? They might be marveling at the recent discovery of an unlimited number of superb jobs for recent law school graduates in a place with a wonderful climate and local laws that make student loans uncollectible. Why, as soon as you see the talking heads, will you change the channel so fast that you will never learn of this remarkable place? Because, like most people, you dislike being put in a passive position while somebody talks at you.

In client counseling, a lawyer who is a talking head might explain the choices nonstop for perhaps a half hour and then ask the client whether she has any questions. The client then says her first word: "No." The lawyer concludes by saying, "Well, go home, think about it, and call me when you've decided."

Be an active listener, using all the techniques you learned.

Give the client helpful respect. You may know some things the client does not, but the client hired you, can fire you, and therefore is your boss. Moreover, the client has to live with the consequences of this decision long after you have forgotten about it.

Why do some lawyers forget this and patronize clients? "[I]n almost every advisory relationship, the client is usually untrained in the professional's specialty, while the professional may have seen the client's problem (or variants of it) many times before. There is thus an almost natural tendency to come across to the client as patronizing, pompous, and arrogant. . . . Although advising clients sometimes feels like explaining things to a child, the secret to becoming a good adviser is to do exactly the opposite: Act as if you were trying to advise your mother or father . . . with immense amounts of respect. . . ."[1]

Consider in advance how you will explain legal concepts and terminology. If you try to find the right words off the cuff, they will either be incomprehensible or sound condescending. You want plain words that accurately describe the concept without implying that you are talking down to the client. Compare three examples, the second of which flunks these criteria:

1. A doctor, speaking to a patient with a neurological disorder.

You feel a tingling in your knee sometimes, but nothing is really happening in the knee. When that tingling happens, it is because of something going on in your brain. Every part of your body is controlled by nerves that report to some specific part of your brain. The nerves use low levels of electricity to report, and your brain also uses low levels of electricity. The part of your brain that controls your knee sometimes has a kind of short-circuit in which the brain thinks it has received a signal from the knee, but it hasn't. That part of your brain, which is very small, probably has been slightly damaged in some way. But even if that weren't true, the brain can still fool itself. People who have had a leg amputated sometimes report that shortly afterward they can still feel their toes wiggling.

2. A lawyer, speaking to a client who owns a gas station and who has just been served with a temporary restraining order.

A TRO can be granted while a motion for a preliminary injunction is pending for the purpose of preserving the status quo until the motion can be decided. You have been restrained from selling gasoline from the pumps alleged by the Department of Environmental Protection to be an environmental hazard, and violation of the order is punishable as a contempt. The order is effective until it is vacated, which probably will not be before the court decides the pending motion for a preliminary injunction, which has a return date of next Friday.

3. Another lawyer, conveying the same information to the same client.

A judge can command you not to do something for a short period, which is what has happened here through this order, which lawyers call a temporary restraining order or TRO. This TRO orders you not to sell gas from the pumps that the DEP complained to you about last week. If you do that anyway, the judge can make you pay a fine or even lock you up in jail. The DEP has also asked for another kind of order called a preliminary injunction, which would do the same thing but for a much longer period of time. The judge has not given DEP a preliminary injunction, although she might do so later. The TRO — the order that was delivered to

---

[1] David H. Maister, *How to Give Advice*, The American Lawyer, Mar. 1997 57, 57–58.

you yesterday — will last until the judge decides whether to issue the other order, the preliminary injunction. We go to court on that next Friday, but the judge will not decide on that day.

Do doctors usually talk to you the way the doctor in the first example does? Do you wish they would? In the third example, has the client been given all the information contained in the second example? Is the third example more clear to a client?

Do not talk to a client using words you would say to another lawyer. Clients want you to respect their intelligence but to use words that nonlawyers can understand. This requires careful forethought. Before you sit down with a client, ask yourself what words will most clearly communicate to the client the legal situation.

Ignore your own emotional needs.   Do not show off. Be patient even if you have a lot of other things to do. If the meeting is taking longer than you thought it would and if you are due in court or elsewhere, break off the meeting and reschedule as soon as possible. Do not try to do an hour job in a half hour.

Explain the options neutrally.   Remember everything you've already learned about client-centered lawyering. Do not let your wording or body language convey that you like some options better than others. That would put pressure on the client to make a choice she might not make otherwise. If the client wants your recommendation, the client will ask for it (see §25.4 for how to answer that question). If the client has not asked for your recommendation, keep it to yourself and do not even hint at it.

Give the client empathy.   If you were in the client's position, you would want the person advising you to be supportive and understanding, but you would not want that person to be unctuous and insincere about it.

Face the harsh facts.   If the client gets an unrealistically optimistic picture, the decision will probably be the wrong one. And clients poorly advised in this way are tempted later to consider ethics complaints and malpractice actions.

Use an appropriate seating arrangement.   You should not be behind a desk, where you look authoritative, distant, and uninterested. (If you were interested, why would you put a big piece of furniture between you and the client?) Sit together at a conference table or in chairs together so you can talk close at hand. The best seating arrangement lets you and the client look at pieces of paper at the same time. The seating arrangement should allow you to use a large note pad or a whiteboard on the wall or an easel, or some other way of outlining the options visually.

§25.2 Beginning the Meeting

When scheduling the meeting, you undoubtedly told the client what decision you would be asking the client to make, and you probably also explained the reason for the decision and its importance (unless the client already knew anyway). If not, now is the time to do so. Even if you have said these things before, it helps focus the client's attention if you at least summarize them as you begin the meeting.

Depending on how experienced the client is in dealing with lawyers, you should explain that this is the client's decision; why it should be the client's decision; how you can help the client make the decision by framing choices and working out their advantages, costs, risks, and chances for success; and how you and the client can work together at doing this. You can dispense with much of these explanations with repeat business clients, who would find them pedantic. But if a client has dealt with lawyers only infrequently, or has dealt in the past with lawyers who have not been very good counselors, the client might really need an orientation.

Before explaining the choices, make sure that you have understood the client's goals and that they have not recently changed. If they have, you will need to adapt. If they have changed greatly, you may be able to do only some of the counseling job in this meeting because you may need a break to prepare some things anew.

If any facts or aspects of the law will dominate the decision, you can describe them to the client (or remind the client of them if she already knows). Do not give a detailed recitation unless the client asks for it. (You are trying to avoid being a talking head.) But if something will be a theme from option to option, it helps to explain it early.

Warn the client against premature judgment. Brainstorming will happen only if the client keeps an open mind.

Then, simply outline the options, letting the client see the outline on paper or on a whiteboard. Describe each one only enough so that the client knows what it is. Then go on to the next option. (Do not evaluate the options yet. You are just trying to give the client an overview before you go into the details.) In what sequence should you mention the options? Put yourself in the client's position and ask yourself which sequence would help this client understand the nature of the decision. For example, you might start with the options the client already knows about and work toward the ones that would be news to the client. Or you might start with the most serious options and then mention the more marginal ones.

In preparing for this meeting, you worked out in detail each option's advantages, costs, risks, and chance of success. The client can better see how these all fit together if you show the client something visual. It can be as simple as a handwritten list on a notepad. If the choices and their ramifications are complicated, you might want it typed to get everything on a single page. (If the client has to turn from one page to the next, the big picture can disappear.)

Afterward, ask the client whether she sees any additional options. Clients can be pretty creative about this. Sometimes they can change some of your ideas into new and additional potential solutions. Sometimes they can remember ideas that you have mentioned in the past but have unaccountably forgotten about now. (Your memory is not perfect.) And sometimes they can think of potential solutions that have escaped you. Clients are closer to the problem than you are, and many of them spend more time than you can thinking about the problem.

You are now ready to explain each choice's advantages, costs, risks, and chances of success.

§25.3 Discussing the Choices and What They Would Do

The best transition is to ask the client which options she would like to talk about first. If the client has no preference, you might discuss them in the same sequence in which you introduced them earlier.

Brainstorming with a client is different from brainstorming with another lawyer. Many clients will assume that their problem-solving skills are inferior to yours, and they will need your encouragement to believe otherwise. The best encouragement is not flattery, but instead a sincere interest in how the client thinks and feels about the problem and how it might be resolved. Treat the client as an equal whose views you respect.

Seek additional insights from the client frequently. Every time you find yourself finishing some aspect of a particular option (its risks, for example), ask the client whether she sees something else. If the client offers something, ask again until the answer, finally, is no. A person with several related pieces of information will usually offer them only one at a time when being asked questions. If you ask once, get one piece of information, and then go onto something else, the client might not tell you the others. After going through all the options, you might ask the client whether any new ones have occurred to her during the conversation. Do not be surprised if the answer is yes.

Be clear about what will happen upon success or loss. Suppose your client has read in the newspaper of multimillion dollar jury verdicts. You have drafted a complaint seeking two million dollars in damages. You fail to tell the client that a complaint customarily asks for the most the lawyer thinks the client could possibly get from a jury. You also do not tell the client that a typical jury verdict in this kind of case would be less than half a million; that local judges might reduce a verdict like that by one-third or even one-half; that nothing will be paid during the pendency of an appeal; and that a reasonable settlement offer by the other side — before or after a verdict — would probably be less than you predict that a jury would award. By failing to tell your client all this, you are not treating your client fairly, and you are asking for trouble.

Also be clear about what your efforts will cost the client. For the client, cost is not limited to your fee. In litigation, the client will also have to pay some itemizeable costs within your office (photocopying and messenger expenses, for example, and perhaps fees for court reporters at depositions). The client also might have to pay court costs. And even in regard to your fee, when does it end? Many clients are astonished to learn that even if they win at trial, they will have to keep paying your hourly rate while the other side appeals.

There are also less tangible costs to the client — in time, missed vacations, annoyed employers, and pure stress. Intangible costs are too often overlooked in counseling. Clients who have never been litigants sometimes find it hard to imagine the frustrations and anxiety litigants suffer, or the ways in which the opposing side in litigation might try to impugn their motives or character.

§25.4 If the Client Asks For a Recommendation, Should You Give One?

In the client-centered lawyering explained, the lawyer helps, but the client decides. In counseling, that means laying out the choices neutrally — without telling the client which ones you like.

This book assumes that most clients want client-centered counseling, and that client-centered counseling produces better decisions. Some clients, however, really do want to be counseled in a different and more traditional way, and a client is entitled to have advice given in a style with which the client is comfortable. If the client is uninterested in an array of options and wants to focus immediately on the one you would recommend, you should try to persuade the client to choose without your recommendation.

But if the client persists and wants your recommendation at the beginning, then the client is making a decision about how she wants to be counseled, and that decision is one you should respect. But be very careful not to let your own needs — your ego or your tight schedule — delude you about what a client really wants. *If it is absolutely clear, despite your attempts to persuade otherwise, that this really is what the client feels most comfortable with,* you should counsel the client in the manner the client prefers. In client-centered lawyering, the client is, after all, the boss. Recommend a solution while explaining its benefits and drawbacks, but mention the alternatives and explain why they are worth considering.

Clients who want to hear *only* your recommendation tend, paradoxically, to be either sophisticated or unsophisticated.

Some unsophisticated clients might not function well in a participatory relationship with a professional and might want guidance from an authority figure in the old tradition where "[t]he client is expected to stand by passively while the lawyer lays out what he considers to be all the relevant legal considerations and selects for the client's rubber-stamping the course of action" that the lawyer thinks best.[2] But, in our experience, that is *not* true of most unsophisticated clients. Some unsophisticated clients have very good problem-solving skills which you will, with pleasure, learn to respect. For some, brainstorming with you is an opportunity to awaken skills and thus gain some mastery and empowerment. And for some, when you presume to recommend, your "opinions may tend to silence and dominate"[3] — rather than enlighten.

At the opposite extreme, a repeat business client who has dealt with lawyers often and who knows you and trusts your judgment might not want to hear about other options because she is confident that the one you would recommend is the best one. Successful business people know how to use time efficiently, and to them a 30-minute conversation seems to be a mistake if a 5-minute conversation would yield the same result.

---

[2] Martin J. Solomon, *Client Relations: Ethics and Economics*, 23 Ariz. St. L.J. 155, 181 (1991).
[3] Robert D. Dinerstein, *Clinical Texts and Contexts*, 39 UCLA L. Rev. 697, 710 (1992).

Only with caution should you accede to a client's preference for "recommendation only" counseling. Three things disappear when you give your recommendation and mention the alternatives only as an afterthought.

The first is an opportunity to brainstorm the options with the client. Not only are two minds better than one, but the client usually knows more than you do about some or most of the factual situation as well as the kinds of solutions the client feels more comfortable with. If you suspect that brainstorming might improve the options in a significant way, say something like: "If we can work together for a few minutes to think about the options, it might be a good investment of time. Before I make a recommendation, I want to be sure about the situation."

The second is a process that can give both you and the client assurance that the right decision is being made. People sometimes think of a process as an inconvenient thing one has to go through in order to get a certain result. But a good process often has its own value even if the same result might be obtained without it. Among other things, a good process creates or deepens confidence that the result is the best one available.

For example, you meet with a client on a Monday. At the client's request, you state your recommendation, and the meeting lasts only ten minutes because the client makes a fast decision on the spot. On Tuesday, you and the client act on that decision, and the action is irrevocable. (No matter how hard you try, you will never be able to undo it.) On Wednesday and Thursday, lots of unexplored issues keep popping into the client's mind. Finally, on Friday, the client cannot stand it any longer and calls you, listing all these issues for you. You explain how, although they are reasonable concerns, none of them would change your recommendation. You have very good reasons, and the client is completely persuaded. After that conversation, the client thinks of a few more unexplored issues. The client might call you again. Or the client might be too embarrassed to do so and might go for a very long time wondering whether what you recommended was really the right thing to do.

Some lawyers would dismiss this client as antsy, but the real problem is that you did not insist on a process that was thorough enough to give this client confidence from the very beginning that your recommendation was the right thing to do. Some things are too important to be settled on your recommendation, even if at the time that is how the client wants to handle decision-making.

The third thing that disappears when you give "recommendation only" counseling is full disclosure sufficient to protect you from the law of malpractice if your recommended solution fails. You recommend option A and do not mention option B. Based on what you and the client know at the time, option A is so much better than option B that no reasonable person would seriously consider option B. (In other words, you have given exactly the right advice.) But later the situation changes. New facts cause option A to fail and to make option B much more attractive. The client hires another lawyer, who sues you in malpractice because you never mentioned option B. You say that it would not have made any difference because the client would still have chosen option A, which was the better choice at the time the client had to make a decision. The client says otherwise. You might win at trial, or you might lose, or your liability insurer might settle before trial. Even if you "win" this dispute, you will lose an enormous amount of time (probably in hours that would otherwise be billable) as well as peace of mind. You may suffer some bad publicity. Your insurance rates will probably go up. *And*, you might not win.

In addition, "recommendation only" counseling creates a potential for confrontation, which might be either open or hidden. You describe option C and recommend it, telling the client that it is the only thing that will work. The client dislikes option C and says, "But what about option D? There are things about it I like, and I really hope it will work." You have researched this thoroughly and know that the last time option D worked for anybody was in 1919, and even then on distinguishable facts. You try to explain why option D will not work. You might persuade the client, and the conversation might end with sincere friendliness on both sides. But two other things are just as likely, or even more likely. One is that you and the client argue about it. The other, which is worse, is that the client does not argue, but you see some stiffening body language, after which the client goes away and follows your advice reluctantly, or does nothing, or hires another lawyer. The problem is that you have taken a position, and once you do that, conflict rather than brainstorming is the usual result. An assertive client might argue with you, and it is difficult to convert arguing into brainstorming. An unassertive client would rather go away than argue, but the problem remains.

Everything said in this section is different from the scene in which the client asks you *what you would do if you were in the client's situation*. In our experience, that is a very good question from a smart client. You should ask the same question of a mechanic who tells you that your eight-year-old car needs a valve job ("if this were your car, what would you do?") or a home contractor who is giving you a quote on an expensive but not urgent repair ("if this were your home, what would you do?").

The client is not really asking for your recommendation. The client wants to know how other informed and responsible people — for example, you — deal with problems like the client's. You can answer while at the same time explaining exactly how your values, goals, tolerance for risk, taste, and situation in life are different from the client's. If you have enough experience to be able to describe how most people in your community decide similar questions, the client might also find that helpful.

§25.5 Asking the Client To Decide

Ask the client to decide among the options. Understandably, the client might want time to think about it. In fact, you ought to encourage that unless there is some reason for an immediate decision. And don't be surprised if the client telephones with one or two follow-up questions before deciding.

If the decision will be delayed, try to work out a "soft" (flexible) deadline before the client leaves the meeting. Legal work seems to go on interminably because few of the people involved impose deadlines on themselves. A client faced with a tough decision may delay making it but then regret the delay. You can help by asking the client if she wants to set a date by which she will get back to you.

After the client decides, the counseling job is complete, and you and the client then act on that decision.

§25.6 What To Do If The Client Is Persuaded By Cognitive Illusions

A cognitive illusion — also called a cognitive bias — is a pattern of thought that causes a person to reason unrealistically, especially about predictions. Here is an example:

> In researching what classes he wanted to take for his third year, [Frank] had examined the course catalogue and looked up the student evaluation results for all the classes and professors in which he was interested. Having done an exhaustive review of all the possibilities, Frank completed his registration form and got on line at the Registrar's office to turn it in. While on line, he got into a conversation with a student from his first-year section, not his friend or someone he knew well, but an acquaintance. They compared their registration lists to see what they were going to take, and the other student commented that he had heard that a professor teaching a course Frank was signing up for was a real bore and that the course sounded a lot better than it really was. This surprised Frank, because he had looked up the course evaluations, and the students in the classes the previous few years had given the professor above average reviews. Nevertheless, Frank . . . changed his registration form right there on line to substitute a different course.
>
> [Frank was later asked why he did this.] . . . did he have any particular reason to trust the other student's opinion (no, he did not really know the student very well); did he change his mind because the opinion expressed related to something that would not be captured on an evaluation, such as whether the teacher was a tough grader (no, it was based purely on the "boring" comment, which was one of the subjects covered in the evaluations); had the spontaneous hearsay opinion confirmed anything else he'd heard about the professor (no, in fact all he knew about the professor was the generally positive commentary from the published evaluations). Having done exhaustive research into course evaluations, Frank had accumulated dozens, if not hundreds, of student evaluations of the professor that convinced him that the course was worth taking. But all that research got pushed aside on the hearsay opinion offered by a student that Frank did not even know very well.[4]

Frank might have acted on any of several cognitive illusions, and without asking him further questions, it's hard to say which persuaded him. One might have been a false assumption that anecdotal evidence trumps empirical evidence. The anecdotal evidence here amounted to rumor from a student Frank did not know to be reliable, and the empirical evidence that Frank himself had studied was

---

[4] Joseph W. Rand, *Understanding Why Good Lawyers Go Bad: Using Case Studies in Teaching Cognitive Bias in Legal Decision-Making*, 9 Clinical L. Rev. 731, 751–752 (2003). See also Ian Weinstein, *Don't Believe Everything You Think: Cognitive Bias in Legal Decision-Making*, 9 Clinical L. Rev. 793 (2003).

impressive. But people often do what Frank did because empirical evidence seems cold and distant while anecdotal evidence is more immediate and vivid (though often unreliable). Another cognitive illusion is a false assumption that the most recent information we are offered (or the first we are offered) is more valid than other information. People are often persuaded by *when* they get information, although its quality has no relationship to when it is delivered, which may be merely coincidental. Other cognitive illusions are explained in the next section of this chapter.

Most clients are tempted by cognitive illusions when making decisions. If you ask clients how they are making decisions, you will hear cognitive illusions regularly, though not always.

Trying to argue a client out of a cognitive illusion usually does not work and can make a client resentful. What can you do? The most effective thing is to ask questions — like the questions Frank was asked — and to ask them respectfully and with genuine curiosity (not like a classroom Socratic dialogue). It's easier for the client to abandon the illusion if we *help* the client see the problem than if we force the client to see the problem.

What if the client will not give up the illusion? That's the client's right. We have fulfilled our obligation if we make it possible for the client to see that it is an illusion.

§25.7 Guarding Against Your Own Cognitive Illusions

What causes doctors to make mistakes? Much research has been done to answer that question, and the studies appear to show that a large proportion of the diagnostic errors made by doctors are caused by cognitive illusions.[5] Although the legal profession has not been studied in the same way, it seems likely that cognitive illusions cause a substantial proportion of lawyers' mistakes.

"Most physicians are not aware of their cognitive mistakes."[6] Probably, most lawyers aren't either. While you're interpreting facts and evidence and making predictions about what will happen, examine your own thinking to make sure that you are not being influenced by any of the following:

Availability bias is "the tendency to judge the likelihood of an event by the ease with which relevant examples come to mind."[7] This is why Frank (in §25.6) rejected his own empirical evidence after someone told him an anecdote. Suppose that last month Judge Patel sentenced one of your clients to the maximum penalty available for the crime of which the client was convicted. You will appear before Judge Patel again tomorrow with Lusardi, another client who has been charged with the same type of crime. Lusardi asks you to predict what will happen if he pleads guilty. Will Judge Patel again impose the maximum sentence, or something close to it? You're tempted to predict exactly that because you saw her

---

[5] Jerome Groopman, *How Doctors Think* (2007).
[6] *Id.* at 277.
[7] *Id.* at 64.

do it only last month. And many lawyers would be tempted to make the same prediction.

But what do you really know? Suppose that in the past 12 months Judge Patel has sentenced 100 defendants for this type of crime. Of that data, you know only 1 percent — your client from last month. It's possible that Judge Patel sentenced all the other 99 defendants to the maximum, which would give her a 100 percent maximum-sentence rate for this crime. It's also possible that your client from last month was the only one sentenced to the maximum, and that Judge Patel was remarkably lenient with each of the other 99. If that's true, she sentences to the maximum only 1 percent of the time — not 100 percent.

You don't know any of this. All you know is what you saw last month. You're tempted to say to Lusardi, "You're looking at something like the maximum sentence, which is what she did to one of my clients last month." No — don't say that. If you do, you will have been seduced by an illusion caused by availability bias. An example was available — an anecdote, really — and it biased you so that you didn't investigate further. You assumed that the anecdote was representative of everything. To avoid this, refuse to be seduced by the example and instead investigate the whole picture. Find out what Judge Patel did in *many* of the cases where a defendant was convicted of this crime. You might not be able to find out what she did in all of them. But learn enough so that you can estimate what the pattern is. (Ask lawyers who are in her courtroom constantly.)

Confirmation bias causes you to focus on information that confirms your preconceptions while ignoring information that challenges your preconceptions. When you first meet your client, you become convinced that he's not guilty of the crime. The story he tells is utterly convincing, and the witnesses against him are inherently incredible. You know that they have testified in other cases, and that no judge or jury has ever believed them. Now you have a preconception — that your client is innocent — and you are at risk for confirmation bias. If you brush off evidence that might challenge your preconception, you will make mistakes. (Here's a preview of what the future might bring in this case: The prosecutor knows the witnesses are liars and won't use them. The prosecutor instead has far better evidence: a recording of your client admitting to a friend that he committed the crime. If you're subject to confirmation bias, you might learn of this recording for the first time when the prosecutor plays it for the jury.)

Search satisficing or *satisfaction of search* is the tendency to stop searching for explanations once you've found one. The explanation you found might not be the right explanation or the best one. It's nothing more than the first one you found. If you call off the search because you've found an explanation, you won't know about the other explanations because your mind closed as soon as you found one. You assumed there were no others. The one you found might not be the best one. Some of the others may be so much better that the one you found might be wrong.

Confidence illusions frequently infect professionals who are aware of their own expertise. All around us, experts confidently predict the future and turn out to be wrong. Predictions by experts in the stock market, for example, are wrong more often than they're right. On the cable news channels, commentators confidently make predictions that are interesting at the time but later turn out to be flat-out wrong. The experts making these predictions are often victims of confidence illusions. Even nonexperts over-estimate their own abilities. Most drivers believe they have above-average driving skills, which is mathematically impossible.[8] But expertise can actually cause errors by inducing confidence illusions. If you're an expert lawyer, you may overestimate your tendency to be right.

---

[8] Tom Vanderbilt, *Traffic: Why We Drive the Way We Do (and What It Says About Us)* (2009).

CHAPTER 26

OVERCOMING SPECIAL PROBLEMS IN COUNSELING

§26.1 When the Client's Goals Cannot Be Accomplished

Suppose the client wants something that the legal system will not deliver, and you are unable to find or create any other solution to the problem. This is much worse than the situation in which some of the client's goals cannot be accomplished but others can.

How do you break this bad news to the client? After examining the research on how doctors do a bad job of delivering bad news and how they can do it better, Linda F. Smith made some suggestions for lawyers in similar circumstances.[1] Among them are the following:

Do not deliver bad news without thinking long and hard about what you will say and how you will say it.   If in the initial interview, you think that the client cannot have what the client wants, do not say so then unless the client's goal is plainly impossible. There are three reasons. First, if you give yourself a few days, you might be able to think of a way of accomplishing at least some of the client's goals. Even if you can deliver only 10% of what the client is after, that is better than nothing. Second, clients can accept bad news better if they are told all the reasons why it's bad, and in an initial interview you are usually not prepared to do that. It can take more time to prepare a solid explanation that a layperson will understand. Third, for the client it can be traumatic to be told immediately in an initial interview that what she wants is impossible. It can feel as though the lawyer is not willing to take some time to try to solve even a part of the problem. If in the initial interview you feel that the client will not get what she wants, it would be more appropriate to say that it will be difficult to do so while empathizing with the client's needs.

---

[1] Linda F. Smith, *Medical Paradigms for Counseling: Giving Clients Bad News*, 4 Clinical L. Rev. 391 (1998). The next eight paragraphs in the text rely on pages 418–424 of Professor Smith's thorough article.

When you do give bad news, allow plenty of time to explain it.   A thorough explanation helps the client accept the situation. And the client will need time to talk about frustration and disappointment.

"Be clear, direct, and candid in giving information." [2]   Sometimes lawyers communicate bad news ambiguously because they are afraid of a client's negative reaction. But clients are entitled to truth rather than misleading ambiguities. And it is part of a lawyer's job to help clients deal with negative reactions.

Begin by saying that what you have to report is disappointing. Then give a quick summary ("Your great-aunt's will cannot be successfully challenged even though she left you nothing") and explain in detail why it is so. To avoid ambiguity, keep the discussion focused on the news you are delivering and what it means for the client.

Listen to the client's reaction and empathize with it.   It can be brutal to hear bad news from a person who does not seem to care about its effect. Legal rules are designed to do the fair thing in most situations. No rule can cause justice 100% of the time. And many situations are themselves unfair because they cannot be resolved without hurting someone. Your client deserves the same human response that you would give a friend in similar circumstances.

But if you overdramatize your empathy, a resilient client might become depressed because you are treating as tragic something that for the client is only frustrating and disappointing. Listen carefully to what the client says and match it with empathy. If, on the other hand, the client reacts harshly, do not change your prediction for that reason alone. If the news really is bad, you would not be doing the client a favor if you imply false reassurance in order to avoid the client's fury or anguish.

Before ending, develop a plan for handling the situation.   What is needed to keep matters from getting worse? Even if the client's goals cannot be accomplished, could anything be done that might benefit the client?

§26.2 When the Lawyer Suspects That the Client's Stated Goal Might Not Represent What the Client Really Wants

What clients tell us about their goals is entitled to respect. Many clients have thought about this deeply and know themselves and their situations far better than we ever will.

But sometimes what a client most needs is for a detached observer, such as a lawyer, to sense an inner truth about the client's situation and then help the client face it. That is particularly so when a client assumes or has been forced into thinking that a particular legal solution is what they should be seeking. How can you help here? Start by listening with your heart rather than with the rational part of your brain. Then ask questions that probe the client's feelings. When you read the following article, notice how the lawyer listened and the questions the lawyer asked.

---

[2] *Id.* at 419.

Steven Keeva, *What Clients Want*

ABA Journal, June 2002, at 49

[The approach of attorney Arnie Herz to counseling] is based on certain premises that in most cases aren't taught to law students. . . . Chief among them: Every legal situation holds the seeds of transformation, once the larger business and life goals are understood.

"If you can discover what your clients really want — and it is rarely what they initially say they want — then, as a lawyer, you are really empowered," Herz says. "We're trained to size up a situation — the client has X problem or Y problem. We pin things down, then move through the process with blinders on. But life's not like that; human beings are constantly changing, evolving. Growth is inherent, and lawyers need to respect that."

A case in point: Macie Scherick. When she hired Herz two years ago, all she needed was for him to draft documents so she could sell her 50 percent share of a SoHo art gallery. At least, that's all she *said* she needed. Indeed, it's all she *thought* she needed.

But Herz sensed there might be more to think about. He asked Scherick about the business and about her partner of 15 years, and he listened carefully to her answers.

The result? Well, here's how Scherick puts it: "He profoundly transformed my life." . . .

. . . Whether clients come to discuss a business dispute, a will or a contract, they almost invariably bring confusion, fear and anger, Herz says. "The problem," he adds, "is that when they come in such a condition, they are apt to accept legal solutions that don't serve them as well as they might."

That's exactly what Scherick was ready to do. But as she talked about selling her stake in the gallery, Herz didn't hear a woman who wanted out. He heard a woman who loved her work but had been intimidated by her business partner. At the time, Scherick had a 2-year-old child, plus another one on the way. Her partner was insisting that the demands of motherhood were inhibiting the gallery's success and, therefore her own. Scherick said she was willing to step aside.

But Herz heard between the lines. "For Macie, what first appeared to be a simple legal transaction powered by a solid business rationale turned out to be a complex situation involving two disempowered people," says Herz. "She . . . was fearful of confrontation, intimidated by her partner's emotions and aggressiveness, and not aware of her legal rights. So she was brought to the brink of selling a business she loved, was good at, and that was rightfully hers."

When Herz explained to Scherick that she was legally entitled to stay in the business, and that her partner could not force dissolution or push her out, she didn't believe it. "But then she began to see that she was not powerless," says Herz. "In fact, it became clear to her that, with all the legal leverage she had, she held the power and not her partner."

This gets at another premise that underlies Herz's work. "You have to identify and acknowledge any fear and/or anger or confusion that clients may be experiencing. When you do that, the relationship is totally transformed. They then know what it means to be heard, because you're seeing their true interests — which they rarely know they have — rather than a mixture of emotions that sets them off balance. With Macie, I had to lead her through the fear and give her some place to stand."

When he did that, says Scherick, "I never felt so understood in my life." Realizing that she had let herself be taken advantage of, she began to express her anger about the situation. Because Herz had helped her reclaim her own sense of self-worth, she realized she wanted more of a fair shake than she had sought.

Then Herz asked her to do what he asks all his clients to do. "I ask them to step outside the legal situation, to forget about all the drama of the moment and instead think about what they'd like their lives to look like three or four months down the line. Suddenly they see possibilities that never would have occurred to them before."

Once the shift occurred in her understanding of what brought her to Herz in the first place, Scherick allowed him to negotiate a fair deal for her. The result was that the partner left the business to start her own.

Scherick, along with a new partner, continues to run the business, which has grown substantially in both revenues and square footage. Their Sears Peyton Gallery is about to double its space in a move to Chelsea, the very epicenter of the New York art world.

§26.3 When the Client Makes a Decision the Lawyer Considers Extremely Unwise

Looking at the client's interests alone, a decision is *extremely* unwise if it would cause *a great deal more* difficulty for the client than it would solve, or if it would do a *much* less effective job of solving the client's problems than other options that the client does not choose.

This is not the same as a decision that you would not make if you were in the client's position. The client, not you, has to live with the consequences of the decision. If the decision reflects the client's tastes and values rather than yours, there is nothing troubling about that.

Why might a client choose an option that would cause many more problems than it would solve or that would do a much less effective job of solving the client's problems than other options would? Here are the three most common possibilities: The client might be ineffectual at making decisions in general. Or the client might be either much less willing or much more willing to take risks than you expected. Or the client might disagree with your predictions of what the various options will cause.

Among the things clients hire us for is to warn them of trouble, and the client who makes an extremely unwise decision is entitled to warning. That client is also entitled to ignore your warning after hearing it. It is not just that the client has to live with the consequences of the decision: The client also decides whether to make risky bets or safer ones. And sometimes clients are right when they disagree with their lawyers' predictions.

How can you deliver this warning? First, do not give a lecture. Instead, raise the matter through questions and through statements of concern about the client's needs. The questions should probe so you can find out why the client is making this decision. You are looking for the places where the client's thinking diverges radically from your own. (The client's thinking might diverge radically from your own in only a very few ways, but you do not understand the client's reasoning unless you find those points of disagreement.) Second, do not argue with the client. Arguing accomplishes nothing in this situation, and most clients will experience arguing as abuse. A good way to express your concern is to say that you are worried about the client or about some aspect of the situation (see the sample dialog below). Third, check your own thinking to make sure that you really do accept the client's goals and values and are not substituting your own. And fourth, make it clear that you will act faithfully on whatever decision the client makes, but because of the matter's importance, you want to make sure that the client understands the risks and consequences.

Here is an example. The client is a plaintiff, and the defendant has offered to settle on the eve of trial. The lawyer believes that the client has only two chances in five of winning.

Client: I want to reject their offer to settle. They're not offering enough money.

Lawyer: I'm fully ready for trial. Our witnesses are ready, and we can start picking a jury in the morning. But this might be the most important decision you'll make in this case. Let me ask some questions so that I understand not only what you want me to do, but also why you want me to do it.

Client: OK.

Lawyer: Are you more optimistic than I am about what will happen at trial?

Client: I'm a little more optimistic. I don't feel like I'm losing. I feel as though it's a toss up now, a fifty-fifty shot.

Lawyer: That is just a little more optimistic than I am. What worries me is that you expressed real concern last week about getting money for you and for your family. How comfortable do you feel risking all or nothing like this? Because if we lose at trial, there will be nothing. . . .

This conversation would probably go on for some time.

§26.4 Ethical Issues in Counseling

Candid and complete advice.   Rule 2.1 of the Model Rules of Professional Conduct requires lawyers to "render candid advice," and in doing so, the "lawyer may refer not only to law but to other considerations such as moral, economic, social and political factors, that may be relevant to the client's situation." The Comment to Rule 2.1 elaborates:

> A client is entitled to straightforward advice expressing the lawyer's honest assessment. Legal advice often involves unpleasant facts and alternatives that a client may be disinclined to confront. In presenting advice, a lawyer endeavors to sustain the client's morale and may put advice in as acceptable a form as honesty permits. However, a lawyer should not be deterred from giving candid advice by the prospect that the advice will be unpalatable to the client.
>
> Advice couched in narrow legal terms may be of little value to a client, especially when practical considerations, such as cost or effects on other people, are predominant. . . . It is proper for a lawyer to refer to relevant moral and ethical considerations in giving advice. Although a lawyer is not a moral advisor as such, moral and ethical considerations impinge upon most legal questions and may decisively influence how the law will be applied.

Rule 1.4 requires you to "explain a matter to the extent reasonably necessary to permit the client to make informed decisions." The Comment to Rule 1.4 notes that, in many instances, the client can make an informed decision only if you explain the damage that some of the options under consideration might cause to others:

> The client should have sufficient information to participate intelligently in decisions concerning the objectives of the representation and the means by which they are to be pursued, to the extent the client is willing and able to do so. . . .
>
> . . . In litigation a lawyer should explain the general strategy and prospects of success and ordinarily should consult the client on tactics that are likely to result in significant expense or to injure or coerce others. On the other hand, a lawyer ordinarily will not be expected to describe trial or negotiation strategy in detail. The guiding principle is that the lawyer should fulfill reasonable client expectations for information consistent with the duty to act in the client's best interests, and the client's overall requirements as to the character of representation.

If you receive an offer of compromise from an opposing party, you must inform the client of the offer and counsel on whether to accept or reject it unless in earlier counseling the client has already decided which offers will be accepted and which rejected.[3]

When the client decides to do something illegal. Illegality can happen on more than one level. For example, one client might decide to commit a crime. Another client might decide to do something that involves an increased risk of negligence liability. Ethics law treats these possibilities differently.

Under Rule 1.2(d) of the Model Rules:

> A lawyer shall not counsel a client to engage, or assist a client, in conduct that the lawyer knows is criminal or fraudulent, but a lawyer may discuss the legal consequences of any proposed course of conduct with a client and may counsel or assist a

---

[3] Comment to Rule 1.4 of the Model Rules of Professional Conduct.

client to make a good faith effort to determine the validity, scope, meaning or application of the law.

This means that in counseling you may not suggest an option that involves committing a crime or civil fraud. But if a client asks you whether a particular act would be illegal, you may answer the question, regardless of what the answer might be.

If you say that the act would be illegal and if the client then asks what would happen if the client were to do it anyway, you may answer that question as well. Depending on the act at issue, you might say that the client could be made to pay damages in tort or contract, or you might explain the judge's sentencing discretion if the act is a crime. If the client further asks you to predict whether the client would be held liable or prosecuted or convicted, you may answer that, too. For example, if the client has a store and wants to open it for business on Sundays, and if your state or county has a Sunday-closing law that has not been enforced in generations, you may tell the client that opening on Sundays is technically illegal, but that there is virtually no chance of the client's being prosecuted. Why may you do that? If law — as practicing lawyers know it — is "[w]hat officials do about disputes,"[4] you are explaining the law to your client.[5]

Rule 1.4(a)(5) requires that a lawyer "consult with the client about any relevant limitation on the lawyer's conduct when the lawyer knows that the client expects assistance not permitted by the Rules of Professional Conduct or other law." That means that if the client asks you to help plan an act that would be criminal, you must say that you cannot and explain why. What's the difference between this and answering the client's question about opening a store on Sunday? It is the difference between describing what the law will do and helping to plan an act. You did not help the client plan to commit the crime of opening on Sunday; you simply predicted the consequences.

When the client makes a decision that you consider immoral. Ethics law gives you a choice between two alternatives. You may act on the client's wishes. Or you may withdraw from the case.[6]

Your withdrawal will probably not cause the client to change the decision. Another lawyer can probably be found who will not pose the objection that you made. And if you represent the client in litigation, the court might order you to continue to represent the client "notwithstanding good cause for terminating the representation."[7] If you try to withdraw on the eve of trial, for example, the harm withdrawal would cause to the opposing party, the court, witnesses, and others might outweigh the harm caused by your continuing to represent the client.

Usually, it's more effective to appeal to the client's self-interest. If the client might be able to see a connection between self-interest and moral values, you might try linking them in an approach something like this:

---

[4] Karl N. Llewellyn, *The Bramble Bush* 3 (1930).
[5] Monroe H. Freedman, *Lawyers' Ethics in an Adversary System* 59–60 (1975).
[6] Model Rule 1.16(b)(4).
[7] Model Rule 1.16(c).

Lawyer: I can understand why you would want to treat your neighbor this badly. If I had a neighbor who behaved that way, I think I would be as upset as you are. But I'm worried about the future. Sometimes, in the heat of hurt feelings, we do things that we later regret. We behave harshly while angry. And later when anger has cooled down, we think that that is not how we want to be remembered by anybody else or even by ourselves. I'm worried that a few years from now you might wish that you had treated your neighbor less harshly on this occasion. I'm not talking about forgiving him. I'm only talking about being less vengeful.

If the client is not likely to see a connection between moral values and self-interest, you might develop a creative plan that does something special for the client's own self-interest in a way that eliminates or reduces the moral problem without describing it as a moral problem.

For example, suppose the client is a real estate developer who has quietly bought up two city blocks of apartment houses. The tenants are all low-income, and the client wants to tear down the buildings and construct a large corporate office complex with upscale stores on the street level. The client has already emptied most of the apartments by refusing to renew leases as they expire and by offering a few thousand dollars each to tenants who would move out while their leases are still in effect. The client predicts that, if this continues, nearly all the apartments will be empty within a few months. But about a dozen tenants have declared that they refuse to move, and each of them has a lease that extends long past the scheduled date of demolition. The client calls these people "the resisters."

The client intends to demolish, on a 24-hour-a-day schedule, the buildings in which the resisters do not live, which is legal in that part of town even though the resisters would not be able to get much sleep. The client will make no effort to make access to the resisters' apartments easy during demolition, and the client will cut off the resisters' utilities from time to time, using "demolition safety" as an excuse. You told the client that it would be illegal to cut off utilities unless it was really required for safety reasons, and the client asked whether the resisters could easily prove that the cutoffs were unnecessary. When you answered that proof would be hard, although not impossible, the client chuckled.

What can you do to persuade this client that it would be in the client's own self-interest to treat these people better? Sometimes a client may be influenced if you were to predict that terrible things would happen to the client if the client were to persist. But the facts here will not support that. This client can probably get away with it if the client is cunning enough. You are not willing to withdraw, and even if you were, it would make no difference because the client can replace you with another lawyer who is not bothered by such things.

The key is to find an incentive that makes sense within the client's way of thinking. Can you show the client that more civilized methods of persuading the resisters to leave would cost less? Can you think up an act of generosity on the client's part that would solve the resisters' housing problems while producing a benefit for the client that the client considers worthwhile? Some clients instinctively think narrowly while ignoring the effect of good and bad publicity. And the tax code can at times be helpful. Money spent in some ways is not taxed or is taxed less than money spent in other ways. You cannot know the true cost of any transaction until its tax consequences are factored in. If Plan X will cost the client $1,000 and is fully taxed, it is more expensive than Plan Y, which will cost $1,150 and is not taxed at all.

In general, there is a limit to the number of times you can tell a client that the client is behaving immorally. With some clients, you will lose your credibility if you do it even once. Even with a particularly fair-minded client, you begin to lose credibility if you do it with any regularity.

When the client is disabled from making a decision. A minor or a person suffering from a mental disability might not be considered by the law to have the capacity to make legally binding decisions. (The definition of incapacity differs slightly from state to state.) But most people who are incapacitated from making legally binding decisions are still entitled to some autonomy and no less respect than anyone else.

The Model Rules take both of these problems into account. Under Rule 1.14(a), "[w]hen a client's capacity to make adequately considered decisions . . . is diminished, whether because of minority, mental impairment or for some other reason, the lawyer shall, as far as reasonably possible, maintain a normal client-lawyer relationship with the client." The Comment to Rule 1.14 explains that "a client with diminished capacity often has the ability to understand, deliberate upon, and reach conclusions about matters affecting the client's own well-being. . . . [For example,] some persons of advanced age can be quite capable of handling routine financial matters while needing special legal protection concerning major transactions."

Rule 1.14(b) provides that

> When the lawyer reasonably believes that the client has diminished capacity, is at risk of substantial physical, financial or other harm unless action is taken[,] and cannot adequately act in the client's own interest, the lawyer may take reasonably necessary protective action, including consulting with individuals or entities that have the ability to take action to protect the client and, in appropriate cases, seeking the appointment of a guardian ad litem, conservator, or guardian.

NEGOTIATION

CHAPTER 27

How Negotiation Works

§27.1 Aims of Negotiation

Some scholars estimate that as much as 90% of the legal matters handled by lawyers eventually involve negotiation.[1] One study of tort, contract, and real property cases in urban state trial courts found that 61.5% of cases were disposed by a settlement or voluntary dismissal.[2] Approximately 60% of criminal cases are disposed with guilty pleas.[3] In federal courts, 88% of criminal cases end in guilty pleas, presumably negotiated.[4]

Like all other work done by lawyers, negotiations can be separated into two general categories: transactions and dispute resolution. In transactional negotiations, the parties try to enter into relationships in which they voluntarily agree to terms that will govern their future conduct. Examples include transferring or renting real estate, buying and selling goods and services, creating business partnerships and joint ventures, and merging and acquiring companies. In dispute negotiations, the parties are in conflict, and they try to resolve the conflict themselves. The alternative is to have a third party, such as a court, decide. Examples include settlement discussions in a lawsuit, plea bargaining, and negotiations between the Federal Trade Commission and a company before the filing of an antitrust case.

Some negotiations have both dispute and transaction aspects. Labor negotiations, for example, might concern both disputes about safety or other working conditions regulated by legal rules and transactional aspects relating to the long-

---

[1] Robert M. Bastress & Joseph D. Harbaugh, *Interviewing, Counseling, and Negotiating: Skills for Effective Representation* 341 (1990).

[2] Brian J. Ostrom & Neal B. Kramer, National Center for State Courts, *Examining the Work of State Courts, 1996: A National Perspective from the Court Statistics Project* 24 (1997).

[3] See Shauna M. Strickland, *Beyond the Vanishing Trial: A Look at the Composition of State Court Dispositions,* http://www.ncsconline.org/WC/Publications/Trends/2005/ADRArbVanish-Trends2005.pdf at 2 (visited Oct. 23, 2006) (examining trends in 19 states).

[4] *Judicial Business of the United States Courts, Administrative Office of the United States Courts* (2009) (Table D-7), http://www.uscourts.gov/uscourts/Statistics/JudicialBusiness/2009/JudicialBusinespdfversion.pdf (visited October 2, 2010).

term relationship between labor and management. Similarly, international trade negotiations may involve disputes about the meaning of provisions in existing contracts and bargaining about future contract terms. Even in an ostensibly "pure" dispute negotiation, transactional issues may arise. In a commercial land-lord/tenant case, for instance, in which the tenant alleges breach of contract because of the purported failure of the landlord to provide services required under the lease, the parties may attempt to resolve the dispute by rewriting the terms of the lease to make the requirements more explicit.

Whether transactional or dispute resolution, the goal of any negotiator is to communicate persuasively with the other side. Communication can take many forms: threats that your client will take certain actions or assert power against the other party if a deal is not reached; arguments that a certain case, statute, or rule supports your position; promises that will bind your client in return for conces-sions from your opponent; appeals to your adversary to display some sympathy to your client; recognition of the views of the other party in an attempt to solve prob-lems collaboratively; or intentional silences to promote discussion with the other side. The forms of communication you choose will depend on the strategy you develop. But, in essence, negotiation — like interviewing, counseling, or legal storytelling — is a communication skill.

Your aim is to get the other party to make an agreement on terms as favorable as possible to your client. It is not to vent your or your client's anger, to show your prowess in researching obscure legal issues, or to demonstrate your ability to dis-play rhetorical flourishes. Negotiation is not a monologue with the other party's lawyer as a passive audience. Rather, it is a dialogue in which you intend to per-suade the other party to reach a mutually agreeable decision on issues.

§27.2 Context of Negotiation: Interests, Rights, and Power

To understand how negotiation works, consider each party's interests, rights, and power.[5] Every dispute or transaction occurs against a backdrop of these three factors. The differing interests of the parties, of course, bring them to the bargain-ing table. But the rights and power of the parties influence the result because the parties know that if an agreement is not reached, "a more coercive process will ensue."[6] In that more coercive process — litigation or economic conflict, for example — each party will ask for vindication of its rights and use its power. These concepts are introduced here and explained more fully in Chapter 28.

§27.2.1 Interests of the Parties

"Interests are needs, desires, concerns, fears — the things one cares about or wants. They underlie people's positions — the tangible items they say they

---

[5] William L. Ury et al., *Getting Disputes Resolved: Designing Systems to Cut the Costs of Con-flict* 4–8 (1988).

[6] Sally E. Merry, *Disputing Without Culture*, 100 Harv. L. Rev. 2057, 2066 (1987) (reviewing Stephen B. Goldberg et al., *Dispute Resolution* (1985)).

want."[7] Common interests are resolving the matter promptly, maximizing financial position, developing or maintaining long-term relationships, or addressing psychological needs.

Consider, for example, a case called *Ransom v. Dusak*, where the tenant, Ransom, sought damages from her landlord, Dusak, for breach of the warranty of habitability. This case will be used throughout this section as a platform to illustrate various aspects of negotiation. There, Ransom sought damages for breach of the warranty of habitability. Underlying that legal position could be a number of interests: compensation for the partial loss of use of her apartment, for her suffering, and for her medical bills; the desire to have the problems in her home repaired; development of a good relationship with the landlord; peace of mind; revenge. And behind Dusak's defense of the case could be several other interests: protection of his reputation in the community, the desire to get a new tenant, compensation for the money he expended to defend the case, and peace of mind.

Likewise, in the transactional context, the parties will usually have multiple interests. In an employment negotiation for a management position in a company, for instance, an applicant may be concerned not only with the amount of the salary, but also the nature of the fringe and vacation benefits, the title and responsibilities of the position, payment of moving expenses, possibilities for promotion, or geographic location of the office. The company's interests may include not only the applicant's training and experience but also her ability to work with supervisors and subordinates, consistency of salary and benefits with comparable managers, the applicant's willingness to make a long-term commitment, or her professional growth potential.

Each party might have many interests, and some of them might conflict. Although in a commercial transaction, a buyer may want quality goods, timely delivery, and a low price, she may not need to obtain all three. In a plea bargaining negotiation in a case with multiple defendants, an individual defendant might have an interest in reducing the risk of a long sentence but also might have some loyalty to codefendants and want to avoid reprisals. And in an international negotiation, a country might have concerns about secure borders but also want to develop long-term trade relations with neighboring countries.

§27.2.2 *Rights of the Parties*

"Rights" are independent standards that demonstrate the legitimacy or fairness of a party's position. They can be based on formal legal rules (case law, statutes, and regulations) or contracts between the parties. Or they can be grounded on socially accepted standards of behavior, such as reciprocity, precedent, equality, and seniority.[8] In the *Ransom v. Dusak* case, for example, Ransom might rely on the statutory warranty of habitability, a common law claim for negligent maintenance of the premises, or the argument that, as a matter of fairness, if she pays her rent, she should be entitled to a habitable apartment. Dusak might base his

---

[7] Ury et al., *supra* note 5, at 5.
[8] *Id.* at 7.

defense on Ransom's failure to prove all the elements on her claim for breach of warranty of habitability or might argue that Ransom's refusal to allow the admittance of the exterminator absolves him of any obligation to pay damages for the vermin infestation.

In dispute-resolution negotiations, bargaining occurs in the "shadow of the law"[9] — in the context of the legal claims and defenses raised by the parties before the particular tribunal. And aside from the substantive legal positions taken by the parties, they may also have different procedural rights that frame the negotiation. Examples are rights to discovery, to joinder of additional parties, to pretrial motions, or to interlocutory appeals. Even a motion for an adjournment or continuance of the proceedings might be a significant right for a party in a particular case.

Unlike dispute negotiations, transactional negotiations do not technically take place in the "shadow of the law." But the rights of the parties do provide some context for transactional bargaining. Sometimes, the parties are limited in their options by specific statutory or regulatory requirements. Usury statutes, for example, limit the amount of interest that a lender can charge a borrower, even if the two want to agree otherwise.[10] Beyond the law, transactional negotiators frequently rely on "common business practice" or "form provisions" in their bargaining.[11] And the parties often refer to socially accepted standards of behavior as a basis for their position. In a negotiation for a sale of residential property, for instance, if the buyer wants a ten-day period to withdraw from the contract after an inspection report, the seller may request that, in return, the buyer give her ten days to withdraw from the contract if she does not want to make the repairs listed in the report.

§27.2.3 Power of the Parties

Power is "the ability to coerce someone to do something he would not otherwise do."[12] Although rights can coerce the party against whom they are enforced (see §23.2.2), power — in the sense used in this book — is coercion *without resorting to enforcement of legal rights*. A party asserts power in two common ways. One way is "aggression, such as sabotage or physical attack" (or more commonly, the pressure of bad publicity); the other way is "withholding the benefits that derive from a relationship, as when employees withhold their labor in a strike."[13]

For some people and in some negotiations, relative power is the determinative factor. For example, when you want to buy a computer, the basic terms of the contract — the price, available accessories and software, and warranty — are not negotiable. When you find the computer you want to buy, you must accept the

---

[9] This term was coined in Robert H. Mnookin & Lewis Kornhauser, *Bargaining in the Shadow of the Law: the Case of Divorce*, 88 Yale L.J. 950 (1979).

[10] See, e.g., N.Y. Gen. Oblig. §5-501(1) (McKinney Supp. 2010).

[11] Carrie Menkel-Meadow, *Toward Another View of Legal Negotiation: The Structure of Problem Solving*, 31 UCLA L. Rev. 754, 766 (1984). She terms this kind of negotiation bargaining in the "shadow of the form contract."

[12] Ury et al., *supra* note 5, at 7.

[13] *Id.* at 8.

terms on which the manufacturer will let it be sold. But when General Motors wants to buy a computer, it can either dictate terms to a much smaller company or negotiate on an equal footing with a company large enough to have market power that matches GM's.

Even in a setting where one party starts out with a substantial power disadvantage, relative power does not necessarily determine the result. For example, car dealers have bargaining resources vastly superior to those of most car buyers. But dealers must make sales in a competitive market. Indeed, during certain times of the year, dealers need to sell cars to get them out of inventory. At those times, buyers may have significant power, at least in regard to the valuing of the trade-in, the financing package, or the availability of some options. Thus, relative power can be variable and does not always determine the negotiation's outcome.

§27.3 Approaches to Negotiation

The two primary approaches to negotiation are adversarial and problem-solving.[14] The adversarial approach focuses on the rights and power of the parties. The problem-solving approach focuses on the interests of the parties. Nearly all negotiations involve some degree of both approaches, but a description of the distinction between these two types of negotiation will help you make appropriate choices in selecting negotiation strategy and tactics.

§27.3.1 Adversarial Approach to Negotiation

A negotiator taking an adversarial approach views bargaining as an issue of distribution of limited resources. This type of bargaining is also called "zero-sum" negotiation because each dollar that one side receives (or does not need to pay out) is one dollar that the other side loses. If there are three claimants to a $3,000 pot of money, and if one claimant takes $1,500, the other two must split the remaining $1,500. Haggling over the price of a new car is a classic example of distributive bargaining. For every dollar that the price comes down, the buyer gains a dollar, and the seller loses a dollar.

In an adversarial negotiation, each party takes a position that she or he is entitled to something. In a personal injury case, for example, in which the plaintiff seeks $500,000 damages for injuries incurred in an automobile accident, the parties view the negotiation in terms of a continuum between zero dollars (the amount the defendant initially says it will pay) and the $500,000 demanded in the plaintiff's complaint. Depending on their assessment of the strength of their respective cases, the plaintiff and the defendant will each select an "opening position" on this continuum and determine a "bottom line" — the position at which the particular party will walk away from the negotiation. Negotiation then becomes a contest in which each party makes concessions, adopts fallback

---

[14] Other approaches exist, such as game theory, economic models, and bargaining theory, but they are less helpful when first learning basic negotiation skills.

positions, and either eventually agrees to a compromise or leaves the bargaining table (see §27.4).

In the legal context, the adversarial approach to negotiation focuses on the rights and power of the parties. In dispute resolution cases conducted in the "shadow of the law," the negotiators typically — and sometimes wrongly — assume that the bargaining is limited to the judgment that could be entered by a court or other tribunal in deciding the case: "who will get the most money and who can be compelled to do or not to do something [by the court]. Indeed, it may be because litigation negotiations are so often conducted in the shadow of [a potential] court [decision] that they are assumed to be zero-sum games."[15] In a personal injury automobile accident case, for example, parties using an adversarial approach limit their discussions to the strength and weaknesses of the legal claims and defenses and each party's predictions of a jury verdict. Similarly, in transactional negotiations, negotiators adopting the adversarial approach assume that bargaining is limited to the options available under common business practices or form contracts and agreements. Even though a court will probably not render a judgment in the transactional negotiation, prevailing practices in the trade or business can become the "rights" about which the parties negotiate. Moreover, the relative power imbalance between the parties can affect the ultimate distribution of the pot.

When is it wrong to assume that the range of possible settlements is limited to what a court could decide or what one would find in common business practices or form agreements? It is wrong whenever a problem-solving approach would get more for your client. Subsections 27.3.2 and 27.3.3 explain how and when that might occur.

§27.3.2 *Problem-Solving Approach to Negotiation*

While the adversarial approach to negotiation focuses on the distribution of limited resources, the problem-solving approach emphasizes the *integration* of the resources each side brings to the table so that each side ends up better off. Earlier in this book, we used the expression *problem-solving* to describe general methods of identifying a client's problem, predicting what will happen in the future, and creating and implementing strategies to control what will happen in the future. In the negotiating chapters, we use that term to refer to a lawyer's use of some of these same methods — especially solution-generation and solution-evaluation — to negotiate a settlement or deal that will meet the interests of all parties.

In the problem-solving model, each side is assumed to bring something of value to the deal that can create benefits to both parties, and the negotiators try to integrate these interests in a settlement or deal. A good illustration is a negotiation to create a joint business venture in which one party puts up the capital and the other provides the research and labor. Such negotiations are not viewed as zero-sum games but win-win situations. Many negotiations present integrative opportunities — even those which initially may appear to be purely distributional.

---

[15] Menkel-Meadow, *supra* note 11, at 766.

In a personal injury setting, for example, the plaintiff's interest in a quick resolution of the dispute and the defendant's interest in delayed payment of full damages might be conducive to a structured settlement with a lengthy payout schedule. (A structured settlement is one in which the defendant makes payments stretched out over a period of years rather than in one lump sum immediately.)

Rather than concentrating on the rights and power of the parties, problem-solving negotiators focus on accommodating the interests of all the parties). As you saw in §27.3.1, the adversarial approach to negotiation results in positional bargaining: each party takes positions based on its evaluation of the strength or weakness of the parties' "rights" in the case. In their well-known book on problem-solving negotiation, *Getting to Yes*, Roger Fisher and William Ury reject this approach:

> When negotiators bargain over positions, they tend to lock themselves into those positions. The more you clarify your position and defend it against attack, the more committed you become to it. The more you try to convince the other side of the impossibility of changing your opening position, the more difficult it becomes to do so. Your ego becomes identified with your position. You now have a new interest in "saving face" — in reconciling future action with past positions — making it less and less likely that any agreement will wisely reconcile the parties' original interests.[16]

Fisher and Ury argue that by focusing on interests and not positions, parties can generate a variety of options that will provide for mutual gain for both of them.[17] By identifying their own interests and recognizing the interests of the other party, both parties can collaborate to develop an agreement amenable to both.

To illustrate such an approach, they point to the Camp David treaty between Egypt and Israel negotiated in 1978. After the Six Day War of 1967, Israel occupied the Sinai Peninsula. In the 1978 negotiations, Israel took the position that it retain some part of the Sinai, and Egypt insisted that Israel return the entire Sinai. Positional bargaining about alternative boundary lines took the parties nowhere. But then the negotiators began to consider their different interests: Israel was concerned about its security interests and did not want the pre-1967 situation with a military presence on its border. Egypt, after centuries of colonial occupation, did not want any infringement on its sovereignty. The interest-based approach to negotiation led to a solution: Israel returned the Sinai to complete Egyptian sovereignty, but Egypt agreed to demilitarization of large parts of the peninsula to assure Israeli security.[18]

Nonetheless, problem-solving negotiators do recognize that there are instances where interests cannot be integrated satisfactorily, and negotiation will fail. While adversarial negotiators select "bottom lines" at which they will walk away from the bargaining table, problem-solving negotiators identify a BATNA — a Best Alternative To a Negotiated Agreement — as a standard against which any proposed agreement should be measured. A BATNA is more flexible than a bottom line position.

---

[16] Roger Fisher et al., *Getting to Yes: Negotiating Agreement Without Giving In* 4–5 (2d ed. 1991).

[17] *Id.* at 10–11.

[18] *Id.* at 41–42.

To develop a BATNA, a negotiator predicts the best thing the negotiator would be able to do if the negotiation fails and an agreement is not reached. In a transactional negotiation where a drug store chain wants to lease space in a building, for example, the building owner will wonder: "What other potential tenants might I lease the space to? Are there any alternative uses for the building? Are there any tax advantages to keeping the store vacant?" Each of these represents a potential alternative to signing an agreement with the drug store chain: finding a different tenant or using the building in a way that does not involve leasing space or leaving the space empty for a time and taking a tax loss. The most profitable of them is the building owner's BATNA — the owner's best alternative to a negotiated agreement with the drug store chain. If during the negotiation, the BATNA looks better than any possible deal with the drug store chain, the building owner can walk away. If not, the building owner will come to an agreement.

Or in a dispute resolution negotiation for settlement of a lawsuit, the plaintiff will wonder, "If this case goes to trial, will I win, how long would I have to wait to win, and how much will it cost to win?" Trial is the only BATNA. The issue is whether it is better than negotiating a settlement, and that depends on the chances of winning at trial, the delay before victory, and the cost of winning.

Good planning involves imagining the other party's BATNA as well. Unless you have a good idea of the other side's alternatives to settling with you, you really do not know how strong or weak you are in the negotiation.

§27.3.3 Use of the Different Approaches

Many commentators express a strong preference for problem-solving as a substitute for adversarial negotiation.[19] Others tout the effectiveness of adversarial methods, arguing that the problems often identified as inherent in such an approach are the result of incompetent bargaining, not the method itself.[20] The approach described in this book is more flexible. Most negotiations are not purely adversarial or problem-solving. Even a usually adversarial negotiator in a personal injury case, for example, might engage in problem-solving on an issue such as the payout schedule, taking into account the plaintiff's immediate financial needs and the defendant's preference to pay at least some of the money later rather than now. And in many problem-solving negotiations, the parties may engage in bazaar-style haggling when it comes down to "nickel and dime" issues at the conclusion of the bargaining.[21]

These mixed approaches reflect the reality of how lawyers really do negotiate effectively. It is a complex process involving both distributive and integrative

---

[19] Menkel-Meadow, *supra* note 11, at 771–772.

[20] See, e.g., Robert J. Condlin, *"Every Day and in Every Way We Are All Becoming Meta and Meta" or How Communitarian Bargaining Theory Conquered the World (of Bargaining Theory)*, 23 Ohio St. J. on Disp. Resol. 231, 241 (2008); Robert J. Condlin, *Bargaining with a Hugger: The Weaknesses and Limitations of a Communitarian Conception of Legal Dispute Bargaining, or Why Can't All Just Get Along*, 9 Cardozo J. Conflict Resol. 1, 79, 88 (2007).

[21] See generally Gerald B. Wetlaufer, *The Limits of Integrative Bargaining*, 85 Geo. L.J. 369, 390 (1996).

issues, all against a backdrop of the parties' interests, rights, and power. As you will see in Chapter 29, understanding the differences between the two approaches can be helpful in developing effective strategies on behalf of your client and crafting arguments or appeals to the opposing party.

If you assume that one approach is always preferable to the other, you will be less effective at negotiation than another person who can function well using either approach.

§27.4 Roles of the Lawyer in Negotiation

In negotiations, a lawyer often acts in four capacities: evaluator, advisor, negotiator, and drafter.

1. *Evaluator.* At a minimum, you can help a client by providing a third party's evaluation of the situation. Sometimes clients become fixated on a relatively small part of a dispute or transaction, and the lawyer, who has no personal stake in the matter, can provide some perspective on the problem. Some clients in personal injury cases, for example, encouraged by press reports of huge verdicts in high-profile cases, expect the same results in their cases. One of the functions of a lawyer is to give clients a reality check as to the actual experience in your particular jurisdiction.

2. *Advisor.* Lawyers counsel their clients as to their options during the negotiation process, particularly in regard to what offers to make and whether to accept an offer made by the other side. The client, however, decides whether to make an agreement (see §28.5).

3. *Negotiator.* In many dispute situations, the lawyer is the exclusive communicator with the other party or its lawyer, and the client does no more than authorize the lawyer to act (see §28.5). But sometimes the client is an active participant in the negotiations, and the lawyer plays the role of a co-negotiator or backseat advisor. The decision as to who should be the negotiator is a strategic one, depending in part on the communication skills of the client, the expertise of the lawyer or client on the issues raised by the transaction or dispute, the advantages or disadvantages of having a person with authority present, and the concern of the client to be intimately involved in the discussions. In most transactional situations, on the other hand, the clients themselves negotiate the key elements of the deal, such as price, what is being purchased, and when it will be delivered. Lawyers are brought into the picture to draft the contract, and the lawyers conduct a second negotiation over how the contract will allocate various risks between the parties and other aspects of contract drafting. Occasionally, a transactional client will turn the negotiation of the entire deal over to a lawyer, but that is unusual.

4. *Drafter.* Once an agreement is reached, it usually must be reduced to writing (see Ch. 33). Even in those situations where the agreement is made orally, such as stipulations on the record in a courtroom, the lawyers need to work out the precise language of the agreement. When reducing the agreement to

writing, other issues often arise, and, as the saying goes, "the devil is in the details." More negotiation is often needed when pinning down the exact language of the agreement.

§27.5 Discharging Your Ethical and Legal Responsibilities

When representing your client in a negotiation, you not only have to examine the different approaches to the process and your role on behalf of your client, but you must also consider your ethical and legal obligations both to your client and the other party. The Model Rules of Professional Responsibility create ethical obligations for attorneys in the negotiation process. And recently, the ABA's Section of Litigation adopted *Ethical Guidelines for Settlement Negotiations*. Although these guidelines are not binding authority, they provide more detailed guidance than the Rules in regard to a lawyer's responsibility to clients and opposing parties during settlement talks.[22] Finally, a lawyer should be aware of the potential tort and contract liability issues that can arise in the negotiation process.

In any negotiation, you will make representations: in regard to particular facts in the case; as to assessments of the strengths and weaknesses of the different parties' cases; or of your opinions about proposed solutions to problems. Indeed, most arguments and threats contain representations of fact, which can raise ethical issues if you misrepresent the facts or omit certain facts.

As to misrepresentations, under Model Rule of Professional Conduct 4.1(a), a lawyer "[i]n the course of representing a client, a lawyer shall not knowingly . . . (a) make a false statement of material fact or law to a third person. . . ."[23] The comment to the rule provides, however, that "[u]nder generally accepted conventions in negotiation, certain types of statements *ordinarily* are not taken as statements of material fact. Estimates of price or value placed on the subject of a transaction and a party's intentions as to an acceptable settlement of a claim are in this category. . . ."[24]

The line between actual misrepresentation and "puffing" is not always clear. And the interpretation of the rule and comment varies from state to state and is influenced by prevailing local practices.[25] The weasel word "ordinarily" in the comment does not necessarily give you broad leeway in your representations in negotiation. In the Ransom case, for instance, consider these three statements by Dusak's lawyer, all of which he knows to be misrepresentations:

1. My client will not agree to exterminations every month.
2. My client has signed an agreement with an exterminator for service every month.
3. My client tells me he thinks it will cost over $150 a month to have an exterminator.

[22] http://www.abanet.org/litigation/ethics/settlementnegotiations.pdf (visited Oct. 7, 2010).
[23] Model Rules of Professional Conduct 4.1(a).
[24] Comment 2 to Model Rule 4.1 (emphasis added).
[25] Charles W. Wolfram, *Modern Legal Ethics* §13.5.8 at 727 (1986).

In most jurisdictions, Statement 1 is probably permissible because it merely reflects his client's intentions as to an acceptable settlement and Statement 2 is probably impermissible because it states an untrue fact that materially relates to the negotiation. Statement 3, however, is on the borderline: it could just be Dusak's opinion about a negotiating position, but, by referring to an estimate of cost, it could be considered a statement of fact made to induce a concession by Ransom.

Certainly, then, before you engage in bargaining, research the applicable ethics opinions for that particular jurisdiction.[26] Even as to your assessments of the strengths and weaknesses of your client's case, "a careful lawyer, intent on negotiating a legally protectable bargain, would be very circumspect in making or implying false and misleading statements about intention."[27] A material misrepresentation not only poses an ethics problem but also permits a challenge to the entire agreement. If the other party can establish the elements for a fraud in the inducement claim, the agreement may be rescinded.

In regard to omissions of fact, Rule 4.1(b) provides that a "lawyer shall not knowingly . . . fail to disclose a material fact to a third party when disclosure is necessary to avoid assisting a criminal or fraudulent act by a client, unless disclosure is prohibited by Rule 1.6."[28] With narrow exceptions, Rule 1.6 prohibits a lawyer from revealing "information relating to representation of a client unless the client gives informed consent [or] the disclosure is impliedly authorized in order to carry out the representation. . . ."[29] Generally, under these rules, a lawyer is not obligated to disclose information that will harm her client's negotiating position. Indeed, a lawyer who discloses confidential information without the client's consent commits an ethical violation.

Besides the rules of professional responsibility, you should consider the possible tort and contract liability which can arise from misrepresentations in a negotiation. Because every negotiated agreement, including one entered in court, is a contract, tort liability for fraud in the inducement can result from a misrepresentation.[30] As agents of their clients, lawyers can share in liability for such damages.[31] In addition to tort liability for damages, a fraudulent or material misrepresentation can lead to the voiding of the contract.[32] Your client, then,

---

[26] A lawyer admitted to practice in a jurisdiction where the Model Rules apply is subject to the disciplinary authority of that jurisdiction although engaged in practice elsewhere. Model Rule 8.5.

[27] Wolfram, *supra* note 25.

[28] Model Rule 4.1(b).

[29] Model Rule 1.6(a).

[30] See Restatement (Second) of Torts §525 (1977) ("One who fraudulently makes a misrepresentation of fact, opinion, intention or law for the purpose of inducing another to act or refrain from action in reliance upon it, is subject to liability to the other in deceit for pecuniary loss caused to him by his justifiable reliance upon the misrepresentation.").

[31] See Restatement (Second) of Agency §348 (1958) ("An agent who fraudulently makes representations . . . is subject to liability in tort to the injured person, although the fraud . . . occurs in a transaction on behalf of the principal.").

[32] See Restatement (Second) of Contracts (1981) ("If a party's manifestation of assent is induced either by a fraudulent or material misrepresentation by the other party upon which the recipient is justified in relying, the contract is voidable by the recipient."). Under this Restatement, non-disclosure of a fact can be equivalent to an assertion. See *id.* §161.

could face not only the possibility of losing the benefits of the deal but also a judgment against her for damages.

Some threats are unethical. In some states, a lawyer may not threaten presentation of criminal charges solely to obtain an advantage in a civil matter.[33] In those states, any threat to bring criminal charges may be risky, as may be a threat to file disciplinary charges with a grievance committee. The best policy is never to threaten criminal or disciplinary consequences in those jurisdictions.

Finally, you should be aware that in most states clients are permitted to sue their attorneys for malpractice for negligently negotiating an agreement even if they consented to settlement.[34] While most courts acknowledge the policy of encouraging negotiated settlements to disputes, they also recognize that lawyers owe their clients the duty to know the law and obtain accurate information upon which the client can make an informed decision. "The test for purposes of malpractice is commonly stated as whether the attorney exercised that degree of skill, prudence, and diligence in investigating the facts, in legal research, and in giving legal advice that lawyers of ordinary skill and capacity would do in similar situations."[35]

---

[33] See generally 2 Geoffrey C. Hazard & W. William Hodes, *The Law of Lawyering* §40.4 [Stefan H. Krieger and Richard K.Neumann, Jr., *Essential Lawyering Skills: Interviewing, Counseling, Negotiation, and Persuasive Fact Analysis*, 4th ed., (2011)] at 40-8 to 40-11 (2010).

[34] See Lynn A. Epstein, *Post-Settlement Malpractice: Undoing the Done Deal*, 46 Cath. U. L. Rev. 453 (1997).

[35] Jay Folberg & Dwight Golann, *Lawyer Negotiation: Theory, Practice, and Law* 272 (2d ed. 2011).

NEGOTIATION PREPARATION: ASSESSING THE PARTIES

§28.1 Interests, Rights, and Power

You saw in §27.2 that all negotiations are greatly affected by the parties' interests, rights, and power. Prenegotiation preparation necessarily includes an assessment of the interests, rights, and power of both your client and the other side.

§28.2 Assessing the Parties' Interests

This process requires identifying the interests of each party, prioritizing your client's interests, and predicting the other party's priorities.

§28.2.1 Types of Interests

Interests are the needs, desires, concerns, fears, and expectations of a particular party. Although this definition seems quite simple, the process of identifying the interests of your client and those of the other party is not so easy. Your client may be unsure or ambivalent about what she really wants. Or she may be absolutely certain about her needs at the initial interview, only to change her mind completely on the eve of the deal closing or trial.

In regard to identifying the interests of the other parties, your access to them is limited, and their communications to you might not be totally forthright. Your task, therefore, is a reconnaissance mission to learn as much as possible about the other side's interests.[1]

To engage in this process, think of various types of interests to explore. Although the following categories may not be applicable to all cases and some of

---

[1] For an extended discussion of this process, see Carrie Menkel-Meadow, *Toward Another View of Legal Negotiation: The Structure of Problem Solving*, 31 UCLA L. Rev. 754, 801–803 (1984).

them overlap, they provide a framework to assure a thorough investigation of interests:

1. Financial interests.   These include not only the short-term money effects of the transaction or dispute but also any long-term financial ramifications or tax consequences for the party.

2. Performance interests.   Especially in transactional settings, performance concerns may be just as important as price. In an installment sales transaction, for example, the seller might be as interested in the security and nonperformance remedy provisions of the agreement as in the payment schedule. Or in the sale of a house, the seller who is relocating to another area in a short time may be willing to accept a much lower price if the buyer pays cash (so that the seller does not have to worry about whether the deal might collapse if the buyer cannot get a mortgage).

3. Psychological needs.   In many transactions and disputes, one or more of the parties has an emotional stake: a seller has lived in her house for 25 years and is ambivalent about having to move; each spouse in a child custody dispute feels that the other is an unfit parent; a commercial buyer feels that it was overcharged in a previous transaction; a plaintiff in an action against an insurance company may have mixed feelings, wanting both vengeance and the certainty that compensation will be forthcoming; an environmental group may be up in arms because it feels that a factory deliberately and greedily ignored clean air standards. Although these feelings might not be rational, they are real and certainly affect the dynamics of bargaining. Indeed, in some dispute resolution negotiations, the primary interest of a party is not the relief requested in the complaint but an apology or public recognition of wrongdoing.

4. Reputational interests.   Some parties might be concerned about the effect of the transaction or dispute on their reputations. They may fear, for example, that this case might set a harmful precedent in the future or that adverse publicity will embarrass them. In the plea bargaining context, some prosecutors may want to buttress their reputations by racking up good win-loss records in which a guilty plea to a reduced charge counts as a win but trials risk being losses. They may also offer less favorable pleas in strong, high-profile cases than in similar low-profile cases hoping to win well-publicized convictions.[2]

5. Relationship interests.   Many transactional and some dispute-resolution negotiations involve repeat players: buyers frequently purchase from particular sellers; unions regularly bargain with management for collective bargaining agreements; parents in a custody dispute may continue to be in close contact with each other; or public interest groups may consistently litigate against the same governmental regulatory bodies. In those situations, although the relationship between the parties on some level will be adversarial, on another level it will require cooperation. After a collective bargaining agreement is reached, for

---

[2] Stephanos Bibas, *Plea Bargaining Outside the Shadow of Trial*, 117 Harv. L. Rev. 2463, 2471, 2474 (2004).

example, the employees will be working for management, and, even after the public interest group has settled or litigated its case, it will probably be dealing on a regular basis with matters before the regulatory body. In many cases, therefore, parties may have a stake in maintaining a working relationship.

6. *Liberty interests.* These may include not only freedom from incarceration in a criminal case but also freedom to travel, to engage in a particular occupation, or to spend time with one's family. Criminal defendants nearly always want to avoid imprisonment. But other dispositions can also have a significant impact on the defendant's liberty: community service obligations may interfere with the defendant's job obligations; a record of a conviction might preclude employment in a particular occupation; or participation in a drug program might interfere with family life.

7. *Basic human needs.* This catch-all category is a useful tool in double-checking your investigation of the parties' interests. It includes security, economic well-being, a sense of belonging and of being appreciated, and control over one's life. These needs are not exclusive to individuals. Groups, corporations, government agencies, and nations, to some extent, all have these interests, and they should not be overlooked.

§28.2.2 *Identification of Parties' Interests*

When interviewing and counseling your client to learn the client's interests, begin with open-ended, rather than closed or leading questions. Ask your client what end results she desires, and then why this outcome is so important. Do not rush into accepting the initial response, but try to obtain a complete listing of all the client's concerns. If the client defines her needs and interests only vaguely, you will want to narrow your questions, perhaps by exploring whether the client has any interests in the categories described in §28.2.1. If you do not succeed with this approach, ask about the kinds of concerns that other clients have had in these situations. It is often helpful to write down your client's responses on a pad or whiteboard which the client can read while you write; seeing the answers charted out, the client may be encouraged to articulate other concerns.

During this process, your client may be reluctant to express some concerns, especially those of a psychological nature. In a child custody dispute, for example, a parent may not want to litigate aggressively an issue because she feels that she lacks the stamina to do it. Sensitive, active listening helps in such situations. To obtain a thorough account of all your client's interests, be nonjudgmental so that your client feels that she can openly confide in you.

A client's interests will shift often during your representation. Some clients may not be ready to commit and reach a deal; others might be ambivalent about what they want; and still others may view the case differently at the end of a negotiation when faced with concrete options than at the beginning. While you may be tempted to take control and tell the client what to do, we suggest that you work with the client to determine what she genuinely wants. Find out the reasons that the client changed her mind. If the client is not ready to reach an agreement, explain the consequences of her shifting positions, the possibilities of delaying negotiations, and the risks inherent in changing positions.[3]

You also need to identify the interests of the opposing party or parties to understand fully the context for the negotiation. Sometimes the other party articulates its needs and interests clearly and forthrightly. Other times, however, your opponent will leave you bewildered either because of its own negotiation strategy or because it has not thought out its concerns thoroughly. In those situations, you may want to adopt an approach similar to the one you use with your client and ask the other party's lawyer why the other party has adopted a particular position and why the other party rejects your client's position (see §32.1.1).[4] If this does not work, you might want to explore possible interests with your opponent by asking questions such as "it seems to me that you are interested in . . ." to evoke an affirmative or corrective response. A similar technique is to make a proposal, tell the other side that you think the proposal helps to satisfy an interest that you assume it has, and then listen carefully to its reaction. Sometimes phrasing a proposal as a hypothetical results in helpful discussion because the other side may not feel as threatened by it as by an actual offer ("If we were to offer X, what effect would that have on your client's situation?").

The other party and its lawyer, however, are not the only sources for identifying its interests. Your client may know the other side's interests and concerns from personal experience. This is certainly true in domestic relations or labor management disputes. And many commercial and corporate transactions involve repeat players who have intimate knowledge of each other's interests. Try to get your clients to put themselves in the role of the other side and argue its view of the case. Ask them how they think the other side feels about them and what it hopes to attain in the case.[5]

Additional information can be obtained from other lawyers or third parties who have previously dealt with your opponent. And in a dispute or transaction with an organization, news articles or Web postings might reveal its financial, reputational, and policy priorities. Consider the other parties' behavior in similar settings both in style and substance; their training, political, and professional affiliation; the organizational position of the person who has authority for negotiation decisions; and the persons to whom the other side defers or tends to admire.[6] Use your fact investigation not only to explore the substantive issues in the case but also the underlying interests and needs of the other side.

§28.2.3 Prioritizing Interests

The final step in assessing the interests of the parties is to prioritize the interests of your client and the other party. Obviously, the lists you compile in regard

---

[3] See generally Robert H. Mnookin et al., *Beyond Winning: Negotiating to Create Value in Deals and Disputes* 201–203 (2000).

[4] Roger Fisher et al., *Getting to Yes: Negotiating Agreement Without Giving In* 44–45 (2d ed. 1991).

[5] Mnookin et al., *supra* note 3, at 180–182.

[6] David A. Lax & James K. Sebenius, *Interests: The Measure of Negotiation*, 2 Negot. J. 73, 89 (1986).

Figure 28.1   Assessment of Parties' Interests

Types of Interest	Client's Interests	Other Party's Interests
1. Financial		
2. Performance		
3. Liberty		
4. Psychological		
5. Reputational		
6. Relationship		
7. Basic Human Needs		
HIGHEST PRIORITIES		

to your client's interests and your guesses as to the other party's interests will in many cases be lengthy. (See Figure 28.1 for the list's basic structure.) And some interests on a list might be inconsistent with others on the same list. In negotiating a business partnership, for example, your client may articulate interests both in retaining control over the direction of the business and in limiting the time he wants to spend on it.

To get an adequate assessment of the interests of both parties, work with your client to determine her two or three most important interests in this transaction or dispute and try to speculate on the priorities of concerns for the other party. Remember that each of the parties' interests may change as the bargaining progresses. As that happens, you may want to revisit your assessment of interests and priorities. By identifying these priorities you lay the groundwork for determining whether or not a problem-solving approach will settle the issues (see §29.3).

§28.3 Assessing the Parties' Rights

Novice lawyers tend to think of negotiations as driven primarily by legal concerns. You saw in §28.2, however, that nonlegal interests — financial, psychological, relationship, reputational needs — can be the driving force behind the parties' behavior. Still, legal negotiations do take place in the "shadow of the law," and it would be a mistake to ignore totally the legal rights of the parties in preparing for negotiation. Although many negotiations do not include lengthy legal arguments, the parties' evaluation of their respective rights can have a significant impact on the outcome. Robert Condlin writes that although explicit legal argumentation is

common among novice negotiators, [it] is less prominent in negotiations between experienced lawyers who bargain with one another regularly (e.g., personal injury plaintiffs' lawyers and insurance company counsel, prosecutors and criminal defense lawyers). Perhaps this is because personal familiarity and common experiences give lawyers shared views about what law is settled and what evidence counts as persuasive, and enable them to play out arguments privately in their heads so that they need discuss only novel or controversial points openly.[7]

In dispute resolution negotiations, assessment of the parties' rights requires predicting the possible outcome if the case were to be tried in court. This includes evaluating the strengths and weaknesses of the parties' legal and factual theories (see Figure 28.2). The lawyer for the party going forward (the plaintiff, the prosecutor, or the movant) should identify all possible claims for relief (or, in a criminal case, the range of charges) and the legal elements for each. The lawyer should then determine whether the evidence will establish a prima facie case. Finally, the lawyer should identify the possible legal remedies that would be available if the case is proved. (Sometimes, a plaintiff in a civil case will have a strong case establishing liability, but only be entitled to limited relief.)

The resisting lawyer (representing the defendant, for example) should consider whether any of the claims is based on an accurate understanding of the law. Then, the resisting lawyer should marshal the available evidence to determine whether the party asserting the claim can establish a prima facie case. Finally, the resisting lawyer should consider whether any affirmative defenses can defeat any of the claims and whether the evidence will establish the minimum facts to prove those defenses.

When considering legal theories in preparation for negotiation, be especially careful about burdens of production and persuasion. In litigation, the winner is the party who either carries all of her burdens or prevents an adversary from carrying all of his. The question is not whether a defendant is liable or guilty, but whether the evidence proves the claim or charge according to the applicable standard. And negotiation "in the shadow of the law" inevitably takes burdens into account. In a criminal case, for example, the prosecution's need to prove its case beyond a reasonable doubt has a substantial effect on the plea bargaining process. (Remember to evaluate not only the strength and weakness of each party's legal theory in the abstract, but also try to predict the probable rulings on these legal issues by the tribunal that will actually decide the case.

In regard to factual theory, consider the persuasiveness of the parties' facts. Evaluate the credibility of each parties' sources of facts, contextual facts, and circumstantial evidence and assess the structural integrity of their stories. Then try to forecast, given the nature of your audience (the particular judge, hearing examiner, arbitrator, or jury), the ultimate judgment. (See §24.3.1 on how to predict damages.)

Rights assessment is also necessary in preparation for a transactional negotiation (see Figure 28.3). Here, the inquiry is not about the possible outcome of the case at trial, but about legal requirements governing the transaction or the common business practices that create context for the deal. Many legal form books provide not only sample forms for similar deals but also relevant case law and statutory authority on these transactions. Although you should avoid using form

---

[7] Robert J. Condlin, *"Cases on Both Sides": Patterns of Argument in Legal Dispute-Negotiation,* 44 Md. L. Rev. 65, 69 n.14 (1985).

Figure 28.2   Assessment of Parties' Rights — Dispute

Analysis of Claims	Plaintiff/Prosecutor	Defendant
Legal Theory(ies)/ Defense(s)		
Strengths		
Weaknesses		
Factual Theory(ies)		
Strengths		
Weaknesses		
WHAT ADDITIONAL INFORMATION IS NEEDED TO REACH A DEAL? **WHO IS LIKELY TO PREVAIL?** **HOW CAN THE RIGHTS RELATIONSHIP BE CHANGED?**		

books as the sole basis for your proposal, they can help to identify key legal issues. If you have not handled such a deal before, get copies of similar agreements from experienced lawyers. With the help of your client, investigate also the common business practices for such transactions, such as pricing, performance, and quality control standards. Certainly, you should not feel bound by the sample agreement in the form book or common business practices, but you need to understand that the other parties may be entering the negotiation presuming that these customs constitute their informal "rights."

Often, novice lawyers — out of fear that the negotiations will fail — will prematurely reach a deal with an opponent without learning crucial facts. Identify the information that is indispensable to your appraisal of the situation so that you can adequately prepare a negotiation strategy. In a transactional setting, obtain facts about industry customs, information about past dealings between the parties, and technical information about the products or services involved. In a dispute negotiation, examine your chronology, and identify the missing witnesses, documents, and facts that are essential to a basic understanding of the events. (See Figure 28.2 and Figure 28.3)

The rights context of most negotiations is not stagnant but can change drastically depending upon the legal maneuvering of the parties. You often have the

Figure 28.3   Assessment of Parties' Rights — Transaction

Rights	Client's Rights	Other Party's Rights
Statutory/Regulatory Requirements Common Business Practices for Transaction		
WHAT ADDITIONAL INFORMATION IS NEEDED TO REACH A DEAL? **WHAT EFFECT DO THESE RIGHTS HAVE ON THE TRANSACTION?** **HOW CAN THE LEGAL RELATIONSHIP BE CHANGED?**		

ability to change the legal relationship of the parties before or during negotiation. In the dispute resolution context, for instance, you can add leverage by suing, making strategically sound motions, conducting extensive discovery, filing a counterclaim, or seeking sanctions for unreasonable conduct. Similar moves can be made in transactional negotiations. For example, in a commercial real estate sale where the price is deflated because of zoning restrictions on the property, the situation will be changed radically if the owner succeeds in getting a zoning variance. In preparing for your negotiation, you should identify those possible changes. (See Figure 28.2 and Figure 28.3.)

§28.4 Assessing the Parties' Power

Power is the ability to coerce someone to do something that person would not otherwise do. Assessing the parties' rights means examining how legal or other objective standards affect the parties' strengths and weaknesses. But assessing the power context explores how *nonlegal*, coercive factors do the same thing. Although, as we shall see, power differentials do not necessarily determine negotiation outcomes, they can have a significant impact on the bargaining process. In fact, several studies have shown that power symmetry rather than power imbalance is the most favorable condition for reaching agreement because the more powerful party's coercive tactics can often lead to resistance from the weaker party, suspicion of even its reasonable offers, and extreme threats by the less-powerful party to counter the stronger party's power plays.[8] In your preparation for a negotiation, therefore, you need to assess the potential effects of power imbalances.

§28.4.1 Types of Power

The primary sources of power in legal negotiations are economic, social, psychological, and political power, and expertise. (See Figure 28.4.)

1. Economic power.   Obviously, the ability of a party to bring its resources to bear on a transaction or dispute can impact the negotiation. When a large corporation negotiates to acquire a smaller, family-run business, for example, the acquiring company will probably have at its disposal a much greater staff of lawyers, accountants, and tax experts. Similarly, in a criminal case, the state can overwhelm many defendants with its cadre of assistant district attorneys, investigators, and expert witnesses. And in the labor-management context, the company, as owner of its facilities, has the right, within legal limits, to set the conditions of work for its employees. In many cases, the dynamic of the negotiation is driven by these types of power imbalance.

Nevertheless, parties with large resources may suffer from limitations on their power, and parties with ostensibly fewer resources may have access to other means of economic power. The large corporation seeking to acquire the smaller company may be involved in numerous other transactions and litigation and may be able to devote only limited staff to this deal. And the privately-owned company may have retained a small, boutique law firm that specializes in representing "underdogs" in such negotiations. Likewise, while the heavy caseload of many urban prosecutors may severely inhibit their ability to press all cases to the fullest extent possible, some white collar defendants may have the ability to retain legal "dream teams." And in labor-management negotiations, the employees may have an advantage if they are few in number, have highly specialized skills, and operate expensive and complicated machinery. The company may have invested heavily in equipment, and it may be cheaper to raise pay than to let that equipment lie idle while hard-to-replace workers are on strike.

2. Social power.   Some transactions and disputes occur within a context where the parties can wield significant power within a given geographic, fraternal, religious, or similar community. For instance, suppose a young retailer has recently opened a business in a small town and negotiates a contract with a well-established and prominent wholesaler. Both parties certainly know the pressures that the wholesaler can exert on the retailer's business relationships in the town, on his position in the community, and on his family and personal life. Or, within some traditional religious communities, parties can apply pressure from religious authorities to attempt to influence negotiations on child custody and property

---

[8] Robert S. Adler & Elliot M. Silverstein, *When David Meets Goliath: Dealing with Power Differentials in Negotiations*, 5 Harv. Negot. L. Rev. 1, 16–18 (2000).

Figure 28.4   Assessment of Parties' Power

Types of Power	Client's Power	Other Party's Power
1. Economic 2. Social 3. Psychological 4. Political 5. Expertise		
WHAT EFFECT DO THESE POWER RELATIONSHIPS HAVE ON THE TRANSACTION/ DISPUTE? **HOW CAN THE POWER RELATIONSHIP BE CHANGED?**		

distribution issues.[9] Even within the more cosmopolitan world of regulatory trans-actions and litigation, social power can play a role. Studies have shown, for instance, that because of the ongoing, day-to-day personal relationship between public utilities and their regulators' staffs, close and informal ties develop between them, often resulting in the companies having an undue influence over the process of regulatory negotiations.[10]

And differences in social status between the parties can create power imbalan-ces in the bargaining process. A visit to a high-volume urban eviction or misde-meanor court will starkly reflect this problem. Court personnel and judges often treat the assistant district attorney assigned to a particular courtroom or a "regular" landlords' lawyer who consistently appears in a court with a deference that is not shown to low-income litigants or defendants of color. Indeed, in some of these courtrooms, African-American and Latino lawyers are often frequently mistaken by the regular lawyers or court personnel for one of the defendants. A defendant who does not speak English is at an even greater disadvantage in attempting to

---

[9] See, for example, *Fred Kaplan, Orthodox Jews Struggle with Divorce*, Boston Globe, May 3, 1998, at A-1, available in LEXIS, News Library, Globe File (describing problems created in civil divorce proceedings when Orthodox Jewish men refuse to give their wives religiously required divorces and the religious authorities side with the husbands).

[10] David M. Welborn & Anthony E. Brown, *Regulatory Policy and Processes: The Public Service Commissions in Tennessee, Kentucky and Georgia* 66 (1980). See Stefan H. Krieger, *Problems for Captive Ratepayers in Nonunanimous Settlements of Public Utility Rate Cases*, 12 Yale J. on Reg. 257, 306–308 (1995).

maneuver through the court process. In such an environment, social factors obviously influence negotiations.

3. *Psychological power.* All parties to a negotiation have certain psychological needs: desires, fears, anger, and other emotions (§28.2). And sometimes one or more of the parties try to exploit those needs in negotiations by wielding psychological power. In a child custody dispute, for example, one parent might threaten to poison the children's minds against the other unless the latter agrees to more liberal visitation terms. Likewise, in some landlord-tenant negotiations, the landlord might threaten to lock the tenant out of his apartment or disconnect the utility service, even though the landlord has no legal right to take such action. Threats like these can have profound effects on low-income tenants who do not know their rights — or on anybody who wants to live in his home in peace. Even in corporate bargaining, negotiators often attempt to play psychological games with their adversaries to obtain an advantage.

4. *Political power* is the ability to influence public officials, decision-makers, or opinion-makers. In high-profile civil rights, antitrust, or products liability cases, parties often attempt to enlist the support of government agencies or key media figures to influence the negotiations.

But even in less dramatic cases, parties can try to exert political power. Consider the *Ransom v. Dusak* case for example. On the one hand, the landlord might attempt to influence the political context by contacting friendly officials in the Department of Health to discourage the filing of any formal charges against him for the conditions at Ransom's apartment. On the other hand, Ransom might work with a community organization to organize the tenants to pressure Dusak to repair the property and to demand prompt action by the Health Department. She might also try to interest a local newspaper in her story. In either case, these political actions or threats of political action by the parties would certainly affect any negotiation of the dispute.

5. *Expertise.* In some negotiations one party has greater expertise on certain issues involved in the transaction or dispute, and that knowledge can result in a power imbalance. Moreover, the more information that a party has about a particular situation, the more likely that she will understand its context and will be able to make a quick decision even with limited resources.[11] Imagine, for instance, a company official with no computer background who is negotiating for the purchase of a software program for all his firm's accounts and records. Even if he educates himself on the basics of computer software, the salesperson will probably be at an advantage because of her superior knowledge about the product.

This situation frequently arises with novice lawyers. Suppose you are negotiating with an experienced lawyer in a routine matter, such as a real estate closing or settlement of a divorce case, and your adversary says, "This is the way attorneys in this area always handle escrow accounts for real estate taxes that will become due," or "They may have taught you this in law school, but let me tell you, Judge Lavagetto won't even countenance a request for joint custody."

---

[11] Adler & Silverstein, *supra* note 8, at 26.

You may have carefully researched the law on the subject and spoken to other experienced practitioners about the issue and come to the conclusion that your adversary is dead wrong — but you might still have the nagging feeling that he knows what he is talking about. Your adversary may have nothing more than psychological power over you because your inexperience makes you insecure. But unless you are willing to stand up to your adversary, that psychological power can be intimidating.

6. Moral power.   Even parties with limited economic or political resources may be able to exert power through appeals to fairness or morality. Day laborers negotiating with a town for the establishment of a hiring site, for example, may have very little political clout but might be successful by appealing to notions of basic human dignity and the right of every person to a job. Although moral power depends in large part on the ability of the more powerful party to empathize with the other side, it can carry a degree of sincerity that is lacking with other assertions of power.[12]

§28.4.2 Shifting the Power Relationship

The power relationship between the parties is not static. You or the other party can take steps either before or during the negotiation to change the power balance. And those changes can significantly impact the course of the negotiations. In preparing for your negotiation, you should also identify those possible changes. (See Figure 28.4.)

1. Using the party's own power to affect the power balance.   Obviously, if one party in a negotiation has substantially more power in a particular area, the other party can either try to increase its power in the same area or develop power in some other area. For instance, a small company with limited resources locked in an antitrust dispute with a large manufacturer that has huge resources can increase its economic power by forging alliances with other small firms that are experiencing similar problems. Or a community organization challenging a powerful corporation's siting of a hazardous waste dump in a low-income neighborhood might attempt to reduce the power imbalance by using media pressure to influence government officials.

2. Asserting rights to affect the power balance.   Often when a power imbalance exists between the parties to a dispute, the less powerful party can attempt to equalize the playing field by seeking rights-based relief. Litigation, for example, can be used by less powerful parties to protect their interests against more powerful opponents.

The prime example of the use of adjudication for this purpose is a federal civil rights action against a school system alleging racial discrimination, in which the plaintiffs rely on the protections of the civil rights laws and the procedural protections of the federal courts to rectify the power imbalance between themselves and local government officials.

---

[12] *Id.* at 28.

3. *Reducing the perception of powerlessness.* Some power imbalances are more perceived than real. Although the threats of a spouse in a child custody dispute or of a landlord against a low-income tenant may be empty, they may still cause your client to feel inordinate fear. Likewise, even though your experienced opponent may be completely wrong in his interpretation of the law or his understanding of how a particular judge handles a matter, you, as an inexperienced lawyer, may feel intimidated by his pressure.

A partial remedy is to change the perception of powerlessness. To address your client's fear, counsel her about the actual risks involved in the situation. Certainly, you do not want to downplay actual dangers. But, in many instances, your client will not have been involved previously with a similar transaction or dispute, and the client's fears will be unfounded. In a calm setting, describe to the client your experiences or those of your colleagues in comparable cases, lay out the advantages and disadvantages of different options, and then let the client decide.

Psychological power plays — aimed at you, your client, or both of you — often occur in hallway negotiations just before trial or at the last minute before a deal closes. To alleviate the impact of this conduct, prepare your client for the contingency that it will happen, and, if it does occur, counsel your client in a private setting where you and the client can coolly reflect on the odds that the opponent will in fact exercise his power. And be prepared in advance for situations where more experienced lawyers might try to manipulate you because you are still a novice lawyer. If you come prepared with cases and statutes in support of your position or have consulted with other lawyers about the habits of a particular judge, you will be in a better position to resist. Moreover, you should consider the kind of impression you want to give the other attorney. Research suggests that the entire tone of a negotiation may be established through the parties' tones and gestures at the beginning of the discussions.[13] If you initially appear hesitant or tentative, a more experienced lawyer will likely try to take advantage of you. While false bravado will seem phoney, you will most likely set the right tone for the negotiation if you appear comfortable in the situation and are prepared to respond directly and confidently to the other attorney's arguments.

4. *Using information to increase power.* In some situations the other side initially has more power because it has access to more information. In an employment discrimination case, for example, much of the evidence about the company's personnel policies, its treatment of similar workers, and the personnel records of the offending supervisor will be in the company's files. The plaintiff can level the playing field through the fact investigation process, by both formal discovery of the company's documents and informal interviews with knowledgeable third parties. Even in cases in which both sides have equal access to information, you may be able to challenge a more powerful opponent effectively with exhaustive fact investigation. In a high-volume criminal courtroom, for example, the prosecutor may get deference from the judge and court personnel but probably will not have the resources to investigate thoroughly every case. A defense

---

[13] *Id.* at 81–82.

attorney whose investigation uncovers major holes in the prosecution's case may use that information to obtain strong leverage in plea bargaining. Finally, when confronted with an experienced attorney, a novice attorney often can equalize any power imbalance in a negotiation with an effective demonstration of her command of the facts in the case.

§28.5 Obtaining Your Client's Authority

Now that you have assessed the interests, rights, and power of the different parties, you can start to develop a strategy for the negotiation. When engaging in this process, remember that your client has the ultimate authority to accept or reject a settlement or plea bargaining offer. Under the ABA Model Rules of Professional Conduct, "[a] lawyer shall abide by a client's decision whether to settle a matter. In a criminal case, the lawyer shall abide by the client's decision, after consultation with the lawyer, as to a plea to be entered."[14] Thus, you are always obligated to inform your client of a settlement offer, even if you suspect that the client will reject it.[15]

Because the client has the ultimate authority in the negotiation process, you should consult with the client from the beginning of your preparation for the negotiation. Have the client identify the core of what she wants in this transaction or dispute and what would be "icing on the cake." As we see in Chapter 29, this process requires a determination of the client's Best Alternative To a Negotiated Agreement. Before the negotiation, ask the client to decide how much authority to settle she will give you. This process consists of counseling the client about her BATNA and exploring with her hypothetical settlement packages, the acceptability of these packages, and the possibility of other packages that are more or less favorable to her.[16] This, of course, is not a one-time process. As the negotiation proceeds, as you learn new information, as you receive offers from the other party, and as your client reevaluates her feelings about the transaction or dispute, your counseling will continue, and your client will determine whether to modify the authority she has given you.

Although your client has the ultimate authority to decide on any agreement, the type of authority your client gives you before and during the negotiation can vary greatly. Sometimes lawyers negotiate "without authority." You can say to the other party's lawyer, "I don't have authority to negotiate those particular type of terms," or "At this time, I don't have authority on anything," and then try to work out the most favorable deal to present to the client for approval. Often your clients will want you to take such an approach, telling you to see what you can get and asking you to report back to them. On the other hand, a desperate client might give you unlimited authority, saying to you, in effect, "Get me the best deal you can" and pre-authorizing you to accept it. In most instances, however, clients will

---

[14] Model Rules of Professional Conduct Rule 1.2(a).
[15] ABA Comm. on Professional Ethics, Formal Op. 326 (1970).
[16] Paul R. Tremblay, *"Pre-Negotiation" Counseling: An Alternative Model*, 13 Clinical L. Rev. 541, 547–556 (2006).

give you limited authority, and you will continually consult with them for increased authority as the negotiation progresses.[17]

Two problems can arise from unlimited authority. One is that the client loses a lot of control over her own lawyer's conduct during the negotiation because the lawyer has not been asked to report back for approval at various stages during the negotiation. The other problem is that a lawyer negotiating with unlimited authority can more easily be swept up in the heat of negotiation. Reporting back to the client before the deal is closed provides an opportunity for reflection before making a commitment.

On the other hand, if you have no authority to settle, you might be able to brainstorm more openly and flexibly with the other side, unconfined by limits set in advance by your client. But when you have no authority to settle, your client may delay making a realistic assessment of her case and expect more from the negotiations than is possible. You might solve that problem before negotiating by explaining to the client the possible deals that might result, given the practicalities of the situation.

We suspect that most lawyers generally feel comfortable negotiating with limited authority, which encourages the client to assess the case seriously before negotiation and allows the client to keep control over the process. But there are disadvantages to limited authority, too. For example, social science studies show that lawyers with only limited authority are more likely to be more vigorous and tough in their use of competitive tactics than lawyers who have unlimited authority.[18]

The decision of how much authority you will be given is a strategic one and should fit the situation. What works well in one negotiation for one client might work badly in the next negotiation for another client.

§28.6 Is a Structured Settlement in Your Client's Interest?

A structured settlement is an agreement in a damages case through which a defendant pays a plaintiff money over a period of time, usually years, rather than all at once.

Structured settlements can look like an easy way to find agreement. A defendant does not need to pay immediately all the money agreed to. And to a plaintiff's lawyer who ignores the time value of money (see §24.3.2), agreeing to accept the money later seems like a small concession to facilitate agreement. But because of the time value of money, payments later are worth less than payments now.

payment	future value	present value
immediate	$100,000	$100,000
1 year	100,000	94,340
2 years	100,000	89,000
3 years	100,000	83,962

---

[17] Donald G. Gifford, *Legal Negotiation: Theory and Applications* 70 (1989).
[18] *Id.*

payment	future value	present value
4 years	100,000	79,209
5 years	100,000	74,726
		total = 521,237

Looking at the deal from the defendant's point of view, if the defendant were to fund this obligation right now by paying $100,000 up front and investing enough to produce the $500,000 for future payments, that would cost the defendant $521,237 in today's money if the rate of return on the investment were 6%.

Some settlements, such as those for personal injury, are not taxable income to the plaintiff. But if the settlement would be taxed, the tax consequences could change the value calculation above.

A structured settlement is an extremely complicated arrangement. If you are about to participate in a negotiation where a structured settlement might be proposed, you should spend some time in the library with books or other materials designed to show practitioners how to handle structured settlements. Do that regardless of whether your client is the plaintiff or defendant.

CHAPTER 29

Developing a Negotiation Strategy

§29.1 Determining Your Client's BATNA

The first step in developing a negotiation strategy is to identify your client's BATNA or Best Alternative To a Negotiated Agreement (see §27.3.2).

> Your BATNA is your walkaway alternative. It's your best course of action for satisfying your interests without the other's agreement. If you're negotiating with your boss over a raise, your BATNA might be to find a job with another firm. If you're negotiating with a salesperson, your BATNA might be to talk to the store manager or, if that fails, you might go to another store. If one nation is negotiating with another over unfair trade practices, its BATNA might be to appeal to the appropriate international tribunal [or impose a tariff].[1]

Determining the client's BATNA is valuable whichever approach you eventually use in the negotiation — adversarial, problem-solving, or a combination of both.

Only after your client has identified her BATNA should she translate it into a bottom line, the minimum amount she would accept rather than pursue her BATNA. Identification of a bottom line prior to the exploration of different BATNA's has several disadvantages.[2] First, premature identification of bottom lines reduces the potential for problem-solving negotiation. By focusing too early on a fixed preconception of what outcome is acceptable, it ignores the possibility of unforeseen solutions that might develop during the negotiation.[3] If, for example, a client in a contract negotiation initially focuses solely on a monetary bottom line, she may overlook the possibility of other nonmonetary options for addressing her interests. By holding off on the identification of a bottom line at least until the

---

[1] William Ury, *Getting Past No: Negotiating Your Way from Confrontation to Cooperation* 21–22 (1993).

[2] See Robert H. Mnookin et al., *Beyond Winning: Negotiating to Create Value in Deals and Disputes* 20 (2000).

[3] Roger Fisher et al., *Getting to Yes: Negotiating Agreement Without Giving In* 98–99 (2d ed. 1991).

client has considered her BATNA and perhaps until negotiations have begun, you leave open the possibility of productive problem-solving brainstorming.

Second, bottom lines are sometimes set too high. At the beginning of the negotiation process, your client's expectations may be unrealistic. But once they are crystallized into a bottom line, those expectations become a position that is hard to abandon even when it turns out later to be unrealistic. The converse can also be true. In some circumstances the bottom line may be too low, but because it is a position, the client might abandon it only reluctantly.

To determine your client's BATNA, you and your client should review your assessments of the parties' interests, rights, and power (Figure 28.1, Figure 28.2, Figure 28.3, and Figure 28.4). From these assessments, generate options by identifying the possible alternatives to a negotiated settlement. From your interests assessment, consider the alternatives that your client can undertake herself to pursue her interests outside of any relationship with the other party. Then, from the rights assessments, identify what rights the client can assert before a court, agency, or arbitrator to address her interests. Finally, from the powers assessment, consider alternative ways that your client can wield power to coerce the other side into meeting her interests.

Assume, for example, that you represent an electric utility that is negotiating for an easement to install a high-voltage transmission line over some farmland. In reviewing its interests, your client might develop a number of possible alternatives to negotiation that it can pursue without any relationship with the property owner: obtaining an easement on other, nearby property; purchasing other property in the area for the installation of the line; enlarging an existing line; or abandoning plans altogether for the new installation. In reviewing its rights, your client might identify still another option: an eminent domain proceeding to obtain a condemnation order allowing an easement on the property. And in reviewing its power, your client might consider the possibility of raising its electric rates to the property owner (because of the extra cost of service) to force the granting of the easement.

Or consider a negotiation in the *Ransom v. Dusak* case. Assume you are counseling Ransom. After reviewing her interests, you might identify several alternatives to negotiation: repairing the conditions herself, moving out of the apartment, or just giving up. Turning to her rights, you might determine that Ransom has other options: withholding her rent and raising the inadequate conditions as a defense in an eviction action, filing an affirmative case against Dusak for breach of the warranty of habitability, or bringing a class action against him on behalf of all the tenants in the building. And, finally, considering her power, you might develop even more options, such as persuading the Health Department to prosecute Dusak for his failure to maintain the premises or organizing the tenants to pressure him to sell the building.

After identifying possible alternatives to negotiation, you and your client should evaluate each of them to determine one or two BATNA's. You and the client should try to imagine the potential consequences of each option and consider its advantages and disadvantages. Although there is no simple formula for this evaluation, the client should consider: (1) whether a particular option meets those interests the client considers to be top priorities, (2) the strengths and weaknesses of the different parties' legal and factual theories, and (3) any power imbalance in the relationship with the other side.

In the utility easement hypothetical, for instance, where your client's primary interest is minimizing costs, the utility will need to consider the potential expense of obtaining an easement from other property owners in the area, the costs of enlarging existing lines, the financial necessity for an easement on this particular property, the costs (and risks) of eminent domain litigation, and the dangers of trying to impose increased rates on the property owner. And, in *Ransom v. Dusak*, if Ransom's principal interest is peace of mind and the safety of her children, she will need to weigh seriously the psychological pressures and time delays inherent in rights-based or power-based alternatives to negotiation.

Identification of a BATNA serves several functions. First, it helps your client decide whether to negotiate. If, for example, your rights-based BATNA is very strong and the client has little interest in any compromise, trial may be better than negotiating.

Second, a BATNA sets a standard by which to measure settlement proposals. If the client's BATNA is a very strong legal case which she is willing and financially able to pursue, she will probably reject an offer that does not address most of her interests adequately. If, on the other hand, the BATNA is a difficult defense of a lawsuit, the adjudication of which will strain the client's limited finances, she will be more likely to accept that very same offer.

Finally, as you will see in §29.3, the process of identifying a BATNA helps you select the most effective overall approach to the negotiation.

§29.2 Determining the Other Party's BATNA

After identifying your client's BATNA, go further and try to predict the other side's BATNA. Reviewing the assessment of the other party's interests, rights, and power, you and your client should imagine the other side's alternatives to negotiation. Then, weighing these options in light of their imagined priority interests, try to identify the one or two that would best accomplish the other side's goals. By comparing your client's BATNA with the other side's BATNA, you get a good sense of the settlement range and the probability of achieving a negotiated agreement.

§29.3 Selecting an Approach to the Negotiation

As you know by now, a lawyer using an adversarial approach to negotiation views what is happening as a conflict over distribution of limited resources and tries to persuade the other side to concede that the adversarial lawyer's client is entitled to the maximum gain. A lawyer using a problem-solving approach tries to integrate the resources of each side to reach a settlement or deal and works with the other party to develop mutual agreements. Often a lawyer will use both types of approaches in the same negotiation (see §27.3.3). In preparation for a negotiation, determine the most effective approach or approaches for the situation in which you find yourself. Most of what you do and say while negotiating will depend on the approach you have selected.

The approach you take will depend, in large part, on the kind of authority the client has given you and the BATNA she has identified. Many proponents of problem-solving negotiation assert that almost all transactions and disputes are not zero-sum games, and they argue for the use of such an approach in most negotiations. "While there may be some paradigmatic zero-sum games in legal negotiations," one scholar asserts, "most are not zero-sum. For example, in a random search of 240 cases taken from 15 federal and state reporters most cases, in terms presented to the court, were not zero-sum disputes. . . . Child custody can become joint custody, zoning cases permit variances, and bankruptcy can become financial reorganization."[4]

Although this might be admirable theory, it ignores the fact that the client has the ultimate authority to accept or reject a proposal. Thus, even if the most efficient and reasonable solution to a child custody dispute might be a joint custody agreement, if your client insists on sole custody, a problem-solving approach to negotiation will probably not be useful in addressing her interests. You, of course, can counsel your client as to the benefits of a joint custody arrangement and warn her of the disadvantages of relying on a court proceeding as her BATNA, but the client does have the final say — and, in the end, a court case might be right for her needs, even if we would rather she chose otherwise.

In determining the approach to take, consider the following factors:

1. Integrative versus distributive aspects of the transaction or dispute. While a problem-solving approach works better when there is good potential for joint gain, an adversarial approach works better when distributive issues predominate. To choose between them, consider the "Highest Priorities" section of your interests assessments chart (Figure 28.1) and determine whether any viable solutions are suggested by these priorities that would be mutually acceptable to both parties. In a negotiation for the commercial sale of goods, for example, if the parties care about price more than anything else, an adversarial approach probably will protect each party's interests better because distributive issues predominate. But in a negotiation to create a joint venture, many common interests may exist that allow for a problem-solving approach; the joint venture will fail if the parties do not develop a sound relationship.

2. Relationship interests versus one-shot deal.   If your interests assessment reflects important relationship interests between the parties, a problem-solving approach may be strongly warranted because positional bargaining can be highly disruptive to relationships. In situations where an ongoing relationship exists between the parties — for example, labor and management, tenant and landlord, spouses, merchants who engage in frequent transactions — an adversarial approach

---

[4] Carrie Menkel-Meadow, *Toward Another View of Legal Negotiation: The Structure of Problem Solving*, 31 UCLA L. Rev. 754, 785 (1984).

has the potential for adversely affecting that relationship. "Even if you win the battle, you may lose the war. In the process you may destroy your relationship with the other side. And they will often find a way to renege or retaliate the next time they are in a position of power."[5] In contrast, if the dispute or transaction is a "one-shot" deal with a party with whom your client has little or no relationship — and anticipates none in the future — the interest of maintaining the relationship does not predominate and the problem-solving approach is not so strongly indicated. You might, of course, still want to use a problem-solving approach for other reasons — for example, if your client wants to minimize the costs of litigating a dispute.

3. Impact of psychological and reputational interests. In some negotiations, if your client's psychological or reputational interests matter most, they will dictate the approach you take in bargaining. If, for example, you represent a criminal defendant who is afraid of the effect of a lengthy trial on his family, you may opt for a problem-solving approach even if you believe you can achieve the maximum gain for your client using adversarial methods. Or, if in an action alleging a Clean Air Act violation, in which you represent a defendant company that believes the plaintiffs are unfairly attacking its environmental record and that wants to vindicate its reputation, you may choose an adversarial approach even if your evaluation of the different interests suggests possible integrative solutions.

4. Strength or weaknesses of the rights-based or power-based BATNA's. Your approach to negotiation may be significantly affected by the strength or weakness of your rights-based or power-based BATNA's. On the one hand, if your client has a strong legal claim or power resources that could coerce the other side into submission, an adversarial approach may be warranted. Unless your client can realize maximum gain from the negotiation, she probably should resort to her BATNA. On the other hand, if her legal claims are more tenuous and you are litigating before a hostile judge or agency or the power balance tips in your opponent's favor, a problem-solving approach may be advisable.

5. Importance of a definitive ruling. In some disputes one or both of the parties might need a definitive ruling on a particular legal issue. In certain constitutional, civil rights, environmental, or other "public interest" litigation, the plaintiff may have a strong interest in attaining a clear vindication of its rights either through a ruling from the court or agency or through a consent decree or other agreement under which the defendant acknowledges some liability. Likewise, in an intellectual property dispute, the plaintiff may want to demonstrate clearly its right to a patent or copyright. In such cases, even though a problem-solving approach might efficiently resolve the dispute, the plaintiff's lawyer may want to adopt an adversarial approach to achieve the maximum gain in the negotiation: an admission of wrongdoing by the defendant.

Consider three cautions about these factors. First, they are merely guidelines to suggest ways of selecting your approach to negotiation; they are not mechanical

---

[5] Ury, *supra* note 1, at 132 ("[as] the great Chinese strategist Sun Tzu wrote, "To win one hundred victories in one hundred battles is not the acme of skill. To subdue the enemy without fighting is the acme of skill").

rules. In some cases, for example, where your client wants a definitive ruling, you may select a problem-solving approach because other overriding client interests, such as maintaining a good relationship with the other side, suggest that an adversarial approach is not warranted. Second, in some if not most cases, different issues in the negotiation will be more amenable to one approach than to another. Third, you may find that your initial approach simply does not work with the other side. Be prepared to adapt your strategy to the negotiation behavior of the other party.

§29.4 Crafting a Plan: Adversarial Approach

In a negotiation in which you have chosen to take an adversarial approach, or for those issues in a particular negotiation for which you have selected that approach, your goal is to maximize your client's gain and minimize your client's loss. To accomplish this goal, you engage in an exchange of offers and counter-offers with the other side until you either reach an impasse or agreement. Along the way, you attempt to persuade the other party to make concessions based on different arguments, threats, warnings, or appeals. On a very basic level, this is not very different from the everyday dickering on a New York street corner between a vendor and a tourist:

Vendor: It sure looks like it's going to rain. These umbrellas are a great buy for $15.00!

Tourist: I saw them on sale at my local Walmart in Tulsa for $5.00 a piece. Fifteen dollars is a rip-off. I'll only pay $7.50.

Vendor: Come on, you know as well as I that a Walmart umbrella would fall to pieces in one wind gust. These umbrellas are high-quality. They have a special patented lining to protect against wind gusts. But, I like you; I once had a good friend from Tulsa. For you today, I'll give you one for $12.50.

Tourist: You have to be kidding! There's no difference between one umbrella and another. I bet you think I'm some sort of hick. In fact, I can go into Macy's basement right now, and I'm sure I can get one for much less than $12.50. [*walking away*] Bottom line, I'll give you $9.00.

Vendor: Wait a second! Do you want to stand in line at Macy's for an hour and then end up paying $20.00. Listen. I need to make a living too; I have a family to support. Did you hear that thunder? OK, for you today, I'll give it to you for $11.00.

Tourist: [*with raindrops falling on his head*] $10.00 and that's it.

Vendor: [*grumbling*] I'm making nothing on this sale, but I'll give it to you for $10.00.

The street vendor and tourist probably did very little, if any, planning for their bargaining. You, on the other hand, will be negotiating for much more than an umbrella. Adversarial exchanges in important matters require serious preparation, including the creation by you and your client of a game plan for the exchange. This plan should identify several key positions in the exchange: (1) the opening offer; (2) the bottom line; (3) the target point (the position on the continuum of offers and counteroffers where you imagine the parties will agree); and (4) concession points (the moves you might make between the opening offer and your bottom line.[6] Section 29.1 warned against premature identification of a bottom line and advised that you initially look for a BATNA instead. Once you decide to take an adversarial approach, however, the identification of a bottom line is essential to effective planning. But counsel your client that circumstances might change, and that she should not become entrenched with that position.

To understand such a plan, consider a simple automobile accident personal injury case in which the plaintiff seeks a judgment of $150,000, and the insurer denies any liability. After meeting with its lawyer and considering the circumstances of the case, the insurer prepares the game plan graphed in Figure 29.1.[7] Although we graphed this game plan in terms of dollar amounts, the same format can be used when the controversy is not about money. In a plea bargaining situation, for example, the parties might graph a continuum of different sentences, or, if the defendant has been charged with many crimes, the parties might chart the range of offenses from the major one to all the lesser included ones. Or, in the *Ransom v. Dusak* case, they might graph both monetary and nonmonetary positions, including not only compensation for Ransom, but also different repairs and the time when they will be completed.

After drawing up your own range of positions, graph your prediction of positions the other side will take. The insurer's lawyer, for example, might develop the diagram in Figure 29.2. From this diagram, the insurer's lawyer can estimate a settlement range of $50,000 (the plaintiff's bottom line) to $85,000 (his client's bottom line). His goal in the negotiation will be to convince the plaintiff to concede all the way to her bottom line and to fend off the attempts of the plaintiff's lawyer to force the insurance company to its bottom line. Most of the time, your predictions of the other party's positions will not be completely accurate. This process helps, however, to give you and your client a rough estimate of the relationship between the other side's bargaining range and yours.

Although these ranges, by their very nature, are merely estimates, do not pull them out of a hat. You and your client should return to your assessment charts (Figure 28.1, Figure 28.2, Figure 28.3, and Figure 28.4) and evaluate your client's and the other party's positions in light of each parties' interests, rights, and power. In the personal injury hypothetical, the insurer's lawyer will certainly consider the strengths and weaknesses of each party's case in terms of both legal and factual theory. But he will also want to examine the interests and power of the

---

[6] Robert M. Bastress & Joseph D. Harbaugh, *Interviewing, Counseling, and Negotiating: Skills for Effective Representation* 475 (1990).

[7] Similar graphs appear in *id.* at 476–477 and Thomas F. Guernsey, *A Practical Guide to Negotiation* 2 (1996).

Figure 29.1   Your Own Bargaining Range

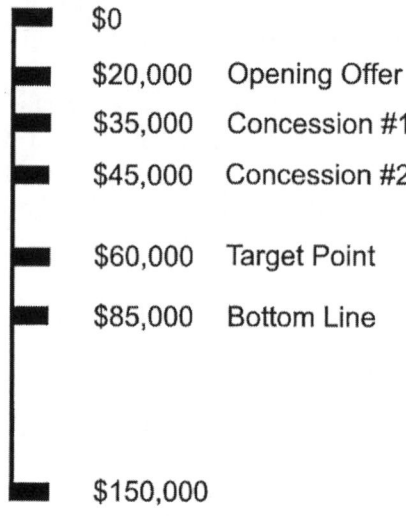

Figure 29.2   Both Parties' Bargaining Range

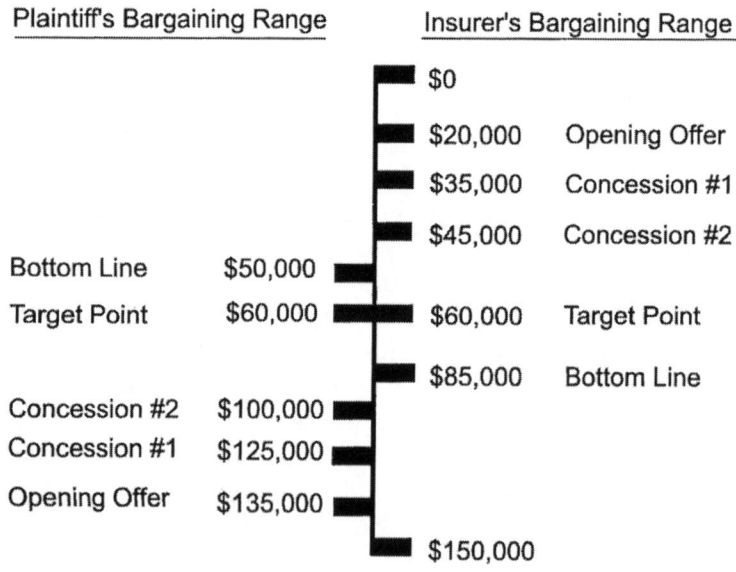

plaintiff and its effect on her bargaining range. If the plaintiff is strapped for funds, for example, or at the deposition appeared very reluctant to proceed with the case, these facts will certainly affect the estimate the insurer's lawyer makes of the plaintiff's bottom line. Additionally, he might want to consider his own client's economic and financial interests in developing its bottom line and concession points.

Evaluating interests, rights, and power in terms of the parties' respective bargaining ranges will also help you develop arguments, threats, warnings, and appeals to convince the other side to make concessions. In order to elicit concessions from the other side, you must demonstrate that your offer is better than its BATNA. The process of estimating these ranges helps you to develop ways of causing the other side to make concessions and to know when you should make concessions (see §31.1.4).

Finally, in making these estimates, your client needs to consider the time value of money (see §24.3.2) and the transaction costs of a trial. Even if the recovery at trial is the same as the settlement amount, a dollar now is worth more than a dollar after trial and possible appeal. Attorneys' fees and litigation expenses decrease even further the future value of an eventual award at trial.

§29.5 Crafting a Plan: Problem-Solving Approach

§29.5.1 *The Brainstorming Process*

When you decide to take a problem-solving approach, your goal is to find solutions that will integrate the resources of both sides or to increase the resources available so that a mutually agreeable solution is more likely. You and your client should consider the priorities of each party's interests (Figure 28.2) and explore any possible solutions suggested by these priorities. Unlike the adversarial approach, where you concentrate on maximizing the interests of your client and consider the most obvious distributive options, here you try to broaden the number of options for settlement beyond obvious issues of dividing a fixed pie. You attempt to "create value" by considering ways of reaching a deal that makes both parties better off without making the other party worse off.[8]

Problem-solving negotiation then requires brainstorming the sources of value to each party beyond the most obvious. While there are numerous methods for engaging in this process, here are a few suggestions.

1. Consider differences between the parties.   Focusing on different interests of the parties may actually be a better basis for problem-solving negotiation than concentrating solely on similarity of interests.

The notion that differences can create value is counter-intuitive to many negotiators, who believe that they can reach agreement only by finding common ground.

---

[8] The following discussion of methods for creating value is based in part on Mnookin et al., *supra* note 2, at 12–17.

But the truth is that differences are often more useful than similarities in helping parties reach a deal. Differences set the stage for possible gains from trade, and it is through trades that value is most commonly created.[9]

The different resources of the parties, for example, may become the basis for a negotiated solution. In a commercial leasing transaction where the property needs a major renovation, the landlord is strapped for cash, and the potential tenant, an excellent handyman, is worried about whether a profit can be made within the first year, a potential solution might be a reduced rent for the first year, in exchange for which the tenant will repair the property. The different time preferences of the parties may also provide the foundation for a settlement. In a personal injury case, for instance, the plaintiff may need money for medical and rehabilitation expenses in the future, and the uninsured defendant may need to limit his short-term expenditures. With an adversarial approach, the parties simply try to reach an agreement as to the amount of a lump-sum recovery. Under a problem-solving approach, the parties might agree on a structured settlement, paid over time, that might meet the needs of both parties. Likewise, the parties' different risk preferences or valuation of the goods in question might create opportunities for a solution.

2. Concentrate on noncompetitive similarities between the parties. In some cases, parties share similar, noncompeting interests so that one party's gain does not mean the other party's loss. In an acrimonious divorce case, for example, the parties may disagree about almost every issue but both are very concerned about the well-being of their children. That shared and high priority interest might form the basis for an overall settlement. In fact, the parties may be willing to compromise on many other very contentious issues for the sake of their children.

3. Focus on ways to expand existing resources. In developing different solutions, look beyond the resources of the parties and ask yourself whether there are ways of creating resources elsewhere. One commentator tells the story, for example, of a large antitrust case against drug manufacturers in which a subgroup of plaintiff drug wholesalers and retailers rejected as inadequate the $3 million allocated to them of the $100 million total settlement. Because of time and other logistic constraints, the settlement terms could not be modified, and it appeared that the deal was a failure. The parties developed a solution, however, under which the drug manufacturers placed a large portion of the total settlement in a bank account for one year in trust for the plaintiffs. After that year, the trust account accrued interest, and the protesting drug wholesalers and retailers were able to take a larger award. The bank provided the mechanism for augmenting the resources available to the parties.[10] By considering expansion of resources, the negotiation becomes less of a zero-sum game.

To plan for a problem-solving negotiation, encourage your client to break out of the tendency to view the issues as a simple distributive problem. Ask the client

---

[9] *Id.* at 14 (footnote omitted).
[10] Menkel-Meadow, *supra* note 4, at 810.

to help you brainstorm other solutions. For example, in representing the buyer in a negotiation for the sale of a house, ask her, "If the seller won't decrease the price, is there anything else he can do that would make you willing to pay that amount?" Another way of increasing the range of options is to enlist the assistance of an expert. Accountants and other financial consultants, for example, can be helpful in devising methods for organizing a settlement or transaction to meet the interests of both parties.

§29.6 Information Gathering, Disclosing, and Concealing

Whether you are planning an adversarial approach, a problem-solving approach, or a combination of the two, you need to prepare for "information bargaining." A negotiation involves not only an exchange of offers and counteroffers or brainstorming of possible solutions, but also attempts by each party to learn more information from the other. Bargaining is as much a learning experience as a contest.[11] With this information, each party can readjust its concession strategy in adversarial bargaining or its brainstorming approach in problem-solving negotiation. To prepare, identify: (1) information you want to obtain from the other party so you can understand its bargaining stance; (2) information you want to disclose voluntarily to the other party to facilitate your overall plan; and (3) information you want to conceal that might weaken your negotiation posture. The next few pages explain how to identify information in each of these categories. We later describe techniques to use during the negotiation to elicit or conceal this information (see §32.1).

1. Gathering information.   Remember that the negotiation process itself is by no means the only vehicle for gathering information about the other side's position or interests in the dispute or transaction. Significant information can be obtained through your client, third parties, the Internet, library research, public records, and, in the dispute context, formal discovery. In a negotiation for a sale of a business, for example, if the seller had previously engaged in failed negotiations with another potential buyer, that party might be an important source of information for the new buyer about the seller's "bottom line." Likewise, in a medical malpractice suit, the defendant's lawyer may be able to discover much more about the plaintiff's interests in the case at a deposition than might be learned during settlement talks. In other words, before relying on the bargaining process as a means to gather information, try to develop other sources of proof.

In adversarial negotiations, the most important information you need is the other party's bottom line. For that very reason, most opponents will not disclose that information. Your goal, then, is to gather as much circumstantial evidence as

---

[11] Robert J. Condlin, *"Every Day and in Every Way We Are All Becoming Meta and Meta"* or *How Communitarian Bargaining Theory Conquered the World (of Bargaining Theory)*, 23 Ohio St. J. on Disp. Resol. 231, 244 (2008) (observing that "[n]ot all bargainers start with a complete understanding of the issues in a controversy, or access to all of the relevant data. . . . As a consequence, even highly skilled bargainers change their minds about what cases are worth.").

possible about the other party's assessment of the transaction or dispute so that you can better estimate its bottom line. Start with your interests assessment of the case and identify what particular interests of the other party might affect its determination of a bargaining range. You might want to explore, for example, the other side's psychological or reputational interests in a lawsuit or its concerns about the transaction costs of the case.

Then, examining your rights assessment of the case, identify both the issues about which your position is strong and the ones in which your position is weak. By obtaining information about the other side's views on these issues, you will learn whether or not its assessment coincides with yours and how it evaluates the merits of its position.

Finally, in regard to your power assessment of the case, consider the types of potential power the other side might wield and how the likelihood of the exercise of that power would affect that party's bottom line. In most cases, you obviously do not want to ask the other side directly if it will exercise a particular form of power if bargaining fails. But if the other side threatens the exercise of that power, you probably will want to gather information to determine whether it is bluffing or is serious.

In problem-solving bargaining, the types of information you want to obtain flow from your interests assessment of the case. Consider the priority interests you have predicted for the other side that lead to the integrative solutions you have brainstormed. In the negotiations, you will want to gather information to confirm whether or not those forecasts are correct.

2. Disclosing information.   The process of identifying information that you should disclose during the negotiation requires an analysis converse to the one you used in regard to the information you want to gather from the other side. Thus, in an adversarial negotiation, you want to disclose information that will apprise the other side of facts showing a strong bottom line for your client: that your client's interests support few concessions in bargaining, that your legal and factual theories are convincing, and that you will use power alternatives if negotiations fail. And, in problem-solving negotiations, you will want to reveal information about your client's interests that will facilitate a solution that will integrate both parties' concerns. Indeed, in some cases, your open disclosure of information can reduce the transaction costs for fact investigation and help to neutralize your opponent's adversarial bargaining stance.[12] In any case, however, your disclosure must be limited by tactical considerations (it must be credible or it will not persuade) and ethical constraints (it must be permitted by the rules of professional responsibility; see §27.5).

3.   Concealing information.   Although many lawyers consider the concealment of damaging information an absolute rule of negotiation, it is better to think of the issue as a tactical one. Initially, consider whether the other side has — or will have — access to the information. If the other side will learn it from other sources anyway, it might be useless to hide it. Second, examine whether candid

---

[12] Mnookin et al., *supra* note 2, at 25–26.

acknowledgment of damaging facts may have the potential to increase the strength of your negotiating positions. In a negotiation for the sale of a house, for example, consider the impact on the buyer if the seller's lawyer admits, "I know that the ceiling in the upstairs bedroom had some water damage a few years ago, but it was fixed, and there hasn't been a problem since then." Finally, analyze whether the disclosure will facilitate the negotiation. Especially in problem-solving bargaining, your openness as to the interests of your client — even if you disclose some weakness of your client — might encourage a similar response from the other side. If, however, the damaging information is not easily accessible and its disclosure serves no tactical purpose, consider ethically acceptable means of concealing it (see §27.5).

§29.7 Planning the Agenda

You need to decide the best sequence in which to address issues as well as where and when to negotiate.

§29.7.1 *Issues*

After you have decided on an approach to the negotiations and considered information issues, plan your issues agenda. Most negotiations concern multiple issues. In the settlement of a police brutality case, for example, the parties might negotiate over the proportionate liability of the different officers, the amount of actual damages, any entitlement to punitive damages, admissions of liability, and the plaintiff's right to attorney's fees. A number of issues can arise even in a routine negotiation for a home sale in those states where lawyers represent the parties to such a transaction. Examples might include responsibility for performing and paying for certain repairs, deadlines for required inspections and obtaining financing, date for closing, and liability for real estate taxes. As part of your strategy development, consider the sequence in which you want to address these issues.

Although there are no hard and fast rules for designing your issues agenda, the primary consideration is whether your sequencing facilitates the overall plan you have developed for the negotiation. Initial consideration of minor issues can be effective if you want to establish a cooperative relationship with the other party that facilitates the negotiation of more difficult issues.[13] This approach can help if you are using problem-solving methods in the negotiation and are concerned about the other party's willingness to engage in such bargaining. But it might delay the inevitable negotiation over the major issues. For that reason, you may want to begin with bargaining over one or two major issues to evaluate the possibility of any settlement or deal. In an adversarial context in which your client has a very strong rights-or power-based BATNA, consideration of a major issue first can give you control over the negotiation. Finally, you might want to negotiate

---

[13] Donald G. Gifford, *Legal Negotiation: Theory and Applications* 76 (1989).

multiple issues simultaneously. In adversarial bargaining, this approach can lead to "logrolling" or trading off of concessions. In problem-solving negotiation, it can assist in mutual brainstorming of solutions.

Development of your own agenda, of course, does not assure that the other party's lawyer will agree with your sequencing of issues. Therefore, be prepared to explain the advantages of your approach and how it will lead to a quick resolution of the issues. In a negotiation where you want to take a problem-solving approach, this explanation might help you persuade the other side to take such an approach. You might also want to present an initial draft agreement to the other party and propose that you both work off of it. This approach helps you to take control of the negotiation. If, however, you want to develop a cooperative relationship with the other side, the surprise presentation of the document at a negotiation session can be viewed as too controlling and can alienate the other attorney.

§29.7.2 Venue: Telephone, E-mail, Location

Where will you negotiate: on the phone, by e-mail, at one of the lawyers' offices, at one of the parties' homes or businesses, or at a "neutral" location such as the hallway outside the courtroom? In some disputes, you may have the option of holding negotiation sessions at a pretrial conference in court. And in many cases, the bargaining will entail multiple negotiation sessions with the possibility of using different venues.

Telephone: Although some lawyers believe that they are always at an advantage if the negotiation takes place at their office, the issue of turf, as with all the other issues of negotiation strategy, is not so clear-cut. Again, consider the overall plan you have developed for the negotiation and the impact, if any, of the venue on this plan. The use of the telephone as the medium for bargaining, for example, can be effective for "short and sweet" exchanges in an adversarial negotiation. Where your client has limited resources, it is also less expensive than a face-to-face meeting. If you want to use a problem-solving approach, however, and the other side is reluctant to engage in mutual brainstorming, the phone can be very limiting. In fact, research shows that less rapport develops in non-face-to-face negotiations than during in-person meetings.[14] Moreover, the parties to the phone conversation can become distracted by other calls or office interruptions. On the other hand, unlike written or e-mail communication, telephone negotiations allow for small talk and other rapport-building communication techniques. They also give each party the ability to control the agenda simply by hanging up.[15]

E-Mail: Like the telephone, e-mail provides lawyers with a cost-effective means to negotiate at great distances. Unlike the phone, it also gives attorneys the flexibility to communicate at times convenient to each of them and to plan carefully each response. E-mail negotiations, however, can have some significant

---

[14] Carrie J. Menkel-Meadow et al., *Negotiation: Processes for Problem Solving* 309 (2006).
[15] Jay Folberg & Dwight Golann, *Lawyer Negotiation: Theory, Practice, and Law* 164 (2d ed. 2011).

disadvantages. Even more so than phone communication, electronic messages are highly "flammable": they are not readily put in context by facial expressions or voice inflection. They, therefore, run the risk of being misunderstood by the other attorney. Moreover, most of us use an informal and abbreviated style in our e-mail messages which usually is not appropriate to serious negotiations especially when precise wording of an agreement is at issue. Finally, we sometimes do not have the same inhibitions in electronic communication as we do in face-to-face meetings. Accordingly, we may respond rapidly and quickly in an e-mail message in a manner that will negatively impact further negotiations.[16]

To address these problems, we suggest the use of e-mail combined with other, more personal means of communications. Small talk in a telephone conversation, for example, can help the parties develop the kind of rapport to lessen misunderstandings about the tone of electronic messages.[17] Moreover, we suggest that you present your arguments in a formally drafted attachment rather than in the message itself.[18] When the precise wording of an agreement is at issue, this method will especially help you carefully prepare your argument and lessen the tendency to quick, flammable responses.

Location: In regard to the location of face-to-face negotiations, an advantage to hosting the negotiation is that you can have the resources you need under your command — your files, research materials, and support staff. You feel more in control of the situation. But there are also advantages to negotiating on the other party's turf. You can demonstrate your intent to cooperate by consenting to meet at the other lawyer's office. And when you are away from your own office, you can honestly excuse yourself if you do not have the necessary materials on hand.

Consider also the person you are and where you will perform best. One of the authors of this book believes that the sales operations of new car dealerships are designed to confuse buyers into making mistakes. He never conducts a serious negotiation at a car dealership. Instead, he uses two or three online car brokerage services to establish a low price and then by e-mail asks several local dealers to beat that price. After some of the dealers respond offering prices lower than the online brokerage price, he telephones each of them and tries to get them to beat each others' prices. After everything is agreed to by e-mail and telephone, he signs a sales contract. The other author of this book believes that he is at his best in face-to-face negotiations and does all his negotiating at the dealership. Neither author gets better deals than the other. But each gets better deals than he would if he were to negotiate in a way that did not fit his personality.

§29.7.3 Timing

Most bargaining does not occur in a vacuum where the parties have infinite time to resolve the transaction or dispute. Negotiators regularly face deadlines imposed either by the circumstances of the case (the date when the seller wants to

---

[16] *Id.* at 166, 178.

[17] *Id.* at 169-70; Janice Nadler, *Rapport in Legal Negotiation: How Small Talk Can Facilitate E-Mail Dealmaking*, 9 Harv. Negot. L. Rev. 223 (2004).

[18] Folberg & Golann, *supra* note 15, at 178.

leave her home, the time when the manufacturer needs the goods for production, or the expiration of the collective bargaining agreement); by third-party requirements (a scheduled trial date); or by limitations set by one or both of the parties themselves (an offer that expires next Tuesday). As part of your strategic planning, you should consider how to handle these deadlines.

As to external deadlines — those imposed by circumstances outside of the negotiation — examine the pros and cons of different timing agendas. The most propitious time to negotiate may not be the earliest. You may, for example, need additional information to assess adequately the strengths and weaknesses of your legal case; you may feel that the case is not "ripe" for serious bargaining because the other side has not seriously considered the merits of the case; or you may want to wait until the trial court has decided a pivotal motion. Indeed, especially if you are using the adversarial approach, you may want to wait until the eve of trial or other deadline to pressure a less powerful opponent into a deal.

On the other hand, delay has its disadvantages. The more resources the other party has devoted to preparing for trial, the greater may be the possibility that it will take its risks going to trial. If your client wants to conserve resources or panics at the thought of going to trial, or if you fear that the opposing lawyer will try to take advantage of your client in the court hallway on the eve of trial, you also may want to forgo waiting until the last minute. Moreover, if you are using a problem-solving approach, you need to allow enough time to work out a mutually agreeable solution. The time pressures of deadlines are not always conducive to such a process.

When the other side sets a deadline on an offer, you can try to persuade the other lawyer that deadlines like that are counterproductive. But if that fails, your client will need to decide, based on her BATNA, whether to accept or reject the offer as made.

If you want to make an offer with a deadline, remember that while that might be effective in adversarial bargaining, it can harm a problem-solving negotiation. It not only hinders the development of a cooperative atmosphere but can also harm any long-term relationship your client might want to maintain with the other side. And unless you are serious about such self-imposed deadlines, your credibility will be significantly damaged if the other side calls your bluff and you have to renege on your threat (see §32.2.2).

§29.8 Adapting Your Strategy

The strategy that you initially develop should not be set in stone. As bargaining proceeds, the interests, rights, and power context of the negotiation may change; your client may modify her BATNA; speculation about the responses of the other party may simply be wrong; the information you gather during the negotiation may significantly affect your client's and your own perception of the situation; and the overall approach you have selected for the negotiation (adversarial or problem-solving) may turn out to be ineffective. Despite your valiant efforts to use a problem-solving approach to negotiation, for example, the other side might simply ignore your entreaties and bulldoze ahead with an adversarial approach. On the other hand, you may find that adversarial bargaining by both sides has worn both parties down to such a small bargaining range that a problem-solving approach helps to obtain a final agreement. "Competitive tactics early in the negotiation, perhaps ironically, sometimes increase the prospects for successful use of . . . problem solving tactics later in the negotiation."[19]

Accordingly, throughout the negotiation process, reevaluate your initial strategy and be open to adapting it to any changed circumstances. The analysis will be the same as the one you used in your initial planning: go back to your assessment of the parties' interests, rights, and power (Figure 28.1, Figure 28.2, Figure 28.3, and Figure 28.4), have your client fine tune her BATNA, consider what additional information might be helpful, and reexamine the approach you have selected for addressing the different issues.

---

[19] *Id.* at 35.

CHAPTER 30

STYLES AND RITUALS

§30.1 Creating Negotiating Styles

In conducting any negotiation, you should select for yourself a negotiating style that will work well in the circumstances. You should also recognize any issues raised by cultural differences between you and the other side.

§30.1.1 Selecting a Style for a Particular Negotiation

As you have learned, negotiating, like most other lawyering skills, requires the ability to communicate. You may have developed the most creative and clever strategy possible, but you will fail unless you can communicate effectively with the other side. Your style is an important aspect of this ability to communicate. Style is the manner in which you personally relate to the other side — for example, your word choice, tone of voice, body language, and eye contact.

Strategy is the overall approach you have chosen to achieve your client's goals — adversarial, problem-solving, or both. Style is the personal manner in which you execute this strategy: how you present your proposals, listen to the other side's proposals, and respond. Obviously, this distinction is a bit artificial (often your tone will reflect your strategy). But the distinction helps in understanding the conduct of a negotiation. Strategy is the content of your presentation to the other side (*what* you say). Style is the way you package this presentation (*how* you say it). Just as you select a strategy for a particular negotiation, you also select a style (or styles).

We do not suggest that you try to become someone who you are not. How you negotiate — as well as how you examine a witness, counsel a client, or argue to a judge — will grow out of who you are. You can change your negotiation style or modify it to meet the needs of a particular situation, but to some degree the ways you negotiate or try a case will be determined by your personality. If you are naturally abrasive and aggressive, for example, it will be difficult, if not impossible, for you to come across as a Milquetoast.

But you cannot ignore the fact that the style you use in your communications with your adversary may have an important effect on its outcome. Part of becoming an effective lawyer is learning how to act. As you become more experienced, try to develop a repertoire of negotiating masks that grow out of your personality but also communicate effectively in the particular situation. Indeed, this approach is applicable to all aspects of the lawyering process. Consider, for example, the cross-examination of witnesses in an assault case. The defense lawyer might very well wear a very different mask in her questioning of the eighty-year-old grandmother who allegedly witnessed the incident and the detective who obtained the confession from her client.

Two categories of negotiating style are *combative* and *cordial*. While a combative style is tough, dominating, forceful, aggressive, and attacking, a cordial style is personable, friendly, and tactful.[1] Obviously, there is a broad continuum between these two styles. And in any given negotiation, a lawyer might switch from one to another style depending upon the impact the lawyer wants to make on the other side. Moreover, since style depends in large part on the perception of the listener, the precise attributes of a particular style will depend significantly on the culture in which the negotiation is taking place. That perception might vary from one region of the country to another, and it might vary from one type of law practice to another. What is combative in a complex federal antitrust negotiation might be considered very tepid in high-volume urban eviction bargaining.

In choosing your negotiation style, consider a number of factors. Sometimes your selection will be based on the strategy you choose. If you are using an adversarial approach, if your client has a strong rights or power-based BATNA, and if she is willing to make few concessions, you may select a combative style to demonstrate to the other side your client's confidence in her position. On the other hand, if you are using a problem-solving strategy, if your client has a strong interest in maintaining good relations with the other side, and if she is open to a wide variety of solutions to the issues, you might choose a cordial approach to encourage mutual brainstorming.

One factor that should not affect your style is your client's or your own emotions about the other side or the other side's lawyer. As Fisher and Ury advise, you need to "separate the people from the problem."[2] While novice lawyers often select a combative approach against an experienced lawyer to show that "they know what they

---

[1] See Gerald R. Williams, *Legal Negotiation and Settlement* 21, 23 (1983). Williams's definition of competitive and cooperative conflates both strategic and stylistic aspects of the negotiator. We focus solely on the stylistic considerations. We use "combative" and "cordial" because they clearly connote the tone, rather than the substance of the communication. The terms "competitive" and "cooperative," although used by other authors, are ambiguous because they could refer either to substance or tone. See Robert M. Bastress & Joseph D. Harbaugh, *Interviewing, Counseling, and Negotiating: Skills for Effective Representation* 390 (1990); Donald G. Gifford, *Legal Negotiation: Theory and Applications* 18 (1989). Actually, *all* negotiations are competitive in the sense that each side tries to satisfy its own interests. Problem-solving and adversarial approaches and combative and cordial tones are just different ways of accomplishing that.

[2] Roger Fisher et al., *Getting to Yes: Negotiating Agreement Without Giving In* 11 (2d ed. 1991). For a different opinion on this issue, see Daniel L. Shapiro, *Emotions in Negotiations: Peril or Promise?* 87 Marq. L. Rev. 737, 745 (2004), in which the author observes

are doing," their bravado may not communicate effectively with the opposing lawyer, who will probably see through the mask and might even break off the negotiation. Other inexperienced lawyers, intimidated by their first negotiations, will mistakenly use a cordial approach because the other lawyer seems so "nice."

Communicate as effectively as possible. Your goal is not to score points or make friends.

§30.1.2 Recognizing Cross-Cultural Differences

Although most legal negotiations occur between lawyers within the same local community, in recent years lawyers have become more involved in transactions and disputes with their counterparts from other cultures. Traditionally, such cross-cultural bargaining arose in the context of international diplomacy. Nowadays, however, it occurs regularly in negotiations between private lawyers and official representatives of other nations, and in commercial transactions between companies in different countries.

Since styles of communication may vary significantly from culture to culture, consider the nature of the culture of the other side and its lawyer in selecting your negotiation style for effective cross-cultural bargaining. Even when negotiating with an attorney or party from another region of the country, you may want to think about the effect of cultural differences on negotiation style. Consider, for example, the characters of the soft-spoken Southern judge and abrasive New Yorker in the movie *My Cousin Vinnie*. Likewise, the gender of the participants may affect the style of the negotiation. Studies are inconclusive, however, on whether female and male lawyers behave significantly differently in negotiations.[3]

While it is beyond the scope of this text to discuss in depth methods for selecting a style in cross-cultural negotiation, it is helpful to identify some of the factors which should be considered.[4]

1. Language. What you might consider standard norms of discourse in America may be viewed as abrasive and rude in another culture. In some negotiations, you will be communicating through an interpreter. You need to understand the limitations of translation and the effects of language structure on communication.

While it is true that emotions can be a barrier to value-maximizing agreement, the common advice "to get rid of emotions" is infeasible and unwise. On the contrary, research suggests that negotiators can improve the efficiency and effectiveness of a negotiation by gaining an understanding of the information communicated by emotions, their own and those of others, and enlisting emotions into the negotiation.

[3] See Lloyd Burton et al., *Feminist Theory, Professional Ethics, and Gender-Related Distinctions in Attorney Negotiating Styles*, 1991 J. Disp. Resol. 199; Thomas F. Guernsey, *A Practical Guide to Negotiation* 26–27 (1996).

[4] See David A. Victor, *Cross-Cultural Awareness*, in *The ABA Guide to International Business Negotiations* 15 (James R. Silkenat & Jeffrey M. Aresty, eds. 1994); John Barkai, *Cultural Dimension Interests, the Dance of Negotiation, and Weather Forecasting: A Perspective on Cross-Cultural Negotiation and Dispute Resolution*, 8 Pepp. Disp. Resol. L.J. 403 (2008). See also Raymond Cohen, *Negotiating Across Cultures* 19–32 (1991); Geert Hofstede et al., *Cultures and Organizations: Software of the Mind* (3d ed. 2010) (describing authors' empirical studies of cross-cultural differences throughout the world during the past three decades).

2. *Environment.* While in the United States, for example, the conference room or formal boardroom is the principal setting for bargaining, in other cultures, the real negotiations occur elsewhere: in hotel lobbies, dining rooms, or private homes.

3. *Social organization and hierarchy.* In crafting a style for a negotiation with someone from another culture, consider aspects of that culture's social hierarchy. In societies with strict vertical hierarchies, it is considered inappropriate to bargain with someone of a different status. This can cause problems for an American lawyer in countries where lawyers have a lower social rank than they do here.

4. *Contexting.* Social scientists distinguish between high context cultures in which the participants rely most heavily on how a statement is said rather than what is said and low context cultures in which the participants rely primarily on what is said.[5] In a high context culture, such as Japan or the Arab countries, the parties rely a great deal on nonverbal communication and pay less attention to detail. In lower context cultures, such as Germany and the United States, the focus is on the words and literal meaning of the communication.[6] Accordingly, while a direct, combative style may be effective in many American negotiations, it may not work, and in fact may be counterproductive, in dealings with negotiators from high context cultures.

5. *Conceptions of time.* Some cultures, such as the United States, understand time in a monochronic manner: time is inflexible, and schedules should be adhered to as closely as possible. In other cultures, time is understood polychronically: it is flexible, and schedules are not closely adhered to. When an American negotiates with someone from a culture with a polychronic conception of time, the American may become impatient with the delays inherent in such a context and may respond combatively. The American may need to adjust style to that of the other side's culture.

6. *Individualism vs. collectivism.* The vast majority of people in the world live in collectivist societies in which the interests of the group prevail over individual interests, and harmony and loyalty are valued more than honesty. Only a minority of people live in societies like the United States in which individual interests predominate, and everyone is expected to look after herself or her immediate family. When Americans negotiate with someone from a collectivist culture, they most likely will be considered suspiciously as outsiders and may encounter deceptive negotiation tactics used against persons who are not part of the group. In such a context, American negotiators will need to take the time to build stable relationships with their collectivist negotiating partners to become accepted as insiders.[7]

7. *Gender roles.* In some cultures, men are expected to be assertive, tough, competitive, and focused on material success, while women are expected to be modest, cooperative, and concerned with the quality of life. In other cultures, gender roles overlap, and both men and women are expected to act cooperatively.

---

[5] Cohen, *supra* note 4, at 25. ("A high-context culture communicates allusively rather than directly.")

[6] Victor, *supra* note 4, at 20.

[7] Hofstede et al., *supra* note 4, at 89–134, 400; Barkai *supra* note 4, at 412–414.

Unfortunately, when bargaining with a man from a culture with distinct gender roles, you may confront someone who expects ego-boosting treatment and who seeks to resolve conflicts with threats and displays of force. And when bargaining with persons from a culture with less distinct roles, your counterparts are more likely to resolve conflicts by cooperation and to strive for consensus. They may respond quite negatively to a domineering, assertive, loud demeanor.[8]

8. *Uncertainty avoidance.* In every culture, people to some extent fear uncertainty and ambiguity. But in some cultures, members feel especially threatened by unstructured and unknown situations. Accordingly, bargainers from cultures with high uncertainty avoidance will likely have a need for structure and ritual in the negotiation process. They also likely will prefer predictable solutions and shy away from the unconventional.[9]

Given these variables in cross-cultural communication, you should consider the sensibilities of the other participants before you embark on negotiations that cross profound cultural divides. Lawyers who have participated in similar negotiations can provide helpful assistance. And you may want to consult the significant body of literature that is being developed on bargaining with negotiators from particular regions or countries.[10]

§30.2 Negotiation Rituals

Negotiations often follow set patterns. In some fields these rituals have become so well established that they are entrenched social expectations. Some labor negotiations between unions and management, for example, often entail months of useless bargaining between low-level representatives until the principals sit down at the table on the eve of a strike deadline to work out a contract. And experienced plaintiff personal injury lawyers and insurance claims agents who know each other well engage in almost ritualistic exchanges of information and offers and counteroffers before agreeing on a deal. In some urban eviction practices, lawyers for both parties know that the real bargaining will only take place in the hallways between the first and second calls of the cases.

Some rituals can serve useful psychological functions such as building trust, maintaining comfort levels, and setting a tone. You should investigate any customs or conventions that local practitioners usually follow for the kind of bargaining you will conduct. Your client or more experienced lawyers who have engaged in similar negotiations may have this information.

On the other hand, some rituals serve no useful purpose for your client and can actually be harmful. Novice lawyers conducting dispute negotiations often

---

[8] Hofstede et al., *supra* note 4, at 135–185, 400; Barkai *supra* note 4, at 414–415.

[9] Hofstede et al., *supra* note 4, at 187–234, 400; Barkai *supra* note 4, at 415–417.

[10] For example, see Urs Martin Lauchli, *Cross-Cultural Negotiations, with a Special Focus on ADR with the Chinese*, 26 Wm. Mitchell L. Rev. 1045 (2000); Rona R. Mears, *Contracting in Mexico: A Legal and Practical Guide to Negotiating and Drafting*, 24 St. Mary's L.J. 737 (1993); Robert J. Walters, *"Now That I Ate the Sushi, Do We Have a Deal?" — The Lawyer As Negotiator in Japanese–U.S. Business Transactions*, 12 Int'l Bus. 335 (1991). An excellent website on which you can compare cultural factors between two countries is http://www.geert-hofstede.com (visited Oct. 11, 2010).

engage in a ritual that goes something like this: Each lawyer brags about the quality of the lawyer's evidence ("we have three witnesses who say your client ran the red light") and the likelihood of prevailing at trial ("the jury will be upset about my client's injuries"), while insulting the other lawyer's evidence ("nobody's going to believe your pathologist") and the other party's chance at trial ("I think you're going to lose"). This goes on like a barroom argument, each lawyer trying to top the other and each getting angry at the other, until finally both realize that time is running out and their clients need a deal. Then, without much thought about why, the lawyers quickly come to an agreement that is about halfway between the positions they started with. This is not really negotiation at all. It is a prolonged threat display, followed by a quick splitting of the difference. Neither side has really influenced the other, and neither has thought about interests, rights, or power enough to plan a careful negotiation.

In your conduct of a negotiation, weigh the advantages and disadvantages of following established bargaining patterns. Examine the effect of these rituals on your overall negotiation strategy. If you decide to break with established local tradition, consider ways to handle the situation without jeopardizing the negotiation. In an environment where swift adversarial bargaining is the norm, for instance, and you want to engage in a problem-solving approach, you may want to begin the negotiations by acknowledging explicitly that you know the usual custom in the area is to have quick exchanges of offers, but that you think it is in the interest of both parties to spend at least a short while brainstorming mutually agreeable solutions.

Besides learning your area's negotiation customs, learn the local bargaining semantics. These coded signals send messages — either intentionally or unintentionally — about a particular side's position or attitude in the negotiation. They differ by geographic region, cultural environment, and practice area. For example, in some places the phrase "I think we can work this out" is just an opening pleasantry to the bargaining, while elsewhere it is a message that the parties are on the brink of a deal. Likewise, the outburst, "This is hopeless! We're going to trial!" in one locale can literally mean that there is deadlock while in another merely that the other party is frustrated and will quickly be back to the table. Sensitivity to these different signals can help you maneuver your way through the bargaining.

The best way to become familiar with these signals is to play the role of an anthropologist during your initial negotiations in a particular locale. Be sensitive to the signals used by various negotiators and the way others respond to them. Think about this not only during negotiation, but also afterward when you have an opportunity to reflect on the bargaining dynamics.

CHAPTER 31

FOLLOWING THROUGH ON YOUR PLAN

§31.1 Adversarial Approach

Remember that your goal in adversarial bargaining is to maximize your client's gain and minimize your loss (see §29.4). You need to communicate your offers and concessions in a way that persuades the other party to agree on terms most favorable to your client.

§31.1.1 *Making Initial Offers*

Should you make your initial offer before the other side makes theirs? Or should you wait to hear their initial offer before you make yours? Many lawyers feel that it is always a sign of weakness to be the first party to make an offer. Lawyers often engage in a ritual dance at the beginning of a negotiation, each lawyer trying to delay making an initial offer until the other side has done so first.

While some empirical research has shown no apparent correlation between those who make the first offer and the eventual outcome of the negotiation, recent research has shown that making first offers can improve the outcome through strategic use of "anchoring."[1] Researchers have found

> that how we perceive a particular offer's value is highly influenced by any relevant number that enters the negotiation environment. Because they pull judgments toward themselves, these numerical values are known as *anchors*. In situations of great ambiguity and uncertainty, first offers have a strong *anchoring effect* — they exert a strong pull throughout the rest of the negotiation. Even when people know

---

[1] Compare Robert M. Bastress & Joseph D. Harbaugh, *Interviewing, Counseling, and Negotiation: Skills for Effective Representation* 493 (1990) (concluding that no apparent correlation exists between first offers and outcomes) and Robert S. Adler, *Flawed Thinking: Addressing Decision Biases in Negotiation*, 20 Ohio St. J. on Disp. Resol. 683, 770 (2005) (observing that "first offers can markedly improve one's outcome"); Dan Orr & Chris Guthrie, *Anchoring, Expertise, and Negotiation: New Insights from Meta-Analysis*, 21 Ohio St. J. on Disp. Resol. 597, 621 (2006).

that a particular anchor should not influence their judgments, they are often incapable of resisting its influence.[2]

Accordingly, an aggressive, but not absurd, first offer can set the tone for further negotiation and may have a positive effect on the outcome. If, however, you have inadequate information about the value of the negotiated object or the relevant market, you may want the other side to make the first offer. From that offer, you can learn something about how much they think it is worth. In those circumstances, if you make the first offer, it might be too pessimistic and lead to a smaller return for your client.

Attorneys can avoid or minimize the impact of anchoring on negotiation by adopting certain de-biasing strategies. First, when confronted with an anchoring offer, you should consciously resist the urge to accept it. Stand back and evaluate it from both your own and your adversary's perspective rather than focusing solely on the amount of the offer. Second, rather than allowing yourself to be unduly influenced by the initial offer in your case, you should assess it based on an investigation of decisions in other similar cases or the handling of other transactions in your community. For example, consult with expert attorneys who have handled such cases or transactions or gather information from resources such as verdict reports on Lexis or Westlaw (see §24.3.1).[3]

§31.1.2 Deciding How Much to Offer

To determine your initial offer, return to your assessment of interests, rights, and power (Figure 28.1, Figure 28.2, Figure 28.3, and Figure 28.4). Then, try to predict the possible outcomes of the case — including your BATNA — by using the same methods you would use in preparing for client counseling (see §24.3.1).

Research does show a correlation between a forceful, but credible, initial offer and a better result for the party making the offer.[4] Apparently, such offers can convey the message that you are convinced of the strength of the case. The danger, of course, is that the other side will immediately reject it. If you stick to your guns, the other party might remain at the bargaining table — or might not. If the offer is rejected, you might have to make a quick concession that would send the exact opposite message — that you were really bluffing — unless you are committed to your offer and are willing to pursue your BATNA instead of negotiation.

---

[2] Adam D. Galinsky, *When to Make the First Offers in Negotiation*, Harvard Business School Working Knowledge for Business Leaders, at *http://hbswk.hbs.edu/archive/4302.html* (visited Oct. 26, 2006). Some scholars have questioned both the methodology of the research on the effect of anchoring on negotiation and the applicability of this research to legal bargaining. See, e.g., Robert J. Condlin, *Legal Bargaining Theory's New "Prospecting" Agenda: It May Be Social Science, But Is It News?*, 10 Pepp. Disp. Resol. L. J. 215 (2010) (observing that most of the anchoring research involved simulated negotiations with student subjects who were bargaining for the first time and simple problems lacking the information-rich context of most legal negotiation).

[3] Orr & Guthrie, *supra* note 1, at 625–628.

[4] Donald G. Gifford, *Legal Negotiation: Theory and Applications* 99 (1989); see generally Andrea Kupfer Schneider, *Aspirations in Negotiation*, 87 Marq. L. Rev. 675 (2004).

You might decide instead to demonstrate the strength of your case through persuasive arguments rather than by inflating your initial offer.

Credibility problems can arise through "Boulwarism" — making only one offer, which you believe is reasonable and just, and telling the other side that you will settle on no other terms. Boulwarism is named after a former vice-president of General Electric who used this tactic in labor negotiations in the 1950s. Although his offers might be considered fair objectively, they generated controversy and friction and made settlement more diffucult. When the other side has hired someone — a union leader or a lawyer — to do the bargaining, one of the other side's interests may be to get enough out of the negotiation to make it appear the bargainer was worth hiring.

Most negotiators enter the bargaining process intending to give and take. Boulwarism, by challenging that basic notion, raises significant risks. Boulwarism can be effective only if three things are true: you have enough information to be reasonably certain that your one offer is better than the other side's BATNA; you can convince the other side of that; and you can convince the other side that you will not make any further concessions. If you try Boulwarism and it fails, you must either make a concession, losing credibility in the process, or stick to your initial offer and retreat to your own BATNA when it is rejected.

Generally, a good initial offer — a forceful, but credible one — is aimed further, but not too much further, than the best terms on which you think the other side might settle. Suppose you represent a plaintiff who is suing for $150,000, and you believe that the most the defendant might be willing to settle for is $85,000. Your initial offer should not be $85,000. If you offer that, the defendant will insist that you retreat — the process of give and take — and retreating would produce a settlement of less than $85,000. Instead, you offer to settle for more than that, but not so much more that you lose credibility. If you were to offer to settle for $150,000 — the amount you sued for — the other side would laugh and ask you to get back in touch with them when you decide to negotiate. Instead, you offer to settle for the highest figure that does not hurt your credibility, perhaps $135,000.

§31.1.3 Presenting Your Initial Offer

As with so much of lawyering, the way you communicate the initial offer is crucial to its effectiveness. You must convince the other side that your bottom line is high (even if your client has not set a bottom line).[5] The key to such a presentation is *credibility*. Unless the other party believes that you are committed to your position, you will not induce it to reassess its bargaining position.

Compare two versions of initial offers from Ransom's lawyer in *Ransom v. Dusak*:

---

[5] Bastress & Harbaugh, *supra* note 1, at 507.

Initial Offer — Example 1

Unless repairs are made to Ransom's apartment within the next few weeks, we're going to take this case to trial. We also want $5,000 in damages. That's for the loss of use of her apartment for the last few months and for her medical bills. You know that because of the lack of heat in her apartment last winter her two-year-old and four-year-old came down with bronchitis, and my client had to pay the doctor bills. And there were other expenses resulting from the wretched conditions too. You know what they are; we've laid them out in the complaint. We also want punitive damages for her mental anguish. We are willing to waive some of those damages if the repairs are made as soon as possible.

Initial Offer — Example 2

We demand that the following repairs be made to my client's apartment by August 8: the roof must be repaired in the master bedroom by a licensed contractor; the entire apartment must be fumigated by a licensed exterminator; and the heating system must be repaired by a licensed plumber. By August 10, a representative from the Health Department will inspect to verify the fulfillment of these conditions. For breach of the warranty of habitability, we demand actual damages in the amount of $1,950 — that's one-half of the rent paid from January to June. As I'm sure your client will acknowledge, the bedroom is one-half of the usable space in the apartment. Also, we want reimbursement for the $250 doctor bill my client paid because of the bronchitis caused by the lack of heat. Here's a copy of the bill. We'll also agree to only $250 in punitive damages if the repairs are made by August 8. As you know, Judge Lopez is hard on landlords who breach the warranty of habitability. Just last month, she assessed $2,000 in punitive damages against A & E Realty in a similar case.

These two examples illustrate the factors that most affect the credibility of initial offers: *specificity, justification,* and *consequence.*

Specificity reflects a firmness of the negotiator's commitment.[6] Specific facts are more credible than mere conclusions because specific facts paint a clear and vivid picture while conclusions are ambiguous. Similarly, by presenting specific offers and demands in negotiation, you show your client's commitment to a position in clear terms. In Example 1, the lawyer ambiguously says that her client wants "repairs made . . . within the next few weeks," "damages for the loss of use of her apartment for the last few months," "other expenses," and "punitive damages." By not specifying the exact conditions her client wants repaired, the time deadline for the repairs, the amount of damages, and the precise basis for damages, she gives the impression that her client is ambivalent about her demands. Indeed, without an exact offer, the client appears to be unsure of her bottom line and open to making concessions.

---

[6] Richard E. Walton & Robert B. McKersie, A *Behavioral Theory of Labor Negotiations* 93–94 (1965). Of course, if the offer is unrealistic, no degree of specificity will increase its credibility (see §31.1.2).

The specificity in Example 2, on the other hand, demonstrates a strong commitment of the client to her particular positions: she knows when she wants the conditions remedied; what exact amount of damages she wants; and what the grounds are for her claims. And by specifying that she wants all the work performed by licensed contractors and to be confirmed by the representative from the Health Department, the lawyer tells the other side her client "means business" when she says she wants the work done properly.

Justification means clearly communicated reasons for your client's offer. Sound reasons give a ring of legitimacy to an offer. Your client did not arbitrarily pick this amount or take this position but instead has seriously considered it and is committed to it for the reasons you describe. And you rely on the logic of the justification to convince the other side that your offer is better than its BATNA. For this reason, the stronger the logic of your reasoning, the more credible is the specific justification.

Again, consider the two examples from *Ransom v. Dusak*. In Example 1, the lawyer gives no justification for her demand for damages for the loss of the use of her apartment. She vaguely refers to "other expenses resulting from the wretched conditions," does not explicitly point to any claims for relief in the complaint, and gives no reasons for the punitive damages except for a feeble reference to "mental anguish." The overall impact of this justification is weak. It appears that the lawyer has not done her homework, that neither she nor her client has seriously thought through the $5,000 demand, and that, therefore, her client is not firmly committed to the offer.

In contrast, the lawyer in Example 2 gives the legal basis for her claim, provides explicit arguments for the 50% abatement in rent, and even provides the other party's lawyer with evidence of damages. And by agreeing to only $250 in punitive damages if the repairs are made by August 8, she furnishes a credible rationale for the offer.

You develop your justifications from your assessments of interests, rights, and power (Figure 28.1, Figure 28.2, Figure 28.3, and Figure 28.4). Sometimes, you can use a particular interest of your client — or of the other side — to establish the credibility of your offer. If, for example, Dusak worries about his reputation in the community, Ransom's lawyer might use that interest as a justification for an expedited schedule for work on the apartment. In other situations, you might want to visit the strengths and weaknesses portions of the rights assessment chart (Figure 28.2 on page 293) to develop a justification. And in still other situations, you may want to rely on power imbalances to "leverage" a deal. If, for example, Ransom is a member of a tenants group whose members are ready to withhold rent, she may have a very strong justification for requesting substantial damages.

Consequence means that the offer communicates the consequences that will ensue if the other side rejects it. Your statement of consequences will be credible only if the other side knows that you are willing and able to follow through with it. A strong commitment to the offer can be demonstrated by an explicit description of the consequences of its rejection. Often, but not always, the consequence is that you will pursue your BATNA rather than continue negotiating.

In Example 1 the lawyer vaguely refers to the consequences of "going to take this case to trial" — as though she is going through the motions of stating a consequence, rather than developing one persuasively. In Example 2, on the other hand, the lawyer specifically spells out the consequences: "As you know, Judge Lopez is hard on landlords who breach the warranty of habitability. Just last month, she assessed $2,000 in punitive damages against A & E Realty in a similar case." By providing a detailed account of the possible consequences, this lawyer communicates both her knowledge of the legal situation and her conviction as to the merits of her case. In framing your initial offer, always try to describe your BATNA in the most persuasive way possible.

§31.1.4 Making Subsequent Demands and Concessions

Unless the other side immediately accepts your initial offer, it might make counteroffers, and you will have to determine how to follow through with your strategy. One thing, however, is almost certain: you will not want to increase your demands. Although the law of professional responsibility does not prohibit such a tactic, it can cause you to lose a great deal of credibility and severely damage your relationship with the other side. If you have demonstrated a firm commitment to your initial offer, it seems illogical to be augmenting it. Moreover, the other party will most likely consider an increase in demand as an act of bad faith and mistrust your motives in any future bargaining. That tactic is warranted only when a surprising piece of important information appears and significantly changes the complexion of the case in your favor. If that happens, explain to the other side clearly and logically the reasons for your reverse in course.

Accordingly, after the initial offer and counteroffer, both sides will eventually have to make concessions of some kind. Indeed, in your planning for an adversarial negotiation, you identify various concession points between your initial offer and your bottom line (see §29.4). The fact that you identify these points in your preparation, however, does not mean that you automatically make a concession when your receive a counteroffer. Remember that your goal in adversarial bargaining is maximizing your gain. One of the ways of achieving this goal is to give the other side the impression that your client's bottom line is higher on the bargaining range than your client has actually placed it. Research has shown that a grudging approach to concessions pays off with better outcomes.[7] Rapid, and especially large, concessions, on the other hand, send the opposite message: after making an inflated initial offer, your client is willing to make substantial and continuing concessions. Similarly, if you make a series of concessions without receiving any from the other side, you communicate a weak commitment to your positions.

Nevertheless, concessions will be required in certain circumstances.[8] First, concessions may be needed to prevent deadlocks. Lawyers generally understand

---

[7] Bastress & Harbaugh, *supra* note 1, at 520.
[8] See generally *id.* at 516–518; Gifford, *supra* note 4, at 147–149.

that in adversarial bargaining a deal is possible within the two bargaining ranges only if each party makes at least some concessions. If you are not close to your client's bottom line, failure to make a concession when both parties dig in their heels will harm your client's interests unless your client's BATNA is better than any deal you foresee getting out of the negotiation.

The second reason for conceding something is to persuade the other side to make concessions, too. In some negotiations, the parties get stuck at a given point and refuse to move. Even a slight concession shows some flexibility and may encourage some movement from the other side.

Third, concessions may be necessary to maintain a good working relationship with the other side. If your client and the other side plan to have an ongoing relationship after this particular negotiation, contentious scrabbling at each point in the bargaining can damage that relationship. Again, a flexible concession strategy may be needed.

Finally, concessions may be required when both parties face a deadline. Unless your client wants to abandon the negotiation and pursue her BATNA instead, you may need to make concessions as a deadline approaches. In the dispute context, this reason for concessions can be very important when a judge, hearing officer, or arbitrator is encouraging settlement. If the adjudicator views your intransigence as the reason for the negotiation's failure, you may enter the trial or hearing at a disadvantage.

Once you have decided to make a concession, think about how to package it in a way that will minimize an impression of weakness. Let us revisit the *Ransom v. Dusak* case and assume that Dusak's lawyer has responded to Ransom's initial offer by saying his client will only pay $100 nominal damages. Here are two possible ways of conceding:

Concession — Example 3

All right, to move the negotiations along, my client will agree to damages of $1,550. But that's my client's bottom line. She won't move any further.

Concession — Example 4

I think my client might agree to a slight decrease in damages just to get this case moving. We both know how long it takes to get a case on the trial calendar before Judge Lopez, and my client wants the money now to pay the medical bill. If you look at Judge Lopez's decision in the A & E Realty case, the smallest abatement she will give us is one-half. So to get this case settled now, we'll agree to a one-third abatement plus the $250 medical bill — that's $1,550. That's as generous as we can get. Under no circumstances is my client going to accept nominal damages of $100. Your client will have to get realistic.

In two ways, the concession in Example 4 is much stronger. First, it includes *a specific justification for the concession.* While the Example 3 lawyer gives no justification for her concession, the lawyer in Example 4 gives reasons: her client wants to pay the medical bill and does not have to wait for a trial. Just as in our analysis of the initial offers, a justification adds credibility to the position. Here, the concession does not come out of nowhere but instead reflects the interests of the conceding lawyer's client.

If you force yourself to give a specific justification for each concession, you impose a self-discipline that helps you resist the psychological pressure many novice lawyers feel to make concessions just to "get along" with the other side. If you and your client cannot identify a rationale for a concession, you should probably stand pat. As with initial offers, examine your assessment of interests, rights, and power to identify the bases for each concession.

Second, the lawyer in Example 4 *makes it clear that this concession will not inevitably lead to others.* She refers to Judge Lopez's decision in the A & E Realty case that allowed for a 50% abatement and argues that a one-third abatement is as generous as she can be. The message is clear: the consequence of a rejection of this offer will be trial, not further concessions. The Example 3 lawyer on the other hand merely makes the conclusory statement that her concession is her client's bottom line. By giving no explanation, she appears to be doing little more than bluffing.

The approach taken by the Example 3 lawyer can often lead to "splitting the difference" positional bargaining. By failing to provide Dusak's lawyer with any justification for her concession or explanation why she will not continue to concede, the lawyer in Example 3 opens the door to this kind of response: "All right, my client will only give $100; your client wants $1,550. Let's split the difference, say $725." Although that approach might be efficient near the end of a negotiation when the parties are very close to an agreement (see §28.4), it is dangerous at earlier stages because it focuses exclusively on the numbers rather than the reasons why the numbers exist: an analysis of your client's and the other party's interests, rights, and power. Splitting the difference is not negotiating. It is appropriate only when the parties are so close to settlement that it is no longer cost-efficient to argue about how to divide the last few inches.

The approach taken by the Example 4 lawyer also facilitates the negotiation process. By inviting Dusak's lawyer to make some concessions, she tries to engage in serious bargaining on the damages issue. She ends her concession by flatly rejecting a de minimis offer of damages and asks the other side to become more realistic. If Dusak's lawyer responds with an offer of $150 or $200, she will learn that — at least for now — there is little chance of any movement on the damages issue, and her client will have to decide whether to pursue her BATNA instead of negotiating. If Dusak's counteroffer is more substantial, Ransom's lawyer can decide whether to make further concessions.

§31.2 Problem-Solving Approach

The biggest challenge for the problem-solving negotiator is to bring the other side into the problem-solving process.

§31.2.1 *Making Initial Offers*

Remember that, if you have chosen a problem-solving approach, your goal is to find solutions that will integrate the resources of both parties or increase resources to reach an agreement that will address both parties' interests. To achieve this goal, you want to engage in creative brainstorming with the lawyer for the other side. Fisher and Ury suggest that you try to persuade the other party to participate in an informal brainstorming session, separate from a negotiation meeting, where the parties can educate each other about their interests, and the participants can freely exchange ideas "off the record."[9] Although that might be worthwhile in settling international disputes or negotiations in complex, multiparty cases, in the day-to-day practice of law, it is usually not cost efficient.

Accordingly, in most situations, your initial offer is an invitation to problem-solving brainstorming within the negotiation itself. For this invitation to be effective, you need to accomplish four things: (1) establish explicitly that you want to take a problem-solving approach in the negotiation; (2) identify the interests both of your client and of the other side; (3) present a solution or range of solutions that addresses these interests; and (4) open the door to joint development of other options.

§31.2.2 *Handling the Other Side's Reluctance to Problem Solve*

In many negotiations, after you have made your initial offer of a proposed solution, the other side's lawyer will answer with a classical adversarial response.

To reframe the discussion and focus on interests, respond to the other side's rigid positions with open-ended, problem-solving questions:

1. **Ask "why?"** Try to get the other side to identify the interests underlying their position. When the City Attorney responds that the issue of the closing of the facilities is nonnegotiable, ask directly for the basis for his client's position. If, for example, he says, "because of the political pressure from the neighbors," you may have an opening for brainstorming ways to address that concern.
2. **Ask "why not?"** Some lawyers simply will refuse to answer a direct question about their clients' interests but may be eager to criticize your proposals. So after the other side's lawyer rejects your proposal, ask what is wrong with it, and the other lawyer might start talking about the interests that lawyer is expected to protect. For instance, when the City Attorney rejects Cassini's proposal for additional services because of the strains on the city's budget, her lawyer can start discussing ways to minimize increased costs or obtain funds from other sources.
3. **Ask "what if?"** Another technique for initiating joint problem-solving is to probe specifics of solutions. After the City Attorney has rejected the educational program as ineffective, Cassini's lawyer could suggest alternatives: meetings with Cassini and Board of Health officials in neighbors' homes; visits by the neighbors to the facility; or participation by local clergy in the programs. Some lawyers will feel uncomfortable consistently saying "no" and may actually start brainstorming.

---

[9] Roger Fisher et al., *Getting to Yes: Negotiating Agreement Without Giving In* 63 (2d ed. 1991).

4. ***Ask for their advice.***   Most lawyers love to give advice to their adversaries, especially novice lawyers. By seeking counsel from the other side's lawyer, you may be able to get him to identify his client's interests and spark some problem-solving discussion. Cassini's lawyer perhaps could say to the City Attorney: "I know my client won't close the facilities. She is very committed to helping people with AIDS. What should I tell her?" Although the response might be a lecture on the necessity of obeying zoning laws, the City Attorney might start talking about the pressure from the neighbors and give you an opportunity to start a discussion on the issue.

5. ***Ask "what makes that fair?"***   Outright rejection of the other side's position often leads to adversarial bargaining about that position. To prevent that, you might ask the other lawyer why his client's position is fair. Try to get the other side to refocus from reliance on the rights or power that support its position to an explanation of why, from a practical standpoint, this position is reasonable. Suppose, for example, that Cassini's lawyer were to ask the City Attorney: "I know your interpretation of the zoning law and don't agree with it. But, putting that issue aside, how is displacing these people with AIDS fair and reasonable?" Again, if the City Attorney starts discussing the underpinnings of the city's decision to prosecute, you have an opening for joint problem-solving.[10]

In many cases, the other side's lawyer will remain adamantly adversarial. The City Attorney, for instance, might consistently answer all these questions by saying: "I know your client's position, and it might be very reasonable. But the city is required to enforce the zoning laws, and Ms. Cassini broke them." Faced with such intransigency to the problem-solving approach, you might want to attempt to change the players in the game.[11] If you believe that the other side may be more open to problem-solving than its attorney, you can write a letter to the opposing attorney presenting your appeal for problem-solving and proposing solutions. Since the attorney usually must communicate this written offer to his client,[12] your letter might persuade the other side to instruct its lawyer to change his position. Or you may suggest to the opposing attorney the scheduling of a meeting of clients and attorneys. At that meeting, your direct appeals to the interests of the other party may be more effective than were your arguments to its attorney.

If all of these approaches fail, you have two choices: walk away from the bargaining table or join in adversarial bargaining. But try not to abandon prematurely your efforts to initiate problem-solving negotiation. Some lawyers do not instinctively problem solve, and it might take a while for the other lawyer to adjust to your approach. Moreover, even if you do switch to an adversarial approach, you might try to restart problem-solving efforts after you have demonstrated the strengths of your client's rights or power.

---

[10] For an in-depth description of the use of these different questioning techniques, see William Ury, *Getting Past No: Negotiating Your Way from Confrontation to Cooperation* 78–89 (1993).

[11] Robert H. Mnookin et al., *Beyond Winning: Negotiating to Create Value in Deals and Disputes* 207–209 (2000).

[12] Comment 2 to Model Rule of Professional Conduct 1.4(a)(1).

§31.2.3 *Problem-Solving With the Other Party*

Even if the other lawyer agrees to join you in a problem-solving approach, your work is far from over. The fact that the other party will consider options addressing the interests of both parties does not mean that the solutions you have developed in your planning will be agreeable to the other side. In adversarial bargaining, after the initial offers, there is usually a give-and-take of concessions until an agreement is reached. In problem-solving negotiation, on the other hand, you need to work with the other lawyer to develop alternative solutions and fine tune them to try to reach a deal.

This process — referred to by William Ury as "building a golden bridge"[13] between your client and the other side — can be facilitated by several methods.

1. *Keep focused on the parties' interests.*   For problem-solving to work, the parties need to make their interests explicit and concentrate on developing solutions to meet these needs. If the parties become distracted and entangled in wrangles about rights and power, problem-solving will fail.

2. *Engage in brainstorming.*   Often, especially where the relationship between the parties has been good or the lawyers both have adopted a cordial style, the two sides might want to engage in a brainstorming session as part of the negotiation. This process is quite simple: after identifying their respective interests, the parties can sit facing a large pad of paper or a whiteboard and generate different solutions to the problems; they star those options which seem most promising; and then, focusing on the interests of the parties, attempt to invent improvements in those options. The key to effective brainstorming with another party is separating the inventing of the options from evaluation of their merits.

> A brainstorming session is designed to produce as many ideas as possible to solve the problem at hand. The key ground rule is to postpone all criticism and evaluation of ideas. The group simply invents ideas without pausing to consider whether they are good or bad, realistic, or unrealistic. With those inhibitions removed, one idea should stimulate another, like firecrackers setting off one another.[14]

A neutral third party can even facilitate the discussion.

3. *Try to develop ways to meet unmet needs.* The major hang-up in problem-solving bargaining is usually that a proposed solution fails to meet the needs

---

[13] Ury, *supra* note 10, at 105 (referring to a saying of Sun Tzu, "Build your opponent a golden bridge to retreat across").

[14] Fisher et al., *supra* note 1, at 60. Recently one scholar has urged caution in the use of this type of brainstorming process. Chris Guthrie, *Panacea or Pandora's Box? The Costs of Options in Negotiation*, 88 Iowa L. Rev. 601 (2003). He argues that option generation in negotiation can have negative, as well as positive, consequences to the outcome of the bargaining. He contends, for example, that "negotiators may unwittingly devalue an option once it becomes part of a set of options because options that look attractive by themselves often look less attractive when compared to others" and may irrationally overvalue an earlier option once an inferior option is added to the mix. *Id.* at 608–625. To overcome these problems, he recommends that lawyers play an active role in the brainstorming process helping clients to make rational assessments of different options and to consider how to use option generation to their strategic advantage. *Id.* at 638–651.

of a party. To address this problem, revisit the type of analysis you conducted in planning for problem-solving negotiation. Do not assume a fixed pie (one that cannot be made larger). Instead, think of ways to increase the available resources to meet that need.[15]

Another way of dealing with unmet needs is to create conditional solutions. One of the parties in a negotiation might believe that a particular problem will arise in the future but the other disagrees. Instead of arguing over whether this contingency will occur, the parties can frame their agreement to address it.

4. *Engage in incorporation.*   In a problem-solving negotiation, if each party presents its own proposal, the parties might become so entrenched in their advocacy that the bargaining can quickly become adversarial in nature. To avoid this problem, try to incorporate elements of the other party's proposal into the modification of your own client's proposal. By recognizing some reasonableness in the other side's proposal, you continue to acknowledge its interests and keep the door open to further problem-solving. Suppose you represent the landlord in the *Ransom v. Dusak* case, and the tenant's lawyer has proposed the completion of all the work in the apartment within one week, a completely independent counterproposal might be greeted with the negative reaction that your client does not understand the terrible conditions in which Ransom lives. By agreeing to accept Ransom's repair list, but tinkering with particular work completion dates and the precise nature of the work, you might reach a deal.

5. *Help the other side to save face.*   In many negotiations, the reputational and psychological needs of the parties are so important that any solution must address them. In such situations, think about ways to help the other side "save face" without compromising any of the priority interests of your own client.

---

[15] See §29.5.1; Ury, *supra* note 10, at 118.

CHAPTER 32

NEGOTIATION TACTICS

§32.1 Information Bargaining

As we discussed in §29.6, whether you are bargaining adversarially or in problem-solving, you will engage in information bargaining. This section explains methods for gathering and concealing information.

§32.1.1 Gathering Information

The techniques for gathering information during a negotiation are similar to those used in any other kind of fact retrieval: from client interviewing and witness interviewing to depositions. Your goal is to encourage a free flow of information, and your methods need to facilitate this process. While in a client interview, the client may be unwilling to provide needed facts because of embarrassment, mistrust, or psychological pressures, in a negotiation the other side's lawyer may be reluctant to share information for purely tactical reasons. In either case, you need to break down the barriers to communication.

1. **Broad questions.** As in client interviewing, the use of broad questions can facilitate information gathering in negotiation. Broad questions give the respondent some room to decide how much to discuss the topic. Many novice lawyers view negotiations primarily as a time to pontificate about the merits of their case, making confident statements to the other party's lawyer in hopes that the other side will capitulate. "Statements [however] generate resistance, whereas questions generate answers."[1] If you want needed information to evaluate your bargaining range in adversarial bargaining and to develop alternative solutions in problem-solving negotiation, the easiest method is broad questioning, not lecturing.

---

[1] Roger Fisher et al., *Getting to Yes: Negotiating Agreement Without Giving In* 111 (2d ed. 1991).

Consider, for instance, two approaches by the tenant's lawyer for obtaining information about the landlord's assessment of the conditions in her apartment in the *Ransom v. Dusak* case referenced earlier:

Example 1

My client has been living in those wretched conditions for months: rodents, falling ceiling, lack of heat. She's complained to Dusak, and he has done nothing. The Health Department has been out there — they verify the problems and are ready to take some action. What's your client going to do about it?

Example 2

What does your client think about the conditions in the apartment?

If Ransom's lawyer wants to get as much information as possible about the other side's evaluation of the conditions of the apartment, Example 1 does not accomplish it. By assuming in the question that the contested conditions exist and accusing Dusak of ignoring them, she puts the other lawyer on the defensive and closes the door on disclosure. The opposing lawyer's response will probably be an argument either contesting the particular conditions or whether the landlord failed to act.

The lawyer in Example 2, on the other hand, takes a nonjudgmental approach that invites as full a response as possible. In answering, Dusak's lawyer might divulge new facts — about the conditions in the apartment or about Dusak's conduct. Even if the lawyer asking the question is using an adversarial approach to the negotiation, the question still might help. Its purpose is to obtain information to aid in assessing Dusak's bargaining range — not to compel a concession. Throughout a negotiation, think carefully about the purpose of your communication with the other lawyer. The very same statement or question can be either beneficial or harmful depending upon its context. For example, in adversarial bargaining, Example 1, while it does not facilitate information bargaining, might help in arguing for a concession from Dusak.

After you ask broad questions, you can ask narrow ones to elicit further information. If, for instance, Dusak's lawyer replies to the Example 2 question that his client knows about a heating problem, Ransom's lawyer might want to pose a series of "Anything else?" questions until she has exhausted the lawyer's knowledge. Then she might want to ask narrow questions exploring the specifics of Dusak's information on each condition. And finally, she might use leading questions to pin down the lawyer about particular facts, such as, "So Dusak knew that the exterminator was unable to get into the apartment?" The obvious danger with this approach is that the opposing lawyer may object that you are deposing rather than negotiating and refuse to answer the questions. Therefore, be selective in the areas in which you use this approach, and try to phrase the questions in noncombative ways that do not prejudge the issues or raise the ire of the other side.

2. *Active listening.*   You have already learned about active listening, In interviewing, the primary purpose of active listening is to establish rapport with the client. In information bargaining, it serves another objective as well: by expressing understanding of the other party's situation, you encourage full responses to questions. People feel that if you are willing to understand their point of view, they are comfortable telling you more about it.

3. *Probing questions.*   In client interviewing, situations arise in which your client will simply say, "I just can't remember when it happened." At this point, you do not give up but ask probing questions to try to stimulate the client's memory: "Was it raining out that day?" or "Was it close to Christmas?". In information bargaining, there are times when the other lawyer will simply say, "I can't tell you." This failure to respond is usually caused not by a memory lapse but by the other lawyer's tactical need to keep the information from you. But the same probing technique that helps in interviewing can be beneficial here.

In information bargaining, probing entails giving the other lawyer an incentive to give a response. One technique is simply to ask your counterpart a direct question. Research shows that people are more inclined to lie by omission (not telling the whole truth) than by commission (falsely answering a direct question). By asking your counterpart to elaborate on an evasive answer, he may be reluctant to make a direct statement that is a lie and back away from the previous answer.[2] Another technique is to confront that lawyer with your knowledge of his evasiveness and to state that you assume the answer would be damaging to his client's case.[3] Consider, for example, this exchange in the *Ransom v. Dusak* case:

Ransom's Attorney:	How many times did your client try to send an exterminator to the apartment?
Dusak's Attorney:	I don't think this information is relevant to this case. If you want to negotiate, let's negotiate. If you want to try the case, let's go to trial.
Ransom's Attorney:	I'm sorry, but I do think this information is very relevant to our warranty of habitability claim. And regrettably I have to assume from your response that the exterminator only came once. That certainly strengthens our claim.

---

[2] Peter Reilly, *Was Machiavelli Right? Lying in Negotiation and the Art of Defensive Self-Help,* 24 Ohio St. J. on Disp. Resol. 481, 528 (2009).

[3] See Robert M. Bastress & Joseph D. Harbaugh, *Interviewing, Counseling, and Negotiating: Skills for Effective Representation* 415 (1990).

Although Dusak's lawyer can simply ignore the response, it might motivate him to become more forthcoming about the information requested. A related technique is to tell the other lawyer that the information is essential for your client's assessment of the case, and bargaining cannot continue without it.

4. *Silence.*A final technique for encouraging full responses is to respond to inadequate answers with silence. "If you have asked an honest question to which they have provided an insufficient answer, just wait. People tend to feel uncomfortable with silence, particularly if they have doubts about the merits of something they have said."[4] Using silence in this way may be hard given the tendency of most lawyers to talk more than they need to. But sometimes it can be the most effective technique. For instance, when Dusak's lawyer answered that the number of visits by the exterminator was irrelevant to the case, silence by Ransom's lawyer would have sent the message, "Come on now, let's get real! That's what this case is all about?" Without the combativeness of a verbal response, a long pause and expectant stare by Ransom's lawyer might embarrass Dusak's lawyer into a more acceptable response.

§32.1.2 Concealing Information

Part of your planning for information bargaining is deciding which facts you need to conceal. There are ethical constraints on your ability to hide information; you cannot lie, for example (see §27.5). But within those limitations, a number of techniques can help block disclosure of information.

1. *Under-answering a question.*
2. *Answer a question with a question.*
3. *Answer a different question.*
4. *Ignore the question and shift to another topic.*
5. *Explain why you will not answer the question.*

In this way, you cordially communicate to the other attorney that you understand his strategy, and it is not going to work.

All these techniques have disadvantages. Many experienced lawyers know about them and will persevere, trying to pin you down to an answer. In fact, if a cordial relationship with the other lawyer is important to your strategy, these techniques could actually be detrimental to your bargaining.

Moreover, since, in some instances, the other side will have access to other sources of proof for the requested information, your game-playing might have no effect other than to alienate the other lawyer. For this reason, in many cases where you have a strong need to conceal information, you may simply want to refuse to answer questions about that area and explain the reasons for your refusal.

---

[4] Fisher et al., *supra* note 1, at 112.

§32.1.3 Verifying What You Think You Know

If your willingness to settle is predicated on certain facts, verify them. Do not make assumptions about facts you consider important. If *only* the other side can know whether those "facts" really are true (rather than assumptions on your part), do two things. First, ask them for proof. Second, ask them to represent and warrant in the written agreement produced by the negotiation that the "facts" on which you rely are true.

If the other side lies to you about facts they represent and warrant to be true, the fraud is grounds for opening up the agreement and for getting damages. If the other side says something untrue through an honest mistake on their part, that might provide grounds for recision if your client later decides that the deal is undesirable. *Your goal is not only to get a good deal, but also to get a deal with escape hatches in case your client later needs to get out of it.* One way to do that is to insist that the other side take responsibility, to the extent possible, for facts on which you rely.

§32.2 Communicating About Rights and Power

A party using an adversarial approach will usually use rights-based arguments and power-based threats or warnings in attempts to compel concessions by the other side. In problem-solving bargaining, even though the parties focus primarily on their mutual interests, they often use rights-based arguments to develop possible solutions. If, for example, parties in a sexual harassment dispute are trying to agree on standards for the employer's future policies, they may look to Equal Employment Opportunity Commission regulations for guidance and might argue about their meaning. Likewise, in the negotiation of a commercial contract, the parties may argue about the business norms in that industry in regard to a contested provision of the agreement. And to a lesser extent, problem-solving negotiators also use power-based tactics to accomplish their goals. They may assert their power in the first instance to try to force the other side into problem-solving or, in the midst of the negotiation, power imbalances may set limits on the range of solutions available. If a tenants' group is negotiating with the landlord about problems in the building, for instance, as eager as both sides may be to work together to solve the problem, the landlord will probably not entertain an option that the tenants take over management of the building.

Negotiation is not just a series of offers, counteroffers, and concessions. Nor is it limited to the identification of interests, generation of options, and development of solutions. The energy that fuels both of these processes — what moves parties to concessions or mutual solutions — comes from communications about the parties' rights and power. The ability to communicate effectively about the parties' respective rights and power, therefore, is an essential skill in negotiation.

§32.2.1 Arguing About Rights

An argument is a group of ideas, arranged logically to convince somebody to do a particular thing or to adopt a particular belief. Lawyers argue about rights in a number of contexts — in motion practice in trial courts, in closing arguments before juries, in oral arguments in appellate courts, and in negotiations. Although all legal arguments have some similarities, argument in negotiation is unique. You are not trying to convince a neutral decision-maker but instead are trying to persuade somebody whose interests are at least initially in conflict with yours and your client's. This skill entails a number of important elements.[5]

1. ***Develop a detailed and organized argument.*** To be effective, all legal argument must be both well-developed and organized. That is especially true in a negotiation when you are trying to persuade someone who has the potential for being hostile to your argument. Detailed argumentation requires a crisp, explicit statement of the legal basis of the argument, a specific description of the facts supporting the application of the legal rule in this case, and a conclusion. This is the same kind of analysis as is used in the legal elements model for organizing facts.

   Consider, for example, the persuasive impact of these different arguments of Ransom's lawyer in the *Ransom v. Dusak* case:

   Example 3

   My client is entitled to a $1,950 abatement of rent because your client has breached the warranty of habitability by failing to provide necessary services in Ransom's apartment.

   Example 4

   As I'm sure you know, under section 500 of the Property Code, your client had a duty to provide Ransom with an apartment fit for human habitation. Your client breached this duty when he failed to provide sufficient heat during last winter, to repair a leaking ceiling in the bedroom, and to spray the apartment for roaches. And, I'm also sure you know, under that same section of the Code, my client is entitled to actual and punitive damages for this violation. Here, she lost use of one-half of the apartment for six months, entitling her to a $1,950 abatement and $250 in punitive damages.

---

[5] These elements were adapted from Robert J. Condlin, *Bargaining Without Law*, http://papers.ssrn.com/sol3/papers.cfm?abstract_id=1649467 (2010) [hereinafter Condlin, *Bargaining Without Law*]; Robert J. Condlin, *"Cases on Both Sides": Patterns of Argument in Legal Dispute-Negotiation*, 44 Md. L. Rev. 65 (1985). Condlin calls this type of communication "conversational argument." In arguments of this sort, "it is inappropriate to make speeches, score debater's points, or rely on the mannerisms and maneuvers of public oratory to influence one another. . . . [Such argument] does not preach, impress, hector, or punish." Condlin, *Bargaining Without Law, supra,* at 30.

In Example 3, the lawyer merely states a conclusion without taking the listener through an analysis. (The late Judge Hubert L. Will of the U.S. District Court for the Northern District of Illinois used to call this type of argument "prayer balls to the gods": the lawyer throws out a legal rule and expects the judge or other listener to conduct the analysis herself.) The Example 4 lawyer does much better by providing a step-by-step review of the rules, facts, and conclusion. He provides necessary details to support the argument (citation to the statutory authority, specific description of the conditions, explicit statement of damages) in a clear and tight format.

Obviously, this approach has limits. A lengthy discourse on the nuances of the law or an extensive review of the evidence, especially if both parties have a thorough understanding of the law and facts, can appear pedantic and turn the listener off. Sometimes, you need only mention the legal rules, focusing your presentation on the factual evidence. At other times, when the facts are not in dispute but the law is, you might need to concentrate on the case law supporting your interpretation of the rules. But beware of assuming that the other side's lawyer understands all the issues. Identify the important issues in dispute about the parties' rights and present a detailed and organized argument on those issues.

2. ***Engage in multi-dimensional reasoning.***   An argument can be based on any number of standards: legal rules; policies; common sense; tradition; business standards; professional judgment; or other norms. And often a number of items of evidence support the application of the standard in the case. The strength of your argument can be increased if you can expand the number of standards and/or facts upon which you rely. Your rights assessment in the case (Figure 28.2 and Figure 28.3) can provide you with these additional reasons.

Assume, for example, a lawyer represents a manufacturer that wants to build a small factory near a residential community. In negotiation with a community group, she can argue simply that the local zoning ordinance allows for the siting of the factory on this property. Alternatively, she can make the following argument:

> As I am sure that city officials have told you, the zoning ordinances allow us to build the factory here without the issuance of a permit or variance. Additionally, three similar factories have been built in other areas zoned I-A in the past five years without any city intervention. But most importantly, consider the jobs this factory will create for your community. The other two factories we operate each employs 50 people from the surrounding community. Finally, your fears about air pollution are unfounded. As our consultant's report shows, our environmental safety record is excellent.

While the first argument addresses solely the narrow issue of the zoning ordinance, the second argument raises not only that issue, but also policy reasons (the city's precedent with such projects) and factual support (increased employment and environmental safety). Whether the lawyer is using an adversarial or problem-solving approach, the second argument presents a more formidable presentation to the community group than the first.

3. ***Design a balanced argument.*** In any argument, balance can create an appearance of reasonableness. In negotiation, that is particularly important because the other side starts out with interests opposed to yours and thus treats you warily. By demonstrating that you understand the strengths and weaknesses on both sides of the case, you show that your assessment of rights is solid and that your reasoning is sound. The legitimacy of your argument will be significantly affected by your acknowledgment of any weaknesses in your case.

    In the *Ransom* case, for example, if the landlord's lawyer makes the argument that no problems existed at the apartment, he will have little effect on Ransom's lawyer because the argument is unbalanced or one-sided. On the other hand, if the landlord's lawyer admits that some problems did exist, but that Ransom failed to give adequate notice and even refused entry to the exterminator, the landlord's lawyer increases the odds that Ransom's lawyer will hear and be influenced by the argument. In an adversarial context, this approach may result in a concession from Ransom, and, in a problem-solving setting, it may help to create an atmosphere for joint option generation.

4. ***Present facts persuasively.***   In some negotiations, the most contested issues will concern disputed facts. A dry and antiseptic presentation of the facts may have very little effect on the other side or its lawyer. On the other hand, a persuasive description of the facts may significantly enhance the force of your argument. In presenting your version of the facts to the other side, consider many of the same factors you do when you are preparing for a presentation of facts at a trial or hearing: the nature of your audience, the uncontested facts, a unifying theme, and persuasive images. Think of how you can tell a persuasive story that will have an emotional impact on the other lawyer.

5. ***Ability to persist in face of rejection.***   While it is important in a negotiation to present a balanced argument to show your reasonableness, you can only be effective if you continue to press your principal points in the face of your adversary's rejection. Merely repeating the same points will not move your adversary. When met with resistance, you need to present your arguments in different ways — reframing them, offering new evidence, or probing for details about your opponent's objections, and modifying your positions only after being presented with arguments or information that provide a good basis for the change. Experienced bargainers expect arguments to be rejected, and you have to be ready to respond, not retreat.

6. ***Use unusual or unexpected arguments.***   Argument is most effective if it creates doubts your adversary cannot overcome within the negotiation time frame. If you rely solely on arguments that are obvious to your adversary, either because you have previously used them multiple times or because they are the boilerplate positions taken by parties in such cases, you will make little headway. Your goal, then, "is to tell the adversary something new about the issues in dispute, something he had not thought of on his

own, and something that causes him to have second thoughts about what he believes to be true."[6]

§32.2.2 Making and Handling Threats

Making threats.   A threat is a declaration by a negotiator of an intent to assert a right or power if the other party does not comply with a request or demand. While an argument is an attempt to persuade the other side logically of a client's rights in a dispute or transaction, a threat is an effort to use your client's rights or power to coerce the other side to agreement. Fisher and Ury say that "threats are one of the most abused tactics in negotiation."[7] They warn that threats can lead to counterthreats from the other party, create ill will between the parties, and even destroy relationships between the parties.

All of that is true. But there are times when logical arguments have no effect, and when the other party will not make any further concessions or agree to any alternative solutions. If your client has rights or powers that can be used to force the other party to budge, threats may be an effective tactic.

Threats work only if they are credible and will have a significant impact on the other side. If they lack credibility, the other party will just laugh them off. A threat by Ransom to stage a rent strike, for example, will have little effect if Dusak knows that no tenants organization exists and that Ransom has made no attempt to start one.

To determine whether you have potentially effective threats, consider your assessments of rights and power (Figure 28.2, Figure 28.3, and Figure 28.4). Assess the strengths and weaknesses of your client's possible legal claims and power plays. Imagine what counterthreats could be raised against your client. Think about what steps the other side could take to shift the rights and power balances. Then ask yourself: "In light of these assessments, will a particular threat appear credible to the other side? And what impact will it have on them?"

Even if you can identify effective threats, think of ways of packaging them to lessen the potential for enmity, especially if the parties will have a continuing relationship after the negotiation. The most credible threats are not delivered with table pounding and insult. They are instead presented in the form of subtle suggestions that demonstrate the existence of the right or power without drama. The trick is to make a threat without being threatening.

Fisher and Ury suggest the use of warnings, rather than outright threats.[8] "A threat comes across as what you will do to them if they do not agree. A warning comes across as what will happen if agreement is not reached."[9] Contrast these threats from Ransom's lawyer:

---

[6] Condlin, *Bargaining Without Law, supra* note 5, at 30.

[7] Fisher et al., *supra* note 1, at 136.

[8] *Id.* at 137; William Ury, *Getting Past No: Negotiating Your Way from Confrontation to Cooperation* 136 (1993).

[9] Ury, *supra* note 8, at 137.

Example 5

If you don't agree to make the repairs in my client's apartment by June 15, she will get the tenants organization to start a rent strike and picket the building.

Example 6

If we can't reach an agreement to have the repairs made by June 15, it seems likely that we're not going to be able to control the tenants organization, and it may start a rent strike and picket the building.

Although both threats demonstrate Ransom's power, the second presents the consequences as though they were outside of the client's control. When Dusak's lawyer asks, "Are you threatening me?", Ransom's lawyer can reply, "I'm sorry, this is nothing personal. It's just my opinion as to how the tenants group will respond."[10]

Responding to threats. When you are confronted with a threat, you have several options. First, you can ignore the threat. If you believe that the claimed right or power underlying the threat is weak or that the other side will not carry it out, you might just write the threat off as ignorable bluster or venting by the other lawyer. If your client will not be significantly affected even if the threat is carried out, you might want to explain why it will have little impact and then continue the bargaining. There is a risk, however, that the other lawyer will try to divert you into a discussion of whether the threatened action will have the slight consequences you assert, and you may lose control of the agenda. If you consider the threat meaningless, cut this discussion off and get back to bargaining.

If the threat is credible and will have a significant impact on your client, you might explain to the other lawyer how you are able to equalize the rights or power imbalance. Outline the actions your client can take to neutralize the threat. You can identify these options from your rights and power assessments. For example, consider an employment discrimination dispute in which the plaintiff's lawyer threatens to seek class action certification if the employer does not agree to the plaintiff's offer. In response, the employer's lawyer might assert that the employer will extensively litigate the class certification motion, and if unsuccessful, will take an interlocutory appeal and tie up the case for years.

A third tactic is a counterthreat. From the arsenal of your own client's rights and powers, you can identify a threat that your client will carry out in retaliation if the other side follows through with its threat. In a negotiation for the sale of a house, for example, when the buyer threatens to purchase other property down the street instead, the seller can respond that it just received a call from another eager buyer. To work, this counterthreat has to be credible and has to have the potential for a significant impact on the other side — or it will be considered no more than bravado.

---

[10] For a discussion of the ethical issues raised by this reply, see §27.5.

The danger with a counterthreat, however, is that it can lead to an escalation of tensions and a breakdown in bargaining. If your evaluation of your client's BATNA suggests that further negotiation would help, you may want to try to soften your presentation of the counterthreat. When the buyer's lawyer threatens to buy another house instead, the seller's lawyer might say: "My client also received a call today from Dandy Realty with a serious prospect for a new buyer who wants to see the house tonight. But let's not be distracted by other buyers and sellers and get back to the terms of this deal."

CHAPTER 33

CLOSING THE DEAL: DRAFTING

Wrapping up the deal includes concluding the negotiation discussions with the other side, discussing the final agreement with your client, and drafting the agreement or stipulation of settlement.

§33.1 Concluding the Negotiation and Discussing It With Your Client

Sometimes, toward the end of a negotiation, the parties will reach an impasse. They will be close to settlement, but neither party will make the final concession or agree to compromise a particular interest. At that point, a formulaic approach such as "splitting the difference," might be very helpful. Although splitting the difference is inappropriate earlier in a negotiation (see §31.1.4), at the end when the parties are close to settlement principled negotiation may not be as important as a simple nudge to agreement. At this point even in adversarial negotiations, you want to help the other side save face and make it feel it won (see §31.2.3).

After the parties have reached an agreement, you should review in detail the terms with the other lawyer, confirming all the essential components. You want to make sure there are no misunderstandings.

Then contact your client immediately. If your client did not pre-authorize the exact agreement you reached (see §28.5), the agreement is tentative and does not become real until your client approves (and until the other lawyer's client approves, too, if the other lawyer did not have authority). If your client had pre-authorized the terms of this agreement, at least you want to share the news.

§33.2 Drafting the Agreement or Stipulation of Settlement

The agreement should be memorialized in writing. If the parties have not been litigating against each other, the writing will usually include the word

"Agreement" or "Contract" or the equivalent in big letters at the top of the first page. If the negotiation resolves litigation, the writing is a stipulation of settlement. A stipulation is an agreement between the parties to a lawsuit; if consideration flows in both directions, it's a contract even though it isn't called one. In some litigation settings, the stipulation is recited orally "on the record" in open court, and the transcript is the writing, even though not signed by the parties.

In any event, the precise wording of the agreement is crucial because afterward the parties will be governed by the words and not by your memory of what was agreed to. If possible, write the initial draft of the agreement yourself to assure precision on the provisions that are most important to your client. In certain settings, practitioners start from — but are not limited to — form contracts or stipulations. But even in those situations, make sure that the language conforms to the agreement you have actually reached. If it doesn't, write new language that does. When another lawyer tells you that "we don't need to deal with that particular issue in writing," you probably *do* need to put it in writing. Nothing protects your client better than a written agreement that spells out the deal exactly as you understand it. If there's a later dispute about what was agreed to, you are at a severe disadvantage without a signed agreement drafted to your satisfaction.

The paragraphs that follow are an introduction to — and not a full explanation of — agreement drafting. To learn how to do this well, read Tina L. Stark, *Contract Drafting* (2007). You really should learn how to draft well. Everything you've gained through negotiation can be lost if you make mistakes in drafting the agreement. (A stipulation of settlement in litigation is a contract between the parties and should be drafted like one, even if it begins with a litigation caption.) Here are a few foundational concepts of agreement drafting:

1. Use words that express precisely the agreement you have obtained from the other side.   The Angels are a baseball team in Anaheim, California, which is near but not in Los Angeles. For several decades, they called themselves the California Angels. Many people in Anaheim feel that the team should not be ashamed of where it plays and should call itself the Anaheim Angels. The City of Anaheim owns the stadium used by the team. In 1996, the city and team negotiated a new lease, which included this language:

> Tenant [the Angels] will change the name of the Team to include the name "Anaheim" therein, such change to be effective no later than the commencement of the 1997 Season.

From 1997 to 2005, the team called itself the Anaheim Angels. In 2005, the team decided that it could make more money with a different name, and it began calling itself the Los Angeles Angels of Anaheim. The city thought it had a deal that the team would be called the Anaheim Angels. The team argued that it satisfied the language in the lease if the word Anaheim appeared *anywhere* in the team's name. The city sued and lost. If you open up the sports pages of any newspaper, you'll now see the team identified as the Los Angeles Angels or the L.A. Angels, which is also what you'll hear announcers say on television and radio. The media aren't required to give the full name of an organization they discuss. What words in the lease would have prevented this? Try this:

> Tenant shall change the name of the Team to Anaheim Angels no later than the commencement of the 1997 Season and shall use that name for the Team and no other name throughout the remainder of the Lease Term.

Use words that express *precisely* the agreement you have obtained from the other side.

2. For each issue which you and the other side have settled, choose the appropriate ingredients of an agreement and draft accordingly.   Agreements are made up of covenants, discretionary authority, conditions, representations, warranties, and declarations.

A *covenant* is a promise to do something ("Smith *shall* paint the house") or not to do something ("Smith *shall not* paint the house"). Those promises represent obligations and are the heart of most agreements. To express a covenant, begin with the name or designation of the party who has made the promise, add the word *shall*, and then add the thing the party has promised to do or not to do:

> Smith shall paint the house.
> Smith shall not paint the house.

Never — never — use the word *shall* in any other way. *Shall* means "has a legally enforceable duty to." "Smith shall paint the house" means that Smith has a legally enforceable duty to paint the house created by the contract. Therefore, *shall* should always be preceded by the person or organization that has the duty ("Smith"). And it should always be followed by language that precisely states what the duty is ("paint the house"). You will see countless agreements and statutes where this rule is violated. Every one of them, as a result, is harder to read and understand. And many of them are ambiguous as well. An agreement that does not state duties clearly and unambiguously creates the risk of later disputes and litigation because each side will interpret the vaguenesses and ambiguities to suit its own interest. In addition, an agreement can impose a duty *only* on a person or organization who is a party to it. "Any lawsuit to enforce this Agreement shall be commenced in the courts of the state of New Mexico" is wrong. A lawsuit cannot have a duty; only the parties can.

Discretionary authority is permission to do something ("Smith *may* paint the house"). To express discretionary authority, begin with the party who has the authority, add the word *may*, and then add the thing the party has discretion to do or refrain from doing. A party with discretionary authority is not required to exercise it. It is discretionary. If it were required, it would be a covenant.

A *condition* limits a covenant or discretionary authority to a condition that must be satisfied before the covenant or discretionary authority is effective. Where the condition can be expressed in the same sentence as the covenant or discretionary authority, use an "if" clause to express the condition.

If the outside temperature is 60.0°F or more at 9:00 A.M. on March 15, Smith shall paint the house on that day [a *covenant*].

If the outside temperature is greater than 45.0°F and less than 60.0°F at 9:00 A.M. on May 15, Smith may paint the house on that day [*discretionary authority*].

Where a covenant or discretionary authority is subject to several conditions, a single sentence may be inadequate, and you may have to use some other construction.

A *representation* is a statement of fact intended to induce reliance. If a party misrepresents facts about the present or the past (not about the future)[1] and intends his assertion to induce the other party to enter into contract, the other party has remedies for misrepresentation. Unlike a representation, a warranty does not require inducement. And the warranteed statement can be about the present, the past, or (unlike a representation) the future. A representation or a warranty is made by one party to the other. If in negotiation the other side has made a statement of fact on which you or your client rely or otherwise want to be true, draft the agreement so that the other side represents and warrants that statement ("Jones represents and warrants that she has sole fee simple title, without encumbrances, to the house").

Make the other side *both* represent *and* warrant because in a later lawsuit growing out of the agreement, a misrepresentation and a breach of warranty require different burdens of proof and yield different remedies. Having both theories available gives you the maximum flexibility later. (If the statement is about the future, it can be only a warranty because representations are limited to the present and the past.) Even if the other side has not volunteered a statement on which you want to rely, you can negotiate for it, for example, by asking the other lawyer, "Is your client willing to represent and warrant that she has sole and clear title to the house?" If the point is important to your client, a negative answer to a question like that is a danger sign.

A *declaration* is a statement made by both parties jointly ("This agreement is governed by the law of New Mexico").

While you're negotiating, remember that what you're working toward is a written agreement made up of the ingredients explained above.   As you and the other side resolve each issue in the negotiation, develop in your own mind an approximate sense of how you will express the resolution of that issue in the written agreement. Often, you and the other side will negotiate the words that will appear in the agreement — either as you negotiate the deal itself or as you draft and find yourself negotiating again over the details expressed in words.

---

[1] Under some limited circumstances a promise about future events can be the basis for a claim of misrepresentation. "[A] promise or a prediction of future events may by implication involve an assertion that facts exist from which the promised or predicted consequences will follow, which may be a misrepresentation as to those facts. Thus, from a statement that a particular machine will attain a specified level of performance when it is used, it may be inferred that its present design and condition make it capable of such a level. Such an inference may be drawn even if the statement is not legally binding as a promise." Restatement (Second) of Contracts §159, cmt. c (1981).

Especially in a deal in which performance is required by a party over a period of time, you should include remedies provisions addressing the issue of nonperformance of the terms of the contract. You might want to consider methods for increasing the costs to the other side for noncompliance, such as the forfeiting of funds deposited in an escrow account. If you're settling litigation, the agreement should provide procedures for bringing the case back to court and perhaps sanctions against the offending party. If the tenant in an eviction action, for example, promises to pay back rent on a payment schedule, the landlord's lawyer may request a provision allowing for the issuance of an eviction order upon her default. In response, the tenant's lawyer might request a grace period for payment and the right to notice and hearing before the granting of such an order. And in a transaction, consider possible penalties against the nonperforming party, such as the imposition of liquidated damages.

APPENDIX

Sample Trial-Level Brief

IN THE UNITED STATES DISTRICT COURT
FOR THE DISTRICT OF COLORADO

RANDALL BROWNLEY,
Plaintiff

v.

SCOTT DUNN, d/b/a DUNN
CREDIT BUREAU,

Defendant

Civ. No. 95-14867

BRIEF IN SUPPORT OF DEFENDANT'S MOTION
TO SET ASIDE DEFAULT JUDGMENT

INTRODUCTION

This is an action alleging a violation of Section 607(b) of the Fair Credit Reporting Act (FCRA), 15 U.S.C.A. § 1681e(b) (West 1995). The Complaint was filed and served upon Scott Dunn on October 27, 1995. Default judgment was entered six days ago, on November 17, 1995, just one day after the expiration of Mr. Dunn's time to answer the Complaint. Mr. Dunn now files a Motion to Set Aside this Default Judgment, along with a supporting affidavit and a proposed Answer to the Complaint. This brief is filed in support of Mr. Dunn's Motion.

STATEMENT OF FACTS

In September 1995, a potential lender contacted Dunn Credit Bureau requesting a credit report on the Plaintiff. Aff. Scott Dunn ¶ 10 (Nov. 26, 1995). The Credit Bureau prepared the report, and it contained a reference to an unpaid department store account. Aff. Scott Dunn ¶ 11. Upon the discovery of this item on his credit report, the Plaintiff contacted Mr. Dunn to demand that the item be removed, arguing that the charged merchandise had been defective and that the defect was the reason for his nonpayment. Aff. Scott Dunn ¶ 12. Mr. Dunn asked the Plaintiff to provide this explanation in writing and promised to include it along with the store's version of the account. Aff. Scott Dunn ¶ 13.

The Plaintiff refused to provide the written explanation, but again demanded that the item be entirely removed. Aff. Scott Dunn ¶ 14. Mr. Dunn replied by letter, declining to delete the item entirely but repeating the offer to include the Plaintiff's defense to the item. Aff. Scott Dunn ¶ 14. The Plaintiff did not respond to Mr. Dunn's letter, and Mr. Dunn did not hear from the Plaintiff again. Aff. Scott Dunn ¶ 15.

On October 27, 1995, copies of the Summons and Complaint in this action were served at Mr. Dunn's home by leaving them with Mr. Dunn's sixteen-year-old son, Gregory. (Ret. of Serv. Oct. 30, 1995.) On that day, Mr. Dunn and his wife had traveled to Denver, planning to return the next day. Aff. Scott Dunn ¶ 3.

However, on the evening of October 27, Mrs. Dunn suffered a serious heart attack and was hospitalized. Aff. Scott Dunn ¶ 4. Gregory left immediately for Denver. In the midst of the crisis surrounding his mother's heart attack, Gregory did not think to tell his father about the delivery of an envelope to the family home. Aff. Scott Dunn ¶ 6.

Mr. Dunn remained in Denver with his wife for two weeks until Mrs. Dunn was released from the hospital to return home. Aff. Scott Dunn ¶ 5. Upon his return, Mr. Dunn began going in to his office part-time, while continuing to care for his wife. Aff. Scott Dunn ¶ 7. Mr. Dunn did not find the envelope until November 20, 1995. On that day, Mr. Dunn moved a stack of papers on the table in the family room and found the envelope there. Aff. Scott Dunn ¶ 8.

Mr. Dunn immediately called his attorney and began the preparations to file an Answer to the Complaint. Aff. Scott Dunn ¶ 9. Shortly after the initial telephone conversation with his attorney, Mr. Dunn learned that a default judgment had been entered three days earlier. Aff. Scott Dunn ¶ 9. Mr. Dunn now seeks an order, pursuant to Fed. R. Civ. P. 60(b), setting aside this default judgment.

<u>ARGUMENT</u>

I. THE DEFAULT JUDGMENT SHOULD BE SET ASIDE BECAUSE IT WAS ENTERED AS A RESULT OF INADVERTENCE OR EXCUSABLE NEGLECT AND BECAUSE THE DEFENDANT HAS A MERITORIOUS DEFENSE TO THE PLAINTIFF'S ALLEGATIONS.

Fed. R. Civ. P. 60(b) grants the Court the discretion to relieve a party from a final judgment entered as a result of inadvertence or excusable neglect. When the judgment was entered upon the moving party's default, the moving party must also demonstrate the existence of a potentially meritorious defense. *In re Stone*, 588 F.2d 1316, 1319 (10th Cir. 1978). Any doubts are to be resolved in favor of adjudication on the merits. *In re Roxford Foods, Inc.*, 12 F.3d 875, 879 (9th Cir. 1993). Mr. Dunn's facts easily establish both Rule 60(b) requirements.

A. <u>The Defendant's Default Resulted from Excusable Neglect Because Service Was Effected upon the Defendant's Minor Son and the Crisis of His Mother's Heart Attack Caused the Son to Forget to Inform the Defendant of the Service.</u>

Mr. Dunn meets the first requirement for Rule 60(b) relief because the default resulted from excusable neglect.

The United States Supreme Court has defined the term "excusable neglect," in the context of bankruptcy filings, to include giving "little attention or respect" or "leav[ing] undone or unattended ... esp[ecially] through carelessness." *Pioneer Inv. Servs. Co. v. Brunswick Assocs. Ltd. Partnership*, 507 U.S. 380 (1993). Last year the Tenth Circuit adopted this definition of excusable neglect in the context of a Rule 60(b) motion. *City of Chanute, Kansas v. Williams Nat. Gas Co.*, 31 F.3d 1041 (10th Cir. 1994). The Tenth Circuit specifically held that Rule 60(b) relief is not limited to circumstances beyond the moving party's control. *Id.* at 1046.

The Tenth Circuit's analysis of excusable neglect considers four factors: (1) the potential prejudice to the nonmoving party; (2) the length of delay; (3) the reason for the delay; and (4) the degree of good faith of the moving party. *Id.* at 1046-1047.

The first factor, the prejudice to the nonmoving party, must amount to more than simply delaying enforcement of the judgment. *Feliciano v. Reliant Tooling Co.*, 691 F.2d 653, 656-657 (3d Cir. 1982). Usually cognizable prejudice involves some change of position in reliance on the judgment. The second factor, the length of delay, measures both the time since the entry of judgment and the time since the party became aware of the judgment. *See Lasky v. International Union*, 27 Fed. R. Serv. 2d 473, 477 (E.D. Mich. 1978), *aff'd*, 638 F.2d 954 (6th Cir. 1981).

The third factor examines the validity of the reason for the delay and whether the delay was willful. The Tenth Circuit has consistently affirmed orders setting aside default judgments entered as a result of understandable error or inadvertence as opposed to willful action by the defendant. For example, the court affirmed a decision to set aside a default judgment entered while the plaintiff believed that his new attorney was negotiating a settlement that would resolve the litigation. *Thompson v. Kerr-McGee Ref. Corp.*, 660 F.2d 1380 (10th Cir. 1981). The Tenth Circuit also affirmed an order granting Rule 60(b) relief from a judgment caused by confusion about filing a notice of appeal. *Romero v. Peterson*, 930 F.2d 1502 (10th Cir. 1991).

The excusable reasons for delay in these cases contrast with cases in which the default resulted from a willful decision by the defendant. For example, in *Cessna Fin. Corp. v. Bielenberg Masonry Contracting, Inc.*, 715 F.2d 1442 (10th Cir. 1983), the court affirmed the trial court's decision denying relief to a corporate defendant whose representatives had decided not to answer the complaint because they believed that the corporate defendant would escape liability in bankruptcy. In *United States v. Theodorovich*, 102 F.R.D. 587 (D.D.C. 1984), the court denied relief because the default judgment had resulted from defendant's willful decisions not to attend his own properly scheduled depositions.

The final factor asks whether the defendant has acted in good faith. This factor invites the court to consider the broad equitable question of whether the moving party has dealt in good faith with the court and with the other parties to the litigation.

Applying these four factors to the present case demonstrates that Rule 60(b) relief is certainly appropriate here. First, granting the Defendant's Motion would not cause the Plaintiff to suffer any cognizable prejudice. The default judgment was entered less than one week ago. The only cognizable prejudice that would result from setting aside the judgment stems from the costs the Plaintiff incurred in seeking the entry of the judgment. The Defendant has offered to pay those reasonable costs Aff. Scott Dunn ¶ 16, and an order to that effect would sufficiently relieve the Plaintiff of even this small prejudice. *Littlefield v. Walt Flanagan and Co.*, 498 F.2d 1133 (10th Cir. 1974).

The "length of delay" factor also weighs in favor of granting the motion. Only three days elapsed between the entry of the default judgment and the Defendant's discovery of the litigation. Only three days elapsed between the Defendant's discovery and the filing of the Motion and supporting documents. By comparison, the Tenth Circuit found a delay of thirty-one days "short." *City of Chanute*, 31 F.3d at 1047. A six-day delay is well within permissible bounds.

The third factor, the validity of the reason for delay, is often the most important factor. In the present case, this critical factor is the most compelling of all. Here, the delay was caused by the sudden and serious heart attack of Mr. Dunn's wife and Gregory's mother Aff. Scott Dunn ¶¶ 4-9. That a teenager should forget to tell his father about the Summons and Complaint under such circumstances is certainly understandable. This is precisely the sort of omission that Rule 60(b) is designed to forgive.

Mr. Dunn's good faith also argues for relieving the Defendant from judgment. Mr. Dunn has dealt with both the Court and the Plaintiff entirely in good faith. The delay was not caused by any stratagem or artifice. Mr. Dunn was entirely unaware of the litigation. Immediately upon learning of the Complaint, Mr. Dunn hurriedly contacted his attorney and began the process of responding to the litigation Aff. Scott Dunn ¶ 9. Mr. Dunn's offer to bear the Plaintiff's costs is further evidence of his good faith.

Thus all four factors of the Rule 60(b) analysis place the Defendant's situation squarely within the parameters for Rule 60(b) relief and establish that Mr. Dunn meets the first requirement for setting aside the default judgment.

    B. <u>The Defendant Has a Meritorious Defense to the Complaint Because the Credit Report Accurately Reflects the Plaintiff's Admitted Failure to Pay the Account.</u>

Mr. Dunn also meets the second requirement for Rule 60(b) relief, the existence of a meritorious defense. A plaintiff alleging a violation of 15 U.S.C. § 1681e(b) must establish two elements: (1) that the credit report is inaccurate; and (2) that the inaccuracy flows from the reporting agency's failure to follow reasonable procedures. *Cahlin v. General Motors Corp.*, 936 F.2d 1151, 1156 (11th Cir. 1991). Establishing inaccuracy is a threshold requirement for a Section 1681e(b) claim. *Id.* at 1156.

The accuracy requirement of the FCRA does not require the credit reporting agency to delete all reference to an unpaid account merely because it is disputed. This is true even if the consumer ultimately pays the account. *Id.* In *Cahlin,* the plaintiff's credit report included reference to a disputed account. Initially the account was unpaid, but after it appeared on the credit report, the consumer settled the account for partial payment. The consumer then demanded that the credit agency delete all reference to the account. *Id.* at 1155.

The Eleventh Circuit held that Section 607(b) does not require a credit reporting agency to report only favorable information. The court specifically held that the agency did not have to delete the reference to the disputed account even though the dispute was settled, explaining that such an interpretation would gut the very purpose of a credit report. *Id.* at 1158.

Here the Plaintiff's credit report accurately reflects his failure to pay the balance owed on a department store charge account Aff. Scott Dunn ¶11. Further, unlike the account in *Cahlin,* the Plaintiff's account remains unpaid. The Credit Bureau offered to include the consumer's written statement describing the dispute, as required by 15 U.S.C.A. § 1681*i* (b) (West 1995). The Plaintiff refused. This refusal is the only impediment to a more complete description of the Plaintiff's dispute with the account holder. The Plaintiff's demand that the item be removed entirely would have decreased rather than increased the report's accuracy because it would have omitted all reference to an admittedly unpaid, though disputed, debt. The Act simply does not require this sort of concealment of a consumer's true credit history.

Thus, the Plaintiff's credit report is accurate, and the Credit Bureau did not violate FCRA. Mr. Dunn has a meritorious defense to the Plaintiff's Complaint.

CONCLUSION

Mr. Dunn meets both requirements for Rule 60(b) relief. All four factors for evaluating inadvertence or excusable neglect strongly argue in favor of granting Mr. Dunn relief under Rule 60(b). Further, the Plaintiff's credit report met the accuracy requirement under FCRA, and thus Mr. Dunn has a meritorious defense to the complaint. Mr. Dunn respectfully requests the Court to enter an order setting aside the judgment and allowing him to file his Answer and to otherwise defend this action.

DATED: _____   _____
                                Attorney for the Defendant

CERTIFICATE OF SERVICE

I, _____, attorney for the Defendant, do hereby certify that I have served upon the Plaintiff a complete and accurate copy of this Brief in Support of the Defendant's Motion to Set Aside Default Judgment, by placing the copy in the United States Mail, sufficient postage affixed and addressed as follows:

[name and address of Plaintiff's attorney]

DATED: _____   _____
                                Attorney for the Defendant

SAMPLE MOTION MEMORANDUM

UNITED STATES DISTRICT COURT FOR THE SOUTHERN
DISTRICT OF ILLINOIS

GEORGE VEDITZ,

     Plaintiff

    v.   2010-C-365

AMOS KENDALL,

     Defendant

MEMORANDUM IN SUPPORT OF PLAINTIFF'S MOTION FOR AN ORDER COMPELLING MEDIATION

PRELIMINARY STATEMENT

Mr. Veditz has sued Mr. Kendall for failure to provide accommodations required by the Americans with Disabilities Act. Although Mr. Veditz has sued for an injunction and other relief, he prefers to mediate this dispute rather than go to trial. Mr. Kendall refuses to mediate. Mr. Veditz has now moved for an order compelling mediation.

STATEMENT OF THE CASE

The plaintiff, George Veditz, is deaf. Amos Kendall, the defendant and an attorney, represented Mr. Veditz in a divorce action. During that lawsuit, Mr. Veditz at times had difficulty understanding what was happening and why it was happening because the defendant failed to supply translation services that a deaf person in Mr. Veditz's situation could understand.

Last year, Mr. Veditz suffered a total hearing loss as a result of meningitis. (Aff. Amos Kendall ¶¶ 2 (July 22, 2008).) Since then, Mr. Veditz has learned some Signed Exact English (SEE), but the only way he can fully converse is through Computer Assisted Real-time Transcription (CART). (Pl.'s Cmpl. ¶ 6, 7 (June 1, 2008).) SEE is a sign language grammatically similar to English, and CART is frequently used for communication with deaf people. (Aff. Laurent Clerc. ¶ 4 (July 14, 2008.) A person who has

1

recently become deaf as an adult typically can communicate most effectively through SEE and CART. (*Id.* at ¶¶ 4, 5.)

At the settlement conference in Mr. Veditz's divorce case, both parties and their lawyers were present. (Pl.'s Compl. ¶ 9.) The lawyers and Mr. Veditz's former spouse talked continually for two hours. (*Id.*) Mr. Veditz could not understand most of what they said because the defendant had hired an uncertified interpreter who knew only American Sign Language (ASL)—and not SEE. (*Id.* at ¶¶ 9, 12-16.) Attempts at communicating in ASL, a language that Mr. Veditz does not know, confused him so much that he did not understand many of the details of the discussion and could not participate in it fully. (*Id.* at ¶ 10.) The defendant knew that Mr. Veditz was still learning to sign, but he failed to ask Mr. Veditz how to accommodate his needs. (*Id.* at ¶ 11.)

According to a communication specialist, Laurent Clerc, SEE is the appropriate method of signed communication for Mr. Veditz. (Aff. Clerc. ¶ 8.) Mr. Clerc, who regularly assesses the needs of deaf people, concluded that CART is the ideal means for a hearing person to communicate with Mr. Veditz. (*Id.* at ¶¶ 2, 9.) These services are widely used at a rate of $150 per hour. (*Id.* at ¶¶ 10-11.)

Mr. Veditz believes that the Defendant's failure to provide an adequate means of communication resulted in an unfair settlement because he was unable to participate in the discussions that led to the settlement. (Pl.'s Compl. ¶ 17.) Mr. Veditz will continue to have a maintenance obligation and will need continuing legal assistance from the defendant as a result of the defendant's failure to sufficiently accommodate Mr. Veditz pursuant to Title III of the American Disabilities Act (ADA). (*Id.* at. ¶ 18.) The defendant charged Mr. Veditz $100 per hour of service. (Aff. Kendall ¶¶ 2, 4.) The Defendant contends that "[t]he costs of CART are beyond what my practice can bear." (Aff. Kendall ¶ 14.)

Mediation has not yet taken place because Mr. Kendall has refused. (Aff. Kendall ¶ 4.) He claims that mediation will cost too much of his money and time. (*Id.*)

ARGUMENT

The Court Should Compel Mediation Between Mr. Veditz and Mr. Kendall.

A federal court has the authority to compel mediation in a lawsuit brought under the Americans with Disabilities Act. This authority derives from Rule 16(c)(2)(I) of the Federal Rules of Civil Procedure; Local Rule 16(a); the Americans with Disabilities Act, 42 U.S.C. §12212 (2006), and the court's inherent powers. Because of the relationship between the parties

2

and the nature of the dispute, the court should grant an order compelling mediation of this lawsuit.

A. The Relevant Court Rules and Statute Authorize and Encourage Mediation.

Rule 16(a) of the Federal Rules of Civil Procedure provides that "[i]n any action, the court may in its discretion direct [the parties to] appear before [the court] . . . before trial for such purposes as (1) expediting the disposition of the action . . . and (5) facilitating the settlement of the case." Federal Rule 16(c) provides that "the use of special procedures to assist in resolving the dispute, *when authorized by statute or local rule* . . . may facilitate the just, speedy, and inexpensive disposition of the action" (italics added). Rule 16 thus authorizes District Courts to order parties to participate in alternative dispute resolution. *Federal Reserve Bank v. Carey-Canada, Inc.*, 123 F.R.D. 603, 607 (D. Minn. 1988). "It is hard to imagine that the drafters of the 1983 amendments actually intended to strengthen courts' ability to manage their caseloads while at the same time intended to deny the court the power to compel participation by the parties to the litigation." *Id.*

Local Rule 16.2(a) of the Southern District of Illinois provides that a court may, "in its discretion, set any civil case for . . . [any] alternative method of dispute resolution which the court may deem proper," such as mediation. Local Rule 16.2(b)(3) provides that "any issue which, in the judge's opinion, may facilitate and expedite the trial . . . shall be discussed at the final pretrial conference and shall be included in the final pretrial order." Local Rule 16.3(a) further gives the court authorization to employ "alternative method[s] of dispute resolution which the court may deem proper," in order to "encourage and promote the use of alternative dispute resolution" so that "parties shall use an early neutral evaluation in the form of a settlement conference."

Mr. Veditz has sued under the Americans with Disabilities Act, 42 U.S.C. §§12101 et seq. (2007). Congress found that "communication barriers" are one of the ways in which "society has tended to isolate and segregate" the disabled. §12101(a)(1), (2), (5). The ADA prohibits discrimination on the basis of disability in a number of settings, including a lawyer's office. §12181(7)(F). The ADA also encourages mediation of complaints of discrimination. §12212.

B. Under Its Inherent Powers, the Court Can Order Mediation.

Even if no other law authorized a court to compel mediation, the court would still be able to do so through its inherent powers. Every federal court has inherent powers "governed not by rule or statute but by the control necessarily vested in courts to manage their own affairs so as to achieve the orderly and expeditious disposition of cases." *Link v. Wabash R.R. Co.,* 370 U.S. 626, 630-631 (1962). Mediation in particular can accomplish an "expeditious disposition" of an appropriate case.

Both of the federal courts that have considered this question held that, despite a party's objection, inherent judicial powers can be used to compel mediation. *In re Atlantic Pipe Corp.,* 304 F.3d 135, 140 (1st Cir. 2002); *In re African-American Slave Descendants' Litig.,* 272 F. Supp. 2d 755, 759 (N.D. Ill. 2003). The *Atlantic Pipe* court reasoned that in cases especially difficult to resolve through trial, mediation can turn out to be much more effective than the objecting party imagined. 304 F.3d at 143. Unlike a trial, in which one party wins and the other loses, a mediation can lead to a solution that benefits both parties. *Id.* at 145.

The *African-American* court agreed in general but held that the unique nature of that particular lawsuit made mediation less satisfactory than trial. 272 F. Supp. 2d at 759-760. There, descendants of enslaved African-Americans sued several corporations for reparations on the ground that the defendants had profited from slavery. The defendants argued that they could not be legally liable to the plaintiffs, and that the only way to resolve the dispute would be through a trial, where liability could be determined. *Id.* at 760.

C. The Court Should Order Mediation in This Case.

Because Mr. Veditz will need the defendant's cooperation in the future with issues arising from Mr. Veditz's divorce, trial could not effectively resolve this dispute. Trial is a conflict in which one side wins and the other loses. Mediation seeks a resolution that both parties can accept as fair and reasonable.

In a case analogous to this one, a doctor refused to provide a deaf interpreter when meeting with a deaf patient. *Mayberry v. von Valtier,* 843 F. Supp. 1160 (E.D. Mich. 1994). The doctor argued that paying for an interpreter would prevent the doctor from making a profit from treatment of the patient. The patient was dependent on the doctor for medical care. Unable to pay for an interpreter herself, the patient sued under the ADA for an injunction requiring the doctor to treat the patient and to provide an interpreter at the doctor's expenses. The trial court held that the patient had made out a prima facie case of discrimination under the ADA.

4

CONCLUSION

Local Rule 16.3(a), Federal Rule 16, and the ADA authorize and encourage court-ordered mediation. Moreover, a court can order mediation through the court's inherent powers. Because the defendant is the plaintiff's former lawyer and will continue to play a role in Mr. Veditz's divorce representation, mediation is the most effective method of resolving this dispute. Therefore, this court should enter an order compelling mediation between the parties to this lawsuit.

Respectfully Submitted,

Nathan J. Bailey
Nathan J. Bailey
Attorney for Plaintiff

SAMPLE APPELLANT'S BRIEF

In some ways, the format of this brief does not follow practices in the Seventh Circuit, where the appeal is set. Instead, the brief's format blends practices in many courts so that it is somewhat representative nationally.

In the UNITED STATES COURT OF APPEALS
for the SEVENTH CIRCUIT
Docket No. 2011–Civ.–141

AMOS KENDALL
Appellant
v.
GEORGE VEDITZ,
Appellee

ON APPEAL FROM JUDGMENT OF THE DISTRICT COURT
FOR THE SOUTHERN DISTRICT OF ILLINOIS

BRIEF FOR THE APPELLANT

Joanne Olson
Caroline Borden
Attorneys for the Appellant

TABLE OF CONTENTS

Page

i

TABLE OF AUTHORITIES

---

* Authorities chiefly relied on are marked with an asterisk.

ii

PROCEEDINGS BELOW

George Veditz, Appellee, is a former client of Amos Kendall, Appellant and a member of the Illinois bar. Veditz sued Kendall, alleging that Kendall failed to comply with Title III of the Americans with Disabilities Act and seeking an injunction and court-ordered mediation. (R. at 2, 11.) Kendall denied all the allegations in the complaint. (R. at 6). Both parties waived their rights to a trial by jury. (R. at 11.)

Over Kendall's objection, the District Court ordered both parties to submit to mediation, but stayed the execution of the order pending appeal. (R. at 11.) Mr. Kendall has now appealed to this Court. (R. at 28, 29.)

QUESTION PRESENTED

Mediation is a form of alternative dispute resolution through which disputing parties, with the assistance of a mediator, try to resolve their dispute. It is a collaborative alternative to an adversarial trial. Because mediation is collaborative rather than adversarial, it succeeds when parties discuss their dispute together and work with each other to resolve it. In this lawsuit, Kendall objects to mediation and is convinced that it will fail. He believes that his rights can be protected only through a trial because he provided Veditz with a deaf-signing translator at a settlement conference and because he otherwise communicated with Veditz through typing on a laptop, which Veditz himself uses in his own job to communicate reliably. On these facts: Did the District Court exceed its authority or abuse its discretion in ordering Kendall to mediate this lawsuit? Did the District err in determining that the accommodations provided by Kendall violate the Americans with Disabilities Act?

STATEMENT OF THE CASE

Amos Kendall, a seasoned attorney, is committed to providing clients with disabilities full and equal enjoyment of his legal services. His office is free from physical barriers, and he has represented many disabled clients. George Veditz, a client, has sued Kendall alleging that Kendall failed to provide a Signed Exact English (SEE) interpreter or a Computer Assisted Real Time Transcription (CART) even though Veditz did not request either of these accommodations.

Accommodations Provided to Veditz

While Kendall was representing Veditz in his divorce proceedings, Veditz became deaf due to viral meningitis. (R. at 13.) As a late-deafened adult, Veditz can communicate most accurately through writing, which he has

1

known and used all his life. (R. at 14.) At work, he communicates through writing. (R. at 14.) Veditz has never had formal training in any signed language. (R. at 4.) After the loss of his hearing, he has attempted to teach himself how to sign and now has a small vocabulary of signs. (R. at 14.) Veditz can understand some Signed Exact English (SEE), which has a grammar structure identical to English, but he is not fluent in SEE. (*Id.*) He has a difficult time understanding American Sign Language, which uses its own unique grammar. (R. at 4.) While Computer Assisted Real Time Transcription (CART) is an efficient method of written communication for late-deafened adults, handwritten or typed exchanges are also effective. (R. at 19.)

Initially, Kendall and Veditz communicated in part through written exchanges via a laptop (R. at 15). Kendall typed so that Veditz could read on the laptop screen. (*Id.*) Veditz communicated by speaking. (*Id.*) They also used email. (*Id.*) Veditz testified that although writing was not fast communication, he always understood what Kendall was telling him, and that he uses writing almost exclusively himself to communicate at work. (R. at 14-15.) Knowing that Veditz was learning signs, Kendall hired a sign language interpreter, Jane Fesenden, for the divorce settlement negotiations. (R. at 8.) Veditz did not ask Kendall to provide an interpreter or CART for the negotiation. (R. at 18, 24.)

The Divorce Negotiation

During the negotiation, Veditz told Fesenden he was unfamiliar with the grammar of ASL. (R. at 15.) Fesenden tried to use English grammar when signing to Veditz, but had to repeat herself and occasionally used ASL grammar. (R. at 16.) Regardless of the grammar Fesenden used, Veditz had trouble understanding her because he did not understand many of her signs. (*Id.*) Privately during the negotiation, Veditz told Kendall that he could not understand much of what Fesenden was translating. (R. at 16.) After learning that, Kendall typed accurate summaries of what each person said during the negotiation for Veditz to read. (R. at 16, 23.) Veditz testified that the typed summaries of the negotiation were "a way to be sure" he was understanding things correctly. (R. at 16.) Kendall testified that with the typed summaries Veditz was able to participate in the settlement. (R. at 23.) Veditz did not tell Kendall in any other way that the communication was ineffective, and he did not ask for CART services at that time. (R. at 18.) Moreover, Veditz did not ask that the negotiation be adjourned, and he did not ask that it be reopened later. (*Id.*) At the time of the negotiation, Veditz had never before used CART. (*Id.*)

Adequacy of Accommodations Balanced against Cost

Veditz alleged he was unable to fully participate in the negotiation and now needs continued legal counsel from Kendall to renegotiate the maintenance settlement. (R. at 2, 16.) Veditz also alleged that the communication obstacle would be remedied by the use of CART. (R. at 17.) From these allegations, Veditz claimed that Kendall did not make sufficient accommodations. (R. at 2.) Veditz testified that he wanted Kendall to use CART if he represents him in the future. (R. at 17.)

Kendall has tried but cannot find a certified SEE interpreter in southern Illinois (R. at 8). Although CART is available, it costs $150 per hour, which Veditz wants Kendall to pay (R. at 23). Kendall bills only $100 per hour for his services. (*Id.*) Kendall has made sure his office has no physical barriers that would hinder clients with movement disabilities, of whom he has represented many. (R. at 8.) As far as Kendall knows, every other disabled client has been satisfied with Kendall's work and the disability accommodations that he has provided. (*Id.*)

SUMMARY OF THE ARGUMENT

The finding that Veditz requested CART services is clearly erroneous because it is contradicted and unsupported by the evidence. Even if Veditz had requested CART services, Kendall would not have to provide CART because CART is unnecessary and unreasonable. CART is unnecessary because Kendall provided Veditz with Veditz's own best method of communication, written English in typed summaries. As a late-deafened adult, Vedtiz has communication needs that are unique, and unlike most deaf people, he communicates best with written English. Finally, Kendall does not have to provide CART, which would be an unreasonable accommodation. Providing CART would be an undue burden because Kendall would lose $50 for every hour he supplies CART.

The District Court abused its discretion by ordering mediation over Kendall's objection. Even if the District Court has the power to order mediation in some cases, it should not have done so here because mediation would be pointless. Because Kendall objects to it and believes that only trial can protect his interests, mediation probably would not lead to a settlement.

ARGUMENT

I.

Kendall Should Not Be Required, Over His Objection, to Mediate a Case That He Could Reasonably Win at Trial.

Whether Veditz asked for CART services is a pure question of fact subject to the clearly erroneous standard of review. Fed. R. Civ. P. 52(a). A finding of fact is clearly erroneous if it leaves the court with "the definite and firm conviction that a mistake has been committed." *Anderson v. City of*

3

Bessemer City, 470 U.S. 564, 573 (1984). The Court of Appeals does not have to accept the District Court's findings of fact if they are not supported by the evidence. *Campana Corp. v. Harrison*, 114 F.2d 400, 405 (7th Cir. 1940).

The remaining ADA questions are mixed questions of law and fact. Whether Kendall provided an appropriate auxiliary aid that ensures effective communication is a mixed question requiring the court to apply legal rules to undisputed facts. The last issue under the ADA claim, the undue burden defense, is also a mixed question requiring a court to interpret and apply the undue burden test to the facts of the case. In the Seventh Circuit, a mixed question of law and fact is reviewed *de novo* when "there is a need for uniformity" and "the issue is so important that there is a felt need to authorize second-guessing of" the District Court. *Cook v. City of Chicago*, 192 F.3d 693, 697 (7th Cir. 1999). Both are true here because the court below took the extraordinary step of ordering Kendall, over his objection, to take part in mediation, a process that works only when the parties participate voluntarily.

A. *Veditz Did Not Request CART and Therefore Cannot Win at Trial Concerning That Accommodation.*

Veditz failed to request CART. Even if Veditz had made such a request, CART is unnecessary and unreasonable given the cost, and Kendall still could not be required to modify his practice of providing deaf clients with interpreters and written exchanges, which are generally effective.

When providing auxiliary aids to disabled people, a business subject to the ADA should ask what auxiliary aid will work best, but the business is not obligated to provide the stated preference. *Majocha v. Turner*, 166 F. Supp. 2d 316, 321 (W.D. Pa. 2001). In *Majocha*, the court held that if a business provided an auxiliary aid that ensured effective communication, a disabled person could not insist on a different auxiliary aid. *Id.* at 323. A business is not obliged to change its practices in order to provide a more technologically advanced auxiliary aid so long as the aid in current use ensures effective communication. 28 C.F.R. pt. 36, App. B (2004) (Attorney General's Report).

If a business provides ineffective auxiliary aids, disabled people can request that the business change its practice of providing such aids, and the business is obligated to change the practice if the modification is requested, reasonable and necessary. 42 U.S.C. §12182(b)(2)(A)(ii) (2000); *Dudley v. Hannaford Bros. Co.*, 333 F.3d 299, 307 (1st Cir. 2003). In determining whether a modification is reasonable, courts balance the effectiveness of the modification against the cost of making the modification. *Fortyune v. American Multi-Cinema*, 364 F.3d 1075 (9th Cir. 2004). A modification is necessary if a disabled person would be unable to use the facilities, services or goods without it. *See PGA Tour, Inc. v. Martin*, 532 U.S. 661, 682 (2001).

Here, the District Court found that Veditz requested CART services and that Kendall failed to provide the requested service. (R. at 28.) At the time of the negotiation meeting, Veditz had never used CART. (R. at 18.) He admits that he never asked for CART services. (*Id.*) If Veditz did not ask for the services, the only request that the court could find would be an implied one. But an implied request does not give a business enough notice to change its policy. An explicit request is necessary because without it the business may not know how or why to change its practices. The District Court erred because no evidence in the record supports the District Court's findings.

The District Court's finding that Veditz requested CART is not supported by any evidence in the record and should be reversed.

B.   *Veditz Needed No Accommodation Because Kendall Provided Effective Communication.*

The District Court erred in finding that Kendall did not provide effective communication. The typed summaries Kendall provided resulted in effective communication during the negotiation settlement because Veditz was able to understand and participate in the negotiation settlement.

The evidentiary record does not support the District Court's conclusion that the communication provided by Kendall was ineffective. (R. at 13.) Veditz testified that the typed written communication *was* effective during the office meetings with Kendall. (R. at 13.) During the negotiations, Veditz had trouble understanding the interpreter and he stopped the meeting, seeking to remedy this communication problem. (R. at 16.) He did not object after Kendall began typing summaries. (*Id.*) If the typed summaries were ineffective, Veditz could have easily stopped the meeting a second time. From these uncontroverted facts, the most reasonable inference is that Veditz let the meeting continue because he understood and participated in the negotiations.

The District Court's decision that Kendall failed to provide effective communication is clearly erroneous and should be reversed because Kendall provided Veditz with written English, his best way of communicating.

C.   *Kendall Probably Will Not Be Enjoined to Provide CART Services Because the Cost Would Impose an Undue Burden.*

A business need not provide disabled persons with auxiliary aids if doing so would be an undue burden. 42 U.S.C. §12182(b)(2)(A)(iii) (2000).

Providing an auxiliary aid would be an undue burden if it is overly expensive or difficult to provide. 28 C.F.R. 5 §§36.104, 36.303 (2004). Because of their high costs, the District Court erred in finding that CART services were not an undue burden.

The case law provides examples of how to apply the factors listed in 28 C.F.R. §36.104 (2004). *Roberts v. Kindercare Learning Centers Inc.*, 86 F.3d 844 (8th Cir. 1996); *Mayberry v. Von Valtier*, 843 F. Supp. 1160 (R.D. Mich 1994). In *Mayberry*, the court determined that an auxiliary aid which costs $28.00 per hour would not be an undue burden for a doctor who charges $40.00 per hour. *Mayberry*, 843 F. Supp. at 1160. In *Roberts*, Kindercare did not have to provide a disabled person with a Personal Care Attendant when such an aid cost $200 per week and the cost of the child's weekly tuition is only $105. *Roberts*, 86 F.3d at 844.

The legislative history of the ADA provides the following example of the undue burden analysis which balances the costs of the auxiliary aid against the resources of the business:

> A small day-care center might not be required to expend more than a nominal sum, such as that necessary to equip a telephone for use by a secretary with impaired hearing, but a large school district might be required to make available a teacher's aide to a blind applicant for a teaching job.

H. R. Rpt. 101-485 pt 2. (May 15, 1990). In this example, it would be an undue burden for the small day care to provide an aide, but not for the large school. *Id.* Congress defined undue burden in this way because it was concerned about balancing the needs of disabled people with the high costs of accommodations. *Id.*, pt 3; 136 Cong. Rec. S9686 (daily ed. July 13, 1990). The legislative history shows that Congress intended to eliminate discrimination of disabled people in "a clear, balanced and reasonable manner." H. R. Rpt. 101-485 pt 2.

Here, providing CART would result in an undue financial burden. This case is factually similar to *Roberts,* and distinguishable from *Mayberry*. In *Mayberry*, the cost of providing an interpreter did not exceed the doctor's hourly charge, while in *Roberts*, the cost of providing a Personal Care Attendant did. The hourly cost of CART exceeds the amount of money that Kendall makes representing Veditz. (R. at 23.) If forced to provide CART, Kendall would lose money at a rate of $50 per hour. (*Id.*)

Veditz claims that CART is not an undue burden because Kendall will only have to provide CART when the parties are communicating face-to-face, or during group meetings at which Veditz is present. (R. at 20.) The fact remains, however, that Kendall would still lose money. For every hour that Kendall provides CART, he would not be paid for that hour of work,

6

and his next hour of regular work would be at half pay. Kendall's small private practice, as opposed to a large law firm, cannot absorb this loss. Forcing Kendall to provide CART may lead to substantial monetary loss, especially if future legal matters are long and complex. This evidence establishes that CART is a financial burden and does not support the District Court's findings.

The purpose of the ADA is to prevent discrimination against disabled people while limiting the severity of financial burden on small businesses. The undue burden exception applies differently to large companies and to small business owners. Kendall, as a small business owner, should only have to spend a small sum, such as the cost of an interpreter, and should not be required to pay for CART. The financial burden of CART negates Kendall's obligation to provide it. The District Court's finding that CART would not be an undue burden is clear error because Kendall loses substantial sums of money for every hour that CART is used. Written communication, the auxiliary aid that Kendall has provided, is the best auxiliary aid that Kendall can afford to offer Veditz.

II.
The District Court Lacks the Power to Order Parties to Mediate.

This issue is one of law because it can be decided without reference to the facts of the case. Therefore, it is reviewed *de novo*, "that is, with no deference given to the finder of fact." *Reynolds v. City of Chicago*, 296 F.3d 524, 527 (7th Cir. 2002).

Veditz cites to several authorities, none of which explicitly provide a court with the power to order parties to mediate. In each instance, Veditz's arguments are based on strained interpretations of words that, read in context, mean something other than what Veditz claims they mean.

Rule 16(a)(5) of the Federal Rules of Civil Procedure allows a District Court to "direct" the litigants to "appear" at a pretrial conference, typically in a judge's chambers, for several purposes, among them "facilitating the settlement of the case." To facilitate means "to make easy or easier." *American Heritage Dictionary of the English Language* 653 (3d ed., 1992). It does not mean "order" or "compel." The plain wording of Rule 16 grants only the power to require parties to appear in a judge's chambers where, among other things, they might choose on their own to negotiate with each other. The words do not grant to a court the power to order parties to negotiate with each other, and they certainly do not grant the power to order parties to subject themselves to a mediation conducted by a mediator. The words "mediate," "mediation," and "mediator" do not appear anywhere in Rule 16.

This Circuit has held that Rule 16 does not grant powers others than those specifically mentioned in the Rule. *Strandell v. Jackson County*, 838 F.2d 884 (7th Cir.1987). There, a District Court ordered the parties to take part in a nonbinding jury trial, which is a form of alternative dispute resolution that (like mediation) is not mentioned in Rule 16. *Id.* at 884-886. This Circuit reversed, holding that Rule 16 does not justify "clubbing" the parties into a settlement procedure that one or both parties object to. *Id.* at 888.

Local Rule 16.2(b)(3) of the Southern District of Illinois also does not empower a District Court to order parties, against their will, to mediate. Instead, it provides that certain issues "shall be discussed at the final pretrial conference and shall be included in the final pretrial order," among them "any issue which, in the judge's opinion, may *facilitate and expedite the trial*." (italics added). Mediation does not facilitate or expedite trial. If successful, it settles the lawsuit and thus eliminates trial. The primary function of a pretrial conference is to coordinate getting ready for trial. Local Rule 16.2(b)(3) gives only one example of an issue that "may facilitate and expedite the trial." That is "the feasibility of presenting testimony [at trial] by a summary written statement." Local Rule 16.3(a) permits a District Court to order "summary jury trial or other alternative method of dispute resolution which the court may deem proper." None of these Rules mention mediation, and the example of summary jury trial suggests that the other permitted forms of alternative dispute resolution are limited to adversarial ones.

Although courts have many inherent powers in addition to those provided for in court rules, only one court has ever held that it had the inherent power to compel mediation. *In re Atlantic Pipe Corp.*, 304 F.3d 135, 140 (1st Cir. 2002). Another court recognized that it could have that power but declined to use it in part because parties objected. *In re African-American Slave Descendants' Litig.*, 272 F. Supp. 2d 755, 759 (N.D. Ill. 2003).

III.
Even if the District Court Had the
Power to Order Mediation, It Abused
Its Discretion in Doing So.

"To find an abuse of discretion, a court must have a definite and firm conviction that the district court committed a clear error in judgment." *Bell v. Johnson*, 404 F.3d 997, 1003 (6th Cir. 2005). Even if a court has the power to compel mediation, doing so over the objection of a party is a clear error in judgment. Mediation should not be compelled when one of the parties objects.

In exercising its inherent power, the court must use the power with restraint and discretion to enhance its processes. *In re African-American Slave Descendants' Litigation*, 272 F. Supp. 2d 755 (7th Cir. 2003). Voluntary participation is the key to mediation's success and "when mediation is forced . . . it stands to reason that the likelihood of settlement is diminished." *Id.* Further, when settlement is unlikely, the investment of substantial time and money in mediation is inefficient and an undue burden on the objecting party. *Id.*

Mandatory mediation can be unfair, inefficient, or uneconomical. Mandatory mediation is overbearing when one party exerts its power over the other party, influencing the outcome of the mediation. Forced mediation also pressures parties to forgo trial and delays a party's day in court. Such a delay may effectively be a denial of justice. *G. Heileman Brewing Co., Inc., v. Joseph Oat Corp.*, 871 F.2d 648, 661 (7th Cir. 1987). Moreover, studies have shown that parties who mediate generally do not save time and money, and that courts do not reduce their caseloads, costs or delays. Holly A. Streeter-Schaefer, *A Look At Court Mandated Civil Mediation*, 28 Drake L. Rev. 367, 388 (2001).

In this case, mediation should not have been ordered because it would not produce a settlement. The likelihood that mediation will resolve this dispute is small because Kendall complied with the ADA and made accommodations for Veditz. Mediation, therefore, will not end the litigation, and the District Court will still have to resolve the case as an adversarial matter. Forcing the parties to mediation merely causes delay and adds to their expense.

CONCLUSION

For all these reasons the District Court erred in its findings and order, which should be reversed.

Respectfully Submitted,

Joanne Olson
Joanne Olson
Attorney for Appellant

Caroline Borden
Caroline Borden
Attorney for Appellant

9

SAMPLE APPELLEE'S BRIEF

In some ways, the format of this brief does not follow practices in the Seventh Circuit, where the appeal is set. Instead, the brief's format blends practices in many courts so that it is somewhat representative nationally.

In the UNITED STATES COURT OF APPEALS
for the SEVENTH CIRCUIT

Docket No. 2011–Civ.–141

AMOS KENDALL
Appellant

v.

GEORGE VEDITZ
Appellee

ON APPEAL FROM THE JUDGEMENT OF THE UNITED STATES
DISTRICT COURT FOR THE SOUTHERN DISTRICT
OF ILLINOIS

BRIEF FOR THE APPELLEE

Nathan J. Bailey
Attorney for the Appellee

TABLE OF CONTENTS

Page

i

TABLE OF AUTHORITIES

---

* Authorities chiefly relied on are marked with an asterisk.

Statutes

Regulations, Court Rules, and Legislative Histories

Other Authorities

PROCEEDINGS BELOW

George Veditz is deaf. (R. at 8, 13.) Amos Kendall, a lawyer, represented Mr. Veditz in a divorce case. (R. at 3.) Mr. Veditz complained to Mr. Kendall that he could not understand Mr. Kendall's advice or even what was happening during a settlement negotiation. (R. at 2-16, 23.) Despite this, Mr. Kendall refused to provide an effective means through which he and others involved in the divorce case could communicate with Mr. Veditz. (R. at 18.)

Mr. Veditz, the appellee here, brought an action under the Americans with Disabilities Act against Mr. Kendall, the appellant. (R. at 1.) Mr. Veditz sought an injunction requiring Mr. Kendall to provide legal services in the future in compliance with the Act as well as attorney's fees, costs, and court-ordered mediation. (R. at 2.) Mr. Veditz also moved for an order compelling the parties to mediate their dispute. In granting that motion, the District Court found that Veditz had promptly asked for a type of disability accommodation called Computer Assisted Real Time Transcription (CART), that Mr. Kendall's failure to provide CART had prevented adequate communication between the parties while Mr. Kendall represented Mr. Veditz, and that providing CART would not be an undue burden on Mr. Kendall. (R. at 27.)

This appeal followed. (R. at 28, 29.)

QUESTIONS PRESENTED

1. Did the District Court have the authority under relevant court rules and statutes and through its inherent powers to order a lawyer to mediate a dispute with a deaf client where the client will continue to need the lawyer's services to resolve remaining issues from a prior representation?

2. Did the District Court properly determine that the deaf client had timely requested a method of communication appropriate to his deafness, that the lawyer had failed to provide a communications accommodation and thus prevented communication with his own client, and that a communications accommodation would not cause an undue burden on the lawyer?

STATEMENT OF THE CASE

George Veditz, who is deaf, was represented by Amos Kendall, an attorney, in a divorce action. During that lawsuit, Mr. Veditz at times had difficulty understanding what was happening and why it was happening because the defendant failed to supply translation services that a deaf person in Mr. Veditz's situation could understand.

Accommodations Needed to Overcome Mr. Veditz's Deafness

While represented by Mr. Kendall, Mr. Veditz suffered total hearing loss as a result of viral meningitis. (R. at 8, 13.) Mr. Veditz is a forty-three-year-old self-employed architect who specialized in historic preservation projects. (R. at 13.) Mr. Veditz can communicate fully with the aid of Computer Assisted Real-time Transcription (CART), and he can understand some Signed Exact English (SEE). (R. at 1.)

A highly trained deaf specialist, Laurent Marie Clerc, testified that SEE would be an effective method of signed communication for Mr. Veditz. (R. at 4.) Mr. Clerc, who regularly assesses the needs of deaf people, further stated that CART would be the best means to communicate with Mr. Veditz in meetings with multiple participants. (R. at 4, 19.) These services are easily obtainable at a rate of $150.00 per hour. (R. at 4, 19-20.) The District Court itself used CART services during the District Court proceedings. (R. at 12.).

*Communication Failures During
the Divorce Settlement Negotiation*

During a divorce settlement conference involving both lawyers and their clients, the lawyers and Mr. Veditz's former spouse talked continually for two hours. (R. at 5.) For this meeting, Mr. Kendall did not provide CART services or an SEE translator. Instead, he hired an uncertified interpreter who knew only American Sign Language (ASL). (R. at 4, 25.) The uncertified interpreter is a college student. (*Id.*) Mr. Veditz first met the interpreter immediately prior to the settlement conference. Mr. Veditz does not know ASL, and the interpreter's attempts at communicating in ASL only confused Mr. Veditz during the negotiation. (R. at 2, 15-16.) Mr. Veditz had to ask the interpreter to repeat herself many times because he did not understand all that she was signing. (R. at 16.)

Consequently, for Mr. Veditz the settlement conference was mostly a discussion he could not fully understand. Mr. Veditz privately informed Mr. Kendall that the student interpreter could not translate what was happening. (R. at 16.) After this, Mr. Kendall supplemented the sign language with summaries of the proceedings typed into his laptop. *Id.* Mr. Veditz testified that typing summaries on a laptop gave him only a rough idea of what was taking place and turned him into an observer instead of a participant at the conference. (R. at 14, 16.) Mr. Veditz believes that he missed opportunities to make his needs known at the conference, which lasted two hours and resulted in a written agreement between Mr. Veditz and his wife. (R. at 16, 23.)

Failure to Provide Communications Accommodations

Mr. Kendall knew that Mr. Veditz was still learning to sign but failed to ask Mr. Veditz how his communication needs could be accommodated.

2

(R. at 8.) Mr. Veditz believed that he could trust Mr. Kendall to do his best to obtain effective communication, and hence did not request CART specifically at the conference. (R. at 18.)

Although Mr. Veditz communicates mostly in writing while at work, his communication needs there do not need to be quick. In a law office, however, time is measured by money. Mr. Kendall charges $100 per hour. (R. at 3, 23.) Like many lawyers, he bills in 12-minute increments, which means that every 12 minutes of Mr. Kendall's work cost Mr. Veditz an additional $20. Mr. Veditz paid Mr. Kendall a total of $2,000 for his services. (R. at 24.)

Because Mr. Kendall failed to accommodate Mr. Veditz, Mr. Veditz will continue to have a maintenance obligation and need further legal assistance to resolve it. (R. at 16.)

SUMMARY OF THE ARGUMENT

The District Court correctly mandated mediation pursuant to the Federal Rules of Civil Procedure, the Court's local rules, the Alternative Dispute Resolution Act (ADR Act), and the Civil Justice Reform Act. The District Court also properly used its inherent powers to ensure the speedy disposition of cases. Furthermore, in light of public policy, the Court should compel mediation.

Mr. Veditz thus was denied the opportunity to have full legal representation because he is deaf. The District Court properly found that Mr. Veditz requested CART services, even though he is not required to request effective communication. The District Court also properly found that ineffective communication at Mr. Veditz's negotiation meetings was the result of Mr. Kendall's failure to provide reasonable accommodations. Lastly, the District Court correctly found that Mr. Kendall could comply with the ADA by providing CART services, which do not impose an undue burden on him.

ARGUMENT

I.

The District Court's Order Compelling Mediation Should Be Affirmed Because This Dispute Can Be Resolved More Effectively Through Mediation Than Through Trial.

Whether the District Court has the power to compel mediation is a question of law, to be reviewed *de novo*. *United States v. Weaver*, 234 F.3d 42, 46 (D.C. Cir. 2000); *United States v. Cuffie*, 80 F.3d 514, 517 (D.C. Cir. 1996). A District Court's authority to compel arbitration derives from several sources of law: the Federal Rules of Civil Procedure, the local rules of the Southern District of Illinois, and the court's inherent powers.

A.   Rule 16 of the Federal Rules of Civil Procedure Authorizes a District Court to Order Mediation.

Rule 16(a) of the Federal Rules of Civil Procedure provides that "[i]n any action, the court may in its discretion direct [the parties to] appear before [the court] . . . before trial for such purposes as (1) expediting the disposition of the action . . . and (5) facilitating the settlement of the case." Federal Rule 16(c) provides that "the use of special procedures to assist in resolving the dispute, when authorized by statute or local rule . . . may facilitate the just, speedy, and inexpensive disposition of the action." This Circuit has held that "[t]he spirit, intent, and purpose of [Rule 16] allow[s] courts to actively manage the preparation of cases for trial," while broadening judges' ability to "manage their affairs as an independent constitutional branch of government." *G. Heileman Brewing Co. v. Joseph Oat Corp.*, 871 F.2d 648, 650 (7th Cir. 1989).

When the Federal Rules of Civil Procedure were amended in 1983, the Advisory Committee noted that the goal of the amendments was the use of settlements as a valuable tool in the promotion of case management. *Federal Reserve Bank v. Carey-Canada, Inc.*, 123 F.R.D. 603, 607 (D. Minn. 1988). Rule 16 thus authorizes district courts to order parties to participate in alternative dispute resolution. *Id.* "It is hard to imagine that the drafters of the 1983 amendments actually intended to strengthen courts' ability to manage their caseloads while at the same time intended to deny the court the power to compel participation by the parties to the litigation." *Id.*

On the other hand, in *Strandell v. Jackson County*, this Court ruled out an argument made regarding the 1984 advisory committee comments. 838 F.2d 884, 888 (7th Cir. 1987). In *Strandell*, an attorney was ordered by the District Court to participate in a nonbinding jury trial, and this Court ruled that the District Court did not have the power to compel parties to participate in summary jury trials pursuant to Federal Rule 16. *Id.* The *Strandell* court held that the rule was not designed as a means of "clubbing" the parties into an involuntary settlement. *Id.*

Soon after *Strandell*, however, district courts in three other circuits expressly rejected this Court's analysis and enforced court-ordered alternative dispute mechanisms as authorized by Federal Rule 16. *Federal Reserve Bank*, 123 F.R.D. 603 (concluding that a court's inherent power and Federal Rule 1 & 16 authorize the court to order alternative dispute mechanisms); *McKay v. Ashland Oil*, 120 F.R.D. 43, 47-48 (E.D. Ky. 1988) (holding that both Federal Rule 16 and the District Court's inherent power authorize a local rule for mandatory alternative dispute mechanisms); *Arabian American Oil Co. v. Scarfone*, 119 F.R.D. 448, 449 (M.D. Fla. 1988) (holding that Federal Rule 16 authorizes courts to order parties to engage in pretrial settlements).

In addition, soon after these three circuits rejected *Strandell*, Federal Rule 16(c) was amended, resulting in its current wording. The Advisory Committee noted that:

> The primary purposes of the changes in subdivision (c) are ... to eliminate questions that have occasionally been raised regarding the authority of the court to make appropriate orders designed either to facilitate settlement or to provide for an efficient and economical trial. The prefatory language of this subdivision is revised to clarify the court's power to enter appropriate orders at a conference *notwithstanding the objection of a party*.

Fed R. Civ. P. n. (1993) (Advisory Committee). (Italics added). The committee further noted that the amendments to the "rule acknowledge the presence of statutes and local rules . . . that may authorize use of some of these procedures even when not agreed to by the parties." 28 U.S.C. §§473(a)(6), 473(b)(4).

B.   Local Rule 16 of the Southern District of Illinois Authorizes the District Court to Order Mediation.

Even if Federal Rule 16 were held not to authorize court-ordered mediation, the District Court still has the power to do so under the Southern District's Local Rule 16 which is broader than Federal Rule 16. Local Rule 16.2(b)(3) provides that "any issue which, in the judge's opinion, may facilitate and expedite the trial . . . shall be discussed at the final pretrial conference and shall be included in the final pretrial order." Southern District Local Rule 16.3(a) further gives the court authorization to employ "alternative method[s] of dispute resolution which the court may deem proper," in order to "encourage and promote the use of alternative dispute resolution" so that "parties shall use an early neutral evaluation in the form of a settlement conference."

Local Rule 16.3 was written after *Strandell*. In *McKay v. Ashland Oil, Inc.*, the court distinguished *Strandell* by noting that Eastern and Western Kentucky Joint Local Rule 23—which is identical to Local Rule 16, except that "court" is replaced by "judge"—provides a District Court with the power to compel alternative dispute mechanisms. 120 F.R.D. at 48. In *McKay*, the judge was in an excellent position to determine the intent of Local Rule 23, because he was, in fact, the drafter of that rule. *Id.* The judge held that this language was written for the express authorization of compelled alternative dispute resolution. *Id.* The adoption of Southern District of Illinois Local Rule 16.3 after *Strandell* and the ruling in *McKay*, therefore, shows that compelled mediation is authorized by the local rules.

C. A District Court's Inherent Powers Include the Power to Order Mediation.

"Even apart from positive law, District Courts have substantial inherent power to manage and control their calendars." *In re Atlantic Pipe Corp.*, 304 F.3d 140, 143 (1st Cir. 2002). A court's "ability to take action in a procedural context," therefore, is governed by the "control necessarily vested in courts to manage their own affairs so as to achieve the orderly and expeditious disposition of cases." *G. Heileman Brewing Co.*, 871 F.2d at 650. The Supreme Court held that federal courts have inherent powers that are not dependent upon any express statutes or rules. *Link v. Wabash*, 370 U.S. 626 (1962).

"The exigencies of modern dockets demand the adoption of novel and imaginative means lest the courts, inundated by a tidal wave of cases, fail in their duty to provide a just and speedy disposition of every case." *Lockhart v. Patel*, 115 F.R.D. 44, 47 (E.D. Ky. 1987). While parties are often reluctant to participate in procedures outside the traditional norm, the need to compel the parties to mediation (and other forms of ADR) is an integral aspect of the court's ability to manage its docket. *Federal Reserve Bank*, 123 F.R.D. at 604.

Empirical evidence shows that cases compelled to mediation settle at about the same rate as those voluntarily mediated, and thus compulsion does not impede the effectiveness of mediation. *See* McEwen & Maiman, *Small Claims Mediation in Maine: An Empirical Assessment*, 33 Me. L. Rev. 237, 254 (1981). Even if mediation does not result in a settlement, it may cause a clarification of the issues, which reduce the length and cost of a later trial. *Federal Reserve Bank*, 123 F.R.D. at 605 (D. Minn. 1988).

The overall benefit of mediation is overwhelming. Mediation does not deprive a party of the right to litigate in court. Even when compelled, mediation only provides an alternative to trial, and trial can still occur if mediation fails. Mediation is also less costly and a more efficient method to resolve a dispute.

It is, therefore, within the court's inherent powers to compel mediation in this case. The District Court has already made the decision to order mediation and this Court should uphold that decision. The District Court's use of the "Standard Pre-trial Order" form, instructing that "the parties must mediate their dispute," makes it apparent that the court wishes to compel mediation in situations it deems necessary. Even though Mr. Kendall claims that mediation would impose additional costs on him, the cost of trial would be greater.

6

II.

The District Court Properly Found That Mr. Veditz Requested Cart Services, That the Parties Could Not Adequately Communicate Without Them, and That They Would Not Unduly Burden Mr. Kendall.

Determinations made by a District Court involving the ADA are findings of fact, reviewed for substantial evidence on the record. *See Melendez v. United States Department of Justice*, 927 F.2d 211, 216-219 (2d Cir. 1991).

The ADA provides that "[n]o individual shall be discriminated against on the basis of disability in the full and equal enjoyment of the . . . services . . . of any place of public accommodation by any person who . . . operates a place of public accommodation." 42 U.S.C. §12182 (2000). The ADA defines discrimination to include "a failure to take such steps as may be necessary to ensure that no individual with a disability is excluded, denied services . . . or otherwise treated differently than other individuals because of the absence of auxiliary aids and services, unless the entity can demonstrate that taking such steps . . . would result in an undue burden." *Id.*

A.   *Mr. Veditz Requested Better Communication and Is Not Required to Request CART Services Specifically.*

A business subject to the ADA, like Mr. Kendall's law practice, is ultimately responsible for selecting the appropriate auxiliary aid, provided that the method chosen causes effective communication. 42 U.S.C. §§12102 *et seq.*; *Proctor v. Prince George's Hosp. Ctr.*, 32 F. Supp. 2d 820 (D. Md. 1998). The Supreme Court has held that the basic requirement of the ADA entails "that the need of a disabled person be evaluated on an individual basis." *PGA Tour, Inc. v. Martin*, 532 U.S. 661, 690 (2001). Based upon a careful review of the ADA legislative history, the Department of Justice found "that strongly encouraging consultation with persons with disabilities [concerning their needs] . . . is consistent with congressional intent." *Majocha v. Turner*, 166 F. Supp. 2d 316, 321-322 (D. Pa. 2001), citing, 56 Fed. Reg. 35565-35567 (July 26, 1991). In effect, "the best way to serve hearing impaired clients is to plan in advance" by consulting with the client and researching all possible alternatives. Roy Miller & Sheila Simon, *Lawyers, Hearing Impaired Clients, and the Americans with Disabilities Act*, 81 Ill. B.J. 153, 154 (1993).

In determining whether Mr. Veditz requested CART services, this Court should defer to the District Court's finding of facts. The facts indicate that Mr. Veditz's request for further help should have prompted Mr. Kendall to integrate Mr. Veditz fully into the settlement negotiations. The ADA does not require Mr. Veditz to specifically request CART services. Rather, it requires Mr. Kendall, a practicing attorney, to know the law and insure that he follows it to communicate with his client.

B.   The Inadequate Communications Accommodations Mr. Kendall Provided Violated the ADA.

Title III of the ADA, along with the regulations implementing the Act, provide that a business furnish appropriate auxiliary aids and services where necessary to ensure effective communication with disabled persons. 28 C.F.R. §36.303(c) (2004); 42 U.S.C. §§12102 (2000), *et seq.* The ADA term "auxiliary aids and services" includes "qualified interpreters or other effective methods of making aurally delivered materials available to individuals with hearing impairments." 42 U.S.C. §12102 (2000). The main requirement of the communication method, therefore, is effective communication. *Id.*

While there are no national standards for interpreters, state law can provide useful guidelines for determining whether or not an interpreter is qualified. Under Illinois Law,

> No person may represent himself or herself as an interpreter for the deaf, work as a professional interpreter for the deaf, or use the title "interpreter for the deaf" . . . unless he or she can show proof of: (1) a certificate issued by the Registry of Interpreters for the Deaf (RID); (2) a satisfactory evaluation by the National Association of the Deaf; (3) a satisfactory Interpreter Skills Assessment Screening (ISAS) evaluation; or (4) licensure or certification or a satisfactory evaluation or screening in another state.

225 Ill. Comp. Stat. §442/5(a) (2007). The record contains no evidence that the novice ASL interpreter provided by Mr. Kendall has these qualifications. (R. at 25.) The uncertified interpreter did not know SEE, the language Mr. Veditz was familiar with, and admitted to not being able to communicate effectively. (R. at 16.) Instead, the interpreter knew ASL, a language that Mr. Veditz was not familiar with. *Id.*

Furthermore, the summaries typed on a laptop, in lieu of verbatim dialogue, are hardly sufficient. While the laptop may have been previously helpful between the parties, it cannot be adequate in negotiations or in a situation where more than two people are communicating back and forth. The participants will inevitably speak far more quickly than Mr. Kendall could have typed. And if he was typing, he could not have been using his time fully to argue for his client. The expert witness at trial testified that the laptop method was not effective for meetings with multiple participants, and that, in these instances, CART would be ideal. (R. at 19.)

8

C. *Providing CART Services Would Not Impose an Undue Burden on Mr. Kendall.*

An accommodation under the ADA is not required if it would impose an undue burden on the business involved by requiring "significant difficulty or expense." 42 U.S.C. §§12111(10)(A), 12182 (2000); 28 C.F.R. 36.104 (2004). Mr. Kendall argues that he would suffer an undue burden because he would lose money if he were to pay $150 an hour for CART services while charging Mr. Veditz $100 an hour. That is not true, either factually or legally.

A business the size of Mr. Kendall's law practice is entitled to a disabled access tax credit for part of the cost of providing accommodations to the disabled, including "provid[ing] qualified interpreters or other effective methods of making aurally delivered materials available to individuals with hearing impairments" 26 U.S.C. §44(a) & (c)(2)(B) (2000). The credit equals fifty percent of the costs greater than those that add up to more than $250 for the taxable year, not exceeding $10,250. §44(a). This is not a deduction reducing taxable income. It is a credit that directly reduces Mr. Kendall's federal income tax by half of every dollar he spends on accommodating the disabled over $250 for the taxable year.

Mr. Kendall testified that he billed $2,000 to Mr. Veditz at a rate of $100 per hour for 20 hours of legal services. (R. at 23-24.) Only two of these 20 hours would have required the CART services that Mr. Kendall says would be too expensive. (R. at 23.) At $150 an hour, CART services would have cost $300. If Mr. Kendall spent no other money on disability accommodations during the taxable year, the tax credit would have reduced that to $275 (50 percent of the amount over $250). But if Mr. Kendall spent at least $250 on other forms of accommodations, the tax credit would have reduced the CART expense to $150. Thus, of the $2,000 Mr. Kendall charged Mr. Veditz, either $275 or $150 would have gone to CART services. That effectively would have lowered his hourly billing rate concerning Mr. Veditz from $100 to either $86.25 or $91.25.

Thus, it is misleading to compare the $150 hourly cost of CART services with Mr. Kendall's hourly rate of $100. The practice of law is filled with similar expenses that seem large when compared with a lawyer's hourly rate but do not make representing a client unprofitable when compared to the total paid by the client to the lawyer over the course of the representation. An example is the cost charged by Lexis and Westlaw for computer-assisted legal research.

Concerning the cost of accommodations under the ADA, Dr. I King Jordan, President of Gallaudet University, testified before the Senate that "it needs to be made clear to people that the accommodations are not nearly as large as some people would lead us to believe." 135 Cong. Rec. S10765 (1989). That same day, Senator Leahy stated that "In this country, equality

9

for all Americans is not a matter of cost. It is a matter of justice." *Id*. Under the ADA, therefore, one is "legally required to provide effective communication, and meeting that obligation is simply a cost of doing business" Miller & Simon, 81 Ill. B.J. at 154. In fact, in some instances "the financial benefits of accessibility may outweigh the costs." *Id*.

CONCLUSION

Mr. Kendall can be compelled to mediate and should be required to do so. The order of the District Court should therefore be affirmed.

Respectfully Submitted,

Nathan J. Bailey
Nathan J. Bailey,
Attorney for Appellee

SAMPLE APPELLATE BRIEF

The issue addressed in this brief is essentially a pure question of law, requiring interpretation of a rule of evidence. Therefore, the rule explanation sections focus primarily on the language of the rule, the intent of the rule's drafters, and the policies served by adhering to the rule's plain language. The writer relies on case authorities as well, but because the cases are not mandatory authority for this court, the writer presents the cases as further support for the primary arguments of plain meaning, intent of the drafters, and policy.

In both the "plain language" section and the "intent of the drafters" section, notice how closely the writer focuses on the actual words of Rule 615. If the case authority had defined the Rule's terms more fully, the writer would have relied primarily on case authority for the definitions of the words used in the Rule. Even without strong case authority defining the terms, however, a writer can use legal and other dictionaries to parse each word of a rule or statute, as the writer has done here.

In the "intent of the drafters" section, the writer casts the Rule as primarily defining what restrictions a party can force on other parties as a matter of course, without justifying the need for the restrictions. This section expressly articulates the primary theme of the brief, contrasting the trial court's powers with the powers given to parties. The section relies on a canon of statutory construction to point out not only what is included in the Rule's plain language, but also what is omitted. The writer also discusses the Rule's silence on important questions that would arise routinely if the Rule had been intended to have the scope urged by the appellant. This section ends by pointing out that the trial court, which presumably knew what it meant by its own order, did not intend that the order apply in the manner the appellant has proposed, thus harkening back to the theme of reliance on the court's trial management powers.

Then, after the rule explanation sections, the writer applies the Rule to the facts of the case before the court. The way the Rule will apply to these facts is clear, but the writer uses the rule application section as an opportunity to reinforce the points made in the rule explanation sections and to reassure the court that justice will not be infringed by a ruling in the appellee's favor.

IN THE UNITED STATES COURT OF APPEALS
FOR THE FIFTEENTH[1] CIRCUIT

DENNIS IRVING,
  Appellant

v.

THE UNITED STATES
  OF AMERICA,
   Appellee.

Docket No. 04-1234

BRIEF OF THE APPELLEE[2]

---

1. This is a hypothetical circuit.
2. This brief is based on briefs written by students in the Spring 2005 Advanced Writing Groups at Mercer University School of Law. Professor Beth Cook of the Pennsylvania State University Dickinson School of Law graciously allowed the use of the problem that was adapted for that class.

TABLE OF CONTENTS

TABLE OF AUTHORITIES

QUESTION PRESENTED

Whether Rule 615 of the Federal Rules of Evidence should be expanded to apply to communications outside the courtroom where (1) the trial court did not intend that its routine Rule 615 order should limit outside conversation; (2) the defendant never requested a broad sequestration order; (3) the court did not instruct witnesses to refrain from discussing their testimony; (4) a police officer spoke about his testimony to his co-worker; and (5) during the co-worker's subsequent testimony, the defendant was able to cross-examine the co-worker about the conversation.

RULE OF EVIDENCE INVOLVED

Federal Rule of Evidence 615 provides:

At the request of a party the court shall order witnesses excluded so that they cannot hear the testimony of other witnesses, and it may make the order of its own motion. This rule does not authorize exclusion of (1) a party who is a natural person, or (2) an officer or employee of a party which is not a natural person designated as its representative by its attorney, or (3) a person whose presence is shown by a party to be essential to the presentation of the party's cause, or (4) a person authorized by statute to be present.

STANDARD OF REVIEW

Because rulings on motions to exclude testimony raise predominately legal questions regarding the interpretation of the Federal Rules of Evidence, the appellate court reviews those evidentiary rulings de novo. *U.S. v. Angwin*, 271 F.3d 786, 798 (9th Cir. 2001).

STATEMENT OF THE CASE

On May 8, 2004, the Defendant, Dennis Irving, sold to Nathan Roberts more than 50 grams of methamphetamine, a Schedule II controlled substance. (R. 1.) Officers Miller and Nelson witnessed the transaction and immediately arrested both men. (R. 1.) Subsequently, a grand jury indicted the Defendant for offenses involving the possession and distribution of methamphetamine. (R. 2.)

In pretrial proceedings, the district court granted the Defendant's Motion to Exclude Witnesses Pursuant to Rule 615 of the Federal Rules of Evidence and specifically ordered all prospective witnesses to leave the courtroom. (R. 4.) The court, however, did not instruct the witnesses or counsel that witnesses were prohibited from discussing their testimony with each other. (R. 4.)

On September 22, 2004, the trial began. That day, during the government's case-in-chief, Officer Nelson testified that he had seen the Defendant hand to Roberts the envelope containing the drugs. (R. 5.) Later that

-1-

evening, Officer Nelson had dinner with Officer Miller, who was scheduled to testify the following day. (R. 6.) A research assistant for the Defendant's attorney was seated nearby. (R. 7.) According to the research assistant, as the officers ate dinner, Officer Nelson described the testimony he had given at trial that morning. (R. 7.) In pre-trial statements, Officer Miller had described first seeing the two men at the point where the envelope was already in Roberts's hand. (R. 7.) Allegedly, after hearing a description of Officer Nelson's testimony, Officer Miller stated that he now remembered seeing the Defendant hand the envelope to Roberts. (R. 7.)

The next day, the Defendant moved to exclude Officer Miller's testimony, arguing that the dinner conversation between Officers Nelson and Miller the previous evening violated the court's Rule 615 order to exclude witnesses from the courtroom. (R. 5.) The district court heard argument and denied Defendant's motion. (R. 6.) The court reasoned that a witness's refreshed recollection of events (1) was common when talking to another person involved in the same incident; (2) was not evidence that the witness planned to perjure himself; and (3) did not violate the court's Rule 615 order, which barred witnesses only from being physically present in the courtroom. (R. 6.)

Later that day, Officer Miller testified at trial. (R. 7.) The Defendant's attorney cross-examined Officer Miller, confronting him with his previous statements and questioning him about his conversation with Officer Nelson the previous evening. (R. 6.) After hearing this cross-examination and all of the other evidence in the case, the jury convicted the Defendant on all counts. (R. 7.) The District Judge sentenced the Defendant to serve 56 months in a federal prison (R. 7.), and the Defendant has now filed this appeal.

SUMMARY OF THE ARGUMENT

Federal Rule of Evidence 615 provides that upon the request of a party, the trial court "shall order witnesses excluded so that they cannot hear the testimony of other witnesses." Fed. R. Evid. 615. The Appellant asks this Court to hold that a routine Rule 615 order also prohibits witnesses from discussing their testimony with each other. Neither the plain meaning of the Rule, the intent of its drafters, nor sound public policy support the Appellant's argument.

First, the plain meaning of Rule 615 is limited to physical presence in the courtroom. The Rule provides that witnesses shall be "excluded," meaning "expelled" or "barred"—a reference to physical presence, not to communication. The Rule sets out the reason for the exclusion, "so that" they do not "hear testimony." The word "testimony" means sworn statements of a competent witness in a trial, affidavit, or deposition. Therefore, by definition, witnesses cannot "hear testimony" unless they are present when the testimony is being given. Several courts, including the First and Eighth Circuits, have so held.

Further, the plain language of the Rule indicates the drafter's intention to limit only presence in the courtroom. Because a trial court already has the power to restrict witness communication as part of its inherent authority to manage proceedings before it, the Rule's primary purpose is to define the restrictions a *party* can impose unilaterally upon other parties. By expressly delineating the power to exclude witnesses from the courtroom, the Rule impliedly withholds from parties other, broader powers. Also, the drafters did not address several key questions that would arise regularly if Rule 615 had been intended to apply beyond the courtroom, such as exactly what witnesses are prohibited from saying and whether the prohibition precludes attorneys from preparing witnesses for their testimony.

Finally, application of Rule 615 beyond its express terms would disrupt the Rule's carefully crafted balance of the rights of parties and the efficient administration of trials. Broad witness sequestration is available outside Rule 615 in those cases where restrictions on witness communication are appropriate. Blanket restrictions, however, would be burdensome to witnesses and unworkable for the trial court. Enforcement proceedings would interrupt trials and squander judicial resources. Without guidance about what sorts of communications are prohibited, outcomes of these hearings would be unpredictable. Witnesses unwilling to risk charges of contempt of court would be inclined not to testify at all.

According to its express terms, the drafter's intent, and sound policy rationales, a routine Rule 615 order is limited to excluding witnesses from physical presence in the courtroom and does not apply to conversations between witnesses. Therefore, the Rule 615 order below did not prohibit the conversation between Officers Nelson and Miller. The Government respectfully requests this Court to affirm the trial court's denial of the Defendant's motion to exclude testimony.

<u>ARGUMENT</u>

I. THE COURT SHOULD AFFIRM THE TRIAL COURT'S DECISION BECAUSE RULE 615 PROHIBITS ONLY PHYSICAL PRESENCE IN THE COURTROOM AND THEREFORE DOES NOT APPLY TO OUTSIDE COMMUNICATIONS SUCH AS THE DINNER CONVERSATION BETWEEN OFFICERS NELSON AND MILLER.

Rule 615 provides that, upon a party's request, the trial court "shall order witnesses *excluded* so that they cannot hear the *testimony* of other witnesses." Fed. R. Evid. 615 (emphasis added). According to the Rule's plain language, a Rule 615 order bans prospective witnesses from the courtroom, but does not restrict communication outside the courtroom. The Defendant seeks to extend the scope of Rule 615 beyond its plain language, in contravention of the intent of the Rule's drafters and in derogation of the trial court's inherent discretionary authority to manage its courtroom. The district court rejected such an interpretation of the rule, and this Court should affirm the district court's ruling.

A. The Plain Language of Rule 615 Applies Only to a Witness's Physical Presence in the Courtroom.

The first step in interpreting a rule is to examine the language itself. If the language is plain and unambiguous, a court should not look past this plain meaning. *Shotz v. City of Plantation*, 344 F.3d 1161, 1167 (11th Cir. 2003); *Thompson v. Goeztmann*, 337 F.3d 489 (5th Cir. 2003). Dictionaries often are used to confirm the plain meaning of statutory text.

The issue before the Court concerns only one sentence of Rule 615: "At the request of a party the court shall order witnesses excluded so that they cannot hear the testimony of other witnesses, and it may make the order of its own motion." Fed. R. Evid. 615. The phrase at issue is "*exclude*[] so that they cannot *hear...testimony*." *Id.* (emphasis added). "Exclude" means to "expel or ban." *Merriam-Webster's Collegiate Dictionary* (11th ed. 2003). "Testimony" means "evidence that a competent witness under oath or affirmation gives at trial or in an affidavit or deposition." *Black's Law Dictionary* 1485 (Bryan A. Garner ed., 7th ed., West 2000). The plain, ordinary, straightforward language of the rule, therefore, provides only that witnesses are banned from the courtroom so they do not hear other witnesses *as they testify*.

The Rule goes on to identify the reason for exclusion from the courtroom: "so that they cannot hear the testimony of other witnesses." This phrase does not define a broad category of situations to which the Rule will apply. Rather, the phrase expressly uses the language of purpose ("so that") to set out the reason for the exclusion from the courtroom. The plain language of Rule 615, therefore, says nothing at all about what a witness may say or do outside the courtroom. *See U.S. v. Scharstein*, 531 F. Supp. 460, 462-63 (E.D. Ky. 1982).

Even if the word "exclude" could be redefined to refer to something other than banning an individual from the courtroom, Rule 615, by its own terms, would apply only to hearing *testimony*. A participant in a restaurant conversation over dinner is not "hearing testimony." In that setting, no one is under oath, no one is being questioned by an attorney, and no rules of evidence apply. The express language of Rule 615 does not apply to communications of that sort. *See* 29 Charles Alan Wright & Victor James Gold, *Federal Practice and Procedure* § 6243, at 57 ("Testimony is given only in a formal legal context such as a deposition, hearing, or trial. Thus witness communication outside that context does not enable witnesses to 'hear testimony.'").

Several courts have held that the language of Rule 615 limits only physical presence of witnesses in the courtroom. For instance, in *Sepulveda v. U.S.*, 15 F.3d 1161, 1176 (1st Cir. 1993), the First Circuit held the Rule inapplicable to extra-courtroom communication. In that case, the defendants had been charged with offenses relating to the distribution of cocaine, and the trial court had issued a Rule 615 order before trial began. *Id.* at 1176. Later in the trial, the defendants alleged that extra-courtroom witness contact had violated the Rule 615 order. The court held that a Rule 615 order does not prohibit witness communication, stating that the Rule 615 order had "plowed a straight furrow in line with Rule 615 itself [and therefore] did not extend beyond the courtroom." *Id.* at 1176.

The Eighth Circuit also has held Rule 615 inapplicable to extra-courtroom communications. *U.S. v. Smith*, 578 F.2d 1227, 1235 (8th Cir. 1978). In *Smith*, defendants were on trial for offenses associated with the distribution of heroin. *Id.* at 1229. Early in the trial, the court had issued a Rule 615 order excluding witnesses from the courtroom. As trial progressed, a police officer took notes and relayed information to government witnesses waiting to testify. *Id.* at 1234. The trial court held that this conduct did not violate the Rule 615 order because Rule 615 only excludes witnesses from the courtroom. *Id.* The Eighth Circuit affirmed the trial court's holding, noting that the defendants had not requested additional restrictions beyond Rule 615. *Id.* at 1235. The appellate court stated that the question of whether to instruct witnesses not to communicate with other witnesses is within a trial court's discretion. *Id.* at 1235. Such a discretionary instruction is not, therefore, mandated by the plain language of Rule 615.

Similarly, the court in *Scharstein* held that the plain language of Rule 615 limits only physical presence in the courtroom. 531 F. Supp. at 463-64. In *Scharstein*, defendants had been charged with illegally manufacturing, storing, and transporting explosives. *Id.* at 461. The court declined to expand the application of Rule 615 to prohibit witnesses from conferring with each other outside the courtroom. The court stated, "[T]his court believes that there is no reason to go beyond the plain language of the Rule," observing that the question of whether to instruct witnesses not to discuss their testimony is within the court's discretion and not required by Rule 615. Id. at 463; *see also Lapenna v. Upjohn Co.*, 665 F. Supp. 412, 413 (E.D. Pa. 1987) (declining to apply Rule 615 "beyond the literal meaning of the rule").

B. The Drafters Did Not Intend Rule 615 to Apply Broadly to Communication Outside the Courtroom

Not only does the plain language of Rule 615 call for affirmance here, but indications of the drafters' intent support that result as well. As a trial court already has inherent power to limit witness communication outside the courtroom, *Sepulveda*, 15 F.3d at 1176, the primary purpose of Rule 615 is to identify the restrictions *a party* can impose unilaterally on other trial participants. Therefore, the key inquiry is what unilateral and unrestrained powers the Rule's drafters intended to give to parties.

The drafters of the Rule rightly limited the unrestrained power the Rule would give to parties. At common law, when a court ordered sequestration, the order could include (1) preventing witnesses from hearing other witnesses testify; and (2) preventing prospective witnesses from consulting other witnesses. *Sepulveda*, 15 F.3d at 1176 (citing 6 John Wigmore, *Evidence* § 1840). When the drafters expressly included in Rule 615 the power to "exclude" witnesses, they impliedly excluded the right to impose other more intrusive limitations. According to the canon of statutory construction *expressio unius est exclusio alterius*, the expression of one thing implies the exclusion of another. *Thompson*, 337 F.3d at 499. Rule 615, therefore, does not give parties the unilateral power to prohibit communication outside the courtroom. That power remains within the discretion of the trial court.

In fact, Rule 615 does not use the term "sequester" at all. *Black's Law Dictionary* defines "sequester" to mean "to segregate or isolate [a witness] during trial." *Black's Law Dictionary* 1370 (Bryan A. Garner, ed., 7th ed., West 2000). Tellingly, the drafters did not use the term "sequester" in Rule 615. Rather, they selected only the first aspect of common law sequestration (the aspect that does not "segregate or isolate a witness") and refrained from using the term "sequester" to describe the scope of Rule 615. These drafting decisions provide further indication of an intent to withhold broad sequestration powers from the scope of Rule 615. *Scharstein*, 531 F. Supp. at 464.

Further, the drafters did not define categories of communication allegedly prohibited by the Rule—as they surely would have done had they intended to restrict communication. Violation of a trial court's order constitutes contempt of court, rendering the offending person at risk of fine or imprisonment. *U.S. v. Johnston*, 578 F.2d 1352 (10th Cir. 1978). A reading of Rule 615 to prohibit certain kinds of communication outside the courtroom would mean that witnesses who spoke outside the courtroom would be subject to contempt proceedings. If the drafters had intended to impose such serious individual liability for trial witnesses, they surely would have set out the prohibition clearly and defined its parameters unambiguously. The Appellant's proposed construction would render trial witnesses vulnerable to contempt proceedings without fair notice of what they must not do or what the penalties might be. The drafters cannot have intended such a result.

If the drafters had intended the construction urged by the Appellant, they also would have had to address the question of whether trial attorneys could continue preparing witnesses for their testimony. To prepare a witness to testify, any competent attorney confers with the witness about the status of the trial proceedings and about the testimony to come. *See generally U.S. v. DeJongh*, 937 F.2d 1, 3 (1st Cir. 1991) (A lawyer "would be foolhardy to call an important witness without attempting, first, to debrief the witness."). Because parties adjust their strategies as the trial progresses, these witness conferences are an essential part of trying a case. *Scharstein*, 531 F. Supp. at 463. In fact, the right to prepare a witness for his or her testimony is so fundamental that deprivation of this right may raise Due Process concerns. *Scharstein*, 531 F. Supp. at 463-64 (citing *Potashnic v. Port City Construction Company*, 609 F.2d 1001 (5th Cir. 1980)).

Had the drafters intended Rule 615 to limit extra-courtroom communication, they could have chosen either to prohibit trial attorneys from preparing witnesses or to exempt trial attorneys. Exempting trial attorneys would have rendered the proposed construction of Rule 615 pointless, however. Witnesses who have already testified would be precluded from speaking to prospective witnesses, but trial counsel could still describe prior testimony freely. In fact, because attorneys know precisely what will be most relevant in future testimony, allowing attorneys to describe prior testimony would be far more problematic than allowing other witnesses to describe their own testimony. To hold that Rule 615 prohibits witnesses from talking to each other but allows attorneys to prepare prospective witnesses for their testimony "would be an exercise in futility." *Scharstein*, 531 F. Supp. at 464.

Prohibiting trial attorneys from preparing witnesses, on the other hand, would have resulted in a sea change in standard trial preparation. Again, like the question of individual witness liability, such a drastic result would have called for express language in the Rule itself, language clearly applying the Rule to attorney conduct and identifying what attorneys could and could not say during witness preparation. Because the drafters did not address the question of whether and how Rule 615 would apply to communication with attorneys, it is most likely that the drafters did not intend to apply Rule 615 to extra-courtroom communication.

Finally, the intent of the Rule's drafters is not the only intent relevant to the question before this Court. The trial court issued its order under the authority of Rule 615, but an order limiting outside communication could have been issued as part of the court's inherent powers of trial management. *Sepulveda*, 15 F.3d at 1176. Therefore, the more important inquiry may be what the *trial court intended* by its order. A court's interpretation of its own order is given great weight. *Sepulveda*, 15 F.3d at 1177; *U.S. v. Smith*, 578 F.2d at 1235 ("holding that it is within the discretion of the trial court to determine whether or not a sequestration order has been violated"). If, as here, the *trial court* did not intend it's order to constrain conversation outside the courtroom, that order should not be redefined on appeal.

Both the intent of the drafters and the intent of the trial court issuing the order demonstrate that the conversation at issue did not violate the court's order. Neither the provisions of Rule 615 nor the court's own language reflect an intent to reach beyond the courtroom doors.

C.   <u>Expanding Rule 615 Beyond Its Express Terms Would Disrupt the Rule's Balance Between Providing Truth-Testing Strategies and Minimizing Unnecessary Litigation Costs.</u>

The purposes of the Federal Rules of Evidence are to secure fairness in administration, eliminate unjustifiable expense and delay, ascertain the truth, and determine proceedings fairly. Fed. R. Evid. 102. The Rules aim to balance the need for legitimate truth-testing strategies with the need to minimize unnecessary expense. Expanding the scope of Rule 615 would unnecessarily disrupt the delicate balance Rule 615 has achieved.

Applying Rule 615 to out-of-court conduct is not necessary to obtain truthful testimony. Barring witnesses from the courtroom prevents them from hearing testimony directly, so their only knowledge of prior testimony will be by the general recollection of others. In most cases, this limitation will be sufficient. *Sepulveda*, 15 F.3d at 1176. Further, a party suspecting that witness contact may have influenced testimony is free to cross-examine a witness about that contact and its content, as occurred in the case before the Court. For cases in which greater protection is appropriate, the trial court can, *sua sponte* or on proper motion, impose greater limitations, including ordering witnesses not to disclose their testimony. In fact, this reliance on the discretion of the trial court is fundamental to the federal trial process. *Scharstein*, 531 F. Supp. at 464 ("The general approach of the Federal Rules of Evidence is to place heavy reliance on the discretion of the trial court in conducting a fair trial."). Thus, the very protection the Appellant seeks is already available without stretching Rule 615 beyond its intended application.

Not only is expansion of the Rule's scope unnecessary, but application to out-of-court communications would result in significant and often unnecessary administrative costs. First, enforcement would be extremely difficult. A court can easily enforce an order banning witnesses from the courtroom, but violations outside the judge's presence are difficult to discover. 29 Charles Alan Wright & Victor James Gold, *Federal Practice and Procedure*, § 6243, at 63 (West 1997). Further, enforcing routine orders prohibiting witness contact would require the court to undertake "an undue amount of supervision" over witnesses, distracting the court from its primary function. *Scharstein*, 531 F. Supp. at 464 n.7.

Second, extension of the Rule would result in long delays during trials. Each time two witnesses talked, there could be grounds for a motion alleging a violation of Rule 615 and a resulting evidentiary hearing to learn the content of the conversation. Witnesses would be called upon to disclose publically everything they had said to each other. These hearings would occur frequently, especially in long trials with many witnesses. *Id.* at 464. Constant interruptions would impede trial management, increase litigation costs, and absorb significant judicial resources. Courts would be "bogged down in numerous inquiries…when there is no genuine need to do so." *Id.*

Third, the outcome of these hearings would be uncertain at best. The Rule does not define what kinds of communication would be prohibited. Neither parties nor witnesses nor the district court itself would know whether a violation had occurred if a witness stated that she had testified; that her testimony was over; that the cross-examination had been brief; that she had been nervous; that she had testified about a particular topic; or that a particular question had been asked. With no clear standard of what could and could not be said, hearings would be numerous and issues would be difficult to resolve. *Id.*; 29 Wright, *Federal Practice* at § 6243.

Fourth, extension of the Rule would place unrealistic hardships on witnesses. An order limiting out-of-court communication between witnesses places far greater burdens on witnesses than does mere exclusion from the courtroom. Wright, *Federal Practice* at § 6243. Witnesses testifying in the same case often are spouses or co-workers. Communication between spouses or other close associates should be restricted only when absolutely necessary, not any time a party decides to invoke Rule 615.

Fifth, extending the Rule to out-of-court statements would render witnesses vulnerable to contempt proceedings. The combination of this vulnerability and the lack of clarity about what kinds of communication are prohibited would discourage witnesses from testifying. Discouraging testimony would impede the goal of obtaining truthful testimony to a far greater degree than would a decision to keep Rule 615 within its intended bounds.

Sixth, to apply Rule 615 to out-of-court conversations would be to give any party, as a matter of right, the ability to impose significant limitations on all witnesses in the case, including spouses and co-workers who must continue to have close daily contact with each other as the trial progresses. A party could use Rule 615 as another way to make the trial experience as unpleasant as possible for opposing parties and witnesses. This approach to trial management does not assist in achieving just and fair results at trial.

Only one circumstance—the reading of transcripts of actual testimony—justifies the application of Rule 615 beyond its express terms. In *Miller v. Universal City Studios, Inc.*, 650 F.2d 1365, 1367 (5th Cir. 1981), the trial court had entered an order excluding witnesses under Rule 615. *Id.* at 1372. During the trial, however, the defendant's expert witness was provided with daily transcripts of the trial testimony. The district court held that providing transcripts of testimony violated the Rule 615 order, and the appellate court affirmed, explaining that the harm of *reading* testimony is potentially greater than the harm of *hearing* testimony. *Id.* Accordingly, the court held that a Rule 615 order prohibits witnesses from reading trial transcripts prior to testifying. *Id.* at 1373.

The *Miller* exception does not apply to conversation outside the courtroom, however. The court in *Miller* compared hearing actual testimony with reading a transcript and found the key difference to be that a listener would have to rely on his or her memory of the testimony while a reader would not. *Id.* at 1372. This key distinction does not apply to conversation outside the courtroom. Unlike the reader of a transcript, who can thoroughly study the actual testimony, a participant in a conversation must rely on his or her memory of the conversation. Perhaps more significantly, the *speaker* must rely on memories of the testimony as well. By the very rationale explained in *Miller*, therefore, the danger of casual conversation outside the courtroom is considerably smaller than the danger Rule 615 is designed to prevent. Thus, the *Miller* exception does not apply to extra-courtroom conversation. In fact, *Miller's* very rationale demonstrates a key reason for limiting Rule 615 to "testimony" rather than to mere recollections of testimony.

Further, the narrow *Miller* exception is consistent with the rationales on which Rule 615 is based. The *Miller* exception does not impose the administrative costs and personal impositions on witnesses that the Appellant's construction would impose. Prohibiting the reading of transcripts creates a bright-line test, easily applied in enforcement proceedings. Witnesses need not wonder what they may and may not say. Parties need not wonder what conduct may violate the Rule 615 order. Also, a witness has access to trial transcripts only through trial attorneys, who are officers of the court and therefore more easily and effectively governed by trial court orders. Further, the prohibition on reading transcripts does not interfere with normal daily interactions between witnesses who live or work together or who encounter each other in casual interactions in the hallway.

In all other circumstances, trial judges have broad discretion to limit contact between witnesses when appropriate. *Sepulveda*, 15 F.3d at 1176. In those few cases in which a small nuance in testimony may determine the outcome, a Rule 615 exclusion of witnesses may be insufficient. *Scharstein*, 531 F. Supp. at 464. In such cases, the trial court can use its broad case management powers to determine whether "extra-courtroom prophylaxis" is necessary and what means best accomplishes the goal in that case. *Sepulveda*, 15 F.3d at 1176 (citing *U.S. v. Arias-Santana*, 964 F.2d 1262, 1266 (1st Cir. 1992)). Since trial courts already have the power to restrict communication when appropriate, the only effect of broadening Rule 615 to include such restrictions would be to shift the power from the trial court's discretion and place it instead in the unrestrained hands of a party. Nothing in the language or history of Rule 615 indicates that the drafters intended such a result.

   D.   The Casual Dinner Conversation of Officers Nelson, and Miller Did Not Violate the Rule 615 order.

On September 22, 2004, Officers Nelson and Miller had dinner together. (R. 6.) During their meal, the conversation ranged over topics of common interest. Officer Nelson had testified in the Irving trial that day. (R. 7.) He related to his dinner companion his recollection of his

-10-

testimony, including his testimony of having seen Irving hand the drug-filled envelope to Roberts. Officer Nelson's description prompted Officer Miller to recall that he had seen the transfer as well. (R. 7.)

This dinner conversation between the officers did not violate the Rule 615 order. The trial court's order made reference only to whether and when witnesses could be in the courtroom, exactly as the plain language of Rule 615 provides. At no time during the trial did the court instruct witnesses not to speak to each other. This was no mere inadvertent omission by the court. As demonstrated by the court's denial of defendant's motion to exclude, the trial court did not *intend* that its order should apply to communication outside the courtroom.

Nor does this case fall within the narrow *Miller* exception. In *Miller*, the reading of daily transcripts was held to violate Rule 615. 650 F.2d at 1374. The court concluded that reading transcripts eliminated the need to rely on memory and was thus more dangerous than actual witness presence in the courtroom. Here, however, Officer Nelson had to rely on his recollection of his testimony. Then, Officer Miller had to rely on *his* recollection of what Officer Nelson had recalled. These key differences render the officers' conversation far less problematic than either physical presence in the courtroom or the reading of trial transcripts.

In fact, this double reliance on memory is even less problematic than the situation the Eighth Circuit permitted in *U.S. v. Smith*, 578 F.2d 1227, where an officer in the courtroom was taking notes and relaying information to prospective witnesses. Here, no one was planted in the courtroom taking notes. There was no plot to circumvent the prohibition on access to actual testimony. Two co-workers simply had dinner together and spoke of their day's events, as friends and co-workers often do.

Additionally, prohibiting these officers from speaking to each other likely would have made no difference here. Officers Nelson and Miller had worked together on this case for months. Together, they had arrested the Defendant and worked with the prosecutor to prepare the case for trial. During that process, they would have seen each other daily. Undoubtedly, they had discussed the case on countless occasions. They may well have discussed the case immediately before trial began. Whether or not the officers communicated on September 22, no doubt the prosecutor would have carefully prepared Officer Miller for his testimony the next day. The prosecutor would have highlighted the factual question of the drug transfer and would have told Officer Miller about the status of the testimony on that point. Officer Miller's recollection would have been just as refreshed by that description as it was by the description of his co-worker the night before. In such a circumstance, there is little point in prohibiting a discussion on September 22nd that normally could have happened both on September 21st and on September 23rd.

Further, whether the conversation occurred before or after trial began, the Defendant would have been able to confront Officer Miller with his prior statements and question him about conversations with others—just as the Defendant did. Thus, in either case, the jury would have been fully informed of the circumstances surrounding Officer Miller's testimony. In neither case would there be reason to second-guess the jury's ability to gauge the officer's credibility and the accuracy of his recollection.

Finally, reading Rule 615 beyond its express terms is not necessary to preserve the availability of broad sequestration in appropriate cases. As part of its inherent authority, the court below had the power to impose, *sua sponte*, extra-courtroom restrictions on witnesses. The court did not find those restrictions necessary here. If the Defendant disagreed, the Defendant had the opportunity to request those restrictions, but the Defendant did not make the request. Had counsel sought such an order, and had the trial court issued it, Officers Nelson and Miller certainly would have complied. The Defendant did not seek the order, however, and cannot now bootstrap a routine Rule 615 order into the order Defendant wishes he had sought.

CONCLUSION

Both the plain language of Rule 615 and all available indicators of the drafters' intent show that the Rule governs only physical presence in the courtroom and not conversations such as that between Officers Nelson and Miller. Further, application of Rule 615 according to its express terms preserves the Rule's carefully crafted balance of the rights of parties and the efficient administration of trials. Therefore, the Government respectfully requests this Court to affirm the trial court's denial of the Defendant's motion to exclude testimony.

_____

Counsel for the United States

Six Suggestions for Converting a NYLS Legal Practice Assignment into a Top-Notch Writing Sample

Professor Heidi K. Brown[1]
New York Law School

---

[1] Many thanks to Professor Jodi Balsam and Professor Anne Goldstein for their edits and contributions to this piece.

1. **Choose work product that best reflects your legal writing and analytical abilities:** In Legal Practice this year, you will produce two legal memoranda and two briefs. Your legal writing proficiency likely will improve as each semester progresses, and your analysis presumably will become more sophisticated. When selecting written work product for a writing sample, choose a memo or brief that best represents your ability as a legal writer. You also might think about the substance of the written work, and decide which piece of writing you would feel most comfortable and engaged discussing in a potential interview.

2. **Consider a document of appropriate length for your intended reader:** Attorneys responsible for hiring law students for summer jobs are busy and have limited time. You should refrain from submitting an overly long writing sample. Some employers impose page limits on writing samples. Even if there is no page limit, ideally you should provide a 5-8 page (double-spaced) sample of your writing that demonstrates your ability to analyze a legal question fully. If you believe your Legal Practice Memo 2 or Brief 2 best reflects your writing ability, but the document exceeds 8 pages, consider editing the document to limit the discussion to a single issue. This does not mean you can simply delete a second issue and submit the document. Make sure you read the entire document and edit the introduction, facts, headings, overview/roadmap paragraph(s), and conclusion to reflect your focus on a single issue.

3. **Read your professor's grading comments and revise the document accordingly:** In grading your work product, your Legal Practice professors spend a significant amount of time providing comments and critique that will help you improve your writing. You should review these comments and your scores on the grading rubric in detail to grasp how you can enhance the document. Then set aside some time to do some serious editing, including: (1) studying the rubric to determine what aspects of the paper need revision, (2) incorporating your professor's suggestions throughout the document (not just in the particular sentences or paragraphs where he or she made comments), and (3) making your writing sample the best it can be.

4. **Consider whether party names or details should be modified for a potential employer:** Sometimes your Legal Practice assignments might involve clients with humorous names or other details to keep class discussion dynamic and interesting. Prior to submitting a law school assignment to a legal employer, you should review your work product to determine whether these names or details should be adjusted slightly for a practicing attorney as your audience. If you change names or details, proofread carefully to ensure you have done so consistently throughout the document.

5. **Proofread, proofread, proofread:** A legal employer might make an employment decision based upon a quick review of your writing sample. Enhance your chances of getting hired by presenting a perfectly-proofread document. One cursory proofread is insufficient. Consider reading the document six different times for six distinct purposes to catch any and all grammatical, typographical, citation and logic errors:

a. Read the document overall, focusing on the substantive logic of each section and paragraph. It helps to read the document out loud for this purpose. Ask yourself whether the text will make sense to a reader unfamiliar with the subject matter, or whether you have made assumptions about your reader's background knowledge that necessitate revision.

b. Read the document at the sentence level to tighten phrasing by deleting unnecessary repetition of language or introductory words (such as "one could make the argument that . . ."), convert passive to active voice, and enhance clarity. Ask yourself whether each sentence will make sense to a reader unfamiliar with the subject matter. Are your sentences easy to follow and not run-on? Are the subjects and verbs of each sentence clear? Are there places where you can convert "legalese" to plain English? Have you used proper grammar and punctuation?

c. Visually scan the document at the page level to catch formatting errors (dangling headings, or inconsistent font, spacing, indentations, margins, etc.), and to ensure paragraphs are of appropriate length.

d. Consider reading the document backwards (yes, backwards!) on a word-by-word level to catch typographical and punctuation errors that our eyes skip over when reading the document numerous times (trial v. trail, or statute v. statue).

e. Focus solely on checking the legal citation throughout the document.

f. Check to make sure the document conforms to any specific rules or guidelines provided by the potential legal employer for submission of writing samples.

Finally, have someone else read the document — ideally a lawyer or business professional who is unfamiliar with the assignment — and have him or her identify if and where the document falls short in clarity and professional presentation.

6. **Give your reader context:** Finally, when you submit the document to a potential legal employer, consider whether the reader might appreciate a two- or three-sentence summary of the context of the writing sample, such as the following:

"This writing sample is a legal office memorandum I wrote for my Legal Practice course at New York Law School this past semester. I represented an airline passenger who was involuntarily removed from a flight on the airline JetGreen for an alleged discriminatory reason. My 8-page memorandum summarizes federal law regarding the circumstances under which an airline may remove a passenger from a flight for safety reasons without incurring liability."

The foregoing process will take considerable effort, so try to set aside an appropriate block of time to focus on creating a strong writing sample to enhance your employment opportunities. You might consider dedicating a full day for the substantive editing process, then set the document aside for a day or two, and return to it with fresh eyes for each level of proofreading. Best of luck!

INDEX